THE ECLECTIC HISTORY OF THE UNITED STATES

THE ECLECTIC HISTORY OF THE UNITED STATES

BY

M. E. THALHEIMER

Author of
"A Manual of Ancient History,"
"A Manual of Mediterai and Modern History,"
"An Outline of General History,"
"A History of England,"
etc.

VAN ANTWERP, BRAGG & CO., PUBLISHERS
CINCINNATI AND NEW YORK

COPYRIGHT, 1880, BY VAN ANTWERP, BRAGG& CO.

ISBN: 978-1-6673-0725-1 paperback
ISBN: 978-1-6673-0726-8 hardcover

THALHEIMER'S HISTORICAL SERIES.

————

ECLECTIC HISTORY OF THE UNITED STATES.
HISTORY OF ENGLAND.
GENERAL HISTORY.
ANCIENT HISTORY.
EASTERN EMPIRES (SEPARATE).
HISTORY OF GREECE (SEPARATE).
HISTORY OF ROME (SEPARATE).
MEDIÆVAL AND MODERN HISTORY.

PREFACE.

THE present time seems eminently fitting for a new recital of the facts and principles of American History.

Increased attention of jurists and historians has been drawn to the Federal Constitution by the events of the last twenty years, and its features have been more thoroughly discussed than at any previous time since its adoption. Especially Mr. E. A. Freeman, in his elaborate "History of Federal Government," has set forth the true relation between our Constitution and those of the ancient commonwealths. It seems desirable that the children of the Republic should share, as far as may be, in the result of these discussions.

The writer has endeavored very briefly, but with clearness, to indicate the state of affairs in Europe from which the first colonization and subsequent reinforcement of our nation proceeded, to mark the growth of institutions from the demands of new circumstances, and, without too much meddling with abstractions, to let the moral lessons in which our history abounds be apparent from a plain recital of events. At the same time the book is occupied with facts, not with arguments. As good men have differed from the beginning, so they will doubtless continue to differ concerning the best policy of the Government, and those who are most loyal to their own convictions are not necessarily least tolerant of the opinions of others.

Respect for individual rights and opinions, and a generous confidence in every man's reason and capacity for self-control, have been distinguishing features of American society almost from its beginning, and have resulted in a degree of personal freedom unknown under older governments. Twenty years ago the doubt was often expressed whether this great experiment had not been tried too soon;—whether mankind had yet risen high enough in the moral scale to respect the common good when it chanced to conflict with individual passion or convenience, or with sectional interests. The very existence of a government like ours must depend on the moral worth of its people; and this, it was felt, had not been sufficiently tested.

Now that the strength of the Republic has been proved by storms that have shaken it to its foundations, it is regarded with increased confidence at home and respect abroad, and the new light of experience that has been thrown upon its Constitution may be used for the benefit of its future administrators.

It has been a constant effort not to encumber the student's mind with a mass of details, but to sketch events with a few strokes easily remembered. Paragraph headings in heavier type will serve as topics for recitation, and the teacher is further aided by Review Questions at the end of each Part. A series of questions on the Constitution will, it is hoped, help to make clearer the most important features of that document and thus simplify the teacher's task.

The Publishers have spared neither expense nor effort in promoting the beauty as well as the practical usefulness of the book. The author's thanks are due to Mr. J. T. Stewart, whose intelligent supervision of details has secured so remarkable a degree of accuracy.

The maps by Mr. Russell Hinman, C. E., and the illustrations by Mr. H. F. Farny, leave nothing to be desired in perfection of finish and adaptation to their purpose.

BROOKLYN, N. Y., *Jan.* 10, 1881.

M. E. THALHEIMER

TABLE OF CONTENTS

PREFACE. 4
CHAPTER I. ANCIENT AMERICA. 8
CHAPTER II PHYSICAL FEATURES AND EARLY INHABITANTS. 14
CHAPTER III. DISCOVERIES AND SETTLEMENTS BY EUROPEANS. 26
CHAPTER IV. ENGLISH SETTLEMENTS. — VIRGINIA. 42
CHAPTER V. VIRGINIA AND MARYLAND. 51
CHAPTER VI. PLYMOUTH, PORTSMOUTH, AND DOVER. 57
CHAPTER VII. MASSACHUSETTS, CONNECTICUT,
AND RHODE ISLAND. 63
CHAPTER VIII. NEW NETHERLANDS. THE MIDDLE STATES. 77
CHAPTER IX. ENGLISH REVOLUTIONS. THE SOUTHERN COLONIES. 88
CHAPTER X. PARLIAMENTARY RULE. 99
CHAPTER XI. FRENCH COLONIES. 106
CHAPTER XII. INTERCOLONIAL WARS. 113
CHAPTER XIII. LITERATURE AND GENERAL PROGRESS. 125
CHAPTER XIV. CAUSES OF THE REVOLUTION. 139
CHAPTER XV. OPENING SCENES OF THE REVOLUTION. 152
CHAPTER XVI. EVENTS OF 1776. 163
CHAPTER XVII. EVENTS OF 1777 AND 1778. 173
CHAPTER XVIII. EVENTS OF 1779-1781. 184
CHAPTER XIX. END OF THE WAR. 193
CHAPTER XX. ADOPTION OF THE CONSTITUTION. 206
CHAPTER XXI. FIRST AND SECOND ADMINISTRATIONS,
A. D. 1789–1797. 215
CHAPTER XXII. THIRD ADMINISTRATION, A. D. 1797-1801. 226
CHAPTER XXIII. FOURTH AND FIFTH ADMINISTRATIONS,
A. D. 1801-1809. 232
CHAPTER XXIV. SIXTH ADMINISTRATION, A. D. 1809-1813. 242
CHAPTER XXV. SEVENTH ADMINISTRATION, A. D. 1813-1817. 251

CHAPTER XXVI. EIGHTH AND NINTH ADMINISTRATIONS,
A. D. 1817-1825. 260

CHAPTER XXVII. TENTH ADMINISTRATION, A. D. 1825-1829. 266

CHAPTER XXVIII. ELEVENTH AND TWELFTH ADMINISTRATIONS,
A. D. 1829-1837...270

CHAPTER XXIX. THIRTEENTH ADMINISTRATION, A. D. 1837-1841. 277

CHAPTER XXX. FOURTEENTH ADMINISTRATION, A. D. 1841-1845............281

CHAPTER XXXI. FIFTEENTH ADMINISTRATION, A. D. 1845-1849. 287

CHAPTER XXXII. SIXTEENTH ADMINISTRATION, A. D. 1849-1853. 297

CHAPTER XXXIII. SEVENTEENTH ADMINISTRATION, A. D. 1853-1857. 302

CHAPTER XXXIV. EIGHTEENTH ADMINISTRATION, A. D. 1857-1861..........307

CHAPTER XXXV. NINETEENTH ADMINISTRATION, A. D. 1861-1865. 316

CHAPTER XXXVI. NINETEENTH ADMINISTRATION EVENTS OF 1862. 325

CHAPTER XXXVII. NINETEENTH ADMINISTRATION –
EVENTS OF 1862 (CONTINUED)..333

CHAPTER XXXVIII. NINETEENTH ADMINISTRATION EVENTS OF 1863. 340

CHAPTER XXXIX. NINETEENTH ADMINISTRATION EVENTS OF 1864. 350

CHAPTER XL. TWENTIETH ADMINISTRATION EVENTS OF 1865. 358

CHAPTER XLI. RESULTS OF THE CIVIL WAR. 363

CHAPTER XLII. JOHNSON'S ADMINISTRATION, A. D. 1865-1869.............370

CHAPTER XLIII. TWENTY-FIRST AND TWENTY-SECOND
ADMINISTRATIONS, A. D. 1869-1877..377

CHAPTER XLIV. TWENTY-THIRD ADMINISTRATION, A. D. 1877-1881. 387

CHAPTER XLV. PROGRESS OF THE REPUBLIC. 393

A HISTORY OF THE UNITED STATES.

CHAPTER I.
ANCIENT AMERICA.

1. A Lonely Land. — Four hundred years ago the American continent was unknown to the civilized world. A few tribes of dark-skinned hunters roamed through its forests; a few villages of wigwams dotted the fertile banks of its rivers; but in the whole area east of the Mississippi and south of the Great Lakes, there were probably not (7) more people than are gathered to-day in a single city like Boston, Chicago, Cincinnati, or New Orleans. Far away to the southward, where maize grew without cultivation and where bananas and other tropical fruits were native, the villages of Mexico and Yucatan contained a larger population; but with these exceptions America might be called "an empty continent, — a desert-land awaiting its inhabitants."

An Ancient Mound.

2. The Mound Builders.—The central part of North America had not always been so solitary. The basins of the Mississippi and the Great Lakes contain traces of a numerous and busy people who tilled the soil, worked the copper mines, and built great houses for habitation and defense. Not a word of their speech is known to us; the name we give them is derived from the huge and singular elevations of earth which they left behind them. Probably these were usually surmounted by houses, which were approachable only by ladders, and were thus secure against attack; but many were burial-mounds, and others may have served as foundations for watch-towers and signal-stations. Still others bear evidence of having been used as places for worship and sacrifice. Figures of men and animals were often imitated in the shape of these mounds. One of them, in Adams County, Ohio, represents an enormous serpent which seems about to swallow an egg-shaped figure 164 feet long. One of the largest villages of the Mound Builders, near the present site of Marietta, Ohio, must have been the home of at least 5,000 people.

3. Wares from Ancient Workshops.—Knives, chisels, and axes, both of flint and copper, carved pipes, beads, bracelets, and vases of glazed earthenware are found in the burial-mounds, and all are of finer workmanship than any thing made by the Indians of the coast. When Frenchmen first visited the Mississippi Valley, the homes of the Mound Builders had been deserted for hundreds of years, if we judge from the age of forest-trees which were growing upon the summit of their earth-works; and the relics which the mounds contained were as much a mystery to the savage natives as they are to us.

4. The Indians knew nothing of their history earlier than the memory of their oldest living men. Perhaps the Mound Builders had been conquered and exterminated by the ancestors of those Indians themselves; perhaps the struggle for

Relics from the Mounds.

existence in so cold a climate was too hard for them, and they returned to the warmer regions of Mexico and Central America, whence they had come; but these are only guesses: the beginning and the end of their history are equally unknown to us.

5. Whence came the early inhabitants of America? is a question that can not be positively answered. A tradition still preserved in China, says that a company of sailors, driven off shore by westerly winds, sailed many weeks until they came to a great continent where grew the aloe and other plants that were strange to them, but which we recognize as natives of Mexico. Even within the last hundred years, fifteen vessels have been driven across the Pacific to our western shores; and during all the previous ages we may believe that many similar accidents had occurred. Doubtless, also, Greek and Phoenician sailors may have crossed the narrower and more stormy Atlantic; but if they reached this continent, they never returned to tell their story. The first white visitors of America, of whom we have any trustworthy record, came from Iceland.

6. Northmen in Greenland.—Iceland, that island of frost and flame, had been occupied about a hundred years by a hardy, sea-faring race from Norway, when, in A. D. 985, Eric the Red, an Icelandic chief, discovered Greenland, and planted a colony of his countrymen on its south-west shore. This settlement grew prosperous through its trade with the Esquimaux, and paid 2,600 pounds of walrus-teeth for a yearly tribute to the Pope. One of Eric's comrades, driven out of his way by adverse winds, descried the mainland of NORTH AMERICA stretching far away to the south-west.

7. Leif in New England.—In A. D. 1000, Eric's son, Leif the Fortunate, undertook, with thirty-five brave companions, to examine this more fertile and attractive shore. They saw the flat rocks of Newfoundland, the white banks of Nova Scotia, and the long sandy beach of Cape Cod. From its abundance of wild grapes, the Rhode Island coast was called Good Vinland. Leif's party wintered in New England, and in the spring carried home news of their great discovery.

8. "White-man's land."—Subsequent parties of Icelanders are supposed to have visited the shores of what are now South Carolina and Georgia. The northern natives had told them of a "white-man's land" to the southward, where fair-faced processions marched in white robes, with banners at their heads, to the music of hymns. Though they never found this abode of pale-faces, the Northmen named it by anticipation, *Great Ireland;* and some wise men believe that

Irish fishermen had indeed arrived on this continent.

Northmen in Rhode Island.

9. Thorfinn Karlsefne, a famous sea-king, reconnoitered the bays and harbors of the New England coast. Icelandic settlements were made, and a brisk trade was carried on with the natives, who were glad to exchange their furs for bright-colored cloth, knives, and trinkets. At least one little Northman was born on the American continent. His name was Snorri, and from him, in our day, the great sculptor, Thorwaldsen, and the learned philologist, Finn Magnusson, traced their descent. A. D. 1007.

10. In time, however, the people of Iceland ceased to hear from their brethren in America. The settlers, if any remained alive, became so mingled with the previous inhabitants that, when white men came again, their descendants were not to be distinguished from other barbarians on the coast.

Point out on Map No. 1, Iceland. Greenland. The route of the Northmen. The Mississippi Valley. The Great Lakes.

Read Baldwin's "Ancient America;" Squier and Davis's "American Antiquities" and "Discoveries in the West." L. H. Morgan's "Ancient Society," Part II, Chapter vii; his article in the "North American Review" for 1876, and one in "Johnson's Cyclopædia" on the "Architecture of the American Aborigines;" Leland's " Fusang;" Sinding's "History of Scandinavia;" Beamish's "Discovery of America by the Northmen."

CHAPTER II
PHYSICAL FEATURES AND EARLY INHABITANTS.

11. While North America is again hidden from the rest of the world, let us take a view of the lonely continent and its savage people, learning if we can what is its fitness for a home of civilized men. As before, for the sake of clearness, we shall use names which were given by white explorers long after the time of which we write.

12. Two great mountain systems form the rocky framework of the continent. The eastern or **Appalachian** system, extending in a direction nearly parallel with the Atlantic coast, is divided by several river-valleys into the White Mountains of New Hampshire, the Green Mountains of Vermont, the Adirondacks of New York, the Alleghanies of Pennsylvania and Virginia, the Blue Ridge and Cumberland Mountains of the southern states. The gentle slope and frequent divisions of these mountains permit the navigation of many rivers far from the sea; and the two thousand miles of coast which now form the eastern and part of the southern limit of the United States, are broken by bays, inlets, and fine harbors large enough to shelter the shipping of all the world.

13. The **Cordilleras** of the western part of the continent form a grand mountain-system 1,100 miles across at its greatest width, consisting of elevated table-lands cut by narrow canons and bounded by still higher ridges and peaks. The Coast Range descends abruptly to the Pacific, and its westward-flowing rivers are short and rapid. It is broken in the north by the gorges, or *dalles*, of Columbia River, and farther south by San Francisco Bay, which extends so far into the interior as to receive the Sacramento and San Joaquin rivers from the eastern slope.

14. On the various elevations west of the Sierra Nevada, nearly all the grains and fruits of the world can be made to grow; but the date-palm, most bounteous of the gifts of nature, has been found best adapted to the river-valleys of Arizona. The greatest growth of the soil is the gigantic *Sequoia* of California, whose trunk, twenty feet or more in diameter near the base, rises often to a height of 300 feet.

15. The continuous mountain-wall of the Sierra Nevada arrests the moist winds from the Pacific; and the **Great Interior Basin**, extending from the Sierra on the west to the Wahsatch and Bear River mountains on the east,—with its alkaline plains and salt lakes—resembles the sandy deserts of western Asia. Sage-brush is the only fuel; the largest quadruped is the prairie wolf. The Digger Indians, most wretched of the human inhabitants of the continent, live on roots and insects. A few tribes near the lakes are better fed with fish. The few rivers of the Great Basin lose themselves in the sands, or in salt lakes which have no outlet.

16. Four rivers have their rise in the mountains northeast of the Great Basin. The *Columbia* begins its long course to the Pacific, the *Colorado* to the Gulf of California; the *Yellowstone* and the *Nebraska*, or *Platte*, to their union with the Missouri. The *Rocky Mountains* form the eastern barrier of the Cordilleras, and from their eastern slope many rivers descend to the great central valley.

17. The Mississippi Valley.—North and south through the interior of the continent stretches an immense plain, 1,200 miles in width, browsed over in ancient times by countless herds of bison. Through the center of this plain flows the longest river in the world, measuring from the head of its longest branch to its end in the Mexican Gulf, 4,194 miles, and receiving fifty-seven other rivers from the east and west. The natives called it *Miche Sépé*, — the Father of Waters. The soil of its valley is of inexhaustible fertility, and a distinguished French writer has pronounced it "upon the whole the most magnificent dwelling-place prepared by God for man's abode."

18. Northeastward from the central valley is a chain of **Five Great**

Lakes, containing collectively nearly half the fresh water in the world. Before reaching the last of the lakes, the mass of water plunges over a precipice 160 feet in height, making the great cataract of Niagara. After passing through Lake Ontario, it flows away through a broad and rapid river to the Atlantic. By means of the Great Lakes, and canals which now connect them with navigable rivers, ships from Europe can unload their cargoes a thousand miles inland on the docks of our western cities.

19. Physical Divisions.—With reference to the uses of man, the lands of the United States may be viewed in four chief divisions: (1) The eastern sea-board, bounded by the Appalachian range, is best adapted to manufactures and commerce; (2) the great central valley, to agriculture; (3) the plains east of the Rocky Mountains, to grazing; and (4) the Cordilleras, to mining. No region of the earth is more richly adapted to all human wants, and to intercourse with other lands.

20. Three Regions.—Before men learned to cultivate the soil, fish and edible roots were their chief food; and there were only three regions in North America that could sustain any great number of people at that grade of savagery. (See Table, p. 22.) These were, first and chief, the valley of the Columbia, "the most extraordinary region on the face of the earth in the variety and amount of subsistence it afforded prior to the cultivation of maize and other plants." Its rivers swarmed with salmon, its forests with game; and, beside the shell-fish on the coast, there were a species of bread-root and an abundance of berries on the prairies. From this land of plenty, successive bands of emigrants may have moved out to occupy various regions of North and South America. The second center of population was the lake-region of Minnesota, the nursery-land of the Dakotas; and the third was on the south shore of Lake Superior, whose abundant fisheries afforded food to the Ojibways and many kindred tribes. Thus bountifully supplied by Nature, the natives of the North-west had no incentive to learn new arts. They had no pottery, and they dressed their game or fish with knives of flint, and cooked it. if at all, in ovens dug in the ground.

21. The **River-tribes** of the interior had risen above savagery to the lower grade of barbarism: they cultivated corn, beans, squashes, and melons, and laid up a store of dried berries and grain for winter use. But they had no domestic animals, no knowledge of the metals, and their earthenware was of the rudest and coarsest kind. Their houses were wigwams or lodges, made of saplings joined at the top and covered with sheets of bark, or sometimes with woven mats or skins.

Occupations.—The entire labor of wigwam and garden was performed by the women, who dug up the soil with clam-shells or sharp sticks; planted, tended, and harvested the crops; concealed the next year's seed-grain in vessels underground from the hungry hunters; made clothing of deerskin and sometimes embroidered it with beads; wove the mats and baskets which were their only household furniture; and, on a march, carried all burdens, including perhaps the whole covering of their houses, or at least a papoose bound upon a board and hung at the mother's back. The men, meanwhile, made their canoes of birch-bark, carved their war-clubs and pointed their arrows with bone or flint, and ranged the forest in quest of food.

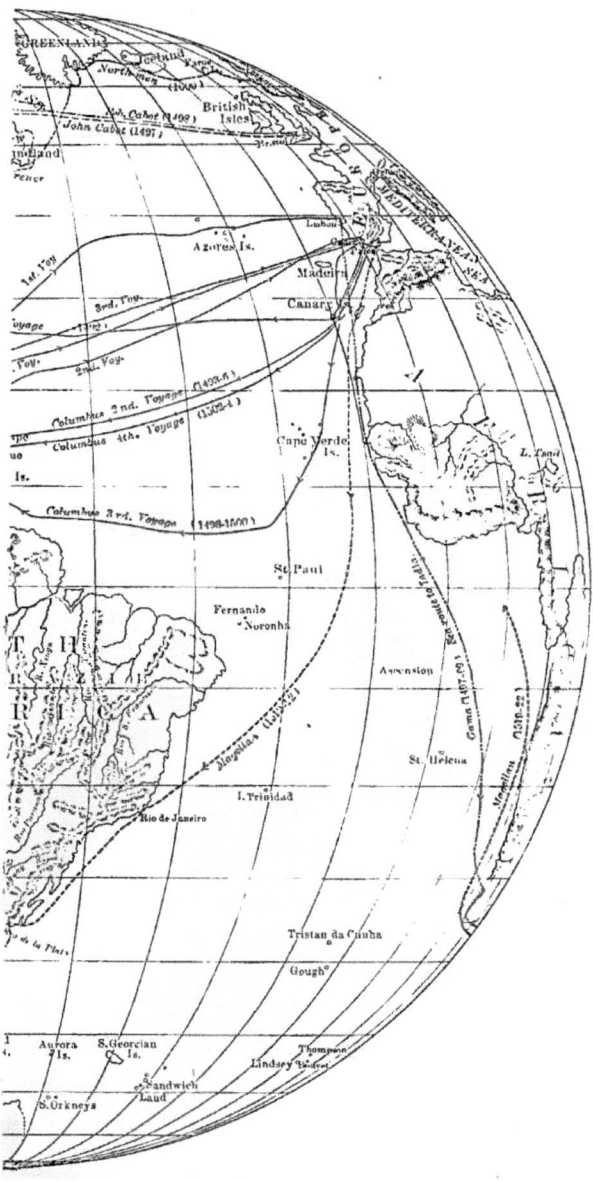

22. The **Village Indians** of the far south-west were in the middle period of barbarism. They built houses of *adobes* (sun-dried bricks) or stone; they made bronze tools, and hardened copper into a very good substitute for steel. The Peruvians tamed the llama to serve them as a beast of burden. In the size and shape of their skulls and in their modes of building, the Village Indians resembled the Mound Builders. Their descendants in Arizona and New Mexico live in the same *pueblos,* or villages, an honest, industrious, and law-obeying people. Their great stone

Pueblo Building.

houses, often four or five stories high, contain several hundred persons. Each story is smaller than the one below it, leaving a long flat terrace or roof through which alone the house is entered, by means of ladders.

23. East of the Mississippi the lands were divided among three great families: (1) The *Algonquin* extended from Hudson Bay to the Tennessee and Roanoke rivers, and from the Mississippi to the Atlantic, excepting the region of the lower lakes which had been wrested from them by the (2) *Huron-Iroquois* ; (3) the *Mobilians,*whose lands were bounded by the Mississippi, the Atlantic, and the Gulf, included the Creeks, Choctaws, Chickasaws, and Seminoles.

West of the Mississippi were the *Dakotas,* or Sioux, and their kindred tribes. These included the Minnitaree, of the upper Missouri, whose fine appearance and superior houses and gardens have led to a conjecture that they may be descendants of the Mound Builders. The *Shoshones* of the south-west, and the *Village Indians* already mentioned, were of a different race.

24. The Iroquois excelled all the northern Indians in the arts of war, government, and agriculture. Knowing well the advantages of their position on the great water-ways which led to the interior of the continent, they made themselves feared by all their race. From Canada to the Carolinas, and from Maine to the Mississippi, Indian women shuddered at the name of the *Ho-de-no-sau'nee** while even the bravest warriors of other tribes went far out of their way in the wintry forests to avoid an encounter with them.

Within sixty years from their first acquaintance with white men, the Iroquois had exterminated the Hurons,—their own nearest kindred and bitterest foes,—the Eries and Neutrals about Lake Erie, and the Andastes of the upper Susquehanna; while they had forced a humiliating peace upon the Lenape, or Delawares, the most powerful of the Algonquins, and had driven the Ottawas from their home upon the river which bears their name. Though now at the height of their power, they numbered only 1,200 fighting men of their own race; but they had adopted a thousand young warriors from their captives to fill the vacancies made by war.

25. Clans.—Throughout the continent families were grouped into *gen'tes,*or clans, which took their names from various animals supposed to be their ancestors. Thus the Mohawks, on the upper Hudson, included the three clans of the Wolf, the Bear, and the Turtle. The Senecas had these three and five more: the Beaver, the Deer, the Snipe, the Heron, and the Hawk. All the members of the same clan,

---

* Or "People of the Long House," the name by which the Iroquois called themselves. The English called them "The Five Nations," and later "The Six Nations." See §172.

in whatever tribe, regarded each other as brothers and sisters, and marriage was not permitted within the limits of the clan. Some believed that after death they would resume the shape of the ancestral bird, beast, or reptile whose form, rudely drawn on bark, was placed over the door of their lodge.

Sachems.—Each tribe had a sachem, or chief counselor in matters of peace, whose place was filled on his death by the election of another member of his family, usually his brother or his sister's son. Women, as well as men, voted in these elections. In time of war, or other emergencies, chiefs were chosen who continued in office as long as they lived. Being chosen for personal qualities, such as wisdom, eloquence, or bravery, these chiefs were often very able men. The sorcerers, called *powwows* or medicine men, had still greater power, owing to the superstitions of the people. They really had some skill in healing sick persons by vapor baths and decoctions of roots and herbs; but to these rational remedies they added howlings and incantations, which were supposed to frighten away the evil spirits that occasioned disease.

26. Religion.—According to the dark notions of barbarians, the Indians were a very religious people. They believed in a Great Spirit, the Master of Life, who had made the world, and whose bounty they celebrated by six annual thanksgivings,—at the first flowing of maple-sap, at planting, at the ripening of berries, when their green corn was ready for eating, at harvest, and at New Year. They believed, also, in an Evil Spirit, who might bring upon them famine, pestilence, or defeat in war, and whom they sought to appease by fastings and sacrifices. They expected another life after death, and desired to have their weapons, and sometimes a favorite dog, buried with them for use in the "happy hunting grounds." The Natchez, on the lower Mississippi, were sun-worshipers, and kept a perpetual, sacred fire in their temples.

27. Dancing and Singing were important parts of every religious observance. No sick person could be cured, no war planned, and no treaty made without a dance, which often continued several days. Their musical instruments were drums, rattles, and a rude kind of flute. The wardance was common to all the tribes, but each clan had peculiar dances of its own, sometimes numbering thirty or more.

Indian Dancing.

Though they had neither books nor letters, some Indian tribes practiced *picture-writing,* which answered all their purposes. They had even a sort of musical notation, by which a leader could read off his song from a piece of birch-bark marked with a stick. Beads made of shells or stones served them for money.

28. Communism was the social law of the whole continent. In some of the "long houses" of the Iroquois, twenty families were fed daily from the common kettle of boiled corn and beans. Hunters left their game to be carried home by other members of their clan, while they pushed on for fresh supplies. The salmon of the Columbia River was speared, dried, and kept in common store-houses for the benefit of the whole tribe. Most of the Mexican *pueblos* consisted of three or four "joint tenement houses," in each of which a hundred or more families lived together.

29. Appearance and Character.—The natives of America were of an almost uniform dark-brown color, with straight, shining black hair and high cheek-bones. With but few exceptions they were treacherous, cruel, and revengeful. Often hospitable and friendly when at peace, they were merciless and brutal in war. Prisoners were tortured with fiendish barbarity. It was thought an ill-omen for the conquerors if they failed to make their victim cry out with pain; therefore though they tore out bits of his flesh with teeth or pincers, night after night, and at last roasted him in a slow fire, he continued to sing his death-song with a calm, unwavering voice until his last breath released him from their torments.

War, famine, and pestilence destroyed so many Indians every year, that we may doubt whether many would now be living but for the interference of the whites, whose cruelties and frauds—though they can never be remembered without shame—were mercy compared with the tortures which the barbarians inflicted on each other. Indians are more numerous now within the limits of the United States than they are supposed to have been when Englishmen first landed on our coasts; and the only tribes which can look forward to continued existence are those which, like the Cherokees, have adopted the thrifty habits of civilized life.

Map No. 2. Name the chief ranges of the Cordilleras. Point out the Great Basin. The Great Salt Lake. The several branches of the Columbia; the Missouri. The course of the Colorado; the Sacramento; the San Joaquin. The longest river in the world. The outlet of the Great Lakes. The country of the Algonquins; the Huron- Iroquois; the Mobilians; the Athabascas ; the Pueblos; the Dakotas; the Shoshones ; and the Apaches.

Consult Walker's "Statistical Atlas of the United States;" Raymond's "Mining Statistics; " Fremont's " Explorations in the Rocky Mountains;" Hayden's "Reports." Read Chapter I of Parkman's "Conspiracy of Pontiac," and the Introduction to his "Jesuits in North America;" Morgan's "League of the Iroquois" and "Ancient Society;" Schoolcraft's "Algic Researches" and other works; Catlin's "North American Indians."

The following Table exhibits seven steps in human progress:

I. LOWEST GRADE OF SAVAGERY.—Mankind lived on fruit and nuts; had no houses, no fire, no agriculture, no animal food.

II. MIDDLE GRADE OF SAVAGERY.—Began with the use of fish for food, and of fire for cooking; ended with invention of the bow and arrow.

III. UPPER GRADE OF SAVAGERY.—Began with use of bow and arrows for hunting, and ended with invention of pottery; included basket-making and use of knives of flint and stone.

IV. LOWEST GRADE OF BARBARISM.—Began with manufacture of pottery, proceeded with cultivation of corn and other plants, and ended with use of sun-dried brick and stone for building.

V. MIDDLE GRADE OF BARBARISM.—Began in Eastern Hemisphere with domestication of animals; in Western, with irrigation of land for tillage. Included use of copper,—which in some cases was hardened like steel,—and building with brick and dressed stone, and ended with the working of iron.

VI. HIGHEST GRADE OF BARBARISM.—Began with iron manufacture, and ended with the invention of the alphabet.

VII. CIVILIZATION.—Began with written language, includes gunpowder, the mariner's compass, printing, steam in manufactures and locomotion, illuminating gas, the electric telegraph, etc., etc.

Of these seven grades, only the third, fourth, and fifth were represented in America at the time of its discovery by white people.

— *Condensed from Morgan's "Ancient Society."*

CHAPTER III.
DISCOVERIES AND SETTLEMENTS BY EUROPEANS.

30. The fifteenth century was a great age in Europe. The art of printing, then newly invented, by diffusing the thoughts of old writers, stirred men's minds to speculation concerning the world they lived in. Improvements in the mariner's compass made navigation safer. Spaniards discovered and colonized the Canary Islands; Portuguese sailors reached the Madeiras, Azores, and Cape Verdes, and, far more important than all, found a sea-route to India.[1]

31. A few bold thinkers had long believed that the earth was a globe instead of the oblong plain which the ancients imagined; but **Christopher Columbus**,[2] a Genoese sailor, was the first to act upon this belief and resolve to sail westward to China and Japan. The means for such a voyage had first to be secured; and Columbus spent many years in begging the various governments of Europe for men, money, and ships. At length the good queen, Isabella of Spain, exclaimed: "I will undertake the enterprise for mine own crown of Castile; and if it be necessary I will pawn my jewels to defray the cost."

32. On Friday, the third of August, 1492, Columbus set sail from Palos, in Spain, with three small ships manned by 120 sailors. He followed first the well-known route to the Canaries, where he took in fresh supplies of food and water, and then stood away forty days westward into the unknown sea, which the imaginations of his men peopled with indescribable horrors. Just as they had resolved to throw their commander overboard, and turn their prows toward Spain,

Christopher Columbus.

a gun from one of the smaller vessels announced a discovery, and the glad cty "Land ahead!" was soon heard from the mast-head of the Pinta. (See Map 1.)

33. The Discovery by Columbus.—On the far horizon the low, green shore of one of the Bahamas was seen by the early morning light. Terror and discontent suddenly gave way to exultant joy. At sunrise of October 12, 1492, the great Admiral landed, and, kneeling on the beach, gave thanks to heaven. He then assumed possession of the country in the name of the sovereigns of Spain, calling it San Salvador (Holy Savior).

34. The people, who were gentle and friendly in appearance, came running to the shore bringing gifts of fruit to conciliate their visitors, whom they supposed to be messengers from heaven. Isabella and Columbus had indeed hoped to convey a message of heavenly grace to these untaught heathen; but the cruelty of most of their representatives defeated their high purpose. Not knowing that a great continent still barred his passage to the eastern seas, Columbus called the people "Indians" and their islands " Indies." With the adjective "West" prefixed, this name has continued in use, while the original natives of the whole continent are known as "Indians."

35. Having visited Hayti and Cuba, Columbus returned to Spain, bearing with him specimens of the people and products of the newly-discovered lands. He was received with a truly royal welcome, and now hundreds of the rich and the great were eager to enlist in his company of adventurers. Knowing nothing, men imagined whatever they most desired concerning the new wonder-land, which was soon said to contain walled cities built of gold and pearls, and to hold, deep in its enchanted forests, a fountain of perpetual youth! But precisely because they were looking for these impossible things, the early adventurers failed. No man came to stay; each hoped to become immensely rich by one fortunate discovery, and return to dazzle his countrymen with a blaze of jewels and rich equipage. The poor natives, who were to help them to this sudden wealth, died by thousands, of unwonted labors, and station after station of the Spaniards was abandoned to solitude.

36. In three subsequent voyages, Columbus discovered Jamaica and others of the West India Islands, and in 1498, touched the continent near the mouth of the Orinoco. But the great Admiral died in 1506, believing that he had only found a new route to Asia; and the *New World,* which he had discovered, received its name, almost by accident, from his friend Amerigo Vespucci,[3] whose description first made it known to central Europe.

37. English Discovery of North America.—When the kings who had refused aid to Columbus heard of his great success, they hastened to seize a part of the newly- discovered lands. Henry VII. of England sent *John Cabot* [4] and his sons to take possession in the king's name of any "islands or regions inhabited by infidels" which they could find,— they taking all the risk and expense of the voyage, to be repaid, if at all, by the profits of trade with the "infidels." *Sebastian Cabot,*[4] one of the sons, was the first to visit the North American continent. In company with his father he descried the coast of Labrador fourteen months before Columbus touched South America (§ 36). The next year he discovered Newfoundland, and extended his voyage to Chesapeake Bay.

38. The **Portuguese**, *Cabral,* discovered, in A. D. 1500, the rich forests of Brazil; while his countryman, *Cortereal,* following the Cabots, explored the North American coasts, and carried off fifty or more of the unoffending natives to be sold as slaves in Europe. A third Portuguese, *Magellan,*[5] found at last a south west passage to the Pacific Ocean through the strait which bears his name, while the notion of a north-west passage is as yet neither realized nor abandoned. For more than a hundred years sailors from all parts of western Europe were sailing into the bays and rivers of the American coast, hoping that each might lead to the Pacific.

39. Spaniards, following Columbus, examined all the coasts and islands of the Caribbean Sea. *Diego Columbus* conquered and colonized Cuba, having inherited his father's title, "Viceroy of the New World." *Ponce de Leon,* a comrade of the great Admiral, but now an old man of damaged fame and fortune, hoped to regain all that he had lost, and more, by finding that fabled fountain (§35) which could restore youth and the vigor of life. On Easter

Day, which the Spaniards called *Pascua Florida,* he came in sight of a beautiful country, bright with spring flowers; and, after exploring its coasts, gave to the whole peninsula the name of Florida. But he never found the Fountain of Youth. In his attempt to gain possession of the country, a few years later, he received a mortal wound, and died in Cuba disappointed in all his hopes. Another Spaniard, *Nunez de*

Balboa,[6] was the first European who crossed the Isthmus of Darien. Advancing waist-deep into the waters of the Pacific Ocean, he drew his sword and swore, as a true knight, that he would defend it, with its coasts, islands, and all that it contained, for his master, the king of Spain!

40. Vasquez de Ayllon, in 1520, visited the coasts of South Carolina, and carried away two ship-loads of natives to toil in the mines of Hayti, or Hispaniola. One ship sank on the return-voyage; the other arrived with only a part of its wretched freight, numbers having perished of suffocation and the barbarities of their captors. Naturally, a later attempt of De Ayllon to plant a colony in the country he had thus despoiled, ended in failure and disgrace. Meanwhile a troop of Spaniards, under Cortez, conquered the rich and populous villages of the Valley of Mexico; but neither this event, nor the subsequent Spanish conquest of Peru, belongs to the history of the United States.

41. Narvaez, in A. D. 1528, landed with 300 men in Tampa Bay, and, marching inland, penetrated through dense pine woods and sickly swamps to Appalachee Bay. Many of his company died of fever and by the arrows of the savages, and neither conquest nor settlement was made. His countryman, *Hernando de Soto,*[7] with a gallant company of 600 men, marched northward and westward into the interior, and during the third year of his wanderings reached the Mississippi near the present city of Memphis. After a winter of untold hardships he died in the wilderness, and was buried beneath the turbid waters of the great river which he had discovered.

42. Coronado, another Spaniard, explored the western shores of Mexico about the same time, ascended the river Gila,

March of De Soto.

visited the magnificent gorges of the upper Colorado, and penetrated probably to the head-waters of the Arkansas. He was seeking the "Seven Cities of Cibola," which the excited fancy of his countrymen had pictured as full of sumptuous palaces blazing with gold and jewels. He found only some village Indians (§22) who offered him a share of their corn, and were amazed by being violently attacked and plundered by the disappointed Spaniards. If Coronado had expected less he would doubtless have admired the fine buildings of dressed stone, whose ruins still attest the industry of the Pueblos.[8]

43. French fishermen were the first to discover the immense shoals of cod-fish on the banks of Newfoundland, and their industry drew thence a steady gain, while the Spaniards were wasting life and fortune in their search for cities of gold. In A. D. 1524, *Verrazzano,* a Florentine in the service of Francis I., king of France, visited the harbors of New York and Newport, and, after exploring the Atlantic coast from Carolina to Newfoundland, wrote the first detailed account of the country, which he called New France. Ten or fifteen years later, *Jacques Cartier*[9] explored the gulf and river St. Lawrence above the sites of Quebec and Montreal, both of which contained a large Indian population.

44. No settlement so far had been made within the present limits of the United States. In A. D. 1562, the French *Admiral Coligny*,[10] a wiser man than most of his countrymen of that day, undertook to establish a home of perfect religious freedom in the American forests. Under his patronage a company of Frenchmen landed on the coast of South Carolina, and built a fort, which they called Caroline in honor of King Charles. The harbor was named Port Royal; the land seemed to them "the fairest, fruitfulest, and pleasantest of all the world." Unhappily they expected the fruitful land to give them harvests unsown. The Indians, who had been friendly at first, grew tired of feeding such lazy guests. *Ribault*,[11] the French captain, returned home for supplies. Hunger and home-sickness conquered the resolution of those who were left, and, building a rude ship, they followed him.

45. Two years later another company of Frenchmen, under Captain Laudonnière,[11] built a second Fort Caroline, on the St. John's River, farther south. Among them were many lawless spirits, who, in defiance of their commander, seized the ships and set off on a plundering cruise among the Spanish West Indies. The Spaniards, who claimed the whole North American continent, and especially Florida, owing to Ponce de Leon's discovery (§39), were made still more angry at the French intrusion by these piracies.

46. Pedro Menendez, in 1565, with nearly 3,000 Spaniards, selected a site for *St. Augustine,* which still exists as

Old Gate at St. Augustine.

the oldest town in the United States. Ribault, who had just come from France, no sooner heard of their arrival than he sailed with a squadron to attack the Spaniards; but Menendez at the same time marched overland to the French fort, and murdered all its occupants. As France and Spain were at peace, he excused the act by an inscription which he nailed to a tree: "Not as French, but as heretics."

When the news of this massacre reached France, the king took no notice of it; but a private gentleman, Dominique de Gourgues, resolved upon vengeance. Selling all his lands,

Champlain among the Indians.

he spent the avails in ships, and with 150 men sailed to Florida. Aided by the Indians, who had learned to dread and hate the Spaniards, he took and demolished Fort Caroline and two other forts at the mouth of the river, hanged all the- men who were not killed in fighting, and wrote over their heads this inscription: "Not as Spaniards, but as traitors, robbers, and murderers."

47. The French in Canada.—Frenchmen were more successful in gaining and keeping a foothold near the St. Lawrence. *Samuel de Champlain* [12]was the "Father of New France." In 1608 he laid the foundations of Quebec. The next summer he joined a war-party of Algonquins (§23), explored with them the beautiful lake which bears his name, and gave diem a victory over the Iroquois by means of fire-arms, which those astonished warriors had never seen nor heard before. Champlain was followed by missionaries, who were the first to discover the salt-springs of Onondaga and the beautiful lakes of central New York. Several of these good men suffered brutal tortures and death from the savages whom they had come to convert.

48. Spaniards in the South-west.—Not only St. Augustine, but *Santa Fé,* [13] the next oldest town in the United States, owes its origin to the Spaniards. Antonio de Es- pejo, [14] starting in 1582 from northern Mexico, explored the upper course of the Rio Grande. He found the people well clothed in cotton and leather, living in houses four stories high, strongly built of stone and lime and with fire-places for winter use. In consequence of Espejo's discovery of rich veins of silver, colonies were sent in 1595 to *New Mexico,* and a town was built near Santa Fé. Late in the following century, Jesuit Fathers established missions in Arizona and California. All the "Mission Indians" were supplied with food and clothing, the former of which they were gradually taught to produce from their fields. Wine, grains, flax, hemp, and wool were among the exports from the Missions; and but for occasional brief relapses into their old wild manners, the people kept for nearly a hundred years the aspect of civilized communities. Then the Fathers left them, and they soon went back into barbarism.

Trace on Map No. 1 the several routes of Columbus. Of Cabot, Cabral, and Magellan. On Map No. 2 the routes of Ponce de Leon, Balboa, De Ayllon, Narvaez, De Soto, Coronado, Verrazzano, Cartier, Chainplain, Espejo. Point out the sites of the two French settlements on the Atlantic coast. St. Augustine.

Read Irving's "Life of Columbus" and "Companions of Columbus;" Hakluyt's "Voyages;" Major's "Life of Prince Henry the Navigator;" Parkman's "Pioneers of France in the New World" and "Jesuits in North America."

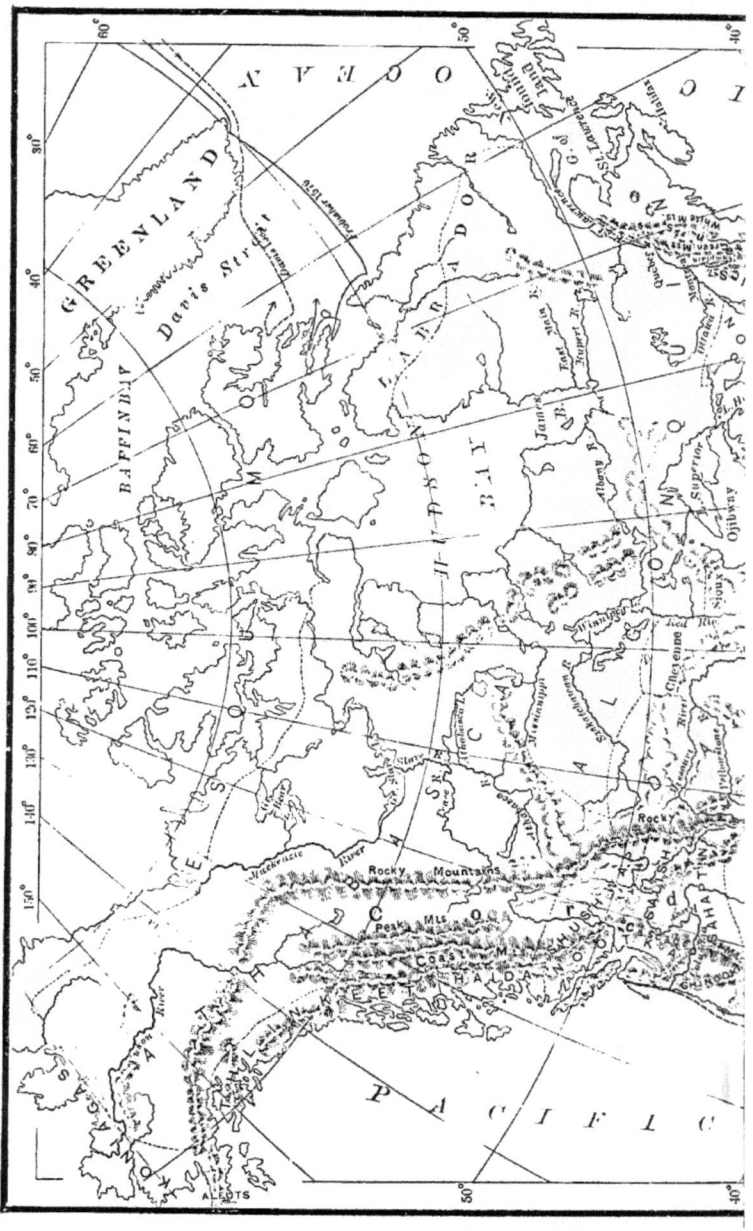

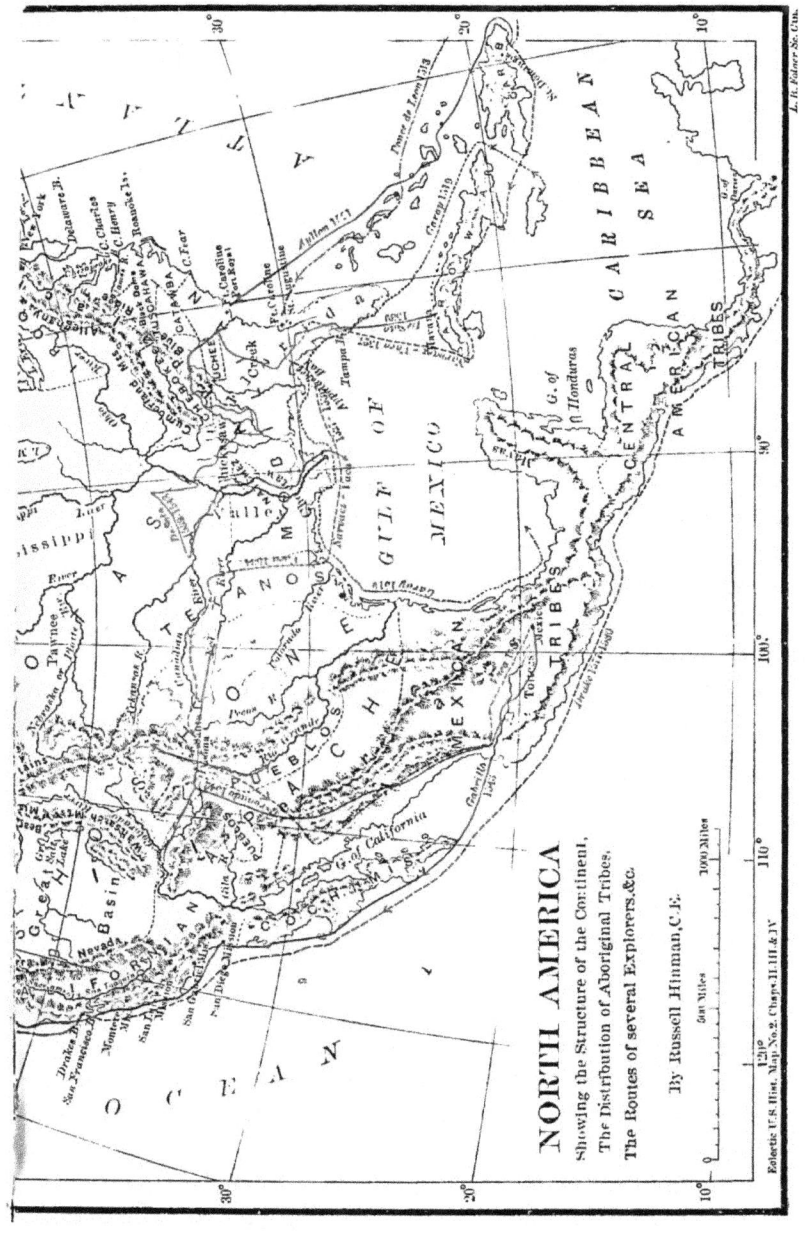

NOTES.

1. **Prince Henry the Navigator** (b. 1394, <1. 1460) was the fourth son of King John I. of Portugal. He established a school of navigation, and introduced the use of the eoinpass and the astrolabe. The discovery of the Madeira Islands and the eoast of Africa southward as far as sierra Leone, was due to his aid and encouragement. The impulse to navigation given by him, caused Portuguese sailors for a time to lead in explorations. The entire western coast of Africa became known when Bartholomew Diaz discovered the Cape of Good Hope in 1486; but this route to Asia was not used for commerce until after 1500.

2. **Christopher Columbus**, the eldest son of a wool-comber, was horn at Genoa, Italy, in 1436. He obtained his education at the University of Pavia, but at the early age of fifteen became a sailor. His experiences at sea embraced all that was then known of seamanship. After his marriage with the daughter of an old sea-captain, he earned his living for some years at the Madeiras by making maps and marine charts. Before he was thirty-eight years of age, he had conceived his grand ideas of the form of the earth and the possibility of reaching Asia by sailing westward from Europe. Columbus was an intensely religious man, and his purpose in seeking unknown shores was "to carry the true faith to the uttermost parts of the earth." Before sailing he was created admiral, and viceroy of the regions he should discover. The incidents of his several voyages are given in the text. His remains are now, after three removals, deposited in the cathedral at Havana, Cuba.

3. **Amerigo Vespucci** was a native of Florence. In 1499 he was agent of a commercial house in Seville, and that year sailed as a pilot in the fleet of Alonzo de Ojeda on an expedition to the " Indies of the West," which had been discovered by Columbus. Vespucci had often talked with Columbus, and the stirring accounts of his travels, related by the great Genoese, had aroused in his own breast the spirit of adventure. Ojeda's caravels readied the island of Trinidad after a smooth voyage, and, sailing through the Gulf of Paria, the mainland was first sighted. In 1501 Vespucci sailed from Spain on his second expedition, this time in charge. He landed on the eoast of Brazil, and cruised north and south from the Florida peninsula to 54° south latitude. His account of this voyage, published at Augsburg, Bavaria, in 1504, was the first printed announcement of the discovery of a western continent, and the zeal of his friends led them to name the new found land " Amerige " (America)

in his honor.

4. John Cabot and Sebastian Cabot.—Very little is known of the lives of the two men on whose discoveries England based her claim to a large part of the New World. It is known that they discovered the mainland of America in June, 1497. John Cabot died before Sebastian's second voyage in 1498. During this voyage the coast was explored 1800 miles. Sebastian Cabot is supposed to have died in 1557, at the age of eighty.

5. Fernando Magellan left Seville, Spain, in August. 1519, and entered the straits between South America and the island of Terra del Fuego, October, 1520. He kept on his westward course, and in April, 1521, was killed in an encounter with natives of one of the Philippine Islands. One of his ships again reached Spain in September, 1522. This was the first circumnavigation of the globe.

6. Vaseo Nunez de Balboa was a freebooter, who, to escape from his creditors in Spain, hid himself in the hold of a vessel bound for the Caribbean Sea. When the ship was several days out, he came forth from this hiding place, and implored the commander on his knees to spare his life and to give him some food. Afterwards the vessel was wrecked on the Darien coast, and Balboa with most of the crew were cast on shore. By his force of character he assumed command of the party, and started to explore the country. They were attacked by hostile Indians, and reduced by starvation ; but, pushing boldly into the interior, they came in a few days to the crest of a mountain range, from which the vast expanse of the Pacifie burst upon their astonished gaze. This discovery was made by Balboa in September, 1513. At the sight he prostrated himself upon the ground ; then, rising to his knees, he thanked God " it had pleased his divine majesty to reserve unto that day the victory and praise of so great a tiling unto him."

7. Hernando de Soto was born in Estremadura, Spain, in 1496. He was of a noble family, and was distinguished for his excellence in scholarship and athletic sports. He accompanied an expedition to America in 1519, and again in 1527. In 1528 he explored the coasts of Yucatan and Guatemala for 700 miles, believing he would find a strait that connected the Atlantic and Pacific oceans. He went with Pizarro to Peru in 1532, and took a prominent part in the conquest of that country. Returning to Spain with an immense fortune, he was received at the court of Charles V. with high honors, and asked of the emperor permission to possess Florida, which was looked upon as a land abounding in native wealth. This being granted, De Soto fitted out a fleet of nine vessels at his own expense, and sailed by way of Havana, in 1539. He had on board, besides his 600 followers, 300 horses, many hogs, and a number of bloodhounds. The exploring party landed at Tampa Bay, in jubilant spirits, on the 30th of May. Their three years perilous wanderings in southern forests, and De Soto's untimely death, are described in the text.

8. The finest existing specimens of the ancient **Pueblo architecture** in New Mexico are the villages of Santo Domingo, San Felipe, Isleta, Aeoma, and others in the valley of the Rio Grande, and Zuñi, near the western border of the territory. These are still occupied by the Pueblo Indians, and many of the houses are in an excellent state of preservation. The ruins of seven great buildings in the valley of the Rio Chaco, 100 miles north-west of Santa Fé, probably mark the sites of the "Seven Cities of Cibola" (§ 12) which Coronado sought. Each edifice contained from 100 to 600 apartments, and was occupied by from 1,000 to 4,000 persons.

9. **When Jacques Cartier**, in 1535, anchored bis ships in the month of the St. Lawrence, he felt confident, from the great width and depth of the river, that he had discovered at last the long sought passage to the Indian Ocean.

10. **Admiral Gaspard de Coligny** was a noted leader of the French Huguenots, and fell the first victim in the Massacre of St. Bartholomew, August 24th, 1572.

11. The expedition of **Ribault** first landed on the Florida coast at the mouth of the St. John's River, which they named the "River of May." On the south bank they erected a stone column, on which were inscribed the arms of France. Laudonnière's party were rejoiced to find this memorial column when they visited the spot two years later.

12. **Samuel de Champlain** was born at Brouage, France, in 1567. His father was a sea-captain,and the son was early skilled in navigation. He visited Canada several times before his appointment as lieutenant-general. He effected the first permanent French settlement in the New World. His expedition against the Iroquois provoked the enmity of that tribe, and the French were compelled to seek lines of exploration and trade to the north of lakes Ontario and Erie, and from thenee to the valley of the Ohio and the Mississippi. He died in Canada in 1635.

13. Santa Fé.—Old Spanish records have recently been discovered in Santa Fé which seem to prove a greater antiquity for the place than has been generally accepted. They indicate that the Catholic chapel of San Miguel, which is still in a fair state of preservation, was originally built as early as 1565. If this be true, Santa Fé was undoubtedly a permanent mission station from that time, and this would make the Spanish settlement as early as that at St. Augustine.

14. Prior to **Espejo's** exploration of the Rio Grande valley, several parties of Spanish adventurers had been over the same region,—notably one under Cabeza de Yaca in 1537, another under Marco dl Niza in 1539, that of Coronado (§ 42) the following year, and one led by Francisco de Bonello in 1581. Between the years 1595 and 1599, Juan de Oñate was sent by the viceroy of Mexico to take formal possession of the country in the name of his Spanish sovereign.

CHAPTER IV.
ENGLISH SETTLEMENTS. — VIRGINIA.

49. The Partition of America.—Spain, Portugal, France, and England were for centuries rival claimants to the New World; while Holland and Sweden kept each a foothold upon its shores, long enough to impress something of their character upon its future inhabitants. But as there was really far more land than either or all of them could use,, the dispute settled itself at last upon

> "The simple plan
> That they should take who have the power,
> And they should keep who can."

50. Eighty years had passed since the discoveries by the Cabots before **Englishmen** made any serious effort to establish homes in North America. English sailors had indeed had their full share in the exploration of the continent. *Frobisher*[1] went beyond all previous mariners into the icy regions west of Greenland; *Davis,* advancing yet farther to the northward, entered the strait which bears his name; *Drake,*[2] in quest of Spanish treasure-ships, explored the Pacific coast as far as Oregon, wintered near San Francisco, and returned to Europe by way of Asia and Africa.

51. Sir Humphrey Gilbert, seeing the failure and misery which had resulted from the eager search for gold, planned a colony for fisheries and regular trade. But his two expeditions failed, and their brave leader was lost at sea. His half-brother, *Sir Walter Raleigh,*[3] was among the greatest and most unfortunate of English adventurers. Under a patent from Queen Elizabeth,[4] in 1585, he sent 108 colonists to occupy the fruitful region from which the French had been expelled (§§44, 46).

52. Virginia. — Delighted with the accounts which reached her of the beauty and wealth of the country, Elizabeth named it *Virginia,* in honor of her own state as a maiden queen. A site was chosen for the colony on Roanoke Island, and a profitable trade was carried on with the friendly Indians. But the misconduct of the white men soon turned these into foes; the situation of the colonists then became unendurable, and they seized an opportunity to return to England.

Sir Walter Raleigh.

53. A second colony,[5] including some women and children, arrived at Roanoke in 1587. But war was now breaking out between England and Spain. Ships which Raleigh sent with fresh supplies for the colonists, went in chase of Spanish prizes, and were themselves taken. When Englishmen revisited Roanoke three years later, no white face was found on the island. Whether the settlers had perished or had taken refuge with some friendly tribe in the interior, can not be known.

54. Though Raleigh derived no benefit from the expenditure of all his fortune, yet his generous efforts had spread through England a knowledge of America, and had given a great impulse to colonization. The voyages of Gosnold,[6] Weymouth, and Pring made known the islands, capes, and noble harbors on the coasts of Maine and Massachusetts; and fleets of English vessels repaired thither for trade and fishing, though for many years no permanent settlement was formed.

55. Colonial Companies.—In 1606 King James I.[7] gave charters to two English companies "for planting and ruling New England in America." The *London Company* might establish a colony anywhere between Cape Fear and the east end of Long Island; the *Plymouth Company*, anywhere between Delaware Bay and Halifax, provided that neither should begin a settlement within a hundred miles of one already made by the other. The king reserved to himself the right to make all laws and appoint all officers for the colonies; and was, moreover, to receive one fifth of all gold and silver, and one fifteenth of all copper obtained from them. For five years every man was to labor, not for himself, but for a common fund.

56. First English Settlement.—The London Company soon dispatched three ship-loads of emigrants, commanded by Christopher Newport, to select and settle lands in Virginia. Of the 105 men who enlisted in the enterprise, 48 were "gentlemen," according to the notions of the times; that is, they despised work, and expected to grow rich either by accident or by the toil of others. The most sensible man in the colony was Captain John Smith,[8] who had gained wisdom by much hard experience; and he was imprisoned on the voyage out, under a foolish charge that he intended to murder the Council and make himself king of Virginia! This accusation sprang from President Wingfield's envy of the superior ability and influence of Smith. Upon trial, the latter was honorably acquitted and restored to his place in the Council.

57. .It was the spring of 1607, when the three vessels entered Chesapeake Bay. Glad to be protected from the storms that were raging without, the adventurers named their first anchorage *Point Comfort*. They called the two capes which guard the entrance of the bay, *Charles* and *Henry*, after their king's two sons; and the noble stream which they soon afterwards ascended, *James* or *King's River*, from the king himself. Fifty miles up the river they chose the site for their first settlement, which bore the name of *Jamestown*.

58. Wingfield's dishonesty soon brought him into disgrace, and Smith became the real head of the colony. He enforced the primitive rule that he who would not work

Settlement of Jamestown.

should not eat; he put an end to quarreling and profanity, and in time he taught the "gentlemen" to swing their axes with the rest. Meanwhile he explored Chesapeake Bay and all its tributary rivers; cultivated friendship with the Indians, of whom a powerful confederacy of forty tribes, called *Powhatans*, occupied the region, and secured from them needed supplies of corn.

59. The "Starving Time."—Compelled by a severe wound to return to England, Smith left about five hundred colonists in Virginia, well supplied with all that was needful for their comfort. Nevertheless, the period following his departure is called the "Starving Time," for the men gave themselves up to idleness and riot, and in six months there were only sixty persons alive in the colony. These resolved to join the fishermen in Newfoundland; but on their way down the river they met Lord Delaware, the new governor, with hundreds of colonists and a fresh supply of stores.

60. A new era soon dawned upon Virginia. Gold-seeking was abandoned after a ship-load of earth containing specks of yellow mica had been sent to England and found worthless. The soil was now perceived to be the true source of wealth, and the allotment of a few acres to each man gave each an interest in his own labor. Unhappily the high price of tobacco in England — where it had been lately introduced and was very fashionable — led most of the planters to raise it to the exclusion of food-products. And though the price soon fell to two-pence a pound, tobacco long continued to be the medium of exchange as well as the chief export of the colony. Ministers' salaries, lawyers' fees, and landlords' rents were all paid in tobacco. But the crop exhausted the soil, and in many cases short-lived wealth was followed by bankruptcy, ruin, and poverty.

61. New Laws. — In 1611 the Company sent out a new code of laws of almost incredible strictness. Theft and disrespectful mention of the king were punishable with death at the first offense. Profane swearing and absence from public worship received the same punishment after two trials of lighter penalties.

62. Introduction of Slavery. — Hitherto there had been very few women in the colony. In 1619, beside nearly twelve hundred other settlers, ninety honest girls came from England and became wives of planters. Another cargo followed, and many colonists now enjoyed the comfort of settled homes. A less valuable acquisition was a company of "jail-birds," who were sold as indentured servants for a limited number of years. Still more serious in its ultimate consequences was an importation of negroes from the African coast who became slaves for life. The first cargo of negroes was brought to Jamestown in a Dutch ship in 1619.

Trace on Map No. 2 the voyages of Frobisher, Davis, Drake. Point out capes Charles and Henry. The site of Raleigh's two colonies. On Map No. 3, point out the site of Jamestown. Point Comfort. The principal rivers that flow into Chesapeake Bay.

Read Smith's "True Relation" and "General History." For this and all following chapters to the end of Part HI: Bancroft's "History of the United States;" Bryant's "Popular History;" Hildreth's "History of the United States."

NOTES.

1. Martin Frobisher for fifteen years cherished the idea that he could sail direct to the coveted " north-west passage," but. he was too poor to fit out a ship. He said " it was the only thing of the world that was yet left undone, by which a notable minde might be made famous and fortunate." At length, the Earl of Warwick provided him with means sufficient to equip two small barks, and he set sail from the mouth of the Thames in the summer of 1576. One vessel deserted him at the first storm, but he fearlessly pressed forward with the other to the coasts of Labrador. Upon entering an inlet north of Hudson Strait., he firmly believed the aim of his journey across the sea was achieved ; for he argued that the land on his right was Asia, while that on his left was the continent of America. A short sail convinced him of his error. The next year Frobisher came with a fleet of several vessels to the same forbidding region, and returned to England laden with worthless dirt and stones which were believed to contain rich traces of gold. In 1578 he commanded a. third expedition, this time under the immediate patronage of Queen Elizabeth. It was composed of fifteen well appointed ships, and carried out many sons of noble English families,besides one hundred persons to form a permanent colony on the inhospitable shores of Greenland. When the flag ship of the Admiral sailed into Hudson Strait, "Now, surely," thought he, "I will go through to the Pacific." But after going sixty miles he concluded that he was upon the wrong course, and turned back with his fleet. With the approach of winter his ships were nearly overwhelmed by icebergs, and the intense cold created mutiny among his men ; so that ali were glad to get away from these polar regions with their lives, and back to their homes without either glory or gold. Frobisher was knighted for bravery at the defeat of the Spanish Armada, and died from a wound received in an attack on Brest in 1594.

2. Sir Francis Drake (b. 1545, d. 1595) was one of the most renowned of British admirals. In 1572, having crossed the Isthmus of Panama from the east, he first saw the Pacific Ocean from the top of a tree which he had climbed; and then and there he resolved "to sail an English ship in these seas." Five years later he left England with five small vessels and nearly two hundred men, to carry out this resolution. In eight months he entered the straits of Magellan with his own ship only, the " Golden Hind ; " and, sailing through, followed the western coast of America. He christened its northern part New Albion, and took possession of it in the name of Queen Elizabeth. Steering westward into the broad, unknown Pacific, he successfully circumnavigated the world, entering once more the harbor of Plymouth two yearsand ten months after his departure. He was the first Englishman, and the second of all navigators, to accomplish this feat. A chair was eventually made of wood taken from the "Golden Hind," and presented by Charles II. to the University of Oxford.

3. Sir Walter Raleigh, born in Devonshire, England, 1552, was beheaded on the charge of conspiracy against the throne in 1618. He was a man of genius and eminent attainments, — distinguished as author, explorer, and courtier. Queen Elizabeth knighted him because of the successful issue of the first expedition which he fitted out to the coast of North Carolina. He became member of Parliament, and was commander of a vessel in the English fleet that annihilated the Spanish " Invincible Armada " in 1588. He explored the coasts of Guiana, in South America, and upon his return to Europe published an account of the expedition. While imprisoned in the Tower of London for a period of thirteen years, he wrote his "History of the World." Raleigh's American colonists have the credit of introducing tobacco and potatoes into Europe.

Concerning Raleigh's execution, his biographer writes that "approaching the edge of the scaffold and kneeling down, he prayed in a very earnest manner, and begged for the prayers of all who heard him. The executioner then kneeled to him for the forgiveness of his office. Raleigh placed both his hands on the man's shoulders, and assured him that he forgave him with all his heart. He then examined the block and fitted himself to it, and asked the executioner to show him the ax. The latter hesitated, but Raleigh repeated the request. Touching the knife-edge with his finger, and then kissing the blade, he said, 'This gives me no fear. It is a sharp and fair medicine to cure me of all my diseases.' He added, 'When I stretch forth my hands, dispatch me.' Kneeling for his last prayer, he laid his head upon the block, calmly stretched forth his hands, and awaited the death-blow. The headsman again hesitated. 'Strike, man, strike! what dost thou fear?' cried Raleigh. Two terrible blows severed the head from the body, and to the last his lips were seen to move in prayer."

4. Queen Elizabeth, the daughter of Henry VIII. and Anne Boleyn, was born in 1533, and ruled over England from 1558 until her death in 1603. She became deeply interested in the marine enterprises of her subjects. Elizabeth was especially jealous of the achievements of Spanish explorers in the New World. When Sir Humphrey Gilbert set out on his unfortunate expedition, she wished him "as great goodhap and safety to his ship as if herself were there in person," and presented him with a golden anchor as a token of her regard Her friendship for Raleigh was manifested in the special patent and licenses granted him, as well as in the marked honors conferred upon him at her court. She showed her approval of Frobisher's first voyage by waving an adieu with her hand from the shore, and sending him a personal message; and of his second and third expeditions by defraying a large share of the expenses.

5. Simon Ferdinando was admiral of this expedition, and John White was appointed governor of the colony. Soon after their arrival at Roanoke Island, Mrs. Dare, the daughter of Governor White, gave birth to a little girl, who was christened Virginia. This was the first English child born within the present territory of the United States.

6. **Bartholomew Gosnold**, in M ay, 1602, discovered and named Cape Cod. He landed there with four men, and these were the first Englishmen who ever set foot upon the shores of New England. Doubling the cape they sailed around Nantucket and Martha's Vineyard islands into Buzzard's Bay (which they called " Gosnold's Hope "),and anchored off the westernmost of the Elizabeth Islands. On this they built a fort and storehouse, purposing to establish a permanent colony, but through fear of the Indians and lack of provisions the party soon returned to England. Until Gosnold's expedition, no English voyager since the Cabots had undertaken the northern or direct course across the Atlantic. His predecessors had followed in the track of Columbus, by the way of the Canary Islands and the West Indies. The distance saved by the new route was between 2,600 and 3,000 miles, and naturally this gave a fresh impulse to colonizing and trading schemes. Gosnold was one of the leaders in the company which founded Jamestown in 1607, and died in the fall of that year from the hardships and exposures of pioneer life. He ranks with Sir Walter Raleigh as one of the wisest and greatest of the founders of American colonies.

7. **King James,** who, in 1603, succeeded Queen Elizabeth on the English throne, was the only son of Mary, Queen of Scots. He was born in 1566, and was crowned King of Scotland when still an infant. James was a weak, cowardly, cruel man. He was constantly under the influence of unworthy favorites, some of whose followers were Hie royal governors of American colonies.

8. **Capt. John Smith** was born in England in 1579 and died in 1631. According to his own account of his life he served as a soldier in the Netherlands, and in the wars against the Turks in Hungary and Austria, where he was taken prisoner and sold as a slave at Constantinople. He slew his master and escaped through Russia. He was also for a time in northern Africa. On his return to England Gosnold persuaded him to join the colony for Virginia. After his return to England from Virginia in 1609, lie made a voyage to New England and constructed a map of the coast from Cape Cod to the mouth of the Penobscot. He published several books relating to America.

CHAPTER V.
VIRGINIA AND MARYLAND.

63. Council of Burgesses.—With the governorship of Sir George Yeardley, the true life of Virginia began. The "cruel laws" were repealed, and, "that the planters might have a hand in the governing of themselves, it was granted that a general assembly should be held yearly once, whereat were to be present the governor and council, with two burgesses from each plantation, freely to be elected by the inhabitants thereof,—this assembly to have power to make and ordain whatsoever laws should by them be thought good and profitable for their subsistence." The "Council of, Burgesses," which met at Jamestown, in July, 1619, was the first law-making body in America which was chosen by the people.

64. Indian Hostilities.—While Powhatan lived,—the chief of that confederacy with which Smith had made friendship,—white men and savages were at peace. His daughter, Pocahontas,[1] married John Rolfe, a young Englishman, and several famous Virginian families are proud to number themselves among her descendants. But Powhatan's successor was hostile to the English. Living in careless security upon their scattered plantations, the colonists had even sold powder and guns to the Indians, who seemed friendly, but who were silently planning the complete extermination of the white intruders. Suddenly at noon of March 22, 1622, every village was attacked. A fierce war followed, in which nearly two thousand colonists perished, and of eighty settlements only eight remained.

65. Changes in Government.—In 1624 King James dissolved the London Company, and made Virginia a royal province; but though the governor and council were appointed by the king, the laws were still made by the representatives of the people. Virginia was strongly attached to both the king and the Church of England. During the changes in the home government, hereafter to be noticed (§125), many royalists found refuge in the colony; and though the Council of Burgesses submitted to Parliament, to avoid the ruin of the tobacco trade, there was great rejoicing when monarchy was restored, A. D. 1660.

66. Condition of Virginia.—Virginia numbered at this time about 30,000 inhabitants. Richmond, in its magnificent position at the falls of the James River, and Williamsburg, on the peninsula between the Rappahannock and the York, were already flourishing settlements. The mildness, beauty, and fertility of the region made it "the best poor man's country in the world." The people wanted only schools for their children to make them perfectly contented. Though "every man instructed his children according to his own ability," this increased the contrast between the families of the educated gentry and the untaught workmen, a distinction which was contrary to the best interests of the colony. The settlers were so scattered that it is said, "no man could see his neighbor without a telescope, or be heard by him without firing a gun."

67. Governor Berkeley.—The joy which attended the restoration of King Charles II. was soon changed to grief and resentment. The right to vote was taken from the mass of freemen to be exercised only by land-owners, taxes were imposed without their consent, and even the settlers of remote and lonely places were not permitted to assemble in arms against the savages, who were murdering their wives and children. Governor Berkeley,[2] an avaricious, selfish, and arbitrary man, was supposed to be selling powder and shot to the Indians contrary to law. Being sent to England to plead the cause of the colony, Berkeley only enriched himself by robbing it of a portion of its lands (§132), which the king was induced to give to a company to which he belonged. In 1673 the same king, in a transient caprice, bestowed "all the dominion of land and water called Virginia" upon lords Culpepper and Arlington for a period of thirty-one years.

68. Bacon's Rebellion.—All this might not have cured the people of their submissive loyalty, but when the governor refused to send troops to oppose a large force of Indians who were coming down the James, they took up arms and chose for their leader Nathaniel Bacon,[3] a gentleman of fortune and influence, who had lately arrived in Virginia. Bacon's little army routed the savages, while the governor was proclaiming him a rebel and traitor, and raising a troop to oppose him. An insurrection in Jamestown compelled Berkeley, however, to disband his army, dissolve his aristocratic council, and call a more popular assembly, of which Bacon was a member.

69. The governor, weak and violent by turns, broke all his promises. Civil war followed, in which Jamestown was burnt, and only a ruined church-tower remains to mark its site. Bacon died suddenly of disease, and his party, for want of a leader, was soon subdued. Berkeley disgraced his victory by the most insolent cruelty. Twenty-two patriots were hanged, and three died from the hardships of their prison. "The old fool," said Charles II., "has taken away more lives than I, for the murder of my father." Berkeley was recalled,[4] and Lord Culpepper,[5] one of the new proprietors, became governor of the Old Dominion.

70. Maryland.—From lands originally belonging to Virginia, a new colony had been formed with a more liberal constitution both as to civil and religious rights. George Calvert, the first Lord Baltimore, obtained from Charles I., in 1629, a grant of lands north of the Potomac, where all persons, but especially members like himself of the Catholic Church, might enjoy freedom of worship. The country was called *Maryland* in honor of the queen, Henrietta Maria; and the first settlement, near the mouth of the Potomac, received the name of *St. Mary's*.

71. Lord Baltimore died before he could revisit America, and the charter was "published and confirmed" in the name of his son. Cecil Calvert, who for forty-three years watched over the prosperity of Maryland. Virginia did not willingly submit to the dismemberment of her territory. William Clayborne, formerly her secretary of state, had occupied the Isle of Kent, in the Chesapeake, with a trading settlement. He considered himself as within the limits of Virginia, and made armed resistance to Lord Baltimore's demand for his allegiance. Three Virginians and one Marylander were killed in battle. Clayborne was sent to England to be tried for treason, but was acquitted, though the right of Maryland to Kent Island was confirmed.

Lord Baltimore.

72. Clayborne's Rebellion.—Some years later Clayborne returned and raised another insurrection in the district which he had once governed. Gov. Leonard Calvert, brother of the proprietor, was forced to retire, but he soon reappeared with superior numbers and put an end to " Clayborne's Rebellion."

73. The Calverts.—The liberal charter granted by Lord Baltimore drew crowds of settlers to the banks of the Potomac. Puritans expelled from Virginia, prelatists from Massachusetts, and refugees from all parts of Europe lived together on equal terms. We regret to record that one party of Protestants made an ungenerous use of their privileges. Resisting both the policy and the rights of the Calverts, they succeeded in banishing all Catholics from the Assembly. Many years of tumult followed. In 1691 the proprietary charter was revoked, and for twenty-four years Maryland was a royal province. In 1715 the Calvert family regained their lands, which they continued to govern until the Revolution.

Point out on Map No. 3, Richmond. Williamsburg. St. Mary's. The Isle of Kent.

NOTES.

1. Pocahontas was born about the year 1595. The long accepted story, that she saved the life of capt. John Smith by interposing her body between him and the war-clubs of the savages who were about to beat him to death, is now discredited. This was one of Smith's wonderful stories in his "General History." That she was much attached to Capt. Smith there is no doubt, for in 1609 she made a long and fatiguing journey by night through the forest to inform him of a plot by her father to murder him. Her marriage with Rolfe, at Jamestown, in 1613, secured many years of peace between the colonists and the Indians. Professing Christianity, she was baptized as "Lady Rebecca." In 1616 she accompanied her husband to England, and was duly presented at court. She was regarded with great interest and curiosity. Pocahontas died in March, 1617, leaving one son, Thomas Rolfe, who in later years removed to Virginia.

2. Sir William Berkeley was appointed Governor of Virginia in 1641, and arrived at Jamestown early in 1642. Being a royalist, he was removed from power by Cromwell in 1651; but, after the Restoration, he again became governor, which position he held until 1677. Berkeley demanded strict loyalty to the civil powers, and conformity to the Established Church. He " thanked God there are no free schools, nor printing, in his colony," and " hoped there would not be for a hundred years ; for learning has brought disobedience into the world, and printing lias divulged them and libels against the best governments." His leniency towards the Indians, who had been committing all sorts of barbarities, and his severity with Bacon and others, who opposed his Indian policy, have led many to believe that Governor Berkeley was in collusion with the savages. Being relieved from office by Sir Herbert Jeffreys in 1677, he returned to England under a sense of disgrace, and died in a few weeks after his arrival. (See Note 4.)

3. Nathaniel Bacon and Governor Berkeley had many bitter personal conflicts, and Bacon was usually more than a match for the governor. At the head of 200 or 300 followers he marched into

Jamestown, halted in front of the state-house, where the assembly was in session, and demanded to see the governor. Berkeley came out, white with rage, and fearlessly went between the lines of soldiers to where Bacon was standing; lie looked defiant, and cried, " Here — shoot me! Fore God, fair mark! Shoot!" But Bacon replied calmly, "No, may it please your honor, — we will not hurt a hair of your head, nor of any other man's; we are come for a commission to save our lives from the Indians, which yon have so often promised; and now we will have it before we go!" And he not only got the desired commission, but the assembly passed an act of amnesty towards himself and his band of rebels They continued, however, to oppose the policy of the governor, and engaged in a vigorous campaign against the Indians. Berkeley once more declared Bacon an outlaw, and led forth his militia to attack the insurgents; but, on approaching their camp, he was dismayed to find most of his men crying, " Bacon ! Bacon ! Bacon ! " and then going over to the enemy.

Bacon said "that it vexed him to the heart that while he was hunting wolves which were destroying innocent lambs, the governor should seek to put him like corn between two mill-stones."

His death oecured in 1676, and the place of his burial was kept secret because Berkeley had threatened to hang his skeleton in chains upon a public gibbet.

4. After Governor Berkeley's removal, Sir Herbert Jeffreys and Sir Henry Chicheley were the successive lieutenant-governors of Virginia, and had the entire control of affairs from 1677 to 1680, when Lord Culpepper assumed the duties of his office.

5. Lord Culpepper was pronounced by a writer of his time, " one of the most cunning and covetous men in England." He was a man of positive character and violent measures. In 1681 the planters in Virginia, became dissatisfied with the extremely low prices paid for their tobacco ; and, in order to create a scarcity of supply, and enhance the value of the remaining crop, an organized band went from plantation to plantation, hacking and destroying the growing plants. Returning from England in the midst of this "strike," Governor Culpepper immediately ordered the leading "plant-cutters" to be hung.

CHAPTER VI.
PLYMOUTH, PORTSMOUTH, AND DOVER.

74. Great religious differences now existed in England. King James, who thought himself at least as wise as Solomon, required all his subjects to believe and worship precisely as he did. A very large party in the nation disapproved some observances of the Established Church, and were especially shocked at the Sunday sports which were recommended and even enjoined by the king himself.

75. Many hundreds of these **Puritans,**[1] finding that there was no toleration for their views in England, separated themselves from the Church, and as many as were able sought an asylum in Holland. They were then called Separatists or Independents, while the great mass of the Puritans remained in the Church, though protesting against some of its practices.

76. The Separatists in Holland were still English at heart, and were grieved to have their children grow up ignorant of the language and customs of their native land. They resolved, therefore, to seek homes in the American wilderness, where, under English laws, they might have freedom to worship God in the way which seemed to them right. From a thousand pilgrims in Holland, a hundred were selected to be founders of the new state; and, after several disasters and delays, they set sail in September, 1620, from Plymouth, in England.

77. The Mayflower.—Though a patent had been secured from the London Company, it proved useless because the person in whose name it was issued did not go with thecolonists; so that the little ship Mayflower set forth on her voyage without warrant or charter from King, Parliament, or Company. Unlike the Virginian adventurers (§62), the "Pilgrims"[2] were accompanied by their wives and children, and expected to live and die in America.

78. Founding of the Plymouth Colony.—Their aim was the

Hudson River; but after a stormy and perilous passage of two months, they came to anchor near Cape Cod.[3] Five weeks were spent in looking for a suitable place for a

Pilgrims Landing.

new home. At last they came to a safe though shallow harbor, to which Captain Smith had already given the name of Plymouth. This they chose, and in remembrance of kindness received at Plymouth, in England, they retained the name. Before going on shore, the forty- one heads of families solemnly combined themselves into a "civil body politic" to "enact such just and equal laws" as should be thought "convenient for the general good." It was the first embodiment, in fact, of the American idea that "governments derive their just powers from the consent of the governed." John Carver was chosen by his associates to be the first governor of Plymouth.

79. The First Winter.—Then came a winter of bitter suffering, bravely borne. Wolves howled about the wretched cabins, and hunger was kept away only by hunting and fishing, which were not always successful. Governor Carver and half the little company died; but of the survivors no man nor woman thought of returning with the Mayflower. Early in the spring a strange voice was heard in the village, crying "Welcome. Englishmen!" It was that of Samoset, an

Indian from beyond the Kennebec, who had learned some words of English from fishermen who visited the coast (§82). A neighboring chief, Massasoit, soon came, and made a treaty of peace which lasted fifty years.

80. The powerful **Narragansetts** were enemies of Mas-, sasoit, and a rattlesnake skin, stuffed with arrows, was sent as a challenge to the colonists. But when Governor Brad- ford, Carver's successor, filled the skin with gunpowder and sent it back, Canonicus changed his mind and begged for peace. Before the coming of the Pilgrims, a pestilence had swept away many hundreds of the Indians near Plymouth, so that the tribes, reduced to weakness and poverty, gave no trouble to the colonists.

81. For several winters food was scarce; but when, in 1623, each settler began to work for his own family instead of putting his earnings into the common stock, plenty came, and the white men were soon able to sell corn to the Indians. Though only forty miles distant from the richer and stronger settlements about Boston, and possessing no charter of its own, Plymouth remained independent until 1692, when it became part of the colony of Massachusetts Bay.

82. Maine.—Sir Ferdinando Gorges, governor of Plymouth in England, was a man of great wealth and influence, and a chief promoter of colonization in New England. In partnership with John Mason, former governor in Newfoundland, he obtained a tract of land extending from the St. Lawrence to the ocean? and from the Merrimac to the Kennebec River;[5] and, in 1623, sent out companies of emigrants
• to find homes where now stand the flourishing cities of Portsmouth and Dover, in New Hampshire.[6] But though among the oldest towns in the United States, these places were little more than fishing stations for many years from their foundation; and, in 1642, the people between the Merrimac and Piscataqua annexed themselves by a free vote to the colony of Massachusetts Bay.

83. Conflicting Grants.—Many scattered settlements were formed along the coast of Maine, and so many conflicting grants were made by the crown that no lawyer could reconcile them. The noble rivers and safe harbors had attracted attention, as promising wealth through commerce. Few attempts were made at farming, for titles were insecure, and the nearness of the French threatened frequent hostilities. Moreover, furs could be taken from the forest and fish from the sea without leave asked of any company. So it happened that the English settlers were little more than scattered companies of adventurers. The "first court ever duly organized on the soil of Maine " was held at Saco, in 1636, by William Gorges, nephew of the proprietor. The land between the St. Croix and the St. Lawrence had been given by James I. to Sir William Alexander,[7] a Scottish poet, and it was called *Nova Scotia,* from his native land; but the French already occupied the same region, to the southern part of which they gave the name of *Acadia,*[8] and it did not become a British possession until a much later date.

Point out on Map No. 3, Cape Cod. Plymouth. Portsmouth. Dover. The boundaries of Gorges and Mason's patent' (§82). Saco. Casco Bay. The Penobscot. The Kennebec. The original boundaries of Nova Scotia (§83).

NOTES.

1. The Puritans.—The term " Puritans " was first applied by way of derision, in 1564, to a large body of non-eonformists in England who were not satisfied with the extent of the reformation in church affairs brought about by Henry VIII. They insisted upon a still further departure from the Church of Rome, and the introduction of purer forms of worship in the Established Church. They were loyal to the throne, and always had at heart the best interests of the Protestants. But they were rigid Calvinists,—men of austere morality yet strong integrity,—and no civil power could make them yield a tithe of their convictions. They willingly suffered death at the stake for their principles. During the reigns of Edward VI., Elizabeth, James I., and Charles I., the Puritans gradually increased in numbers and influence. With Cromwell and the Commonwealth, they came into complete control of the government.

2. Pilgrims.—This name has been applied to such of the Puritans or Separatists as could no longer endure the interference of the national church in their spiritual affairs, and who for conscience' sake left their homes in England to seek lands where they might worship God after their own manner. Their wanderings give them their distinguishing name. They had been told that in Holland there was " freedom for all men." The first band of Pilgrims, under the direction of John Robinson and William Brewster, reached Amsterdam in 1608. The next year they removed to Leyden, and many followed them from various parts of England. Bancroft says of the Pilgrims: "They were Englishmen, Protestants, exiles for conscience, men disciplined by misfortune, cultivated by opportunities of extensive observation, equal in rank as in rights, and bound by no code but that of religion or the public will."

3. **The first landing** of the " Mayflower " Pilgrims was November 11th, on Cape Cod, near the site of the present Provincetown. Captain Miles Standish, with sixteen men, went on shore and explored the dreary, narrow strip of sand. Some distance inland they had their first sight of Indians. On December 11th an exploring party of seventeen men landed at Plymouth, but it was two weeks later before the passengers generally disembarked upon " Forefather's Rock." Indeed, most of the women and children remained on board the vessel until a rude shelter was provided for them on the land.

4. **This was December 21st** according to our present calendar. In the seventeenth century the difference between Old Style and New Style was ten days. In England, however, the old style method of reckoning dates was continued until 1752, when, by act of Parliament, the error was corrected. By adding ten days to the dates given in the text regarding the movements of the Pilgrims, we get the true dates, new style.

5. This tract probably took its name, **Maine** (or the main-land), to distinguish it from the many islands along the coast.

6. New Hampshire was so named by Mason in remembrance of his old home, Hampshire, in England.

7. Sir William Alexander gained little, beside the subject of a rather dull poem, from his vast, domain; his family afterward settled in New York, and his descendant and namesake, William Alexander, Lord Stirling, bore an honorable part in the war of American Independence.

8. Acadia was granted by King Henry IV. to the Huguenot, De Monts, in 1604. Besides the peninsula of Nova Seotia, it included all of New Brunswick and a part of Maine. De Monts was made lieutenant-general of the country, and at once sailed with a company to colonize his

new possessions. Champlain and the Baron de Poutrincourt accompanied the expedition. They settled first upon the little island of St. Croix, in Passa- maquoddy Bay, but a few weeks residence served to show the disadvantages of the location. Cruising along the coast of Maine they entered many of its noble bays and rivers, and were delighted with the land ; but at all points they found the Indians hostile, and reluctantly returned to St. Croix. Thence, in a short time, they crossed the Bay of Fundy, and chose a place of settlement, to which the name Port Royal was given. The site was the same as the present town of Annapolis, Nova Scotia.

The opening lines of Longfellow's beautiful poem, "Evangeline," are descriptive of the region of Acadia:

"This is the forest primeval. The murmuring pines and the hemlocks, Bearded with moss, and in garments green, indistinct in the twilight, Stand like druids of eld, with voices sad and prophetic, Stand like harpers hoar, with beards that rest on their bosoms. Loud from its rocky caverns, the deep-voiced neighboring ocean Speaks, and in accents disconsolate answers the wall of the forest.

In the Acadian land, on the shores of the Basin of Minas, Distant, secluded, still, the little village of Grand-Pré Lay in the fruitful valley. Vast meadows stretched to the eastward, Giving the village its name, and pasture to flocks without number. Dikes, that the hands of the farmers had raised with labor incessant, Shut out the turbulent tides ; but at stated seasons the flood-gates Opened, and welcomed the sea to wander at will o'er the meadows. West and south there were fields of flax, and orchards and cornfields Spreading afar and unfenced o'er the plain ; and away to the northward Blomidon rose, and the forests old, and aloft on the mountains Sea-fogs pitched their tents, and mists from the mighty Atlantic Looked on the happy valley, but ne'er from their station descended."

CHAPTER VII.
MASSACHUSETTS, CONNECTICUT, AND RHODE ISLAND.

84. Salem Colony.—Eight years and more after the settlement at Plymouth, five vessels, bearing two hundred English emigrants, entered the harbor of Salem,[1] in Massachusetts Bay. Their governor, *John Endicott*,[2] had preceded them, and had selected a place for their settlement a year before. The new-comers were Puritans, but not Separatists: they believed in the union of Church and State, and the authority of the civil government in matters of religion; but they availed themselves of their freedom to drop the usages of the Church of England, and there was little apparent difference between them and their neighbors at Plymouth.

85. The Charter.—The next year seventeen ships brought a thousand more emigrants, with horses, cattle, and whatever was needed for prosperous farming. A royal charter[3] for all the new settlements on Massachusetts Bay gave them leave to make their own laws and choose their own rulers, so long as they did nothing contrary to the statutes of England. Among them were men of wealth, influence, and high education, who, distrusting their king, thought to build up better homes for their children in the New World. Their chosen leader was *John Winthrop*, a man of noble character, who continued to be either governor or deputy-governor of the whole colony for twenty years, until his death.

86. Towns about Boston.—Reports of the peace and order to be enjoyed in Massachusetts, drew increasing crowds of colonists. Before 1640 many towns were planted: Roxbury, Dorchester, Lynn, Charlestown, Watertown, and others. Shawmut, or Boston,[4] was chosen, for its "fountain of sweet waters" and its admirable harbor, to be the capital of the colony. Each separate settlement had its town meeting, in which every "freeman" voted for magistrates and delegates to the General Court. Every township was required to maintain a school for reading and writing; every town of a hundred householders must also have a Latin and Grammar School ; and heads of families were subject to fines if they failed to have their children and apprentices taught.

87. Harvard College.—A college,[5] the first in the United States, was established at Newtown, whose name was now altered to *Cambridge,* in memory of the English university-town, where most of the educated men in the colony had spent their years of study. To endow the new college, all the people brought such things as they had. Those who could do no more, gave a peck of corn yearly. Many gave pieces of silver plate, and one rich man gave a flock of sheep. The Reverend John Harvard bequeathed to it all his books and half his estate, and it has ever since borne his name. The first printing-press [6] within the present limits of the United States was set up in the president's house in 1639. Its first publications were the "Freeman's Oath" and a "New England Almanac."

88. Settlements on Connecticut River.—Reports of the rich lands in the Connecticut Valley soon reached the settlers on the coast. As early as 1633 a company from Plymouth built a fort at *Windsor,* on that river, and commenced a fur trade with the Indians. Two years later, parties of emigrants from Massachusetts Bay laid the foundations of *Hartford, Wethersfield,* and *Springfield.* In June of 1636, a hundred persons, led by Rev. Thomas Hooker,[7] whose sick wife was carried on a litter beside him, marched through the woods, driving their cattle and flocks to these far western settlements.

89. Settlements on Long Island Sound.—Two English noblemen, Lord Say and Lord Brook, who had themselves thought of settling in America, sent the younger Winthrop, son of the Massachusetts governor, to establish a fort and garrison at the mouth of the Connecticut. (A. D. 1635.) It wascalled *Saybrook. Guilford, Milford,*

Stratford, and other towns with English names were soon scattered along the Sound. *New Haven*[8] was founded in 1638 by a company of Puritans from England. John Davenport,[9] their pastor, preached to them under a spreading oak. The Bible was their only law-book, and members of the church their only freemen.

90. Religious Intolerance.—Having crossed the ocean at great cost and sacrifice for the sake of enjoying a perfect and peaceful society, the rulers of Massachusetts Bay had no tolerance for opinions different from their own—less, indeed, than had the Pilgrims of Plymouth, who had suffered yet more for conscience' sake, and knew the hearts of strangers and exiles from their own experience in Holland (§§75, 76).

91. The magistrates of Massachusetts Bay held themselves responsible, not only for the orderly conduct, but for the right belief and character of every soul in the colony. They believed that they had gone just far enough in their withdrawal from the English Church. Those who lagged behind them were regarded with suspicion ; but their heaviest penalties were reserved for those who went beyond them in the direction of "soul-liberty."

92. Roger Williams,[10] the eloquent and faithful young minister of Salem, taught that every man is answerable for his belief to God alone, and that governments have no right to interfere in matters of religion. He insisted, moreover, on the payment of the Indians for their lands, while the rulers claimed that their charter from King Charles was a sufficient title. For these and other differences of opinion, Williams was exiled from the colony, and, having wandered fourteen weeks in cold and hunger through the wintry forests, he reached the lands of the Narragansetts (§ 80). Their chief, Canonicus, received him with affection, and gave him a tract of land ; here, with five companions, he began the settlement of *Providence*,[11] and "desired it might be a shelter for persons distressed for conscience."

93. Rhode Island.—Many such persons lived in those days, and of them Mrs. Anne Hutchinson,[12] a woman of great gifts and independent spirit, an exile, like Williams, from Massachusetts Bay ; William Coddington, a former magistrate of that colony, but a steady opponent of persecution; John Clarke, William Aspinwall, and many others repaired to the Narragansett country. They bought the beautiful island of Rhode Island for "forty fathoms of white beads," and there, in 1638, *Newport* was founded.

94. The Pequod War.—Roger Williams had an early opportunity to do good to those who had wronged him. The settlers in Connecticut had for neighbors the Pequods, the most powerful and hostile of New England savages, who, enraged by the intrusion of the white men, tried to engage the Narragansetts and Mohegans in a league for their destruction. The governor and council of Massachusetts wrote to Williams, who lost not a moment, but, crossing Narragansett Bay during a tempest in an open boat, met the Pequod chiefs in the wigwam of Canonicus, and, after three days and nights of violent discussion, persuaded the latter not to grant their request.

95. The Pequods had to fight the English without aid: and in May, 1637, the destruction of their fort at Stonington by only sixty men from Hartford, led to the extermination of their tribe. The few who surrendered themselves were made slaves, and for forty years no serious war troubled the New England settlements.

96. The State of Connecticut.—In 1639, Hartford, Windsor, and Wethersfield joined themselves in one state under the first written constitution which was ever framed in America. In 1641 Massachusetts also adopted a "body of liberties," —a code of well-tried laws, securing to every person, whether resident or stranger, prompt and equal justice in the courts. The education of all children, the training of young men in military exercises, and the security of town meetings were among the chief cares of the law-makers.

97. In 1643 a **league** of the four governments,—Massachusetts, Connecticut, New Haven, and Plymouth—was formed under the name of the United Colonies of New England. Providence and the neighboring settlement on Rhode Island were not admitted, because they refused to be subject to Plymouth. But the League lasted forty years, and was of great importance as a precedent for a more extensive Union.

98. The Charter of Rhode Island.—In 1644, Roger Williams, visiting England, obtained from Parliament a "free and absolute charter of civil government for the plantations on Narragansett Bay," with full power to rule themselves "by such laws as they should find most suitable to their estate and condition." The system chosen was a pure democracy; farmers and shepherds met on the sea-shore or under some spreading tree, and discussed plans for the general good; and though all shades of opinion-were represented in the colony, and debate was often violent, the result was one of the most wise, liberal, and merciful governments that the world has seen. No person was ever disquieted or called in question for his religion; the best men were elected to office; and the seal of the new state expressed the principle of its constitution,—"Love will conquer all things."

99. Society of Friends.—In 1656 the first *"Friends,"* or *" Quakers,"*[13] arrived at Boston, a people who, notwith- standing their pure, peaceful, and upright characters, were destined to be the occasion of great disturbances. They thought it their duty to protest against a paid ministry, civil oaths, military service, and several other established customs of society. Their consciences were, if possible, more exacting than those of the Puritan rulers, and on these points they were directly opposed to them. When they refused to leave the colony peaceably, they were publicly whipped and sent away; some were imprisoned; four, who persisted in returning after exile, were hanged on Boston Common. Two children, whose parents had been banished, were fined for non-attendance at meeting; being too poor to pay the fine, they were ordered to be sold as slaves in the Barba- does. We are glad to find that no ship-master could be induced to execute the commission, so that the order was never enforced. A large number in every community disapproved, and sometimes protested against acts of intolerance, so that the sin of persecution can not be charged upon the mass of the people.

100. John Eliot.—The people of New England were, as a rule, both just and merciful toward the Indians. Never a bushel of corn was taken from them without payment; and offenses against them were punished by the courts, if possible with greater severity than if the victims had been whites. Many good ministers were at great pains to teach them the truths of religion: among these the most celebrated was the Reverend John Eliot[14] the "Apostle of the Indians."

101. Praying Indians.—He translated the whole Bible, as well as other books, into their native language. As the number of his disciples increased, he gathered them into the villages of Nonantum, Natick, and Neponset, where he taught them to support themselves by useful labor, and to live under civilized laws which he wrote for them out of the Bible. These "praying Indians" numbered at one time four thousand souls. They were never fully trusted, however, by the whites, while they were regarded with suspicion and hatred by their own people.

102. King Philip's War.—Metacom, commonly called Philip, chief of the Pokanokets, did not share his father, Massassoit's, friendship for the whites. He saw them encroaching more and more upon the lands of his people, and in 1674, fourteen years after his accession, the smothered flames of his revenge burst forth. Most of the savage tribes joined him in a grand effort to destroy the English. Terror spread along all the borders of the white settlements from Connecticut to Maine. Farm-houses were surprised, women and little children murdered, and of all the men in the colonies one in twenty fell in battle. The Christian Indians were faithful to their teachers, and warned them repeatedly of the coming danger. But in spite of their invaluable services, it is sad to relate that they were treated with suspicion and contempt, and even murdered by white women who were filled with rage at the sight of a dark face. Eliot and his friend Daniel Gookin, for thirty years Indian superintendent in the Massachusetts colony, plead for reason and justice against the popular fury.

103. On the part of the heathen Indians, it was a war of desperation without hope. Canonchet, chief of the Narragansetts, an ally of Philip, was taken and put to death. Philip was driven from his lands; his wife and son were captives. "My heart breaks; now I am ready to die," cried the chief, when he heard of their fate. His own people plotted against him, and he fell by a traitor's bullet. His only son was sold as a slave in the Bermudas. Peace was not restored until 1678, when two thousand Indians had been destroyed,[15] and the scattered remnants of the tribes were unable longer to resist the whites.

Point, on Map No. 3, to the several towns near Massachusetts Bay. The site of Harvard College. Eight towns in Connecticut.

Read Palfrey's "History of New England;" Neal's "History of the Puritans."

NOTES.

1. Salem is a Hebrew word meaning peaceful. The Indian name for the same locality was Naumkeag. Roger Conant and three companions, " religious, sober, and well affected persons," left the Plymouth colony in 1625, and, stopping for awhile on Nantasket beach, finally settled at Nauinkeag in 1627. Conant was disposed to dispute the authority of Endicott upon his arrival, but a peaceful adjustment of the controversy was effected ; hence the name, Salem, was chosen.

2. "Governor Endicott," says Bancroft, "was a man of dauntless courage, and that cheerfulness which accompanies courage; benevolent, though austere; firm, though choleric; of a rugged nature, which his stern principles of non-conformity had not served to mellow." For forty years he played a prominent part in the colonial history ot New England.

3. This royal charter created a corporation styled "The Governor and Company of the Massachusetts Bay in New England," and by this instrument the Massachusetts colony regulated its affairs for more than half a century. The granting of this charter was regarded by the Puritans throughout England as a providential call to them to escape the religious fetters by which they were bound, and to seek new homes in that free land of the west, where they could worship God without restraint. Massachusetts began to be talked about in every Puritan household, and plans were quietly laid by the heads of families to join the tide of emigration at an early day. These resolute men saw that their long struggle for freedom in England had been a failure, and now their grievances were greater than ever under the tyrannies of Archbishop Laud. Even closer conformity to the Established Church was required ; Puritan clergymen were ejected from their livings, and persecution met them at every turn. These things easily account for the rapid accessions to the Salem colony, and to the others that soon sprang up around the shores of Massachusetts Bay. Within ten years from the arrival of Winthrop's expedition, it is thought no less than 20,000 Englishmen came to America.

4. **Boston.**—The earliest settlement was made in the fall of 1630 by some of John Winthrop's party, who had first located at Mishawum (now Charlestown). William Blackstone had lived in the vicinity of Shawmut since 1623, and two other Englishmen had for some time occupied a couple of islands in the harbor; but these were the only white men in the region before Winthrop came. The settlement was called "Boston," in compliment to the Rev. John Cotton, who had been vicar in Boston, Lincolnshire, England, from which locality many of the leading colonists had come.

5. **Harvard College.**—In 1636 the general court of the colony of Massachusetts Bay voted " the sum of four hundred pounds to form a school or college." One half the amount was not to be paid until the building was completed. The management of the institution was intrusted to a Board of Overseers. The Jesuit Fathers at Quebec began a structure for a seminary and college in 1637, one year before the foundations of Harvard were laid.

6. **This was not the first printing-press in America.** As early as 1535, Catholic priests set up a press in the city of Mexico; a second one was in operation at Lima, Peru, in 1586.

7. **Thomas Hooker,** "the light of the Western Churches," was born in Leicestershire, England, in 1586. He was a cousin of the celebrated divine, Richard Hooker. His sermons being offensive to Archbishop Laud, he was compelled to stop preaching in England, and commenced teaching. For throe years he preached with great power to the Puritan

refugees at Delft and Rotterdam. In 1630 he emigrated to New England with his fellow pastors, Cotton and Stone. He and Rev. Mr. Stone were associated in their work for several years, both at Newtown (now Cambridge) and Hartford. Hooker died at Hartford in 1617. We cite a few lines from Bancroft touching the pilgrimage of Hooker and his one hundred companions to their new homes : " Traversing on foot the pathless forest, they drove before them numerous herds of cattle; advancing hardly ten miles a day through tangled woods, across the valleys, swamps, and numerous streams, and over the intervening highlands; subsisting on the milk of the kine, which browsed on the fresh leaves and early shoots ; having no guide through the pathless wild but the compass, and no pillow for their nightly rest but heaps of stones. How did the hills echo with the unwonted lowing of herds! .... Never again was there such a pilgrimage from the seaside to 'the delightful banks' of the Connecticut."

8. New Haven. — The Indian village at this point was Quinnipiack. The colonists paid the natives for a large tract, " twelve coats of English cloth, twelve alchemy spoons, twelve hatchets, twelve hoes, two dozen knives, twelve porringers, and four cases of French knives and scissors."

9. John Davenport (*b*. 1598, *d*. 1670) preached at New Haven for thirty years, and then removed to Boston. He had been a noted Puritan minister in London, and because of the success of his labors in behalf of poor congregations he met with the opposition of Archbishop Laud, and was obliged to flee to Holland. After four years residence there he came to America. He exerted a strong influence in the civil as well as the religious affairs of his community. Davenport was an intense controversialist, but his integrity and ability are conceded by all who were familiar with his life.

10. Roger Williams was born in Wales, about 1606, passed with honors through Oxford University, England, was for a time minister in the Established Church, but soon joined the ranks of the Puritans. He was a fine-linguist, being versed in Latin, Greek, and Hebrew, besides several modern languages. This bent of his mind led him, soon alter his arrival in New England, to study the dialects of the neighboring Indian tribes. He became a master of the speech of the Narragansetts, whose language was understood by all of the Massachusetts Indians and by most of the tribes to the west and south. Williams reached Boston early in 1631, and in a few weeks was called as pastor over the church at Salem. Being a Separatist of most decided views, he had refused to join the church at Boston unless it would publicly repent of having held communion in the past with the Church of England. This defiant stand provoked at once the ire of the council, and the magistrates made it so uncomfortable for him that he concluded to remove to the Plymouth Colony, where he had reason to believe the right of individual opinion was upheld. Williams remained in Plymouth only two years, however, and then returned to Salem. In 1635 he was banished from the colony by sentence of the General Court for teaching:

1st. That the title of the Massachusetts Company, from the king, to its lands, was not valid, but that the Indians were the true owners.

2d. That it was " not lawful to call a wicked person to swear, [or] to pray, as being actions of God's worship."

3d. That it was wrong to listen to any of the ministers of the Parish Assemblies in England.

4th. That the civil power had no authority over the opinions of men.

A warrant was issued to seize Mr. Williams and convey him to England for trial, but when the officer reached Salem the offending pastor had fled. He went directly among his old friends, the Indians, and was received with kindness by the chiefs. Although Canonicus freely offered him the tract of land on which the colony of Providence was planted, Williams insisted upon paying a fair price for it. He was president, of the colony from 1654 to 1657, and from its foundation had been the inspiring genius of its good fortunes. He was independent in spirit, wise in counsel, bold in action, forgiving in disposition, and upright in principle. A writer of his day judges Roger Williams from " the whole course and tenor of his life and conduct to have been one of the most disinterested men that ever lived, — a most pious and heavenly-minded soul."

His death occurred at Providence, in 1683.

11. Providence was so called by Roger Williams in recognition of the sustaining Providence that had preserved him amidst so many dangers and trials, and guided him at last to this selected spot. The incorporated name of the colony, according to the royal charter, was " Providence Plantations in Narragansett Bay in New England."

12. Anne Hutchinson removed from Rhode Island, in 1642, to New Netherlands, and the next year, with all her family but one child, was murdered by the Indians. She was a second-cousin of the poet Dryden.

13. The Quakers, or Religious Society of Friends, had their origin in the preaching of George Fox, of Leicestershire, England, who was born in 1624 and died in 1691. They were called "Quakers" because Fox admonished them to tremble at the word of God. Like the Puritans, they were the outgrowth of the independent religious movements of the seventeenth century. But in their departure from the prescribed worship of the state they were not, like the Puritans, intolerant towards those who did not exactly agree with them. Fox, the founder of the sect, twice visited America, and preached among his followers in this country two years with marked success. The first Quakers who came to Boston were two ladies, Mary Fisher and Ann Austin. Their baggage was broken open and examined, their religious books burned, their persons searched for signs of witchcraft, and both were thrown into prison, although "no token could be found on them but of innocence." For five weeks they were kept shut up in jail, and then banished from the colony. A law was enacted prohibiting the admission of Quakers, and a heavy fine imposed upon any who should keep in his house one of "this accursed sect." A Quaker who should return after banishment was to be "imprisoned, whipped, and otherwise punished ; " should he return again, he was to " lose one ear ; for the next offense, his other ear ; after the third, to have bis tongue bored with a red-hot iron." Notwithstanding these barbarous laws, the Quakers continued to come in considerable numbers, although some were executed. They were not afraid of persecutions. At length, under the leadership of William Penn, they established one of the most successful of American colonies.

14. Many anecdotes are related of **John Eliot** connected with his missionary work among the Indians. He learned the Indian language from a servant in his family. When he first attempted to address the savages, and to teach them concerning God and the Bible, he was asked by one, "How can God understand prayers in the Indian language?" and by another, "How came the world so full of people if they were all once drowned in the flood? " He received a salary of but $250 a year, and nearly all of this he gave to Indians whom he found in want. Knowing the extent of his generosity, the parish treasurer when paying him money would tie it up in his handkerchief with a dozen hard-knots, to prevent Mr. Eliot from giving it away before he got home. On one occasion, just after receiving his pay, he called upon a sick family to share with them his funds, and began to untie the knots successively. But before getting to the money he grew impatient at the delay, and handed over the handkerchief to the mother just as it was, saying, " Here, my dear, take it: I believe the Lord designs it all for you."

15. **"King Philip's War** had lasted for more than a year. Thirteen towns had been destroyed, six hundred buildings burned, countless numbers of stock of all kinds were lost, six hundred men killed in lights or murdered, and great numbers disabled by wounds. There was hardly a family without its scar of sorrow. But the power of the Indians in all southern New England was destroyed forever. Some escaped by flight into the western wilds where the white man had not penetrated; but many small tribes were obliterated ; whole families had perished ; many who were captured were sent to the West Indies, and dragged out the remainder of their miserable lives as slaves." — *Bryant.*

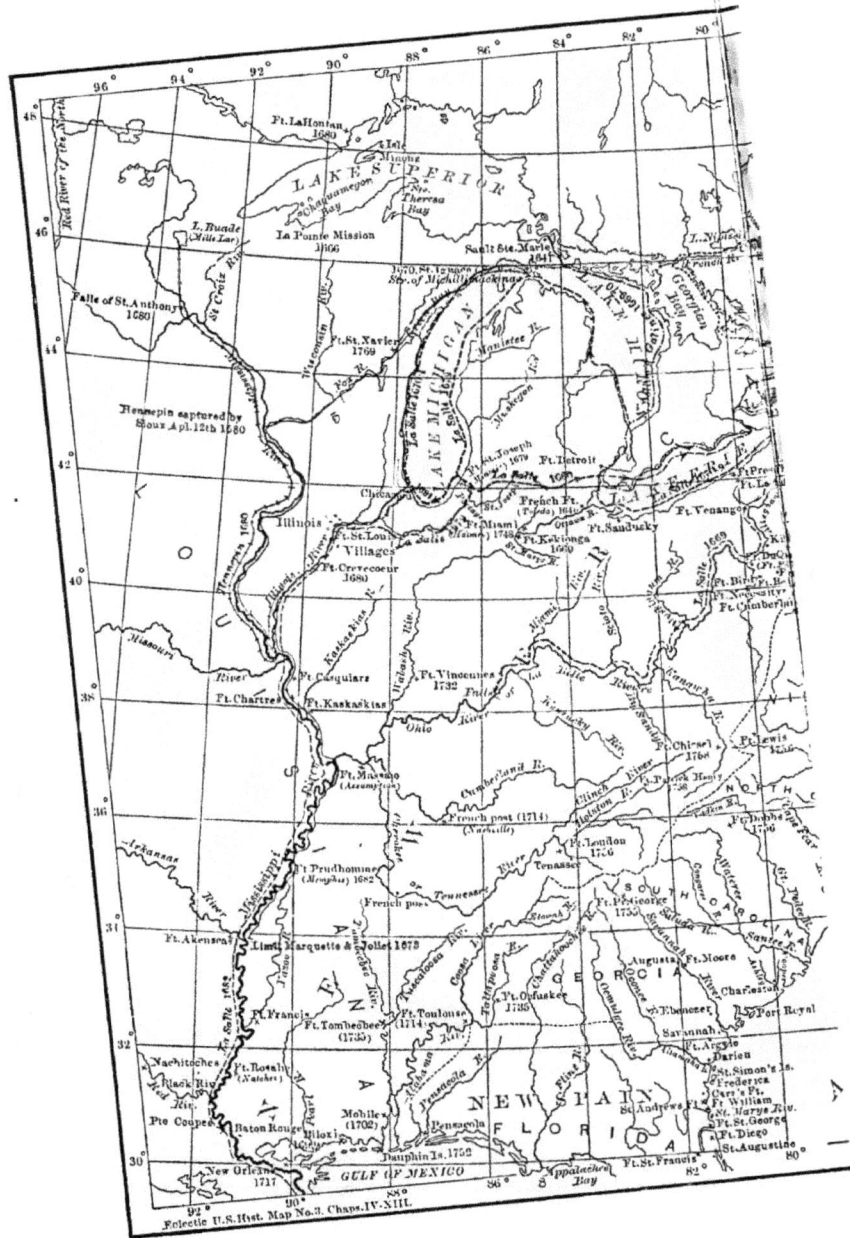

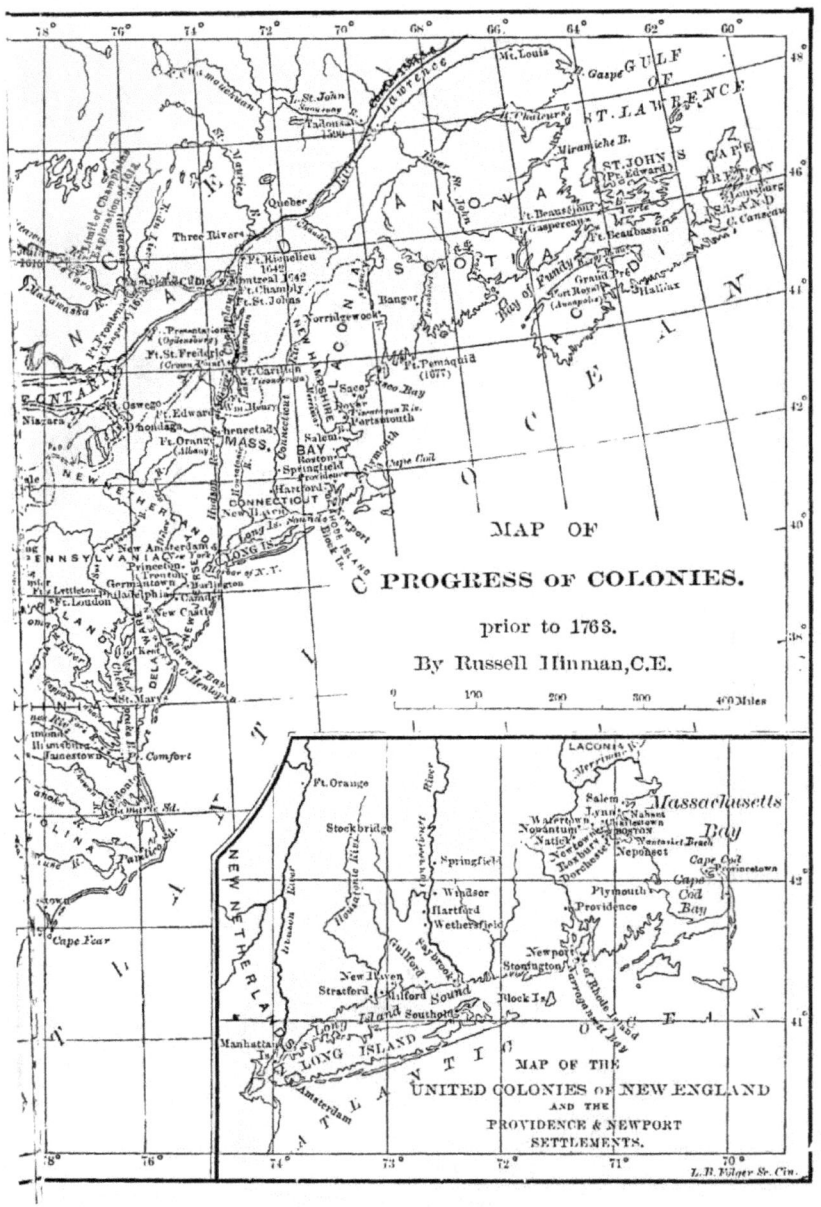

CHAPTER VIII.
NEW NETHERLANDS. THE MIDDLE STATES.

Hudson on the River.

104. The Dutch Republic,[1] lately freed from Spain, was during the seventeenth century the foremost maritime nation on the globe. Its trading stations were scattered along the islands and coasts of Asia, and its ships penetrated the remotest seas. In A. D. 1609, the Dutch East India Company[2] commissioned Henry Hudson,[3] an English captain, to seek for it a nearer passage to Asia than was yet known. Having visited many points on the American coast between Penobscot and Chesapeake bays, Hudson entered what is now the harbor of New York, and found himself at the mouth of a great river flowing between wooded heights to the sea. This he ascended beyond Albany, hoping to find an entrance to the Pacific Ocean.

105. Five years later **Adrian Block** built on Manhattan Island a small ship called the *Unrest*, with which he cruised through Long Island Sound, discovered the Housatonic and Connecticut rivers, gave his name to the island which guards the eastern entrance of the Sound, and followed the coast as far as Nahant. By reason of all these discoveries, the land between Delaware Bay and Cape Cod was called *New Netherlands,* while the noble river which Hudson explored has ever since borne his name.

106. A little trading-post, called **New Amsterdam**, was soon established on Manhattan, where now stands the greatest city of the western continent. Another arose, in 1614, upon the present site of *Albany,* and thither came Mohawks and other Indians to exchange the skins of otter, beaver, and mink for knives, beads, looking- glasses, and, later, the coveted fire-arms. In 1621 a Dutch West India Company[4] was formed, and emigration to New Netherlands was encouraged for purposes of trade.

107. Like their mother country, the Dutch settlements in America were thrown freely open to persons of all nations and religions; and before long, eighteen languages were spoken in New Amsterdam. The Company especially desired to secure "farmers and laborers, foreigners and exiles, men inured to toil and penury." A free passage from Europe was granted to skilled mechanics. Large tracts of land with many privileges were offered to rich men who would bring out whole colonies at their own expense. Such persons were called *patroonsp* and in time some of them had thousands of tenants on their estates.

108. **Forts and trading-houses** were erected on the Delaware and Connecticut rivers, where *Camden* and *Hartford*now stand. But the English refused to recognize any Dutch title in America; though some civilities were exchanged between the rulers of Plymouth

New Amsterdam.

and New Amsterdam, the latter were advised to obtain a title to their lands from King Charles I.; and not only the valley of the Connecticut, but a large part of Long Island was ultimately settled by pilgrims from Massachusetts.

109. Swedes in America.—King Gustavus Adolphus, the greatest and best of Swedish kings, resolved to open for his people a refuge in America from the wars and oppressions of the Old World. His untimely death on the battlefield of Lützen[6] delayed the execution of his purpose; but the plan was taken up by his chancellor, Oxenstiern, "one of the great men of all time." In the spring of 1638, two vessels bearing a company of Swedes and Finns entered Delaware Bay.

110. All the lands bordering upon the bay and river, from Cape Henlopen to the falls near Trenton, were bought from the Indians, and named *New Sweden*.[7] A fort was built within the present limits of Delaware, which received the name of the little queen *Christiana*. The fame of the mild climate and fertile soil drew fresh arrivals of hardy and industrious people from the frozen shores of the Baltic. In 1643 Governor Printz' removed his residence to Tinicum Island, near the confluence of the Schuylkill ; and neat cottages and gardens were soon seen within what are now the suburbs of *Philadelphia*.

Peter Stuyvesant.

111. Indian Troubles. — The people of New Amsterdam and its neighborhood had much to fear from the Indians, to whom they first sold gin, muskets, and gunpowder, and then treated them so unjustly that they might be sure the weapons would be turned against themselves. Governor Kieft, the third of the Dutch chief magistrates, punished the poor savages with wanton cruelty for offenses which his own crimes had provoked. He was recalled in 1647, and Peter Stuyvesant,8 a better man and a brave soldier, was sent in his place.

112. Governor Stuyvesant visited Hartford and made a treaty with the English settlers, which fixed the eastern limit of New Netherlands on the mainland, not far from the present boundary of New York and Connecticut. Half of Long Island was ceded to the English. He made peace with the Indians, and to protect the beaver-trade on the Delaware he built a fort on the present site of Newcastle, near the mouth of the Brandywine.

113. End of New Sweden. — The Swedes resented this intrusion, and in 1654, their governor, Rising, overpowered the garrison and seized the fort. But Sweden was not strong enough to protect her colony. Stuyvesant soon appeared with six hundred men, and, sailing up the Delaware, received the surrender of all the forts without the destruction of a life. The people submitted to Dutch rule, and remained peaceably on their farms. New Sweden had existed seventeen years.

114. Discontent in the Dutch Colony. — Though consciences were free in New Netherlands, the people had no share in the government. Citizenship meant "not much more than a license to trade." Taxes were often oppressive. The Director was haughty and obstinate, replying to all remonstrances, that he derived his "authority from God and the West India Company, not from the pleasure of a few -ignorant subjects." The English, who were now numerous in the colony, envied the greater freedom of their brethren in Massachusetts ; and there were few of any race who would not rather be subjects of England than servants of a trading company.

115. English Conquest of New Netherlands. — During a war between England and Holland, an English fleet entered the harbor of New Amsterdam, and demanded a surrender. Stuyvesant had no power to resist; the citizens had no disposition to aid him. New Amsterdam became *New York,* and Fort Orange, on the upper Hudson, was named *Albany,* from the English king's brother, the Duke of York and Albany, to whom the whole region between the Connecticut and the Delaware had been given.

116. New Jersey. — The Duke in his turn bestowed the land between the lower Hudson and the Delaware upon Lord Berkeley and Sir George Carteret. It received its present name from the island in the English Channel, of which Carteret had been governor. Eastern New Jersey, which fell to Carteret's share, was already settled in part by English Puritans. To attract immigrants, perfect freedom of conscience was guaranteed; and the fertile river banks, so easy of access, were soon occupied by industrious and worthy people.

117. Reconquest by the Dutch. — The hope of English liberty was not immediately fulfilled to the people of New York. The Duke of York was a tyrant, and the groom of his bed-chamber, Richard Nicolls, whom he appointed to govern the colony, levied taxes at his own will. The people of Long Island complained that they were "deprived of the privileges of Englishmen." No one was sorry when a Dutch fleet reappeared in New York Harbor, and the city was quietly surrendered after nine years' occupation by the English. The second Dutch rule lasted, however, only fifteen months; for by the treaty of peace between Holland and England, the New Netherlands were permanently ceded to the latter.

118. England now ruled all the Atlantic coast between New France and New Spain ; *i. e.*, between Acadia and Florida. Berkeley and Carteret resumed their possession of New Jersey. The former, now a very old man, soon sold his half of the territory for $5,000 to an English Quaker, and in 1674 John Fenwick sailed with a large company of "Friends" to the eastern bank of the Delaware. A liberal government was established at Burlington, confiding all power to the people and securing equal rights to every man. East New Jersey was subsequently purchased from the heirs of Carteret by a company of English "Friends," of whom William Penn" was one.

119. Pennsylvania.—In 1681 William Penn obtained from King Charles II. a tract of land west of Delaware River, instead of a large sum of money which the king owed Admiral Penn, his father. The owner of *Pennsylvania* was invested with sovereign rights; but the "Quaker King" desired only to make a "free colony for the good and oppressed of all nations." He had suffered in his own person imprisonment and persecution for conscience' sake; and he wished, as he said, to make the "holy experiment" whether perfect justice and good will toward high and low, rich and poor, heathen and Christian, were not a safe and sufficient foundation for a state.

120. Purchasing land of the Swedes, who had already bought it of the Indians (§110) he laid out Philadelphia, the "city of brotherly love."

William Penn.

In August of that year it contained only three or four cottages; two years later it numbered six hundred houses, and had a school and a printingpress. The Lenni Lenape of the surrounding region had been so humbled by the Iroquois (§24) that they were incapable of making war : their hearts were touched, moreover, by the kind and just words of Penn ; and the treaty which they made with him under the great elm-tree at Shack- amaxon, was " the only Indian treaty never sworn to and never broken."

121. "English freedom" was bestowed upon the Swedes, Finns, and Dutch, who were already numerous in the region. News of the very liberal constitution granted by Penn, drew immigrants not only from Great Britain but from central Europe. "Friends" from Kirchheim, near Worms, settled on lands then six miles from Philadelphia, now forming *Germantown*. All forms of belief were free in

Pennsylvania; superstitions were met by that calm good sense which is their only antidote. Only one trial for witchcraft ever took place; the prisoner, a Swede, was acquitted of the charge, though censured for disorderly conduct. (See §141.)

122. Delaware.—The Duke of York, an old friend and comrade of Penn's father, conferred upon the son the "three lower counties" on

Delaware Bay. They were included for nine years in Pennsylvania; but in 1691 a separate governor and assembly were chosen for the "Commonwealth of Delaware."

123. Duke of York becomes King.—In 1685, the Duke of York became King James II. of England. Penn used all his influence with his royal friend to secure justice for the oppressed, and had the joy of liberating twelve hundred "Friends" from the noisome English dungeons, where some of them had suffered many years for no other crime than obedience to their consciences.

124. Ingratitude towards Penn.—Though the colonies established by Penn flourished, their proprietor became poor. He had spent all bis fortune in the prosecution of his great "experiment." Many settlers refused to pay the moderate rent which he asked, as some little return for all his expense; and the liberator of so many prisoners actually went to jail in his old age for debt.

Trace on Map No, 3 the course of Hudson; of Block. Point out two Dutch settlements on the Hudson. Two on the Delaware and Connecticut (§ 108). Long Island. Two Swedish settlements on the Delaware. The three principal rivers of New Netherlands. Penn's chief city. The capital of West Jersey. The boundaries of Delaware.

Read Brodhead's "History of New York;" Chapters xxii-xxiv of Bancroft's "History of the United Stales;" Mrs. Lamb's " History of the City of New York;" "Lises" of William Penn by Clarkson, Weems, and Ellis.

NOTES.

1. The Dutch Republie, or United Netherlands, in the seventeenth centnrv, embraced the present kingdom of Holland, and a part of Belgium. The remainder of Belgium constituted the Spanish Netherlands.

2. The Dutch East India Company was chartered in 1602, with "the exclusive right to commerce beyond the Cape of Good Hope on the one side, and beyond the Straits of Magellan on the other." It had almost unlimited powers in respect of "conquest, colonization, and government," and soon became the greatest trading corporation in the world.

3. **Hudson's** first two voyages to the American coast (1607 and 1608) were under the auspices of a company of London merchants, and for the purpose of finding the long-sought north-west passage to Asia. He cruised farther north, along the eastern shores of Greenland, than any navigator before him, and, when his progress was stopped by ice, sailed across the polar seas to Spitzbergen, and vainly tried to reach China through the frozen channel between that arctic island and Nova Zembla. He was not discouraged by these repeated failures, but his countrymen refused the means to carry on other expeditions ; so he offered to sail for the Dutch Company, and his services were accepted. His vessel, the " Half Moon," was a yacht of only eighty tons burthen, and with this small craft he first essayed the " north-east passage " around Nova Zembla. Finding it blocked with ice, as be had the year before, he turned his prow westward, and, after a stormy voyage of nearly three months, sighted the foggy banks of Newfoundland. Cruising south, lie landed first on the Maine coast, then on Cape Cod (which he called New Holland), and, before entering New York harbor, explored Delaware Bay. On the 4th of September (1609) a boat's crew from the "Half Moon" landed on Congo (Coney) Island. These were the first Europeans known to have been on the shores of New York Bay. In 1610 Hudson made his last voyage to America. He sailed through the straits and discovered the bay which bear his name. His ship, the " Discovery," was caught in the fields of ice. Dissensions and mutiny broke out among his sailors, and they cast Hudson and bis son, with seven others, into a small shallop, and set them adrift among the icebergs. 'Their sad fate was never known, but the entire party must have perished from cold or starvation.

4. **The Dutch West India Company** was almost as great a monopoly as the East India Company. Its patent prohibited any citizen of the United Netherlands, for the period of twenty-two years, from sailing to the coasts of Africa or America except in the company's service. It exercised all governmental powers over the colonies it established. Besides an immense fleet of merchant vessels, this great company had under its control thirty-two war vessels and eighteen armed yachts', one clause in its charter was that "they must advance the peopling of those fruitful and unsettled parts," and this important feature received the first attention of the company. Early in 1623 their first colonists were brought to the shores of Hudson River, called Mauritius River by the Dutch.

5. **The Patroons**, or proprietary lords of the early Dutch settlements of New York and New Jersey, were granted remarkable privileges, and clothed with almost princely powers. Provided they would bring a colony of fifty persons to America, they were permitted to select lands having a frontage of sixteen miles along any river bank, and extending back " so far into the country as the situation of the occupiers would permit." They appointed officers and magistrates to govern the colony, and their sway over the people was absolute. No man or woman could quit the patroon's service until the time of contract had expired, whether treated well or not; and the only privilege which these tenants enjoyed was an exemption from taxation for ten years.

6. **Lützen** is a small town in Prussian Saxony. The battle in which Gustavus Adolphus lost his life, occurred in November, 1632. The Swedish king, with 20,000 men, was opposed by the great Austrian general, Wallenstein, with an army of 40,000. The tide of battle wavered for some time, when Gustavus Adolphus rode fearlessly to the front to inspirit his soldiery. He received a shot in the arm and one in the back; he fell from his saddle, and, his foot catching in the stirrup, lie was thus dragged by his flying horse. It is thought that the fatal wound in the back was caused by a traitorous eousin in his own ranks.

7. The first director of **New Sweden** was Peter Minuit, a Dutchman who had been discharged from office in the New Netherlands settlement. Governor Printz was a man of immense size, weighing over four hundred pounds, a generous liver, and of violent temper. His house, Printz Hall, was an elegant mansion for the times. From his fort on Tinicum Island he. stopped every passing vessel, and levied tribute for the privilege of trading at any point on the Delaware or Sehuylkill rivers.

8. **Peter Stuyvesant** was warmly welcomed by the people of New Netherlands when, in 1647, he came as director-general to relieve them from the rule of the despotic Kieft. But it did not take them long to find out that lie was as self-willed and violent in temper as his predecessor. He was, however, a man of better judgment and executive ability. He succeeded in making peace with the Indians, and in introducing system and good order in the affairs of government. Stuyvesant was born in Holland in 1602; he lost a leg in a naval attack on the island of St. Martin in 1644, and had it replaced by a wooden one, bound round with silver rings. On account of this he was called by some of his disrespectful subjects, "old Wooden Leg" or "Silver Leg." He delighted in pomp and

in display of authority. As an instance, when he landed at New Amsterdam as the. new governor of the colony, one of the writers of the time says, he "strutted like a peacock, with great state and pomp;" and, being met by a deputation of the leading citizens, who took off their hats as a mark of respect, the governor "let them wait bareheaded for several hours, he himself keeping on his hat as if he was the ('zar of Muscovy; nobody was offered a chair, while he seated himself very comfortably on a chair, the better to give the welcomers an audience."

After surrendering New Netherlands, Peter Stuyvesant lived quietly for eighteen years on his farm, which lay upon both sides of the street now called the Bowery, in New York City. He died at the age of eighty, and his remains are now in a vault in St. Marks Episcopal Church, N. Y̆.

9. **William Penn** was the son of a distinguished English admiral. He was born in London in 1644. From his father he inherited force of character and sprightli liess of disposition; and from his mother, a strong religious temperament. He entered Oxford University at the age of fifteen. During his first year there he heard the preaching of Thomas Lee, an eminent "Friend," and became impressed with his simple doctrines. He grew more and more to dislike the forms and ceremonies of the Anglican Church, and rebelled against the conformity to them required in the University. He refused to wear a surplice himself, and incited a few of his comrades to join him in tearing off the surplices worn by other students. For this he was expelled. During the next few years he traveled in Holland, France, and Ireland, was often presented at court, and led quite a gay life. But again falling in with the Quaker preacher, Lee, he became a convert to his views, and adopted the garb and the professions of the Society of Friends. He gave up his luxurious habits of living, and began zealously to speak and write in favor of the new doctrines. He was thrown into prison for heresy, but improved the time passed in his cell by writing more vigorously than ever. He was a man of strong conscientious convictions, and without a particle of fear. On the death of his father in 1670, William Penn came into possession of a large estate. The grant to Penn comprised 40,000 square miles in the wilderness of America, which King Charles named Pennsylvania. Penn wished to call the territory New Wales or Sylvania, but the king replied that he was "godfather to the country, and would bestow the name."

When James II. was deposed and in exile (A. D. 1692), William Penn was accused of treasonable correspondence with him. On the strength of this charge, his title to Pennsylvania was annulled; but a long and severe trial proved his innocence, and his flourishing province in the New World was restored to him. The business embarrassments of his later life affected his health and spirits. In 1712 a stroke of apoplexy greatly impaired his mind; though his death, in Berkshire, did not occur until six years later.

CHAPTER IX.
ENGLISH REVOLUTIONS. THE SOUTHERN COLONIES.

125. Important changes took place in England during the seventeenth century, which had their influence in America. The Puritans (§§74, 75, Note 1., p. 53) were now a majority of the great middle class of the people and of Parliament. They were the party of freedom in civil as well as religious matters, and they soon came into collision with Charles I., the second of the Stuart kings, whose ideas of royal authority were as absolute as his father's (§74). To escape their opposition, he tried for many years to rule without a parliament, and to support his government by forced loans. Want of money compelled him, however, to summon the representatives of the people, and he found them even less obedient than before.

126. Civil War in England at length broke out. Multitudes of families sought peace and security in America. The king, after many defeats, was taken prisoner, tried, condemned, and beheaded. The last parliament which he summoned, voted itself perpetual by an act which the king signed. It is hence called the *Long Parliament,* for it continued in session twelve years. It contained many warm friends of the New England colonies; but the latter were careful to ask no favors, lest they should confess themselves dependent.

127. Oliver Cromwell,[1] the head of the army, at length dissolved the Pong Parliament, and made himself chief ruler of England with the title of Lord Protector of the Commonwealth. He was a great man, and England was never more respected than when governed by him. But the power of the Commonwealth ended with his life; for his son Richard, who inherited his title, had not the strength to keep it.

128. In 1660 Charles II.[2] was called to occupy his father's throne.' He came with grand ideas of his powers and privileges as a king, and in four years gave away half of North America to men who had shared his exile or helped in his restoration. During the same years several new *Navigation Acts* gave to English merchants all the benefit of colonial trade. No goods could reach the colonies except in English ships; even the exchanges of one colony with another were loaded with heavy duties. Americans could buy foreign goods only in England, and must sell in England all their products which the English merchants would take; the rest must be sold "south of Cape Finisterre," so as to compete as little as possible with the interests *of* the mother-country. Under such ungenerous restrictions, it is needless to say, American merchants had little chance of success, for they bore all the risks and losses, while receiving scarcely any of the profits of European trade.

129. Conflicting Grants.—Probably the years of the king's exile had not been devoted to the study of geography, for while restoring *Acadia* to the French he renewed a grant of *Nova Scotia* to Sir Thomas Temple, who had succeeded the original proprietor (§83). He bestowed upon Connecticut — now made to include Saybrook and New Haven—all the land between Narragansett River and the Pacific Ocean, together with a new and very liberal charter; and at the same time he gave to his brother, the Duke of York, the tract between the Delaware and Connecticut rivers. (See §115.) Wiser men than King Charles had as yet no true idea of the breadth of the American continent, and the boundary lines of several colonies, extending from ocean to ocean, were hopelessly entangled. It was under the charter of Charles II. that Connecticut originally held the lands in Ohio, since known as the "Western Reserve," which afforded the basis of her school-fund.

130. The Carolinas.[3]—Hitherto both French (§§44-47) and English (§§51-54) had failed to make any lasting settlements in the southern half of the United States. In 1663 Charles II. granted to eight of his courtiers[4] the whole vast country southward of Virginia, and extending beyond the Mississippi on the west. Here the English dukes and earls resolved to set up an empire with all the parade of ranks and ceremonies to which they were accustomed in Europe. To this end, John Locke,[5] the great philosopher, together with Lord Shaftesbury, drew up a "Grand Model" of government. The country was divided, — on the map, — into provinces of nearly half a million acres, each to be governed by a landgrave, with a whole order of nobles under him. No settler was to vote unless he owned fifty or more acres of land; the tillers of the soil were to be serfs, and beneath them were slaves.

131. The "Model" proved to be too "grand" for the woods and marshes of the American wilderness. The farmers and lumbermen near Albemarle Sound, while awaiting the arrival of their baronial lords, struck out a plan of government better suited to their present needs ; and the proprietors at last consented to its adoption, only reserving to themselves an annual rent of a half-penny per acre, and the right to appoint two governors, the one for the northern, the other for the southern part of the territory.

132. The Albemarle settlement, though within the original limits of Virginia, was now made the nucleus of North **Carolina.** Its first governor was William Drummond, a Scotchman and a sincere lover of liberty, who afterwards lost his life in Bacon's Rebellion (§69). Its numbers were increased by emigrants from New England, and by a colony of ship-builders from the Bermudas. A company from Barbadoes settled on the south bank of the Cape Fear River,[6] and prospered so well in the exportation of staves, shingles, and boards to the islands whence they came, that in 1666 they numbered eight hundred souls.

133. The first settlement[7] in **South Carolina** was planted by the proprietors themselves, who sent out three shiploads of emigrants in 1670, at their own expense. After one or two experiments a site was chosen at the confluence of the Ashley and Cooper rivers; and in the midst of ancient forests, brightened in the spring by yellow jasmine, a little village was begun which received the name of *Charleston* in honor of the king.

134. French Colonists.—The genial climate attracted crowds of settlers.[8] Among others were thousands of French Protestants,[9] whose own land was made intolerable by persecution, though, strangely enough, they were forbidden to leave it under penalty of death. Their industry, intelligence, and high moral character were what the new colony most needed, and their gentleness and refinement of manners made a lasting impression upon the society of South Carolina.

135. Their plantations of pears, olives, and mulberry trees soon extended along the Cooper and Santee rivers. Rice was introduced from Madagascar, and was found well suited to the lowlands ; indigo flourished, and cotton at a later day became the most important staple. The heat of the summers made labor in the forests and rice-swamps fatal to white men. and negroes[10] were imported in greater numbers than to any other colony. In a few years they constituted nearly two thirds of the population.

136. Monmouth's Rebels.—In 1685 Charles II. died, and his brother, the Duke of York, became King James the Second. His nephew, the Duke of Monmouth, rebelled against him and tried to seize the crown. The movement was put down, and its leader beheaded, but a cruel vengeance was taken upon all who were suspected of having part in it. Hundreds were sold as indented servants to work in the tobacco fields of Virginia, and their wealth, with the price paid for them, went to enrich the king's courtiers. But Virginia was more merciful than her sovereign. In 1689 these exiles were set free, and many of them became honored citizens of the colony.

137. Covenanters in New Jersey.—King James's persecutions of the Covenanters[11] in Scotland led thousands of worthy people to emigrate to New Jersey. Here, instead of being hunted among dens and caves of the mountains, they went to work in peace and security upon fertile fields ; schools and churches multiplied, and it was soon said "there is not a poor body, nor one that wants, in all the colony."

138. Andros as Royal Governor.—As duke, James had unwillingly granted a free constitution to his province of New York ; but becoming king, he took it away, and forced the people to buy new titles to their farms from his agents. After several changes he intrusted Sir Edmund Andros[12] with the government of all the country from the Delaware to the St. Croix. Boston, then the "largest English town in the New World," was the capital of one great despotism. All discussion in townmeetings was forbidden ; public funds for schools and charities were confiscated ; and when it was represented that the new and enormous taxes would ruin the colonies, the oppressors answered, "It is not for his Majesty's interest you should thrive."

139. Lost Charters.—The great seal of Rhode Island was broken, and its government overthrown. The charter of Connecticut was demanded by Andros in person. It disappeared during the discussion, and is said to have been concealed in the hollow trunk of an old oak,[13] which stood nearly two centuries later, a beloved and venerated relic of colonial times. Andros wrote *Finis* at the end of the records of Connecticut, but happily his power, like his master's, was short-lived. The revolution which ended the short reign of James, restored some degree of order and freedom to the colonies (A. D. 1689).

Point out on Map No. - the various territories granted by Charles II. The first city in South Carolina. The limits of Andros's government.

NOTES.

1. Oliver Cromwell was born A. D. 1599, and died in'1658. His is one of the great names in history Cromwell's military genins and practical statesmanship are admitted even by his enemies. " Never," says

Macaulay, " was any ruler so conspicuously born for sovereignty. Insignificant as a private citizen, he was a great general ; lie was a still greater prince." With the Puritans, lie advocated religious liberty; but, like them, he was not tolerant towards those who differed from him. His personal ambition was great, but he refused kingship when it was offered to him. Yet Cromwell's rule was as absolute as any king's: his word was law throughout his reign. During the persecution of English Puritans by Charles 1., Cromwell and Hampden are said to have taken passage for America; but, being discovered on board the vessel before starting, they were ordered by the king to disembark. In after years the lord-protector took great interest in the Puritan colonies of the New World, and proffered them aid against the encroachments of the New Netherlanders.

2. Upon the accession of **Charles II.** to the throne of England, the Massachusetts colonists appealed to him " as a king who had seen adversity, and who, having himself been an exile, knew the hearts of exiles." They besought him for "a continuance of civil and religions liberties," andin response King diaries wrote a letter assuring them of his good will. He granted them amnesty for past offenses, and urged them to repeal all laws which might be opposed to his royal authority. The Navigation Acts bore heavily upon the people of New England, and they sent agents to remonstrate with Charles against the injustice of such laws. But the constant infringement of their charter of liberties, under the open sanction of the king, was hardest to be borne. All entreaty, however, was in vain. In 1681 the Massachusetts charter was declared to be forfeited, diaries II. was ever ready with pleasant promises, but few of them were kept. He was supremely selfish and impure in character. His reign was one of the most corrupt in English history. He died of apoplexy in 1685.

3. **Carolina.**—A grant of the "Province of Carolana" was made by Charles I. in 1630, to Sir Robert Heath, who afterwards disposed of his title to Lord Maltravers. The owners of this claim disputed the rights of the courtiers of Charles II. under their charter of 1663. The Virginia Assembly had made numerous trading grants along the Roanoke River and Albemarle Sound as early as 1643, and a few years later some New England colonists selected tracts of land on the Cape Fear and Chowan rivers. These conflicting claims were the cause of much unpleasant feeling in the early days of the Carolinas.

4. The Earl of Clarendon, the Duke of Albemarle, Lord Craven,

Lord Ashley Cooper, Sir John Colleton, Lord John Berkeley, Sir William Berkeley, and Sir George Carter.

5. John Locke was born in 1632 and died in 1704. He attended the University at Oxford. His great philosophical treatise is an "Essay on the Human Understanding." Locke's system of philosophy became at once widely popular, and exerted a marked influence upon the thought of the civilized world.

6. This settlement was probably about twenty-five miles from the mouth of Cape Fear River. It was called Charles-town. Sir John Yeamans was chosen governor of the province called Clarendon, which extended as far south as the St. John's River in Florida.

7. This settlement was under the direction of Captain William Sayle and Joseph West. Both were afterwards governors of South Carolina. The vessels landed first at Port Royal, at that time the best known harbor on the coast, and then sailed to a point a few miles up the Ashley River, — "the first high land that seemed convenient for tillage and pasturing." Here the immigrants planted a town and built log houses. The site did not prove advantageous, and it was not many years before all the settlers had removed to the present location of Charleston.

8. Several ship-loads of Dutch emigrants eame from Holland and from New Amsterdam ; a company of hardy and intelligent Scotchmen sought new homes in South Carolina; and large numbers of English, both Churchmen and Dissenters, swelled the tide of emigration. The king of England sent out, at his own expense, a small band of Protestant workmen to introduce the productions of southern Europe.

9. These were Huguenots. A century before this the great Huguenot leader Coligny (§44) had selected the shores of Carolina as a place of refuge for their persecuted ancestors. During the three years, 1686-1688, one million inhabitants are believed to have tied from France because of the persecutions by Louis XIV. Besides those who came to America, thousands went to England, Switzerland, and Holland.

10. Negro slaves were brought to the first plantations on Ashley River in 1671.

11. The Covenanters, or Cameronians, were a sect of Presbyterian dissenters in Scotland who rebelled against the use of the liturgy which King James I. had forced upon them. In 1638 they entered into a covenant "In behalf of true religion and freedom of the kingdom." Five years later they formed a new covenant far bolder and more sweeping in its terms than the first. They held firmly to their avowed principles throughout the reigns of James II. and Charles II., and by their tenacity incurred the displeasure of these sovereigns. In 1650 Charles himself, when in exile, had signed the covenant for the sake of gaining popularity and regaining the crown; but after the Restoration lie shamefully broke the covenant and cruelly persecuted the Covenanters. Richard Cameron was the founder of this sect.

12. Sir Edmund Andros was governor of New York from 1674 to 1682; of New England from 1686 to 1689; and of Virginia from 1692 to 1698. His appointment as governor-general was very displeasing to the Puritans. His first acts were arbitrary, and he enforced them rigidly. Not only in civil affairs, but in matters pertaining to worship, did he violate the long established customs of the people. He decreed that no marriage should be regarded as legal unless the ceremony was performed by a minister of the Church of England. His rule became so oppressive that the people of Boston could endure it no longer, and they deposed him by force of arms, He was arrested, and twice escaped from prison, but both times was recaptured. He was permitted after awhile to return to England. The private character of Governor Andros was not bad, and his despotic acts were simply the fulfillment of the policy of his king.

13. Charter Oak.—This famous tree stood on the grounds of Samuel Wallys in Hartford, and was blown down during a severe storm in 1856. It was in 1687 that Governor Andros appeared with a band of soldiers, and commanded the General Court to deliver to him the royal charter of Connecticut. Governor Treat eloquently argued the rights of his people to their charter, which had been endeared to them by so many hardships and sufferings in its defense. The instrument was in a box on the table in front of him while he spoke. Suddenly the candles were put out, and in the darkness and contusion Captain Wadsworth, of Hartford, seized the box and bore the precious charter safely to the hollow oak, where it remained for a long time.

THIRTEEN ENGLISH COLONIES.

VIRGINIA.—Settled first at Jamestown, 1607.

NEW YORK.—Settled first at New York (by the Dutch) 1614; became English, 1664.

MASSACHUSETTS.—Settled first at Plymouth, 1620; at Salem, 1629.

NEW HAMPSHIRE.—Settled first at Portsmouth, 1623; became a royal province, 1675.

CONNECTICUT. — Settled first at Windsor, 1633; at New Haven, 1638.

MARYLAND. — Settled first at St. Mary's, 1634.

RHODE ISLAND. — Settled first at Providence, 1636; at Newport, 1638.

DELAWARE. — Settled first at Christiana (by Swedes) 1638 ; granted to Penn, 1682.

PENNSYLVANIA. — Settled first near Philadelphia, 1643 ; granted to Penn, 1681.

NORTH CAROLINA. — Settled first near Albemarle Sound, 1663.

NEW JERSEY. — Settled first at Elizabethtown, 1665.

SOUTH CAROLINA. — Settled first at Charleston, 1670.

GEORGIA. — Settled first at Savannah, 1733.

ENGLISH SOVEREIGNS DURING THE FIRST COLONIAL PERIOD.

ELIZABETH, A. D. 1558-1603, authorized adventures *of* Frobisher, Davis, Drake, Gilbert, and Raleigh (§§ 50-54).

JAMES I., A. D. 1603-1625, gave charters to the London and Plymouth companies; made laws for Virginia; wrote a "Counterblast" against tobacco; offended English Puritans, who took refuge in Holland and America (§§ 55, 74-76).

CHARLES I, A. D. 1625-1649, gave charter to Massachusetts and proprietary patent for Maryland ; at the end of civil war with Parliament, was condemned and beheaded (§§ 70, 85, 125, 126).

CHARLES II, A. D. 1660-1685, gave popular charters to Connecticut and Rhode Island; proprietary patents for all the country east of the Kennebec, and west and south of the Connecticut as far as Florida and the Mississippi; renewed "Navigation Acts" which bore heavily on the colonies (§§ 128-130).

JAMES II, A. D. 1685-1688, as Duke of York, proprietor of eastern Maine, New York, and New Jersey; as king, sends Andros to govern all the colonies east of the Delaware (§§ 122, 123, 129, 136, 139).

THE ECLECTIC HISTORY OF THE UNITED STATES

QUESTIONS FOR REVIEW. —PART I.

		Section
1.	What is known concerning the Mound Builders?	1-4
2.	How did men first reach America?	5
3.	Describe the cruises of the Icelanders.	6-10
4.	Sketch the main physical features of the United States.	12-19
5.	Sketch the appearance, customs, and tribal divisions of the North American Indians.	20-29
6.	What led to the re-discovery of America?	30, 31
7.	Tell the story of Columbus.	32-30
8.	Describe the consequent maritime adventures of English, Portuguese, and Spaniards.	37-40
9.	Describe the inland explorations of Narvaez, De Soto, and Coronado.	41, 42
10.	French adventures and early attempts at settlement.	43-40
11.	What was done in New York by Champlain and the French missionaries?	47
12.	Describe the Spanish explorations and settlements in the south-west.	48
13.	Describe the English voyages and vain attempts at settlement.	49-54
14.	Describe the first English colony that kept its ground.	55-62
15.	How was Virginia governed ?	63-67
16.	Tell the story of Bacon's rebellion.	68-69
17.	Describe the foundation and government of Maryland.	70-73
18.	Describe the movements of English Puritans and Independents.	74-76

		Section
19.	Describe the foundation of the Plymouth Colony.	77-81
20.	Describe the settlements east of the Merrimac.	82, 83
21.	Describe the beginnings of Massachusetts and Harvard College.	84-87
22.	Describe the beginning of Connecticut.	88-89
23.	Describe the beginning of Rhode Island.	92-93
24.	How were religious differences regarded in Massachusetts?	90-94, 99
25.	Describe the Pequod War.	94, 95
26.	How were the several colonies governed?	96, 98
27.	How were Indians treated and regarded?	100-102
28.	Describe King Philip's War.	102, 103
29.	What was done by the Dutch in exploring and occupying New Netherlands?	104-108
30.	What by the Swedes?	109, 110
31.	What changes were made under Governors Kieft and Stuyvesant?	111–115
32.	How was New Jersey first settled?	116, 118, 137
33.	On what principles was Pennsylvania founded?	119-121
34.	What other state belonged to Penn?	122
35.	What changes occurred in England during the seventeenth century?	125-127
36.	What was done by King Charles II.?	128-130
37.	Describe the settlement and government of the Carolinas.	130-135
38.	Describe the character and policy of James II.	117, 136-139

PART II.—GROWTH OF THE COLONIES.
CHAPTER X.
PARLIAMENTARY RULE.

140. Revolution in England.—James H. had been King of England only three years when the Whig or liberal party, grown strong by his tyrannies, called his son-in-law and daughter, the Prince and Princess of Orange, to supersede him on the throne. The accession of William and Mary was hailed with great joy[1] by the people of New England, who hastened to throw off the hated government of Andros and resume all their chartered rights. A new charter, which was granted in 1690, incorporated the "Old Colony" of Plymouth with Massachusetts, and added to the latter all the country between the eastern boundary of New Hampshire and the St. Lawrence.

141. Salem Witchcraft.[2]—One or two towns in Massachusetts became about this time the victims of a strange delusion. All the world then believed in the possibility of possession by evil spirits. The witch—usually some helpless and harmless old woman—was supposed to issue from her chimney at night, and ride on a broomstick or on the wings of the wind to some assembly of demons. The accused found it impossible to prove their innocence; for envy and spite seized the opportunity afforded by the prevailing panic, and even religion, commonly the protector of the wronged, was now enlisted against them.

142. Twenty innocent persons were put to death as witches, and fifty-five more were only saved by false confessions extorted by torture, before the people awoke from their horrid dream. Then Justice Sewall, who had pronounced sentence against some of the accused, made public confession of his error in the Old South Church at Boston, and to the end of a long life the good man never failed to renew this act of penitence at each annual Fast-day.

143. Death of Leisler.—The Dutch people of New York were rejoiced at the accession of their countryman, the Prince of Orange. In the absence of Andros and his lieutenant, they made Jacob Leisler their chief magistrate until instructions could be received from England. On the arrival of Sloughter, the new governor, with a commission from William III., Leisler sent to surrender the fort. But Sloughter chose to consider him as a traitor, and in an hour of drunkenness signed a warrant for his execution. All the other colonies willingly acknowledged William and Mary as their sovereigns.

144. The English Revolution settled three important principles for all English-speaking nations: that a bad king may rightly be deposed; that Parliament may alter and decide the succession to the throne; and in general, that governments exist for the benefit of the people, and not for the selfish advantage of their rulers. The establishment of this last principle was a long step toward that greater revolution which made the United States independent of Great Britain ; but for a time they were subject to a more irksome despotism than before, namely, that of the English Parliament.

145. Board of Trade.—In 1696 colonial matters were intrusted to a "Board of Trade and Plantations," consisting of five high officers of the crown and eight special commissioners. This Board was to study how to "make the colonies most useful and beneficial to England;" to revise the acts of the provincial governments, and see how all their money was expended.

146. Plans for Union.—For the sake of the common defense, the Board recommended a closer union of the colonies. Postal service, already existing between Boston and New York, was now extended, and letters could be carried eight times in the year from Philadelphia to the Potomac! William Penn drew up a plan for the union of the American states by means of a general congress. But the time had not come for union. If it had been effected then, it would have been under a military despotism.

147. The "Mercantile System," which was already ruining the colonies of Spain, was now adopted in its full force by England. The Navigation Acts (§128) were renewed and stringently enforced. England was to be the only market and the only storehouse for colonial commerce. Wool, being the staple export of England, was forbidden to be carried out of any colony upon horse, cart, or ship. Even a sailor in want of clothes must not buy more than forty shillings' worth in any American port, and even this small purchase was soon forbidden. Not a pine tree could be felled on common lands except by the king's license. Later, all iron-works were prohibited.

148. Courts of Admiralty.—As colonial juries would not pronounce men guilty for evading laws like these, new "Courts of Admiralty" were established to try all offenses against the Navigation Laws. Among the greatest injuries inflicted by Parliament upon the southern colonies was the forced increase of the slave trade. Virginia and Carolina made repeated attempts in their popular assemblies to stop the importation of negroes from Africa. But Queen Anne, the successor of William III., was, by the terms of her treaty[3] with Spain, the greatest slave-merchant in the world. Many English lords and capitalists, also, had large shares in the traffic; and for their advantage Parliament reversed the acts *of* the colonial assemblies, and forced every American port to receive men as merchandise.

149. Literary Progress.—The twelve colonies now numbered about two hundred thousand people. At the accession of Queen Anne, in 1702, they had three colleges: Harvard in Massachusetts, Yale in Connecticut, and William and Mary in Virginia. There was no newspaper printed as yet upon the western continent; but in 1704 the Boston *News Letter,* the first American journal, was established. It was a small sheet which merely reported facts and never meddled with opinions. There were but two public libraries in the whole country; one was in Massachusetts and the other in South Carolina.

150. Georgia.—One more state was yet to be added to the

cluster of English colonies on the Atlantic. The great proprietors of the Carolinas (see §130), weary of endless disputes with the people concerning rents, taxes, and political rights, surrendered their claims to the crown. A part of the surrendered territory was bestowed by King George II. on General Oglethorpe[4] " in trust for the poor." Oglethorpe was not only a famous soldier, but a good and benevolent man. As a member of Parliament, his attention was called to the wretched condition of persons imprisoned for debt under then-existing laws of England. Their sufferings seemed to him needless as well as cruel, while the great, rich lands of America were lying untenanted; and .he resolved to open in the New World a refuge for the unfortunate of every name.

151. He himself came over with the first settlers, and lived for a year in a tent, where he afterwards laid out the broad avenues and spacious squares of *Savannah.* The colon)- was named Georgia, in honor of the king. The neighboring Indians were justly treated, and they repaid the kindness of Oglethorpe by the same loving fidelity which their northern brethren had shown to Penn. German Lutherans and Moravians, Swiss Calvinists, and Scotch Covenanters were among the early settlers of Georgia.

152. So long as he remained with the colony, Oglethorpe refused to admit either slaves or rum, though the latter would have been received at a great profit in exchange for the pine-timber which was the chief natural wealth of Georgia. The great English preachers, John[5] and Charles Wesley, who visited America in 1736, strongly opposed negro slavery ; but Whitefield,[6] a no less celebrated preacher, whose wonderful eloquence swayed all hearts, approved and recommended it ; and after Oglethorpe's departure African servants were soon introduced.

James Oglethorpe.

153. Spain, meanwhile, claimed the whole territory of Georgia as her own (§45). Foreseeing war, Oglethorpe built forts at Augusta, at Darien, and at Frederica, and brought a regiment of soldiers from England. War was declared in Europe in 1739; and in the following winter General Oglethorpe invaded Florida, captured two fortified posts, and besieged St. Augustine, though without success. In return the Spaniards invaded Georgia, but after a severe defeat at Bloody Marsh, on St. Simon's Island, they sailed away to Florida with their forces much diminished.

154. In 1743 Oglethorpe left the colony which he had spent ten years in founding, and returned to England, where for forty years he was known as a warm friend of America. Considered as an institution of charity, Georgia was not altogether a success: the people who had failed to support themselves in England, had seldom the courage and industry needed for life in the wilderness. Happily, more energetic settlers were not wanting, and Georgia became in time one of the richest and most thriving colonies.

Point out on Map No. 3 the enlarged boundaries of Massachusetts (§ 140). Savannah. St. Augustine. Augusta. Darien and Frederica.

NOTES.

1. King William had always been opposed to France and to Catholicism, and as the conquest of New France was now the great ambition of New England, it was hoped by the latter that a common sentiment would unite England and the northern colonies.

2. The spread of this delusion among the intelligent classes is almost incredible. It was not confined to America, but had a much wider prevalence in France. Switzerland, and Germany. In England and Scotland four thousand witches were put to death during the seventeenth century. Among the most ruthless opponents of witchcraft in the colonies was the Reverend Cotton Mather, then a young minister, whose remarkable learning gave a fatal importance to his opinions. His book, entitled " Wonders of the Invisible World," was approved both by the governor of the state and by his father, the president of Harvard.

3. In the words of the treaty: "Her Britannic Majesty does offer and undertake, by persons whom she shall appoint, to bring into the West Indies of America belonging to his Catholic Majesty in the space of thirty years, one hundred and forty-four thousand negroes, at the rate of four thousand eight hundred in each of the said thirty years." It was further agreed that the exclusive slave-trade of all Spanish America, as well as of the British possessions, should be in the Queen's hands.

4. James Edward Oglethorpe was born in London in 1688, and entered the army at the age of fourteen. He served against the Turks in 1716-'17, and in 1722 was elected to Parliament, holding his seat for thirty- two years. Oglethorpe returned to England from America in 1743, and served as major-general against the Pretender in 1745. In 1765 lie was made General of all His Majesty's forces, when he retired upon half-pay. His death occurred in 1785.

5. John Wesley (b. 1703, d. 1791) was the founder of Methodism. He graduated at Oxford in 1727, and the following year was ordained priest in the English Church. From 1729 to 1735 he was an instructor at Oxford, where he became the leader of a set of pious young men, who were derisively called "Methodists," from their methodical mode of living. In 1735, Oglethorpe persuaded Wesley to go to Georgia as a missionary. He was accompanied by his brother Charles and two Oxford friends; his principal object being the conversion of the Indians. It was upon this journey that Wesley met with some Moravian missionaries, who so impressed him that, immediately upon his return to England, he commenced the study of their doctrines, which finally led to his

establishing the Methodist Church.

6. George Whitefield (b. 1714, d. 1770), an associate of the Wesleys at oxford, was the most remarkable preacher of his day, — his audiences frequently numbering ten thousand persons. He was deeply interested in extending Methodist doctrines, and visited the American colonies no less than seven times, preaching wherever he went. Il is death, from asthma, occurred at Newburyport, Mass.

CHAPTER XI.
FRENCH COLONIES.

Marquette on the Mississippi.

155. While Englishmen thus occupied the Atlantic coast, French adventurers were laying the foundations of several important states in the great central valley, and along the southern shores of our country. Missionaries, traders, and soldiers were the three classes who successively planted the lily-standard of France by the lakes of central New York and the northwest, along the Mississippi and its branches, and by the Mexican Gulf. The Franciscan and Jesuit Fathers[1] were moved by zeal for the souls of the savage heathen; and the bells of their little chapels broke the silence of many a wilderness far from the dwellings of white men.

156. In 1673 **Father Marquette**,[2] with six Frenchmen, made his way, first of Europeans, to the upper waters of the Mississippi, and descended it in boats as far as the mouth of the Arkansas. Michigan traces its origin to Marquette, who established the missions of St. Mary and St. Ignace. At Kaskaskia he became, in 1675, the founder of Illinois.

157. Fur-traders.—Next to the missionaries came the fur-traders, pushing their canoes up every navigable stream from the Great Lakes, carrying them over water-sheds to the head-waters of rivers flowing to the Mississippi ; becoming as hardy and skillful in wood-craft as the Indians themselves, from whom they received treasures of rich furs in exchange for knives, trinkets, axes, and guns.

158. The name **Louisiana** was given to the whole region watered by the Mississippi and its branches, by La Salle,[3] the greatest of French adventurers, who aimed to make it a vast inland empire, drawing its wealth from the fur-trade, but subject to the king of France. Launching the first European vessel above the Falls of Niagara, La Salle sailed through the Lakes, establishing trading stations at Michillimackinac and St. Joseph's, in Michigan, — then struck inland, and after many losses and disasters passed through the Mississippi to the Gulf.

159. The French in Texas.—Frenchmen were eager to take possession of the great country thus thrown open to them, and their "Grand Monarch," Louis XIV.,[4] expended more upon one expedition to plant a city at the mouth of the Mississippi than all the English sovereigns in a hundred years had bestowed upon their thirteen colonies. Nevertheless, it proved a miserable failure. The fleet passed the great river, and La Salle never succeeded in retracing his way to it. He was murdered by one of his men, and the colony which he had founded in Texas dwindled away until its site was only occupied by graves.

160. In Mississippi and Alabama.—In 1699 Lemoine d'Iberville,[5] with two hundred French immigrants, arrived at Biloxi, in the present state of Mississippi. *Natchez,* already a cluster of Indian villages, became the site of Fort Rosalie, a French colony, two years later. In 1702 the chief French station on the Gulf was removed from Biloxi to the fine harbor of *Mobile,* and the state of Alabama received its first white inhabitants.

161. Louis XV.—The eighteenth century saw a sudden revival of the scheme for a great French empire in America. The throne of France was inherited in 1715 by Louis XV.,[6] a child five years old, under the regency of the Duke of Orléans. The wars and luxuries of Louis XIV. had left his kingdom buried in hopeless debts. Law,[7] a Scotch banker, formed a wild plan for relieving the treasury by pledging the untold wealth of Louisiana.

162. The "Mississippi Scheme" for a time seemed successful. Rich and poor hastened to exchange their gold for Law's paper money, and the public debt disappeared as by magic. And though the bubble soon burst, leaving France in deeper poverty and misery than before, the colony prospered, for several thousands of people sought homes in the New World, of which they had heard such wonderful reports. The city of *New Orleans*, founded in 1717, took its name from the Regent. Law himself secured a great tract of prairie-land on the Arkansas, and spent a fortune in founding a city and villages. Though his plan was not fulfilled, a new state was thus begun.

163. The Natchez (§ 26) were superior in some respects to other Indians of the region, and their monarch, "The Great Sun," was the proudest of native chiefs. Around him was a race of nobles who were treated with great respect by the common people. They were jealous of the French, whose rapidly increasing numbers threatened to occupy the whole land; especially when Chopart, the commander in their neighborhood, demanded for a plantation the site of their chief village, which contained their holiest temple. Incited by the Chickasaws, they planned a sudden vengeance, and murdered in one morning two hundred Frenchmen. When the news reached New Orleans, a force was sent which surprised and defeated the Natchez. The "Great Sun" and four hundred of his subjects were sold as slaves to the Spaniards in Hayti. All who escaped joined other tribes, and the nation became extinct.

164. New Orleans, which, in 1723, succeeded Mobile as the seat of French government in Louisiana, now contained 4,000 white settlers and 2,000 negroes. It exported to France small quantities of cotton, indigo, and the wax of the candle-berry, a curious production which was much valued in those days. Its most important trade, however, was in the furs which were collected from the northern Indians and brought down the great river in canoes. Discouraged by the first report of the loss of Natchez, the Company decided that the cost of the colony exceeded the profit, and surrendered all its rights to the crown.

165. French Forts.—The French guarded their American possessions by a chain of sixty forts from the mouth of the St. Lawrence to that of the Mississippi. Among the most important, beside the citadels of Quebec and Montreal, were Fort Frederic, Crown Point on Lake Champlain; Frontenac near the outlet of Lake Ontario; Niagara, Detroit, *Chicagou* : forts on the present sites of Vincennes in Indiana, Memphis, and Natchez.

Point out on Map No. 3 the towns founded by Marquette (§156). By La Salle (§158). The French settlements on the lower Mississippi and the Gulf (§§ 160, 162). The boundaries of French Louisiana. The chief military stations of the French.

Read Parkman's "Jesuits in North America" and " Discoverers of the Great West."

NOTES.

1. Jesuit Fathers.-The "Society of Jesus" was founded by Ignatius Loyola in 1540. Its members were pledged to extend the Itoman Catholic religion over the world, at whatever cost of personal sacrifice or suffering. In the early history of America the exploits of Jesuit missionaries among the Indian's furnish some of the most thrilling chapters. Their intense zeal for the conversion of the savages is proven by the terrible privations they endured, many of their number having fallen victims to exposure, starvation, and the scalping-knife. One of them wrote from a Canadian wilderness in 1647, after several of his companions had been murdered by the Iroquois, " Do not imagine we are cast down. We shall die; we shall be captured, burned, butchered. Be it so. Those who die in their beds do not always die the best death."

2. Jacques Marquette was born in northern France in 1637, and became a member of the order of Jesuits at the age of seventeen. He received a good education, was a fine linguist, and possessed rare traits of character. He eame as a missionary to Canada in 1666, and in a short time learned the languages of several Indian tribes. With Louis Joliet, Marquette set out, in 1673, around the Great Lakes, to find the headwaters of the Mississippi. In due time they reached Green Bay, where a Jesuit mission had been established ; they ascended the Fox River to " the portage." A mile and a half brought them to the Wisconsin River; friendly Indians helped them drag their canoes. They drifted down this larger stream for a couple of days, when they were rejoiced to see the waters of the great river they had come so far and toiled so hard to discover. It was the 17th of June, 1673, when these intrepid explorers entered the Mississippi. Their return was through the Illinois River; and Marquette, being taken siek, stopped at the Indian village of Kaskaskia, while Joliet proceeded to Quebec to report the successful issue of their journey. Père Marquette died two years later, in the wilderness on the eastern shore of Lake Michigan, while on his way to the mission at Michilhmackinae.

3. Robert Cavalier de La Salle was born at Rouen in 1643. He was educated for the priesthood, and early joined the Jesuits; but he chafed under their severe discipline, and soon left the order. Becoming interested in the accounts of discovery in the New World, he set out for Canada when twenty-three years old. He was ambitious to add his own name to the list of great explorers, and to extend the possessions of France. Hearing from the Indians at Quebec of the great river of the west, the Miche Sèpè, La Salle conjectured that it must flow into the Pacific. He determined to solve this problem. His first expedition was in the summer of 1669, and resulted in the discovery of the Ohio River, which he followed to the falls at Louisville. The next year he descended the Illinois, though not to its mouth. The vessel which he built above Niagara Falls was named the " Griffin : " in this he sailed around the lakes as far as Green Bay, then crossed Lake Michigan in canoes, and with a small party traversed the lower peninsula of Michigan. They ascended the St. Joseph River, made a portage to the Kankakee, and through this stream reached the Illinois. Just below the present site of Peoria they built Fort Crèvecœur. From this point La Salle went back to

Montreal in midwinter for new supplies, and nearly perished on the journey. But in 1680 he retraced his course to the fort on the Illinois, and thence floated down to the Mississippi. It was two years later before he descended the " great river." On the 9th of April, 1682, he set up a column near the Mississippi's mouth, bearing the royal arms of " Louis le Grand," and claimed the vast stretch of territory from the lakes to the gulf, and from the Alle- ghanies to the Rocky mountains, as the domain of France. Recrossing the wilderness to Montreal, lie sailed for his native land to bring out a colony to Louisiana. In 1684 he left the shores of France with some three hundred adventurers. One ship-load turned back before many days, and many deserted at St. Domingo. But the resolute leader, with a remnant Of his band, reached Matagorda Bay in the spring of 1685, and built a fort for protection against the Indians. Two years of ill success, and heavy losses by disease and Indian attacks, utterly dispirited the settlers. They blamed La Salle for their sufferings, and one or two desperate characters determined to take vengeance on his life. His assassination took place in 1687, on the banks of the Trinity River in Texas. Says Parkman: "America owes La Salle an enduring memory; for in his masculine figure, cast in iron, she sees the heroic pioneer who guided her to the possession of lier richest heritage."

4. **Louis XIV.** was king of France for seventy-two years — A. ID. 1613- 1715. His reign, until towards its close, was marked by prosperity at home and valuable conquests abroad ; while an unusual interest was shown in literature and art. The alliance of the French king, in 1666, with the Butch against England, led Charles If. to urge his American colonists to attack the French in Canada; but the settlers of Virginia and Massachusetts had other work to do, and did not respond to the appeal. Until the great discoveries of La Salle, and the compliment he bestowed upon his king in the name given to Louisiana, Louis XIV. seemed to care little for the enlargement of his territory in America. In 1676 he wrote to Count Frontenac: "With regard to new discoveries, you will not address yourself to them excepting in a great necessity."

5. **Lemoine d'Iberville** was born in Montreal, 1661, and died in Cuba, 1706. He early entered the French navy, and became distinguished as one of its ablest officers. He won many victories over the British in Hudson Bay, Newfoundland, and off the coast of Maine. He was selected to plant colonies in the extreme south-west of New France, where La Salle had set the standard of his king nearly twenty years before. After building Fort Biloxi, d'Iberville sailed for France, leaving his brother,

Bienville, in command. He returned with reinforcements in A. B. 1700. D'Iberville named lakes Maurepas and Pontchartrain. He is regarded as the founder of Louisiana.

6. Louis XV. was the great-grandson of Louis XIV. His reign covered the period from 1715 to 1774. It was a brilliant era in French literature, but the profligacy of the court was notorious, and the wild speculation of the times brought about almost universal bankruptcy. The "French and Indian War" occurred during the reign of Louis XV., by which France lost all her valuable possessions in America.

7. John Law, the founder of New Orleans, was born in Edinburgh in 1671. He was the son of a goldsmith, received a careful education, but preferred gambling to business, and at the age of twenty-three killed a man in a duel, for which he was sentenced to death. Escaping from prison, he tied to Holland and studied banking in Amsterdam. But his favorite resort was the gaming-table, and by this means he is said to have won a large sum, which he took with him to Paris as capital for his future operations. Law's private bank was soon made a "royal bank," the king himself being security. He formed the "Western Company," afterwards the "Indian Company," through which he purposed to control all the commerce of New France from Canada to the Gulf of Mexico. He appointed Bienville as Governor-general of Louisiana. From 1718 to 1721 the number of emigrants to this new region was several thousand. After the collapse of Law's great financial scheme, he left Paris in great disfavor, and died in poverty, at Venice, in 1729.

CHAPTER XII.
INTERCOLONIAL WARS.

166. King William III. was the sworn foe of Louis XIV. of France, and their wars were fought out with even greater violence in American forests than on battle-fields in Europe. For here the French had savage allies, who, falling upon the inland settlements of the English, murdered women, children, and defenseless men, with atrocities which civilized people can hardly conceive.

167. Four distinct wars between the French and English colonies are commonly named as:

KING WILLIAM'S WAR	A. D.	1689-1697
QUEEN ANNE'S WAR	"	1702-1713
KING GEORGE'S WAR	"	1744-1748
THE OLD FRENCH AND INDIAN WAR	"	1754-1763

These wars were ended in Europe by treaties of peace, but fighting could hardly be said to have ceased on this continent at any time within the seventy-four years.

168. Attack on Schenectady.—During that time no mother hushed her babe to its night's rest, in any frontier village of New York or New England, with the least assurance that it would not be snatched from her arms and murdered before morning. The inhabitants of *Schenectady*, in New York, were awakened one wintry night, in 1690, by the savage war-whoop, to find their village in flames. The few who escaped the tomahawk fled, half-clothed, over the snow to Albany. The assailants gained nothing but the addition of sixty scalps to their trophies, to repay them for twenty-two days' march through snows and frozen forests from Montreal. Similar attacks were repeated all along the northern frontier. Hundreds of captives were dragged away on the rapid return-march to Canada, and a single cry of pain or fatigue was answered by a blow from the tomahawk.[1]

169. Congress of the Northern Colonies.—To put a stop to such outrages a congress of the northern colonies at New York planned the conquest of Acadia and Canada. The first was accomplished by volunteers from Massachusetts, who conquered Port Royal; but the attempts against Montreal and Quebec[2] ended in failure and disaster. At the end of the war all conquests were restored, but a few years later Port Royal was retaken and named Annapolis, in honor of the queen of England. Acadia also changed its name to that of *Nova Scotia,* by which the English had always called it.

170. Queen Anne's War was called in Europe the "War of the Spanish Succession," and it ended, after eleven years' conflict by land and sea, in placing a French prince on the throne of Spain. This was a serious matter for the English colonies, as it united in one policy their French and Spanish rivals, who hemmed them in on the north, west, and south. Spaniards as well as French now stirred up the Indians to attack the English towns.

171. In return, Governor Moore, of South Carolina, led a company of volunteers through the pine forests which then covered Georgia, and attacked the Spanish settlements on Appalachee Bay. A force of twenty- three Spaniards and four hundred Indians was defeated; six towns submitted to the English, and many of their people joined the South Carolina colony. A French fleet from Havana attempted the next year to capture Charleston, but so brave was the defense that the invaders had to retire with immense loss. The boundary between Georgia and Florida was pushed far southward of the limit which Spain had claimed before the war.

172. The settlements on Albemarle and Pamlico sounds were nearly destroyed by the Tuscaroras. Their wrath had been excited by a survey of their lands with reference to a new immigration of Germans from the Rhine provinces, and they resolved to exterminate all the white men. The war was fierce and long, but at last the Indians were so far subdued that they abandoned their old hunting grounds, and emigrating northward became the sixth nation in the League of the Iroquois (§24).

173. The French in Maine. — The French, meanwhile, still claimed the greater part of Maine; and their westernmost station was at Norridgewock, on the Kennebec.[3] Here Father Rasles, a pious and learned priest, had gathered a school of Indian converts, who revered him as a saint. The English colonists regarded him, however, as a promoter of savage raids upon their homes, and several attempts were made to capture him. In one of the expeditions an Indian village above Bangor, on the Penobscot, was burned to the ground. At length Rasles's settlement was surprised by a party from New England; he made no effort to escape, but bravely met death in covering the retreat of his flock. His chapel was burnt, with all the Indian cabins.

174. A new war soon broke out between Florida and the English colonies at the south. General Oglethorpe besieged St. Augustine without success; the Spaniards invading Georgia, were repulsed from Frederica with great loss. (See §153.)

All the colonies north of Carolina contributed men to a great English fleet, designed for the conquest of Mexico and the Spanish West Indies. Havana might have been captured, but the admiral missed his opportunity and attacked *Carthagena* on the South American coast. It was taken, and its fortresses were demolished; but there was nothing gained to balance the loss of 20,000 men. Nine tenths of all the colonial troops fell victims to the unhealthy climate.

175. King George's War. — These colonial contests were only a part of the "War of the Austrian Succession," in which nearly all Europe was engaged. In America it was known as "King George's War." Its chief event in the north was the capture of Louisburg, on Cape Breton Island, the strongest fortress in America. The main burden of the undertaking was borne by the farmers and fishermen of New England; and their success was of great service as proving their power.[4] In 1748 peace was restored, one of its conditions being the restoration of all conquests. Eight years of untold suffering and loss left the boundaries of all the nations unchanged.

176. The Ohio Valley.—French forts and English settlements had now extended so far as to meet in the Ohio Valley. In 1753 Governor Dinwiddie, of Virginia, sent George Washington, then twenty-one years of age, to know from the French commander at Venango[5] "his reasons for invading the British dominions." It was replied that the whole country was French by right of La Salle's discoveries, and that it could and would be defended. Washington returned, in imminent peril from Indian bullets and floating ice[6]; and the next year was put in command of an expedition to complete and defend a fort already begun by the English at the forks of the Ohio.

177. Washington's Failure.—Before his arrival the French had seized the fort, which they named Du Quesne in honor of the governor of New France. Washington surprised and defeated a party of the enemy; and while awaiting the promised aid from the colonies, he fortified his little camp in the "Great Meadows," and named it *Fort Necessity*. No help came, excepting a company from South Carolina; and its captain, who held a commission from the king, claimed to supersede Washington, who, though a lieutenant-colonel, had received his rank only from the governor of Virginia. This unhappy dissension ruined tire expedition. Attacked by the French and Indians, Washington was compelled, after nine hours' fighting, to retreat, leaving the whole Ohio basin to the enemy.

178. Union of the Colonies.—The prospect of a general war was now so imminent that the English colonies were forced to unite for the common defense. A convention of all the colonies north of the Potomac was assembled at Albany, and a plan of permanent union was submitted to it by Dr. Franklin. (See §§203-205.) It was accepted by the convention, but rejected by the Board of Trade as tending toward American independence; while the people themselves feared that a central government would interfere with the rights of each colony.

179. French and Indian War.—Though the colonial troops had borne so much of the labor and hardship of the wars with the French, they were despised by the regular British officers, who made no account of their superior knowledge of Indian tactics, and expected to enforce the same rules in the tangled forests of America as upon the fields of Europe. One result of the French and Indian War was that American soldiers, beside profiting by British drill, learned something of their own value.

180. Braddock's Defeat.—In 1755 a combined force of British and colonists undertook the capture of Fort Du Quesne (§177). General Braddock commanded, and Washington was his aid. As they marched through the dense

Braddock's Defeat.

woods in solid columns, to beat of drum, suddenly a swarm of savages seemed to spring from the earth on every side. The British could only fire in platoons, hitting rocks and trees much oftener than Indians, while the colonists, springing behind trees, took aim with effect. Braddock was mortally wounded, and his men fled, while Washington and his "continentals" covered their retreat.

181. **Three other expeditions** occupied the summer of 1755. I. *The forts in Acadia* were taken; but the honor of the victory was effaced by the cruel expulsion of the peasantry from their homes. These poor people had surrendered their arms, and wished only to cultivate their farms in peace, but they were driven on board the British fleet— women and children on different ships from their protectors,—and were scattered through the colonies, wherever it suited their conquerors to leave them. To prevent their return, their cottages were burnt.

182. II. The attempt to seize *Fort Niagara* failed through desertion by Indian allies, and the discouragement caused by Braddock's defeat. III. The portage between *Hudson River and Lake Champlain* was of great importance to both nations. The English built Fort Edward on the upper waters of the river, and encountered the French, under Baron Dieskau, near the head of Lake George. After a frightful slaughter, with varying fortunes, Dieskau was defeated and slain. The English general, Johnson, built *Fort William Henry* near the field of his victory.

183. **The next two years** were disastrous to Great Britain. *Fort Oswego,* with 1,600 men, ships, cannon, and valuable stores, was taken by the Marquis of Montcalm. The Indians of the Ohio Valley, false to their treaties with the English, fell upon the western settlements and made great havoc of life and property. They were punished, however, by a brave company of Pennsylvanians who destroyed Kittanning, the chief village of the Delawares.

184. In 1757 **Fort William Henry** was taken and demolished by the French under Montcalm. The garrison were assured of a safe retreat to Fort Edward, but scarcely had they issued from the surrendered fortress when they were attacked by the savages, and many were killed. The French officers risked their lives and received many wounds in trying to restrain their allies. "Kill me," cried the brave Montcalm, "but spare these English who are under my protection."

185. Of all North America, France now owned *twenty* parts in twenty-five, Spain *four,* and England *one.* But the misfortunes of the latter arose from the incapacity of her officials at home and abroad. In 1757 *William Pitt,* a plain English commoner, came to the head of affairs, and soon new energy was felt in all English movements, from his cabinet in London to the battle-fields of Germany, America, and India.

186. English Disaster.—Before the tide turned, one great disaster befell the English. In July, 1758, General Abercrombie, with the largest army ever yet assembled in America, embarked on Lake George for the capture of the French fort, Carillon, at Ticonderoga. More than a thousand boats conveyed the soldiers; the cannon were mounted on rafts ; and, as the whole force moved down the lake, with waving banners and triumphant strains of music, victory seemed certain.

187. Montcalm commanded the French. His numbers were less than those of the English, but his works were strong, and he was foremost among his men, cheering them by example not less than by words, while Abercrombie remained out of sight and danger. In a skirmish, Lord Howe, the bravest and best of the English officers, was killed. Two days later the main army was defeated, with a loss of nearly 2,000 men, and General Abercrombie, though still outnumbering the French four-fold, hastily retreated in "fright and consternation."

188. Colonel Bradstreet, of New York, with difficulty obtained leave to go with a small colonial army against *Fort Frontenac.* He was completely successful; the garrison surrendered, and an immense quantity of stores and cannon, designed for Fort Du Quesne, was captured or destroyed. A few months later the last-named fort was taken by an advanced guard under Washington's command, and was named *Pittsburgh* in honor of the great English minister.

189. The same year Louisburg, with the islands of Cape Breton and Prince Edward were conquered by the combined forces of Old and New England, and France never regained a foothold on the eastern coast.

Embarkation at Acadia.

190. Capture of Quebec.—The great event of the war was the capture of Quebec in 1759. Quebec was the strongest natural fortress on the continent,[7] and the key to all Canada. Montcalm, vigilant and brave, made the most of every advantage for defense; and for two months the British forces lay beneath the inaccessible heights, surrounded by enemies and scarcely hoping for success.[8]

191. The quick eyes of **General Wolfe**, the brave young British commander, at length discovered a path up the cliff so narrow as hardly to allow of two men walking abreast, and so steep that they needed the aid of projecting roots and branches in the ascent. Landing by night, and followed in silence by his men, Wolfe climbed the dizzy height, and surprised Montcalm at daybreak by the unwelcome spectacle of glittering rows of bayonets drawn up in perfect order on the "Plains of Abraham." The two armies were equal in numbers, but the English were superior in discipline, and the French were soon thrown into confusion.

192. Both **Wolfe**[9] **and Montcalm**[10] received mortal wounds. As Wolfe was carried off the field, he heard a shout, "They run! they run!"

"Who run?" he whispered. "The French." He gave some last orders, then sighed, "Now God be praised, I die happy!" and expired. Montcalm asked his surgeon how long he had to live. "Ten or twelve hours, perhaps less," was the reply." So much the better," he rejoined. " I shall not see the surrender of Quebec."

Wolfe and Montcalm Monument.

193. Treaty of Paris. — The attempt of the French, next year, to recapture their great fortress was defeated by the arrival of a large British fleet. Three English armies were concentrated upon *Montreal,* which surrendered in September, 1760. By the Peace of Paris, signed in February, 1763, France surrendered to Great Britain all the country north of the St. Lawrence and the Great Lakes, with the provinces south of that river, now included in New Brunswick, Nova Scotia, and eastern Maine, and all lands east of the Mississippi. Spain ceded Florida to England, and received from France all the lands west of the Mississippi.

194. The Conspiracy of Pontiac.—The Indian allies of the French did not at once accept the peace. Pontiac, the great Ottawa chief, incensed at the transfer of his lands from one European power to another, stirred up a great conspiracy of the tribes on the lakes for the destruction of all the English garrisons. Eight forts were captured. Hundreds of settlers were murdered along the western borders of Pennsylvania, Maryland, and Virginia. Detroit was saved by an Indian girl who revealed the plot in time, but it had to endure an eight months' siege. At length the savage confederacy was broken up, and Pontiac was slain while on a visit to the Illinois.

Trace on Map No. 3 the nearest route from Montreal to Albany. Point out Annapolis, N. S. Bangor. The Kennebec. The Penobscot. Cape Breton Island. Louisburg. Fort Du Quesne. Pittsburgh. Lake George. Fort William Henry. Fort Edward. Oswego. Niagara. Detroit. Ticonderoga. Quebec. On Map No. 2, Havana. The change of boundaries by the Peace of Paris.

Read Volume I. of Irving's "Life of Washington;" Bancroft's "History of the United States," Volumes II. and III.; Parkman's "Conspiracy of Pontiac;" Longfellow's "Evangeline."

NOTES.

1. "An attack upon Haverhill (Mass.) was memorable for the subsequent exploit of Hannah Dustin, who, with an infant only a few days old, a boy named Samuel Leonardson, and another woman, was carried off to an Indian camp on an island in the Merrimack, near Concord, N. H. The infant, as usual, was killed against the trunk of a tree. The sight of this prepared the mother's heart for her bloody reprisal. One day when the boy was at work chopping for the Indians, he casually asked one of the savages how and where he struck a man with a hatchet. The Indian, pleased to show that bit of sylvan skill, told him. That night the three captives with hatchets slew the ten sleeping guards, and Hannah, remembering her infant, scalped them. Then they dropped down the river in a canoe to Haverhill." —Bryant.

2. A fleet from New England arrived in front of Quebec, but the admiral's demand for a surrender was met with derision. Owing to mismanagement the expedition had been so delayed that the alarm was given of their approach, and the assailants found the strongest fortress in America guarded by a greater force than their own. They therefore

sailed away without attacking.

3. By the treaty of Utrecht, in 1713, at the elose of Queen Anne's War in Europe, Acadia, Newfoundland, and Hudson Bay Territory were transferred to the English.

4. Colonel William Pepperell, of Kittery, Maine, commanded this expedition, and through his success became the first American barouet. The city of London presented him with a silver table and a service of plate, and the king made him a lieutenant-general.

5. **Venango** was a French fort on a branch of the Alleghany River.

6. On his homeward journey Washington was fired upon by an Indian not fifteen steps distant. Fortunately the latter missed his mark, and was captured by Washington and his guide, Christopher Gist. Gist would have killed the savage at once, but, acting on Washington's advice, they merely detained him a prisoner until night-fall, and then allowed hini to depart.

While attempting to cross the Alleghany on a raft, Washington was hurled amidst the grinding ice. He clung to the timbers of the destroyed raft, however, and, reaching an island, he and Gist waited in the freezing weather until morning, when they found ice on the river solid enough to cross on foot.

7. Quebec is built partly on and partly at the foot of a promontory, and is divided into what are known as the "Upper" and the "Lower" Town,—the Upper Town being surrounded by a heavy wall. The highest point of the promontory is 333 feet above the river, and here are built the fortifications which have given to Quebee the name of "the Gibraltar of America." The "Plains of Abraham" are the open fields on top of the promontory, outside the walls. A very correct idea of the city may be obtained from the illustration on page 137.

8. On the 31st of July Wolfe made an unsuccessful attack on Montcalm's forces, which were drawn up in front of the Lower Town. The instant the English landed from their boats they rushed impetuously forward without forming in line or awaiting for orders. Volley after volley mowed them down, and a great storm bursting over the town made the steeps too slippery to elimb. A retreat was ordered, but the flower of Wolfe's army was left on the bloody field.

9. James Wolfe (b. 1726, d. 1759) entered the English army as a second lieutenant at the age of fifteen. He distinguished himself as a brigadiergeneral at the siege of Louisburg (§ 189), and Pitt selected him to command the expedition against Quebec, making him a major-general, with a force of 8,000 men and a strong fleet.

Parkman says of him: " His person was slight, and his features by no means of a martial cast. His feeble constitution had been undermined by years of protracted and painful disease. His kind and genial disposition seemed better fitted for the quiet of domestic life than for the stern duties of military command; but to these gentler traits he joined a high enthusiasm, and an unconquerable spirit of daring and endurance, which macle him the idol of his soldiers, and bore his slender frame through every hardship and exposure." Again, of the night the heights were scaled, he says: "The ebbing tide sufficed to bear the boats along, and nothing broke the silenee of the night but the gurgling of the river and the low voice of Wolfe as he repeated to the officers about him the stanzas of Gray's ' Elegy in a Country Church-yard,' which had recently appeared, and which he had just received from England. Perhaps, as he uttered those strangely appropriate words,

'The paths of glory lead but to the grave,'

the shadow of his own approaching fate stole with mournful prophecy across his mind. 'Gentlemen,' he said, as he closed the recital, * I would rather have written those lines than take Quebec to-morrow.'"

10. Louis Joseph Montealm de Saint-Veran (b. 1712, d. 1759) was a French marquis. He entered the army when fourteen years old, and gained distinction in several European wars. In 1756 he was put in command of the French troops in Canada, and was very successful, despite the much larger and better disciplined forees arrayed against him. His own troops were mainly raw Canadian volunteers, brave, but without experience or discipline, poorly clad and half starved. The governor of the province was at variance with Montcalm, and hampered his movements so that he labored under great disadvantages. Montcalm received his mortal wound within a few moments after Wolfe's fall. Both generals had been wounded earlier in the action, but both kept the field until shot down to rise no more. When told by the surgeons that he could not recover, Montcalm replied, "I am glad of it." He was buried at his own request in an excavation made by the bursting of a bombshell. A monument common to the memory of the two generals now adorns Quebec. See illustration page 106.

CHAPTER XIII.
LITERATURE AND GENERAL PROGRESS.

195. It may be believed that the first settlers in America found enough to do in subduing the wilderness and devising the laws under which their children were to live, without writing books. But so anxious were they to be remembered and understood in England, and to be reinforced by new parties of emigrants; so full of wonder and delight in the new world that was thrown open to them, and so desirous that their children should not lack the advantages that they would have enjoyed at home, that a mass of literature does in fact date from the very earliest years of the colonies.

196. The first book written in America was Captain John Smith's (§§56-59) *"True Relation of Virginia,"* which he sent home in 1608. A few months later he dispatched to the London Company a report of the Jamestown Colony, with a map of Chesapeake Bay and its tributary rivers, and a very lively description of the surrounding country. In spite of the hunger and hardship of those early years, he declares that "Heaven and earth never agreed better to frame a place for man's habitation."

197. Beside many other descriptive works, Virginia made one contribution to elegant letters; for *George Sandys,* treasurer of the colony, A. D. 1621-1625, beguiled the loneliness of his absence from polished society, and the horror attending the Indian massacre (§64) by translating Ovid into English verse. The Roman poet had been an exile in a savage country near the Black Sea, and doubtless his translator sympathized with his condition.

198. The Ministers.—No class of men contributed so much to the intellectual growth of New England as the ministers of religion. All were educated men, and some of them were distinguished by immense learning. As there were yet no newspapers nor lyceum lectures, and few new books, ministers were the authors of public opinion, teaching their people how to think as well as how to believe and act.

Among the greatest was *Rev. John Cotton,*[1] who came to the Massachusetts Colony in 1633. had been rector of St. Botolph's at Boston, in England, and it was in compliment to him that the Trimountain settlement had received the name which has become so famous. He was esteemed the "mightiest man in New England," and "whatever he delivered in the pulpit was soon put into an order of court."

Next were *Thomas Hooker* (§88) whose saintly and kingly presence inspired courage and hope; *Thomas Shepard,* minister of Cambridge; *President Chauncey,* of Harvard; — all men of vast learning. *Increase Mather,*[2] another Harvard president, represented his fellow colonists in England during the troublesome reign of James II. (§§ 136-139). His son, *Cotton Mather,* wrote a prodigious number of books, of which the greatest was his *"Magnolia"*or ecclesiastical history of New England. Another was entitled *"Memorable Providences relating to Witchcraft,"* a subject in which the author had a most unfortunate interest (See Note 2, p. 90).

199. Historians.—*Governor Bradford,* of Plymouth (§80), may be called the father of American history. His *"History of Plymouth Plantation "* is a noble record of events in which he had part. The *Journal* and *Addresses* of *Governor Winthrop,* of Massachusetts Bay, are interesting memorials of that accomplished lawyer and excellent man, who devoted large wealth and great abilities to the service of the colony. His son, *John Winthrop, Jr.,* rendered equal service to Connecticut (§89).

200. Yale College.—*Elihu Yale,* a later governor of Connecticut, was a liberal benefactor of the college which bears his name; but its origin is due to ten clergymen, who bringing each a few books from his own scanty library, met at Branford, in 1700, and, depositing their gifts upon a table, said, "I give these books for the founding of a college in this colony." The first terms were held at Wethersfield, later ones at Saybrook; but in 1716 the college was planted on its present site at New Haven.

201. College of William and Mary,—The desire of Virginians to have a college for their sons was long frustrated by such governors as Berkeley (See Note 2, p. 47). The House of Burgesses, however, set apart lands for the support of a college, and in 1692 the long-desired charter was obtained from King William and Queen Mary, together with grants of money, land, and permanent duties on tobacco. The college took the name of its royal benefactors, and was established at Williamsburg, A. D. 1693.

Other Colleges.—Four more colleges were founded during our second colonial period: at *Princeton, N. J.*, in 1746; *King's,* now *Columbia College,* in New York, 1754; one at Philadelphia, now the *University of Pennsylvania,* 1755; and that of Rhode Island, now *Brown University,* 1764. These colleges, even in their early years, did grand, good service by training the men who were to be the fathers of the Republic.[3]

202. Jonathan Edwards.—Among the writers of the later colonial period the greatest, perhaps, was *Jonathan Edwards* (b. 1703, d. 1758), whose *"Essay on the Freedom of the Will"* revealed to the world the most acute and original mind which America has produced. It was written at the little village of Stockbridge, Mass., where he was acting as missionary to the Indians. His childhood was no less remarkable. Before he was thirteen years old he had read many works in Latin, Greek, and Hebrew, beside the most learned of English books; but his observations in Natural History show that his studies had not been confined to printed pages. He was graduated at seventeen from Yale College, preached in New York before he was twenty, was twenty-four years pastor at Northampton, Mass., and became president of Princeton College two months before his death. His wonderful power as a preacher was ascribed to his immense preparation, long forethought, sedulous writing of every word, touching earnestness, and holy life."

203. Franklin. — But the mind which most perfectly represented and most strongly influenced the character of American institutions was that of *Benjamin Franklin,*[4](*b.* 1706, *d.* 1790), the printer-boy of Boston, the self-taught sage of Philadelphia, the representative of the colonies at London, the embassador of the United States at Paris, whose plain, good sense, genial humor, and honest self-respect made him the favorite of all ranks and classes. He had accustomed himself from boyhood to write on public affairs, and his pamphlets on the interests of England and the rights of the colonies were read with great attention on both sides of the ocean. Examined by Parliament in 1765 concerning the probable effect of the Stamp Act in America (§ 220), he replied with so much firmness, dignity, and intelligence that even the bitterest enemies of the colonies were forced to respect his arguments. A distinguished statesman declared him to be the greatest diplomatist of the eighteenth century. " He never spoke a word too soon; he never spoke a word too late ; he never spoke a word too much ; he never failed to speak the right word at the right time."

204. His most popular work was *"Poor Richard's Almanac,"* whose successive numbers were afterwards abridged and reprinted in one volume under the title of *"The II ay to Wealth."* It contains a fund of homely wisdom, and Franklin himself attributed the rapid increase of prosperity in Philadelphia to the extent to which the people read and followed his good advice. (See Note 6, p. 167.)

205. Among his great services to his country was his organization of its postal service as early as 1754. "Every penny stamp is a monument to Franklin." His simple experiment with the kite, proving lightning and thunder to be caused by electric currents, and his subsequent invention of the lightning-rod, gave him a high place among scientific men. His philosophical writings are in the same clear language as his charming autobiography and almanac, for he aimed to make wisdom useful rather than dignified.

Benjamin Franklin.

206. Science. — From the beginning the colonies contained many noted students of natural science. The soils, minerals, plants, and animals of the new continent were all objects of keen research. Linnæus, the noted Swedish naturalist, declared *John Bartram*, the Quaker gardener of Philadelphia, to be the "greatest natural botanist in the world." Virginia and the more southerly colonies had several botanists of European fame. But the scientific reputation of America was established when Franklin, in 1744, drew about him other gentlemen of kindred tastes, and formed the *American Philosophical Society*. It was an important bond of union among the best men in all the colonies.

207. *John Woolman* is known only by his *"Journal,"* with

The Pillory.

a few tracts and letters; but these are of value as expressing the pure conscientiousness of the early "Friends," and justifying the great influence they had upon the national character. Woolman's efforts went far to put an end to slave-holding among Quakers. He was born in West Jersey, 1720, and died in England, 1773.

208. Pamphlets on questions concerning government and popular rights were the most valuable part of American literature during the second colonial period. The theory of a great, free nation was slowly forming in some of the best minds of the age; and the American state papers of the next generation were recognized in

England as ranking among the wisest productions of all ages.

209. Colonial Habits.—All the colonies had greatly increased in wealth by industry and frugal living, while still among the mass of the people food, dress, and furniture were of the simplest kind. Clothing was usually home-spun and home-woven from the wool of their own flocks or the flax of their own fields. Yet there were some families in every colony that imported costly furniture and silver-plate from Europe, and even plain people often invested their slow savings in strings of gold beads or in laces and satins for great occasions. In some colonies apparel was limited by law to the means of the wearer: the grave magistrates had much trouble with the silken hoods and kirtles of the women, the "great boots," gold buttons, and ornamented belts of the men; but if the accused could prove that their circumstances warranted the expense, they were dismissed without a fine.

210. In New England especially "plain living and high thinking" were the rule. Great respect was paid to educated men. Ministers and magistrates,—with their sons, if college-bred,—alone bore the title of *Mister; Goody,*—a contraction for Goodman or Goodwife,—was the mode of address for ordinary people. Punishments were inflicted without the least regard to the personal dignity of the culprit. When two men quarreled in the Plymouth Colony, they were bound together, head to head and foot to foot, for twenty-four hours. In New York a scolding wife was made to stand all day before the door of her house, having her tongue enclosed in a cleft stick. The *Pillory,* as represented in the engraving, was a wooden frame in which the head and hands of the criminal were held fast, while he was exposed to the taunts and sneers of the crowd. In Virginia, as in the mother-country, this was a common penalty for religious dissent.

211. Roads, in all parts of the country, were few and poor. Whole families went to church through the woods on horseback, the wife, sometimes with a child on her lap, sitting on a pillion behind her husband. In exposed settlements the father carried his gun and left it at the churchdoor in the care of the sentinel who watched for hostile Indians. Long journeys were made, if possible, by water, but stage-coaches connected Boston with Providence, and New York with Philadelphia. Like English vehicles of the same kind, they were called "flying-machines."

212. Manufactures.—At first nearly all the people in the colonies were farmers or fishermen ; but necessity soon compelled them to make salt, glass, paper, farmers' tools, shoes, hats, and gunpowder; and, though almost every home had its loom, cloth factories were also set up. Circumstances favored inventive talent, for which Americans have always been famous. New England had a saw-mill one hundred and thirty years before one was built in the mother-country. But England, far from encouraging manufactures in the colonies, checked and thwarted them, lest they should become rivals of her own.

213. Commerce and Piracy.—The first product of New England which reached Europe was a cargo of sassafras root, taken by Gosnold (§54) in 1602. Before long, furs, fish, lumber, corn, rice, and tobacco furnished freight for multitudes of ships ; and a lucrative commerce sprang up with England and the West Indies, and between the colonies. This commerce was seriously molested by pirates, whose black flags were met in all the seas.

To suppress their ravages the British Admiralty, in 1696, ordered *Captain Kidd*[5] with a ship to the East Indies. But Kidd, after retaking several prizes, thought it more profitable to turn pirate himself. For two years he pursued a reckless career of robbery and rapine, but he was at length brought to justice, and was hanged on "Execution Dock" in London.

Going to Church.

214. Royal Officials.—In a review of civil affairs, it can not be said that England ever employed her best brains in governing America. Younger sons of great families, who were too stupid or too dissolute to find places at home, were made governors, secretaries, or treasurers in the colonies, and used their opportunities for mending their fortunes as rapidly as possible. Such, in New York, was the haughty but imbecile Lord Cornbury, a cousin of Queen Anne, who applied to his own pleasure the funds voted for the defense of the harbor, and told the Colonial Assembly that it had no rights but such as the queen was pleased to allow it. He was more useful to the colony, however, than a better governor might have been, for he effectually taught the people to stand for their rights. Here and there a royal officer may have been more justly and kindly disposed, but as a class they regarded their own interests first, England's next, but a long way after, and those of the colonies last of all.

Even at home the great dignitaries who had charge of colonial affairs were usually less wise than great. The Duke of Newcastle, who for twenty-four years was minister for British America, owed his position partly to his incapacity, being appointed through Sir Robert Walpole, then prime minister of England, who feared to have men of ability about him. The duke is said to have directed letters to the "Island of New England," and to have been unable to tell whether Jamaica was in the Mediterranean Sea or elsewhere.

Read Volumes I. and II. of Tyler's "History of American Literature;" Volume I. of Duyckinck's "Cyclopædia of American Literature;" Franklin's "Autobiography;" Palfrey's or Elliott's " History of New England ; " Irving's " History of New York by Dietrich Knickerbocker;" Longfellow's "Courtship of Miles Standish" and "New England Tragedy;" Whittier's "Margaret Smith's Journal," "Mabel Martin," and "The Changeling;" Hawthorne's "Twice Told Tales," and other stories of the colonies in New England.

NOTE TO TEACHERS. — Younger classes may do well to omit Chapter XIII for the present, or to use it only for reading and explanation in the class-room. Older pupils will be profited by studying the several topics with the aid of the books above mentioned and others, and making them the subjects of written essays.

NOTES,

1. **Rev. John Cotton**, "the patriarch of New England," was a bright scholar at the University of Cambridge, and for twenty years a noted Puritan preaeher in his English home. For refusing to kneel at the sacrament, he incurred the displeasure of Archbishop Land, and was compelled to flee the country. Cotton could write or speak readily in Latin, Greek, and Hebrew. His oratory was simple, and his sermons pointed and eminently praetieal. He originated the practice in New England of observing the Sabbath from Saturday evening until Sunday evening. His more important writings were " Milk for Babes," a religious book for children, and "The Power of the Keys," a treatise on ehureh

government. Mr. Cotton died at Boston in the year 1652.

2. **Increase Mather** was born in Massachusetts, graduated at Harvard, and married a daughter of Rev. John Cotton. He is said to bave passed sixteen hours daily in his study. He was the author of nearly one hundred publications. Cotton Mather was his son. His death occurred in 1723.

3. During the same period " there had been established in the American colonies at least forty-three newspapers, — one in Georgia, four in South Carolina, two in North Carolina, one in Virginia, two in Maryland, five in Pennsylvania, eight in New York, four in Connecticut, three in Rhode Island, two in New Hampshire and eleven in Massachusetts." — *Tyler's "History of American Literature."*

4. **Benjamin Franklin.** — The "Encyclopaedia Britannica" describes Franklin as " the most uniformly readable writer of English who has yet appeared on his side of the Atlantic. An inexhaustible humor, a classic simplicity, an exquisite grace, and uniform good sense and taste informed and gave permanent interest to every thing he wrote. No man ever possessed in a greater degree the gift of putting an argument into an anecdote." His style was largely modeled upon the three books with which he was most familiar in his early life — Addison's "Spectator," Bunyan's "Pilgrim's Progress," and Locke's "Essay on the Understanding." When Franklin was on his way from Boston to Philadelphia, in 1724, the shipeaptain reported at New York that his passenger had "a trunk full of books." This was such an unusual occurrence for the times that Governor Burnet requested an interview with the lad who was possessed of such an evident literary turn. He received him with great cordiality, and manifested a warm interest in the intelligent printer.

When Whitefield visited America in 1740, Franklin went to hear one of his sermons in Philadelphia. Although he did not approve of the great divine's Orphan House scheme in Georgia, he was so moved by the preacher's eloquence of appeal that first he gave what copper eoins he had in his pocket, then added a few silver pieces, and finally could not resist giving all the gold he had about his person.

During his long public career, Benjamin Franklin accepted very meager compensation for his services. He drew principally upon his private fortune for expenses. To show his faith in the value of the continental loan he invested $15,000 in its securities. When president of the Commonwealth of Pennsylvania he devoted his entire salary to charities. Franklin was a signer of the Declaration of Independence, and one of the framers of the United States Constitution. Twenty thousand Americans attended his funeral in 1790.

5. **Captain Kidd** has come to be regarded as the ideal pirate, — a man devoid of all feeling, a buccaneer of the high seas; but he probably was not so bad as he is generally reputed. It is known that he was more merciful than most of the privateers of his time. When Kidd set out under Admiralty orders to suppress piracy, King William was to receive one tenth of the profits of the cruise, and Governor Bellomont of New York eight tenths, leaving but one tenth for himself. This arrangement proved so unprofitable to the captain that he sailed for the eoasts of Africa and Asia, and commenced privateering on his own account. In 1699 he boldly returned to American waters, and sailed into Long Island Sound, Delaware Bay, and several bays along the New England coast. Seventy thousand dollars worth of treasure which he buried on Gar-(liner's Island, was recovered by Bellomont. Traditions are numerous that Captain Kidd also buried rich treasure at Block Island, Monhegan, and several other points on the American eoast, but diligent search has failed to find any of it. Kidd's boldness is illustrated by his appearance in the streets of Boston when he knew a large reward was offered for bis arrest. Within a week tie was seized and sent to jail. He was taken to London, where his trial and execution occurred A. D. 1701.

ENGLISH SOVEREIGNS DURING THE SECOND COLONIAL PERIOD.

WILLIAM III., A. D. 1689-1702, and MARY II., 1689-1694, called by Whigs to the throne, gladly proclaimed by colonies   (§§ 140, 143 144); charter William and Mary College (§ 201).

ANNE, A. D. 1702-1714, takes contract for supplying Spanish West Indies with African slaves (§ 148) ; sends Lord Cornbury to govern New York (§ 214).

GEORGE I., A. D. 1714—1727, Elector of Hanover, in Germany.

GEORGE IL, A. D. 1727-1760, grants Georgia to Oglethorpe as asylum for the unfortunate (§ 150) ; has part in the War of Austrian Succession, known in America by his name (§175).

GEORGE III., A. D. 1760-1820, of despotic temper, but loyally regarded by Americans (§ 219). See also §§ 231, 235, 244, 251.

QUESTIONS FOR REVIEW.—PART II.

		Section
1.	What were the causes and results of the English Revolution of 1688?	140, 143, 144
2.	Describe the Witchcraft delusion?	141, 142
3.	Describe the policy of Parliament toward the colonies.	145-148
4.	State the literary progress of the colonies about the time of Queen Anne's accession.	149
5.	Describe the founding of Georgia.	150-154
6.	Sketch the course of French discoveries in the Mississippi Valley.	155-159
7.	Sketch the course of colonization on the Gulf.	160-164
8.	Name the chief French military stations.	165
9.	Name the four wars between the English and French colonies, giving their dates.	167
10.	Describe King William's War in America, and state its results.	166, 168, 169
11.	Describe Queen Anne's War.	170-173
12.	What were the chief events of King George's War?	174, 175
13.	Give the preliminary events of the French and Indian War.	176-178
14.	Name the chief events in the French and Indian War.	179-192
15.	What territories were acquired by England, and what by Spain?	193
16.	Describe the conspiracy of Pontiac.	194
17.	Name some of the first books written in Virginia.	195-197
18.	Name some of the most distinguished clergymen in New England.	198
19.	What can you tell of Governor Bradford and other distinguished colonists?	199
20.	Who founded Vale College?	200

	Section
21. What was the origin of the College of William and Mary?	201
22. Name the first seven colleges in America.	87, 200, 201
23. What can you tell of Jonathan Edwards?	202
24. Describe the character and public services of Franklin.	203-206
25. What is said of John Bartram?	206
26. What can you tell of other colonial writers?	207, 208
27. Describe the customary dress, manners, and employments in the colonies.	209-212
28. What restrictions and interruptions to commerce?	128, 147, 213
29. What is said of the royal officials?	214

PART III.—WAR OF INDEPENDENCE.

CHAPTER XIV.
CAUSES OF THE REVOLUTION.

215. French Predictions.—"We have caught them at last," said the French prime minister,[1] as he signed the cession of nearly half of North America to the English (§193). "I am persuaded," said another French nobleman, when he heard of the act, "that England will soon repent of having removed the only check that could keep her colonies in awe. They stand no longer in need of her protection ; she will call upon them to contribute toward supporting the burdens they have helped to bring upon her, and they will answer by striking off all dependence."

216. Taxing the Colonies.—These predictions were fulfilled. The English public debt was doubled by the Seven Years' War (§179), and a plan was revived for taxing the colonies with a share of the expense. Now it was a part of the British constitution that the "power of the purse" belonged to the people; *i. e.,* that taxes could be levied only by the representatives of the whole nation ; and violation of this rule had cost one king his head (§126).

217. The colonists insisted upon their privilege as Englishmen,—that as they were not represented in the British Parliament, they could not be taxed by it, but only by their own assemblies, which were to them precisely what the House of Commons was to their countrymen at home;— and some of the best and wisest men in England declared that they were right.

218. Though hard things must be said of the British government as it was then administered, we ought never to forget that our fathers had the spirit and ability to repel English injustice precisely because they had been trained to the rights and duties of Englishmen.

They hoped at first that the French colonists on the St. Lawrence, so few years subject to the humiliating yoke of England, would join them in seeking independence. But under French rule there had been no town-meetings, no colonial assemblies; and the people lacked the power to combine even against a government which they detested.

George III.

219. George III.—The throne of Great Britain was now occupied by George III., a narrow-minded and obstinate young king, who had succeeded his grandfather in 1760. He hated Pitt,[2] the friend of America; and his ruling purpose was to exalt kingly authority at the expense of all popular rights. Yet Harvard College celebrated his accession by a volume of loyal poems in Latin, Greek, and English, promising so to train her sons "that they may be in their future stations grateful as well as useful subjects to the best of kings." Harvard soon saw reason to change her mind.

220. The Stamp Act.—In 1765 the famous "Stamp Act " was made a law. All legal documents were to bear a government stamp, costing from three-pence to thirty dollars, according to the importance of the transaction: every newspaper and pamphlet must be stamped, and every advertisement must pay a tax. The day appointed for the Stamp Act to go into execution was observed by the colonies as a day of mourning. Bells tolled, flags were lowered, and business was suspended.

221. Declaration of Rights.—In the Virginia House of Burgesses *Patrick Henry* carried resolutions declaring that the right to tax the colonies rested solely with the representatives of the colonists, "and that every attempt to vest such power in any person or persons whatsoever, other than the General Assembly aforesaid, has a manifest tendency to destroy British as well as American freedom." Delegates from nine colonies met at New York in October, 1765, and prepared a Declaration of Rights with remonstrances to king and Parliament.

222. The Stamp Act was repealed a year after its passage, but new taxes were imposed on tea, glass, paper, and painters' materials. The government was authorized to send soldiers to America, and the colonists were required to house and feed them. Boston, which was regarded as a "hotbed of revolt," received two British regiments. Frequent collisions took place, in one of which several citizens were killed.[3] The soldiers who had fired on the mob were tried for murder in the colonial court, but they had a fair hearing, their case being defended by some of the best lawyers in the colony. All but two were acquitted on the ground that they had fired in self-defense, and the two were only branded on the hand.

Stamp.

223. In North Carolina the general discontent was aggravated by the misconduct of the royal governor and his officials, who shamelessly plundered the people. The "Regulators,"—colonial volunteers who attempted to put down these extortions,— were defeated by Governor Tryon with a British force, and many were slain, while their estates went to enrich the governor. Disgusted with his

Burning of the Gaspée.

tyranny, many of the planters left the settled limits of the colony, bought lands of the Cherokees to the westward, and laid the foundations of what is now the state of *Tennessee*,[4]

224. The old restrictions upon colonial industry were in full force. Iron, which abounded in Pennsylvania, could neither be sent to

England nor be manufactured at home. The rich pine forests of the southern states were rendered almost useless by act of Parliament, for neither tar nor turpentine nor staves could be made, nor could any tree be cut down without the king's permission. Foreign goods could be bought only of English merchants, and were loaded with duties for the enriching of the mother-country. The natural sense of the people rebelled against such laws.

225. Rhode Island and the Revenue Laws.—Rhode Island, with its bays and inlets, was well suited to the smuggling trade; and, moreover, it was the only colony whose governor at the time of the Revolution was chosen by its own people. All other governors were appointed by the king. A governor had the right to grant flags of truce; and, during the French and Indian War, Newport merchants had availed themselves of these flags, not only as privateers but as smugglers. To stop this illegal traffic, the British schooner *Gaspée* was ordered, in 1772, to lie at the entrance of Narragansett Bay, and question every craft that floated in or out, from tiny market-boats to great East Indiamen.

226. Burning of the Gaspée.—Having run aground by accident, the *Gaspée* was boarded in her turn by eight boat-loads of citizens from Providence; her officers and crew were bound and taken on shore, and the schooner was burnt. Though a reward of $5,000 was offered for the detection of any of the citizens concerned in the affair, and though almost every child in Providence knew the open secret, not a name was ever reported to the king's commissioners, and the inquiry was dropped.

227. Taxes on Tea.—Surprised at the firmness of the colonists, Parliament, in 1773, repealed all taxes excepting that of three-pence a pound upon tea, and so arranged matters with the East India Company that this article could be sold cheaper in America than in England. But the colonists were contending for principles, not pence. New York and Philadelphia sent the tea-ships home with all their cargoes on board. Boston, being held by British troops, could not do this; but after a great meeting in Faneuil Hall,[5] a party of men disguised as Indians boarded the vessels and threw all the tea into the harbor.

228. The **"Boston Tea Party"** occasioned great wrath in England. The port of Boston was closed by act of Parliament, and great distress fell upon the laborers who were thus deprived of employment. Instead of profiting by their neighbor's loss, Salem and Marblehead offered their wharves for the use of the Boston merchants. Tokens of sympathy poured in from all the colonies: even far-off Georgia and South Carolina sent money and cargoes of rice to relieve the suffering poor in the northern city.

229. The House of Burgesses in Virginia appointed a solemn fast on the day when the '' Boston Port Bill " was to go into effect. The governor thereupon dissolved the assembly, but its members only adjourned to another building and unanimously voted that the attack upon Massachusetts threatened ruin to all the colonies alike, and demanded measures for united resistance. In England Mr. Pitt, now the Earl of Chatham, urged Parliament to desist from the cruel injustice of oppressing three millions of people for the act of thirty or forty.

230. First Continental Congress. — The "Sons of Liberty," who had organized themselves in each of the colonies, now sought a closer union. In September, 1774, the First Continental Congress met at Philadelphia. Fifty-three of the best and ablest men in the country were there; men deeply versed in English law, and who knew well that king and Parliament were violating the constitution which they

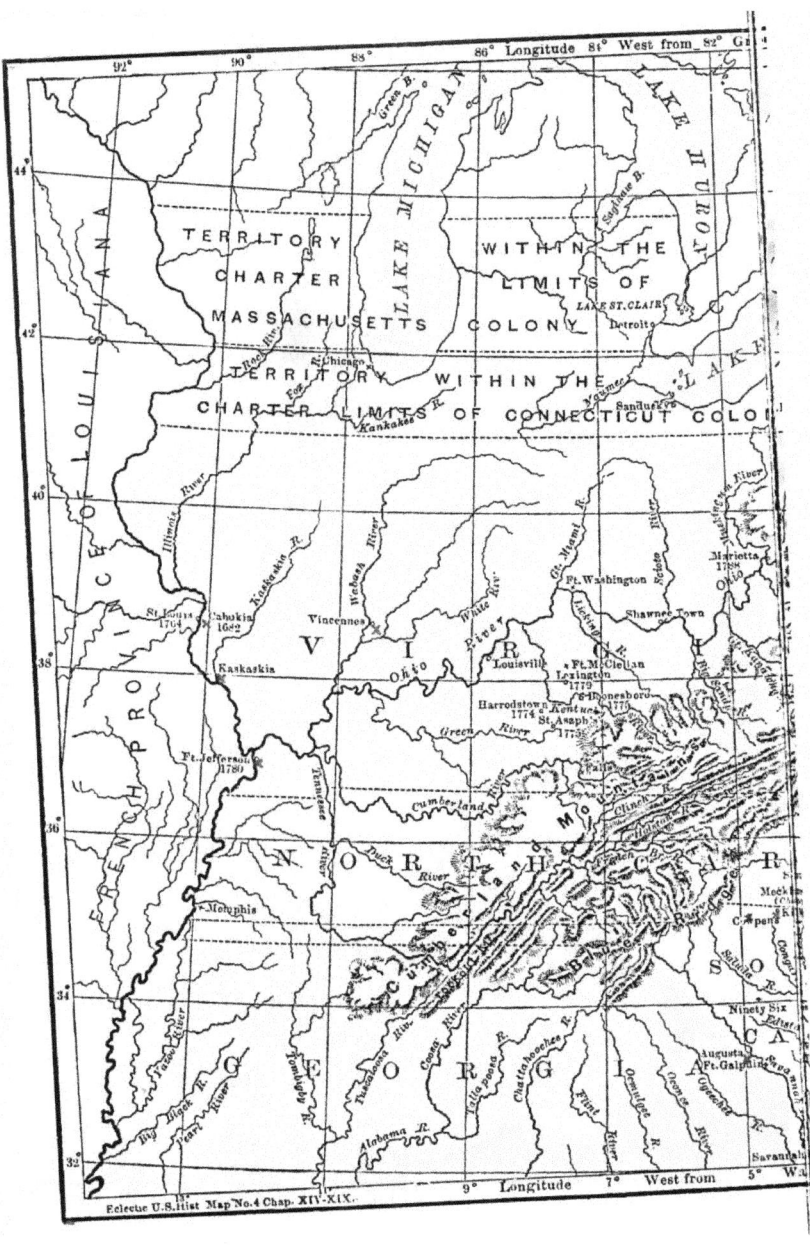

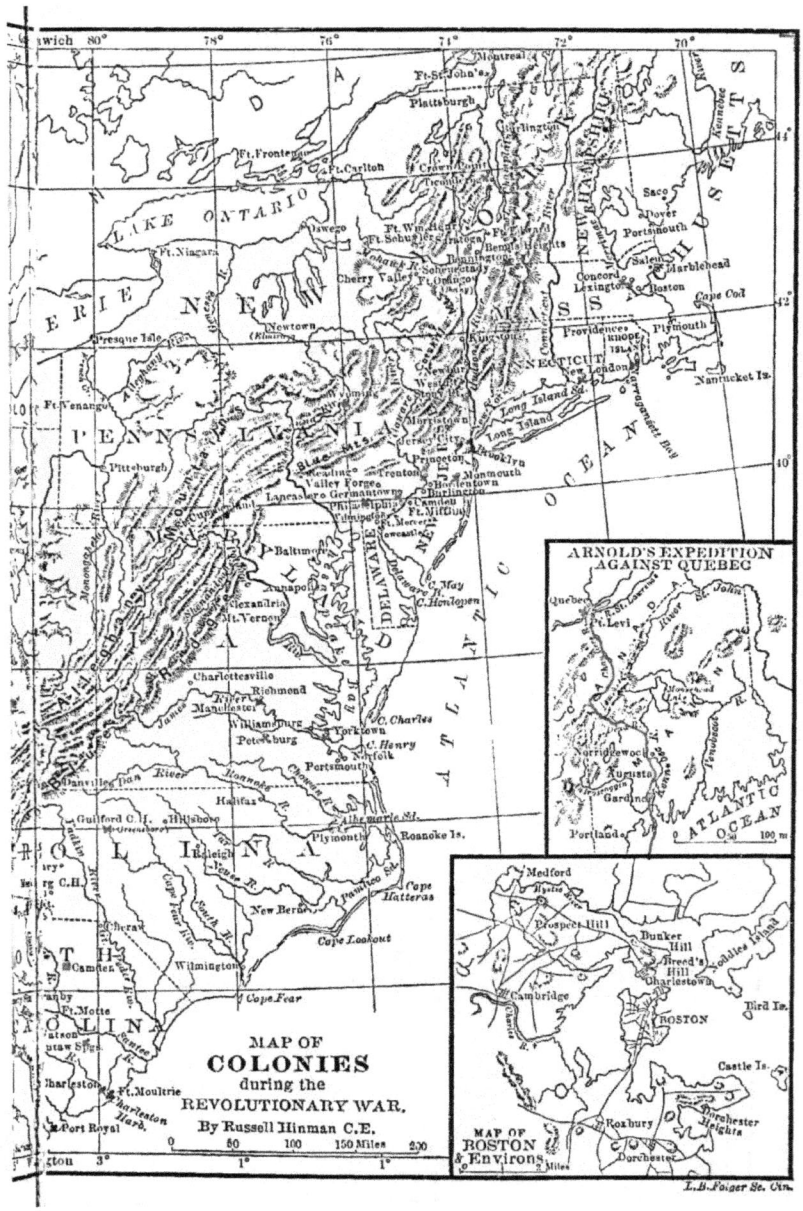

were sworn to maintain. Awed by a feeling of the tremendous results which depended upon their conduct, a long and deep silence fell on all the members of the Assembly. It was broken by *Patrick Henry*,[6] of Virginia,—the greatest orator of his day, and perhaps the greatest that America has yet produced,—who recited the wrongs of the colonies with magnificent eloquence, and yet with strict adherence to the truth.

Patrick Henry.

231. A petition to the king and separate addresses to the people of Great Britain and of Canada were voted. while expressing unshaken loyalty and affection to the king, Congress protested against the keeping of armies in America without the consent of the people, and resolved to hold no commercial intercourse with England until a different policy should be adopted.

Companies of *"minute-men"*[7] were now formed and drilled in all the towns. In the midst of their preparations came news that the British were cannonading Boston. In two days 30,000 volunteers were on the march for that city.

232. The Battle of Lexington.—On the evening of April 18th, 1775, General Gage, commanding at Boston, sent 800 men to destroy some military stores which the Americans had collected at Concord. The movement was signaled by a beacon-light hung in the North

Church tower, and all night long the farmers were gathering to oppose it.[8] At dawn the British, arriving at Lexington, found a company of minute-men drawn up to receive them, and here the first blood was shed in the War of American Independence.

233. The British pressed on and destroyed the stores at Concord; but by this time the whole country[9] was under arms, and on their return they were so hard pressed by the colonists that their retreat became a flight, and all would, perhaps, have been killed or captured had not fresh troops with cannon come out from Boston to aid and protect them. Before long General Gage was besieged in Boston by 20,000 men.[10]

Point out on Map No. 4, Narragansett Bay. Providence. Boston. Salem. Concord. Lexington.

Read Wirt's "Life of Patrick Henry," Parton's "Life of Jefferson;" Jesse's "Life of George HI.;" Greene's "Historical View of the American Revolution;" Lossing's " Field-Book of the American Revolution."

NOTES.

1. This was Choiseul. The other French nobleman was Vergennes, the French embassador to Constantinople, a man noted for his calm, equable temperament.

2. William Pitt (*b.* 1708, *d.* 1778) first Earl of Chatham, was America's warmest champion in England during the troubles that led to the Revolution. He had the reputation of being " one of the most powerful, vigilant, and patriotic opponents in Parliament of unconstitutional and unwise measures." He opposed the stamp act of 1766, and from 1755 to 1757 his voice rang warning and prophecy to the British ministry in their oppression of the colonies. In 1778 he rose from a sick-bed to speak in the House of Lords against a motion to acknowledge the independence of America. At lie close of his speech, he fell in an apoplectic fit, from which he never recovered.

3. This affair is known as the " Boston Massacre : " it grew out of a fight between a soldier and a laborer in a rope-walk. The soldier being whipped brought other soldiers, who were again and again beaten off by the laborers. The following night, Diarch 5th, 1770, the soldiers, infuriated by talking the affair over amongst themselves, rushed about the streets insulting and striking unoffending citizens. An angry mob gathered, and six soldiers under an officer charged through the crowd. A soldier was struck, and the order to fire was given. Three persons were killed outright, and eight were wounded, two of them mortally. "Of all the eleven, not more than one had had any share in the disturbance." This shedding of innocent blood caused the wildest excitement, not only in Boston but throughout the country, and Governor Hutehinson was compelled to remove the soldiers from their quarters in the city.

4. The most prominent among these settlers was James Robertson, who two years before this time had settled in Tennessee. Bancroft says of him: "This year [1770], James Robertson, from the home of the Regulators in North Carolina, a poor and unlettered forester, of humble birth but. of inborn nobleness of soul, cultivated maize on the Wautauga. The frame of the heroic planter was robust, his constitution hardy; he trod the soil as if he were its rightful lord. Intrepid, loving virtue for its own sake, and emulous of honorable fame, he had self-possession, quickness of discernment, and a sound judgment. Wherever he was thrown, on whatever he was engaged, he knew how to use all the means within his reach, whether small or great, to their proper end, seeing at a glance their latent capacities, and devising the simplest and surest way to bring them forth; and so he became the greatest benefactor of the early settlers of Tennessee."

5. **Faneuil Hall** was built in 1749, and was a gift to the town of Boston from Peter Faneuil. The latter was a Boston merchant, born at New Rochelle, New York, of a French Huguenot family. The lower floor of the hall was a market-house; above that was a town-hall, with other rooms attached. This hall was a great place of rendezvous for the patriots at the outbreak of the Revolution, and came to be known as "The Cradle of Liberty."

6. **Patrick Henry** (*b.* 1736, *d.* 1799) was a man of limited education, and in early years displayed few indications of his future greatness. He was exceedingly fond of fishing and hunting, and of social pleasures, all of which were allowed to interfere with his duties. He married at eighteen, failed twice in business, once in an attempt at farming, and finally, when twenty-four years of age, entered the profession of law after six weeks study of the subject. Of course he was ignorant of the simplest details of the profession he had undertaken, but his wonderful gift of oratory stood him in good stead, and after the first trial in which he appeared, at the age of twenty-seven, he never lacked for business, although he was never considered remarkable as a lawyer.

Henry was a man of high moral courage, and the instinctive champion of the wronged and the oppressed. The opening seenes of the Revolution fired his patriotic soul; evidently the time and purpose for which he had been born had arrived. His speech before the Virginia House of Burgesses (§221) electrified the country, and gained him the reputation, at the age of twenty-nine, of being "the greatest orator and political thinker of a land abounding with public speakers and statesmen." From this time forth he was prominent in the political conventions and congresses of the colonies, and, in 1776, he was elected the first republican governor of the state of Virginia. He held this office until 1779, when, being no longer eligible, he returned to the legislature. At the close of the war he was again chosen governor, and served until 1786, when he resigned. In 1794 he retired from the law, and removed to his estate. After this he declined several honorable positions in public life, but was finally persuaded by Washington and others to become a candidate for the Virginia senate, in 1799, in order to oppose certain measures there. He was easily elected, but death interposed before he could take his seat.

7. The minute-men were so called from the terms of their enlistment. They were to serve whenever called upon, and at a moment's notice.

8. This was the occasion of "Paul Revere's Ride" made celebrated by Longfellow's poem. As soon as Warren, an American patriot in Boston, discovered Gage's plan, he dispatched William Dawes through Roxbury, and Revere by way of Charlestown, to spread the alarm. Revere had the beacon-lights hung in the North Church tower, as stated, and then with muffled oars rowed over to Charlestown only five minutes before the sentinels received orders to allow no one to pass. At Charlestown Neck he was stopped by two British officers, but escaped them through the speed of his horse, and proceeded on bis way to Lexington and Concord, rousing each household as lie passed.

> "A hurry of hoofs in a village street,
> A shape in the moonlight, a bulk in the dark, And beneath, from the pebbles, in passing, a spark struck out by a steed flying fearless and fleet
> That was all! And yet, through the gloom and the light, The fate of a nation was riding that night ;

And the spark struck out by that steed, in its flight, Kindled the land into flame with its heat."

9. "The Americans who joined in the pursuit, which began at the old North Bridge in Concord, came from Acton, Bedford, Billerica, Brookline, Beverly, Concord, Carlisle, Chelmsford, Cambridge, Charlestown, Danvers, Dedham, Dorchester, Framingham, Lexington, Lincoln, Lynn, Littleton, Medford, Milton, Needham, Newton, Pepperell, Roxbury, Reading, Sudbury, Stowe, Salem, Woburn, Watertown, and Westford. Thirty-one towns! Such is the distinguished roll of honor represented in the opening fight of the Revolution." — Austin's "History of Massachusetts."

Fatal collisions between the colonists and the British had indeed occurred in the streets of New York and Boston, and in North Carolina (§§222, 223). But these had more or less of a local character, while the armed resistance to a regular British army at Lexington was distinctly a battle for American independence.

10. General Gage was not only military commandant at Boston, but civil governor of Massachusetts. His instructions from the king required him to seize and condignly punish Samuel Adams, John Hancock, Joseph Warren, and other leading patriots, "but he stood in such dread of them that he never so much as attempted their arrest." "He had promised the king that with four regiments he would play the lion," but in truth his arrogance and presumption far surpassed his practical abilities, and "he inspired neither confidence nor fear." It is impossible to say how different might have been the result to the colonies if the king had been better served. America has reason to be thankful that her courage and resources were underrated at this critical time, when even her own best men little understood the gravity of the conflict that was impending.

CHAPTER XV.
OPENING SCENES OF THE REVOLUTION.

234. Second Continental Congress.—In May, 1775, the Second Continental Congress met at Philadelphia, and never had a body of men such tremendous duties with so little power to perform them. There was no public treasury, and no authority to create one ; war was already begun, while there was not a soldier nor an officer enlisted in the name of the whole country. Worst of all, Congress could not bind the people to any measure; but could only advise the thirteen colonial governments what it seemed best for them to do.

235. No wonder that their first steps were hesitating and weak. In appointing a day of fasting and prayer for the "restoration of the invaded rights of America," they desired the people to recognize "King George the Third as their rightful sovereign." They took measures, however, for organizing a "continental army" for seven months, and appointed George Washington, of Virginia, to be its commander-in-chief; while they sincerely "labored for the restoration of harmony between the colonies and the parent state." The responsibility of war was thrown upon Great Britain; for the Americans only desired peace with justice, and Washington wrote at this very time that he "abhorred the idea of independence."

236. The Earl of Chatham declared in Parliament that no body of men ever surpassed the second American Congress in "solidity of reasoning, force of sagacity, and wisdom of conclusion;" and to Franklin he remarked, that the success of the American cause was the last hope of liberty for England. The debates in Parliament proved to the colonists that their contest was with the king and ministry, not with the people of England. Several Englishmen of rank resigned their places in the army and government rather than fight against America. One of them, Lord Effingham, received the public thanks of citizens of London for having acted "as a true Englishman." It was fortunate, however, that Lord Chatham's plan of conciliation failed. If it had succeeded, England might have kept her colonies on the condition of governing them justly. It was better for her, for them, and for the world that she should cease to govern them at all.

237. The communications with Canada were felt to be of great importance. In May, 1775, the forts at Ticonderoga and Crown Point were surprised by Ethan Allen[1] and Seth Warner[2] with a handful of "Green Mountain Boys," and were surrendered without a shot. Ticonderoga had cost England an enormous amount of money and many lives (See p. 104). It was taken "in ten minutes by a few undisciplined volunteers, without the loss of life or limb." In it was an immense supply of cannon and other war materials.

238. Three British generals,[3] soon to become well known in America,—Howe, Clinton, and Burgoyne,—now arrived with heavy reinforcements at Boston. General Ward,[4] still in command of the Americans, resolved to push the siege more closely. To this end he ordered Colonel Prescott[5] to fortify Bunker Hill. At the last moment Breed's Hill was substituted, as a still more commanding position, but the battle which followed took its name from the former.

239. Battle of Bunker Hill.—During the night following, June 16th, a strong earth-work was thrown up. As soon as the morning light revealed it to the British, a cannonade was opened from their fleet and the opposite shore, and 2,000 men were sent to storm the work. The Americans, who had only dropped the spade to seize the musket, waited until they could see the whites of their enemies' eyes, then fired with such deadly effect that the attacking column broke and fell back to the foot of the hill.

240. The village of Charlestown was then fired, and under cover of its smoke the enemy rallied and ascended the hill, only to be repulsed as before. Fresh troops came from Boston, and a third attack was made. The spirit of the defenders had not flagged, but their powder was nearly spent. Still the front rank of the assailants was again mown down; and the Americans fought with the butt ends of their guns, until they retired in good order to Prospect Hill, only a mile in the rear.[6]

General Gage wrote home, "The trials we have had, prove the rebels are not the despicable rabble too many have supposed them to be." He was already superseded in command by General Howe, brother of him who had fallen at Ticonderoga and whom Massachusetts had loved and honored (§187).

241. Washington in Command.—Among the first acts of royal governors when the war broke out, was the seizure of gunpowder belonging to the colonies. The want of this necessary article had occasioned the loss of Breed's Hill and seriously crippled the movements of Washington. On the 3d of July this great general took command of the forces besieging Boston. They could scarcely be called an army: arms, uniform, and drill were lacking; each man had brought his own musket and powder-horn, if he happened to possess them, and subsisted mainly on food which he received from home. Washington's first task was to create an army out of these raw recruits, and happily the inaction of the British gave him a few months for the work.

242. The Mecklenburg Resolutions.—Still very few colonists dreamed of a separation from England. The patriots of Mecklenburg County, in North Carolina, had, however, advanced to a different conclusion, in which the whole country afterwards joined them. In May, 1775, they met at Charlotte, and renounced their allegiance to king and Parliament. The "Mecklenburg Resolutions" were the prelude to the " Declaration of Independence."

243. Kentucky Settled.—During the same year the foundations were laid of a new state west of the Alleghanies. Daniel Boone,[7] the famous hunter, with Kenton, Floyd, Harrod. Shelby, and others, having bought land of the Cherokees, settled the rich meadow-lands on the Kentucky River. Free from the first, they never owned the dominion of England; and they were among the earliest in America to declare their independence, on a footing of obedience to local law. Courts, churches, and schools were established; and order and justice were held as dear as freedom. (See § 277.)

244. Indians and Hessians.—Meanwhile King George, so far from regarding the humble petition he had received from Congress, was sending emissaries to the Iroquois and Canadian Indians to excite their savage wrath against the colonies ; and, as Englishmen enough could not be enlisted, was making bargains with petty German princes, who sold him the services of their subjects at a little less than thirty- five dollars per head. "Every soldier killed was to be paid for at this rate, and three wounded were to be reckoned as one killed." Acts of Parliament forbade any trade with the "rebels," and ordered that American vessels should be seized, and their crews treated as slaves.

245. Invasion of Canada.—These violent measures went far to destroy the love of Americans for England, and it was seen that independence was the only way to honor and safety.

Quebec.

The Canadian peasantry wished well to the cause of separation, but the rich and ruling class were content with the existing order of things.

To sustain the popular feeling, and prevent attacks from the north, a two-fold invasion of Canada was planned for the autumn of 1775.

246. Siege of Quebec.—General Montgomery,[8] descending Lake Champlain, captured St. John's and Montreal. General Arnold,[9] ascending the Kennebec, made a toilsome march through the woods and marshes of northern Maine, and though deprived by hunger and disease of nearly half his men, undertook the siege of Quebec, the mightiest fortress in America. Climbing by Wolfe's path (§191) to the Heights of Abraham, he summoned the city to surrender; but its commander had learned wisdom from Montcalm's disaster, and remained within his fort.

247. Montgomery soon arrived and took command. The garrison numbered twice as many as the combined army of assailants, and had strong walls and two hundred cannon to oppose to the musketry and few small siege-guns from Montreal. Nevertheless the colonists intrenched themselves behind ramparts of ice, since the frozen ground defied their pickaxes. On the last morning of 1775 assault was made. Montgomery led the advance, crying out, "Men of New York! you will not fear to follow where your general leads!" The attack was brave and spirited; but Montgomery fell dead, Arnold was dangerously wounded, and the effort failed.

Still determined, the Americans turned the siege into a blockade, and held out until May, when they reluctantly retreated, wasted by disease and starvation. The British governor, pitying their sufferings and admiring their courage, offered to shelter and care for their sick until they were able to march; but the generous invitation was declined (See § 306). A great British force arriving in the St. Lawrence, Montreal and St. John's were abandoned.

248. Deliverance of Boston.—Against innumerable difficulties, Washington had persevered through the winter in drilling and strengthening his army; and early in March he was ready for a decisive stroke. In a single night works were erected on Dorchester Heights, which forced General Howe to evacuate Boston. Taking on board the fleet not only his army, but eleven hundred Americans who chose to remain subjects of the king, he sailed away to Halifax, to the great joy and relief of the Bostonians.

Washington knew that the breathing-time would be short. New York was of the greatest importance to both parties from its central position, its easy communication with Canada, and the strong Tory[10] interest among its people. Thither Washington soon marched to anticipate the arrival of the British.

249. Siege of Charleston.—Early in June a British fleet from Halifax appeared in Charleston harbor bearing an army commanded by General Clinton. Major-general Lee,[11] second only to Washington among American officers, had been placed in charge of the southern department. But he cared more for himself than for the success of the cause, and wrought more evil than good to the American service. He pronounced Charleston untenable, and was only anxious to secure the retreat of the garrison. Colonel Moultrie[12] was of a different mind. From his fort of palmetto logs on Sullivan's Island, he kept up so steady a cannonade that the fleet, after ten hours' engagement, withdrew shattered and disabled, unfit even to convey the army to New York.[13] The fort has ever since borne the name of its brave defender.

Trace on Map No. 4, the two routes by which the Americans invaded Canada.

Read for the whole Revolutionary period Irving's " Life of Washington," Volumes II.-IV. ; the Lives of Generals Greene, Putnam, Arnold; Lossing's " Field-Book of the Revolution ; " Botta's " History of the American Revolution."

NOTES.

1. Ethan Allen (*b*. 1739, *d*. 1789) was born in Connecticut, but removed to Vermont when about twenty-four years of age. Previous to the Revolution New York and New Hampshire disputed possession of the territory which now forms Vermont, and the New York officers tried to enforce their authority which the settlers resisted. The latter formed an organization known as the "Green Mountain Boys," of which Allen was the colonel. They succeeded in holding their farms, and Allen became so obnoxious that Governor Tryon of New- York offered £150 reward for his arrest.

Just before the attack on Ticonderoga, Benedict Arnold (§292) appeared, and claimed command of the forces through a commission received from Massachusetts. Allen would not give way, however, and they finally compromised by walking at the head of the column side by side. Shortly after the fall of Ticonderoga Allen made an unsuccessful attack on Montreal, and was taken prisoner. He was sent first to England, and afterwards to the prison-ships at Halifax and New York. He was heavily ironed and treated as a common felon. Although rough in manner and appearance, Allen was a man of good intellect. He wrote a history of the dispute in regard to Vermont, a narrative of his captivity, several political pamphlets, and also a work entitled "Reason the only Oracle of Man." He resided in Vermont until his death, serving for some time in the legislature.

2. Seth Warner (*b*. 1743, *d*. 1784) was also prominent In the controversy between New York and Vermont, and like Allen he was outlawed. In the expeditions against Ticonderoga and Crown Point lie was second in command, and personally conducted the attack on the latter place. He remained in the army, doing good service until 1782, when lie resigned on account of ill health, and returned to his native town of Roxbury, Conn.

3. These generals were men of experience. General William Howe had command of the light infantry under Wolfe in the attack on Quebec (§ 190); Sir Henry Clinton had served in the same war; and General John Burgoyne had won distinction as a brigadier-general in Portugal. All of them were severely censured at home for their conduct of affairs in America. Burgoyne and Clinton each wrote a narrative which, in a measure, removed the feeling against them, and Howe was freed from blame by an investigation ordered by Parliament.

"As they entered the harbor, they hailed a tender bound for Newport, and asked the news. When told that Boston was surrounded by ten thousand men in arms, they asked how large was the English force, and were told it was five thousand men. 'Ten thousand peasants keep five thousand king's troops shut up! Let us get in, and we 'll soon find elbowroom.' The story was circulated every-where, and the nickname 'Elbowroom' was applied to Burgoyne all through the war, never with more sting, of course, than at the period of his own reverses." — *Bryant*.

4. After the battles of Concord and Lexington the congress of Massachusetts voted to raise an army of thirteen thousand six hundred men, and called upon the other New England colonies to increase the number to thirty thousand. In response to this eall about sixteen thousand men assembled around Boston. There was no unity among them, however, the men from the several colonies appearing as independent corps under leaders of their own.

Artemas Ward, as captain-general of the Massachusetts forces, held the leading position, but had no commission as commander-in-chief. Bancroft says of him : " He was old, unused to a separate military command, from an infirmity not fit to appear on horseback, and wanting in ' quick decision and activity ; ' lie never could introduce discipline among free men, who owned no superiority but that of merit, no obedience but that of willing minds." About this time the Continental Congress made him a major-general under Washington, but he resigned within a month.

5. William Prescott (*b.* 1726, *d.* 1795), born at Groton, Mass., had served in the attack against Nova Scotia (§181) as lieutenant and captain. He was made colonel of a regiment of minute-men, and marched at their head to Cambridge as soon as he heard of the battle of Lexington. He had sole command of the redoubt on Breed's Hill, and by his remarkable courage and self-possession inspired the men under him with a similar spirit. He was among the last to quit the redoubt, unwounded, although his clothes were pierced and rent by the English bayonets. He remained in the army until the battle of Saratoga, in 1777, where lie served as a volunteer. He then returned home, and in later years was a member of the Massachusetts legislature.

6. In this battle the English had one thousand and fifty-four killed and wounded. The American loss was one hundred and forty-five killed and missing, and three hundred and four wounded. Among the Americans killed was General Warren, He was an ardent patriot and highly esteemed as a statesman as well as a soldier. He had just been appointed a major-general by the Continental Congress, but in this battle was serving simply as a volunteer. He was the last man in the trenches, and fell while endeavoring to rally the men about him.

7. Daniel Boone (*b.* 1735, *d.* 1820) was born in Pennsylvania. When he was eighteen years old, lie removed to North Carolina. He married and passed some years there as a farmer, but during that time made several excursions into the wilds of Kentucky, where lie finally removed with his family. He was captured several times by the Indians, but always managed to escape. Kentucky filling rapidly with settlers, Boone lost all his land there through neglect in making his title good, and left in disgust for Missouri, then under Spanish rule. Here the same tiling happened again, but in 1812 Congress confirmed his claim to another tract of land in return for his valuable public services. Boone and his wife died in Missouri, but in 1845 their remains were transferred to the cemetery at Frankfort, Ky.

8. Richard Montgomery (*b*. 1736, *d*. 1775) was born near Raphoe, Ireland, and entered the British army at the age of fifteen. He distinguished himself in America during the "French and Indian War," but, disappointed at not receiving a promotion, he sold his commission, and in 1772 emigrated to New York. Here he married a daughter of Robert R. Livingston, and in 1773 settled on a farm at Rhinebeck, hoping to lead a quiet, domestic life. At the breaking out of the Revolution lie was appointed brigadier-general. The expedition against Canada fell to his command owing to the sickness of Major-general Schuyler, who was to have conducted the operations. Montgomery soon won the love and esteem of his soldiers, and distinction in the eyes of the country, by his energetic and daring management. He was made a major-general afew days before his death. Congress honored him with a monument, beneath which his remains now lie, in front of St. Paul's Church, New York.

9. Benedict Arnold (*b*. 1740, *d*. 1801) was one of the most conspicuous characters of the Revolution. Bancroft thus concisely describes him : " In person he was short of stature, and of a florid complexion ; bis broad, compact frame displayed a strong animal nature and power of endurance; he was complaisant and persuasive in his manners, desperately brave and sanguinely hopeful, avaricious and profuse, of restless activity, intelligent and enterprising." He was one of the first to march to Cambridge, but unfortunately his early patriotism and daring leadership are utterly overshadowed by his disgraceful treason. (See §§ 292-295.)

10. Tories were those who believed in the "divine right" of the king to be obeyed, whether his commands were just or not—hence, in America, those who still considered themselves subjects of George III. Those who in both countries maintained the rights of the people were called Whigs (§140). It is supposed that twenty-five thousand American Tories were enlisted in the British armies during the Revolution.

11. Charles Lee (*b.* 1731, *d.* 1782) is said to have held a commission in the British army when but eleven years of age. His first actual experience in warfare, however, was at Braddock's defeat (§180). At Ticonderoga, in 1758, he was severely wounded, but continued in service in America until 1760, when he returned to England. He distinguished himself in Spain, but failed in securing further promotion. In disgust he left England, and became "a soldier of fortune," serving in Germany, Poland, and Russia. He twice returned to England and endeavored to secure advancement and active service. His failure to do this soured his disposition; lie violently opposed the ministry, and indulged in newspaper attacks upon them full of irony and sarcasm.

At the breaking out of the Revolution he eagerly espoused the American cause. The Continental Congress appointed him second of five major-generals under Washington, much to Lee's disappointment, who had worked hard for the position of commander-in-chief. Of his conduct during the war little can be said in praise. His bitter jealousy and intense selfishness carried him almost, to the verge of treason (§257). At the battle of Monmouth (§272) he behaved so badly that Washington ordered him to the rear; a court-martial followed, which found him "guilty of disobedience, misbehavior before the enemy, and disrespect to the commander-in-chief." He was accordingly suspended from all command for twelve months. Finally Congress, provoked by an impertinent letter, dismissed him from service. He retired to a plantation, where his only companions were his books and his dogs, of both of which lie was passionately fond. The life wearied him, however, and in 1782 he visited Baltimore and Philadelphia, endeavoring to sell his estate. At the latter place lie was attacked by fever, and died in a very few days.

12. William Moultrie (*b.* 1731, *d.* 1805) was a South Carolinian by birth, and when thirty years old was made captain in a militia regiment which fought in the war with the Cherokees. He served in the beginning of the Revolution as colonel, and superintended the building of the fort on Sullivan's Island. He rose to the rank of brigadier-general, serving with great distinction until his capture by the British at the surrender of Charleston in 1780. While a prisoner lie was offered money and command of a British regiment at Jamaica if he would desert. His reply is worthy of commemoration: "Not the fee-simple of all Jamaica could induce me to part with my integrity." He was exchanged for Burgoyne after two years' imprisonment; rose to the rank of major-general; and after the war was twice elected governor of South Carolina.

13. The fort was built of palmetto logs, laid in two rows sixteen feet apart, and filled in between the rows with sand. This made a most effective defense, as only eleven men were killed and twenty-six wounded out of a garrison of four hundred and thirty-five; while in the ten vessels of the British squadron the loss in killed and wounded was two hundred and five. The British flag-ship was so badly shattered that "but for the stillness of the sea she must have gone down;" another vessel, that had run aground, was set fire to and abandoned.

"In the fort, William Jasper, a sergeant, perceived that the flag had been cut down by a ball from the enemy, and had fallen over the ramparts. 'Colonel,' said he to Moultrie, 'don't let us fight without a flag.'

"'What can you do?' asked Moultrie; 'the staff is broken off.'

"'Then,' said Jasper, 'I 'll fix it to a halberd, and place it on the merlon of the bastion next the enemy; 'and leaping through an embrasure, and braving the thickest fire from the ships, he took up the flag, returned with it safely, and planted it as he had promised on the summit of the merlon." — *Bancroft*.

CHAPTER XVI.
EVENTS OF 1776.

Independence Hall.

250. **Separation from Great Britain could** no longer be delayed. In April, 1776, Congress abolished the "colonial system" by opening the American ports to free trade with all the world excepting the British dominions. On the 7th of June Richard Henry Lee [1] offered a resolution in Congress, "that these united colonies are, and of right ought to be, free and independent states." After due debate the resolution was adopted, and a Declaration, written by Thomas Jefferson, of Virginia, was published to the world on the 4th of July. [2] It recited, in firm and manly terms, the acts of George III. which had rendered the separation necessary, and declared the *United States of America* "absolved from all allegiance to the British crown."

251. **The Declaration of Independence** was received with joy all over the land. It was read to every brigade of Washington's army at

New York; and the soldiers, without leave, pulled down the leaden statue of George III. which adorned the Battery, and converted it into bullets for resisting that king's ascendency. All the colonies now organized themselves into sovereign states. Many of them seized the opportunity to get rid of abuses which had been wrought into their governments. Virginia put an end to the importation of slaves; to all penalties for religious dissent; and to the law of entail, which had accumulated great estates in the hands of eldest sons; and adopted a plan for universal education which, however, was long delayed in its execution by the poverty consequent upon war.

252.   On the 12th of July **Lord Howe**[3] arrived in New York Bay with a powerful English fleet. His brother, the General, was already encamped on Staten Island with 30,000 British and German troops, all thoroughly armed and trained to the highest degree of efficiency; while Washington's recent recruits were scantily supplied with clothing, with weapons, and even with food. The Howes sincerely desired to restore peace without bloodshed; and they issued a proclamation offering "pardon to all rebels who would return to their allegiance." Congress ordered this paper to be printed and distributed among the American people.

253.   **Battle of Long Island.**—On the 26th of August the English General Clinton crossed the Narrows and marched northward to the neighborhood of Brooklyn. Two of three roads through the hills were occupied by the American

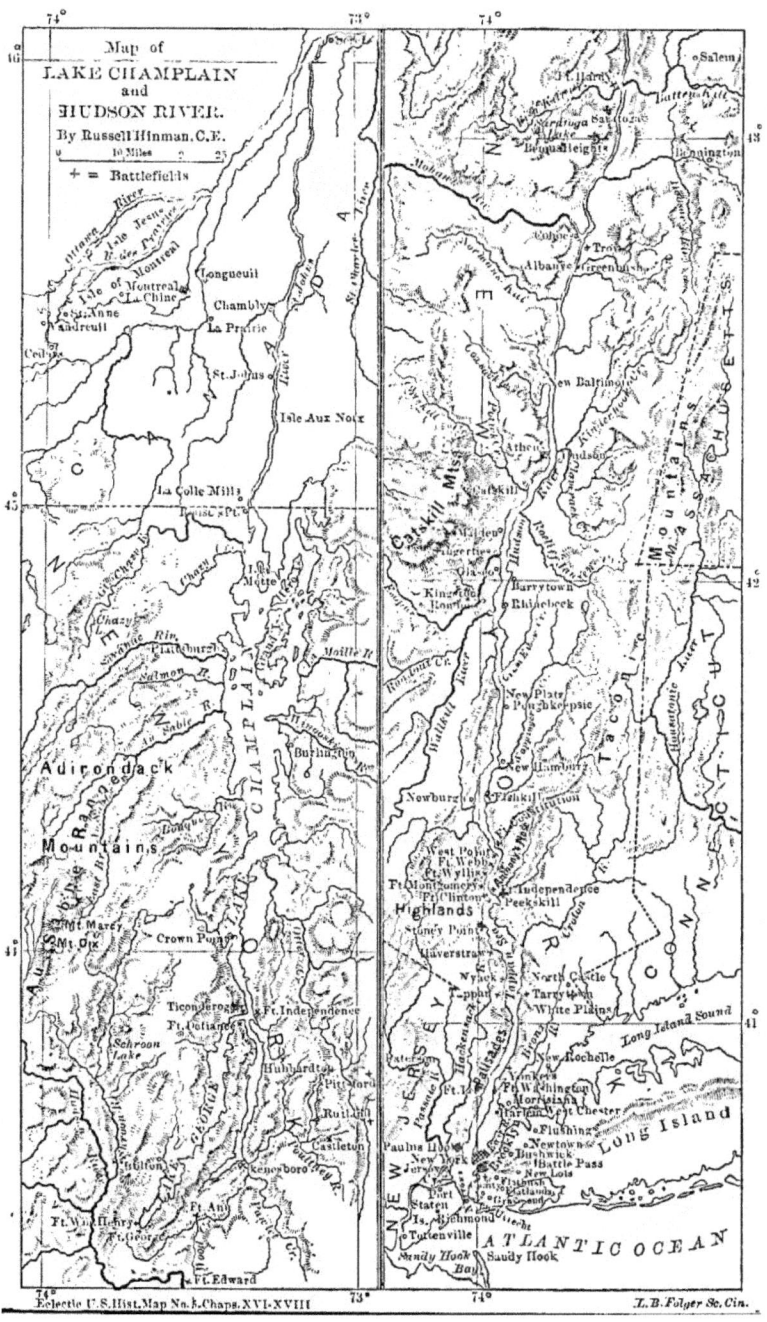

generals Sullivan[4] and Stirling[5] with about 8,000 men. Unhappily the Jamaica road had been left unguarded, and that was promptly seized by the enemy. There was brave fighting, — still commemorated at "Battle Pass;" but, surrounded on all sides, the Americans were forced at length to retreat or surrender. General Stirling held out still longer on ground now within Greenwood Cemetery, and protected the retreat of the greater part of his force at the expense of his own capture and the death of two hundred and fifty-nine brave Marylanders. The Americans lost in all somewhat less than a thousand men, of whom three fourths, more unfortunate than their dead comrades, were doomed to the "prison-ships," where, during the war, eleven thousand perished of fever and starvation.

254. **Washington's Retreat.**—Two days after the battle Washington drew off his forces under cover of a heavy fog, and crossed East River in safety. It was now impossible to hold New York, and during September he entrenched himself on Harlem Heights. His army was disheartened, and nearly dissolved by desertion; terms of enlistment were short, and the work of drilling fresh recruits had to be resumed continually.

255. **Howe took possession of New York** September 13. A fire followed his entrance, in which five hundred houses were burnt. As Washington greatly desired news of the enemy's plans, Captain Nathan Hale, a Yale student who had quitted his college for the colonial service, volunteered to enter the British lines on Long Island and obtain information. He was recognized by one of his own kinsmen, who, being a Tory, betrayed him to the enemy. By Howe's order he was tried and condemned to death as a spy. Even the common offices of religion were denied him, and his farewell letters were destroyed. His last words were, "I only regret that 1 have but one life to give to my country."

Attack on Rall's Camp.

Unable to dislodge Washington from Harlem Heights, Howe resolved to reach his rear by landing in Westchester. Washington met him at White Plains, October 27th, and suffered a partial defeat, but was able to withdraw in good order to North Castle.

256. To protect Philadelphia Washington now removed his army to New Jersey. Contrary to his judgment, Fort Washington was still held. It was captured by the British and Hessians, November 16th, after a brave defence, and 2,600 of our much-needed men went to crowd the prison-ships at Brooklyn. Fort Lee, on the opposite bank of the Hudson, was soon afterward taken, but its garrison was brought away in safety.

257. General Lee, who commanded the rear division, disobeyed all orders to rejoin his chief, hoping by some brilliant stroke to raise himself to the head of the army. Instead, he was taken prisoner, and tried to gain favor with his captors by advising them of the best means to conquer America. But Howe never trusted him, and gladly exchanged him a few months later for the British General Prescott, who was captured in Rhode Island.

258.   Lord Cornwallis,[6] with a large army, was in rapid pursuit of Washington. His German troops robbed and insulted the people ; and many, believing the hope of freedom lost, accepted the royal "pardon" for the sake of security. Washington retreated across the Delaware, and so swept it of boats that the enemy could not follow him.

259.   Battle of Trenton.—Colonel Rall and his Hessians were keeping Christmas at Trenton when the American chief suddenly recrossed the river, amid blocks of ice, in a furious storm, surprised and defeated Rall, and returned to his camp with nearly a thousand prisoners, having lost only two men, who were frozen to death. Rall himself was mortally wounded. This decisive stroke revived hope and courage in all true hearts. The enemy abandoned Burlington and Bordentown, and the people tore down from their doors the "red rags" by which they had claimed British protection.

260.   Washington Dictator.—Congress, finding that their general was not slow and cautious except by necessity, conferred on him extraordinary powers for six months to raise and maintain a larger army. Washington returned to Trenton, where he was soon hard pressed by Cornwallis, with greatly superior forces. Leaving his camp-fires burning, he gave his enemy the slip, moved swiftly by night to Princeton,[7] and defeated three British regiments [777] there, then hastened to the rugged heights of Morristown, where he was safe from farther pursuit.

261.   Foreign Aid.—These brilliant movements commanded admiration in Europe, and secret or open help began to reach the Americans. The young Marquis de La Fayette[8] fitted out a ship at his own expense, and came from France to serve as a volunteer in the American ranks. He was made a major-general, and became the intimate friend of Washington. Kosciusko[9] and Pulaski,[10] Poles of high birth, who had fought in vain for the deliverance of their own land, now offered themselves as "soldiers of liberty," and rendered good service to our cause.

Nevertheless, some of the darkest days were yet to be passed through.

Trace upon Map No. 5 the movements on Long Island (§ 253). Point out Harlem. White Plains. North Castle. Forts Washington and Lee. On Map No. 4, Burlington. Bordentown. Trenton. Princeton. Morristown.

Read Lives of Kosciusko, Pulaski, and La Fayette in Sparks's "American Biographies."

NOTES.

1. Richard Henry Lee (*b*. 1732, *d*. 1794) was one of the most eminent statesmen of American Revolutionary times. He was a native Virginian, a brilliant scholar, a wise politician, an accomplished speaker, a tried patriot. His fiery eloquence and profound political knowledge brought him to the front in the creative days of our national republic. One of his greatest addresses was that to the people of Great Britain in 1775, wherein, after stating the wrongs the colonies had endured, he wrote: "And shall the descendants of Britons tamely submit to this? No, sirs! we never will while we revere the memory of our gallant and virtuous ancestors. . . . . Admit that your fleets could destroy our towns, and ravage our sea-coasts; these are inconsiderable objects, things of no moment to men whose bosoms glow with the ardor of liberty Your ministers (equal foes to British and American freedom) have added to their former oppressions an attempt to reduce us by the sword to a base and abject submission. On the sword, therefore, we are compelled to rely for protection. Of this, at least, we are assured, that our struggle will be glorious, our success certain; since even in death we shall find that freedom which in life you forbid us to enjoy."

2. "It was two o'clock in the afternoon when the final decision was announced by secretary Thomson to the assembled Congress in Independence Hall. It was a moment of solemn interest; and when the secretary sat down, a deep silence pervaded that august assembly.

Thousands of anxious citizens had gathered in the streets of Philadelphia, for it was known that the final decision was to be made on that day. From the hour when Congress convened in the morning, the old bellman had been in the steeple. He placed a boy at the door below, to give him notice when the announcement should be made. As hour succeeded hour, the gray-beard shook his head, and said, 'They will never do it! they will never do it!' Suddenly a loud shout came up from below, and there stood the blue-eyed boy, clapping his hands and shouting, 'Ring! ring!' Grasping the iron tongue of the old bell, backward and forward he hurled it a hundred times, its loud voice proclaiming 'Liberty throughout all the land, unto all the inhabitants thereof.' The excited multitude in the streets responded with loud acclamations, and with cannon-peals, bonfires, and illuminations, the patriots held a glorious carnival that night in the quiet city of Penn." — *Lossing*.

It is a curious fact that this bell, now known as the "Liberty Bell," which was cast twenty-three years before the Declaration of Independance, had around its crown the quotation from Scripture, "Proclaim liberty throughout all the land unto all the inhabitants thereof." The bell, though now cracked and voiceless, still hangs above Independence Hall. Upon the approach of the British in 1777, it was removed to a place of safety; before replacing it, the old belfry, which had decayed, was torn down and a new one built. The illustration on page 143 shows the present appearance of the building.

3. **Lord Richard Howe** (b. 1725, d. 1799) was a noted British admiral. He entered the navy at fourteen years of age, and took part in many important sea-tights. His operations on the American coasts continued for about two years.

4. **General John Sullivan** was born at Berwick, Maine, in 1740, and was a successful lawyer both before and after the Revolution. At the battle of Long Island he was given command of the forces of General Greene, who was sick. Sullivan fought with valor, but was captured by the Hessians. He was not held long as a prisoner, and, returning to duty, did good service throughout the war. Afterwards he was a member of Congress and United States Judge. He died at Durham, N. II.. 1795.

5. **Lord Stirling**, major-general in the American army, was a descendant of Sir William Alexander (§ 83). He was born in New York, 1726, and died 1783.

6. **Lord Cornwallis** (*b.* 1738, *d.* 1805 was a prominent British

commander in the Revolution from first to last. At this time the English colonial officers wrote home, "Cornwallis is carrying all before him in the Jerseys; it is impossible but that peace must soon be the consequence of our success." He opposed the action of the ministry which led to the war in America, but when the conflict opened he took the field with his regiment, and was soon made a major-general. Atter his career in America, Lord Cornwallis filled several public offices with distinction. He was created a Marquis, given a seat in the Privy Council and the Cabinet, became Viceroy of Ireland, and was twice made Governor-general of India.

7. At the **battle of Princeton** the American loss included several gallant officers. Their fall caused a temporary panic among the men, and Washington seeing this rode bravely to the front and rallied the fugitives at the great peril of his own life. The British losses were two hundred killed and wounded, besides two hundred and fifty prisoners, among whom were fourteen officers.

8. **The Marquis de La Fayette**, born in 1757, came of a noble French family, and to the close of his eventful life, in 1831, displayed a nobility of character rarely surpassed. He was an orphan from early childhood, and during his school-days in Paris and Versailles no studies interested him so much as the histories of the world's great struggles for freedom. Thus was kindled in his breast the military ardor which afterwards marked his career. Married at sixteen, he entered the army at nineteen. When he heard that the American colonies had declared their independence, he resolved to enlist in their cause. Franklin, the American agent at Paris, was unable to furnish La Fayette with transportation; so he fitted out a vessel at his own expense, and, notwithstanding the strong opposition of his friends, and the repeated efforts of the government to cause his arrest, he embarked from a port in Spain early in the year 1777. In April he landed on the South Carolina coast, proceeded at once to Philadelphia, and tendered his services to Congress. That body "Resolved, That his services be accepted, and that in consideration of his zeal, illustrious family, and connections, he have the rank and commission of major-general in the army of the United States." From the first meeting he and Washington became warm friends, and their personal attachment continued through life. Although youug and inexperienced, General La Fayette showed, in his American campaigns, soldierly qualities of the highest order, and won a world-wide reputation for great military ability. His influence at the French

court secured the aid of many thousand troops for the patriots' cause. "It is fortunate for the king," said Maurepas. the chief minister, " that La Fayette did not take it into his head to strip Versailles of its furniture to send to his dear America, as his Majesty would have been unable to refuse it!"

After the Revolutionary War he revisited the United States in 1784, and again in 1824, receiving an ovation wherever he went. He visited the chief cities of the country. La Fayette was a prominent figure in France during the "Revolution." He fearlessly denounced the wrongs practiced upon the people, and became their boldest champion. He was made commander of the National Guard, and suggested the national emblem of the "tri-color." In 1792, during the war with Austria, he was captured and confined for five years in a dreary dungeon at Olmutz. For twenty-two months his wife voluntarily shared his imprisonment. He was released upon the demand of Napoleon, but never was a partisan of the great emperor. His death occurred in Paris, and his funeral was a magnificent tribute to hismemory as held in the hearts of the French people.

9. Kosciusko (b. 1746, d. 1817), being opposed in his suit by the father of the lady with whom he was in love, left his native land in 1775 and came to America to join the patriot army. He fought valiantly in many battles, and returned to Poland at the close of the war. From 1791 to 1794 he was the leader and hero of the Polish army in their efforts to regain independence, but fell severely wounded at the battle of Maciejowice.

> "Hope, for a season, bade the world farewell,
> And Freedom shrieked as Kosciusko fell."

He was captured and imprisoned for two years by the Russians, revisited the United States soon after his release, lived the rest of his days in France and Switzerland, and met bis death by falling from his horse over a precipice.

10. Count Casimir Pulaski was born in Lithuania, 1747, and received a mortal wound in the attack on Savannah, 1779, (§ 285). His father and brothers lost their lives in the wars for Polish independence, and he himself was outlawed. In France he met Benjamin Franklin, and through him offered his services to the American army.

CHAPTER XVII.
EVENTS OF 1777 AND 1778.

262. For the campaign of 1777[1] two great movements were planned by the British. Howe was to seize Philadelphia, while Burgoyne, descending from Canada, was to meet Clinton ascending from New York, and secure the whole line of Lake Champlain and the Hudson, thus cutting off New England from the other states.

263. Battles of Brandywine and Germantown.— Washington, who had the care of the whole defense, detained Howe all summer in New Jersey, and prevented any march of British detachments to the north, while he sent Arnold, Lincoln, and Morgan with troops he could ill spare, to aid Schuyler in opposing Burgoyne. He was himself defeated at Brandywine;[2] Congress hastily removed to Lancaster, and Howe entered Philadelphia, September 26. A bold attack, a few days later, upon the British at Germantown,[3] raised the spirits of the Americans, though it did not regain the city.[4]

264. Battle of Bennington.— In the north Fort Ticonderoga was surrendered to Burgoyne, with all its cannon and stores ;[5] Fort Edward was abandoned, and it seemed as if the whole state of New York lay at the mercy of the invaders. The Mohawk Valley was ravaged by a force of Tories and Indians in English pay.[6] The British, however, were scantily supplied with food. Learning that the Americans had stores at Bennington, Burgoyne sent Lieutenant-colonel Baum with a force to capture them. But General Stark,[7] with his New Hampshire militia, and Colonel Warner, with his "Green Mountain Boys," fought with such spirit that Baum and his entire command were either killed or captured.

265. First Battle of Saratoga.— At this point General Gates[8] took command of the army in the north; the New England farmers, inspired with new hope by the victory at Bennington, flocked to his camp at Bemus's heights near Stillwater. Burgoyne came up and a battle was fought,[9] September 19, of which both sides claimed the victory. While the two armies lay facing each other for a fortnight, militia-bands hovered about the British, cutting off their supplies, now and then capturing a picket-guard, and in many ways embarrassing their position.

266.   Surrender of Burgoyne.— A second battle,[9] October 7, was more disastrous to the British, and hunger soon completed what the American arms had begun. On the 17th of October Burgoyne surrendered his whole army, numbering nearly 8,000 men, with all their cannon, muskets, and war material. The men were to have sailed from Boston for Europe; but, some delay occurring, they were cantoned among the fertile fields of Virginia. The Hessian General Riedesel distributed a thousand dollars' worth of seeds among his men, and pretty gardens soon surrounded their barracks. Some of them liked the country so well that they remained willingly after the war was over, and became citizens of the United States.

267.   Winter at Valley Forge.— After remaining in the field until shelter became necessary for the preservation of his army, Washington went into winter-quarters at Valley Forge, twenty miles from Philadelphia. Scantily supplied with food and clothing, and destitute of even straw to sleep upon, 2,000 men were soon disabled by illness. Secret emissaries from General Howe offered them good pay and every comfort if they would desert to the British, but though many of them had been born in Great Britain, scarcely a man accepted the bribe.

268.   The winter at Valley Forge was the severest agony of the war. Washington had to contend not only with cold and starvation, but with envious plots[10] against himself, quarrels among his officers, and weary indifference in the people. While his poor men were starving, farmers sold all their produce to the British, or even burnt it to keep it from being taken by his commissaries. Even the clothing and shoes which belonged to the army, failed to reach it through the disgraceful negligence of the quartermaster-general. Washington was too great to notice injuries which only concerned himself, and some of his secret enemies afterwards bitterly regretted the plots they had made against him.

269. **Baron Steuben.**— Meanwhile a most welcome volunteer presented himself at the camp. It was Baron Steuben," an officer of Frederic the Great,[12] who came prepared to introduce the perfect drill of the Prussian army, and prepare the Americans for future successes.

270. **The good effects of the victory at Saratoga** were yet to be felt. From the beginning France had wished well to the Americans, partly through hatred of England, who had deprived her of so large a part of this continent (§193), and now that the tide seemed to have turned in their favor, she was ready to take their part. Benjamin Franklin and Arthur Lee[13] were sent as commissioners to Paris. The good sense, plain dress, and simple manners of the former struck the fancy of the queen and the court, while his wise and brilliant conversation won the admiration of wits and philosophers. He knew how to turn all his success to the account of his country, and already money, powder, and arms reached America from France. During the winter after the surrender of Burgoyne, the French government made a treaty of friendship with the *United States of America,* being the first to recognize that new nation among the powers of the world.

271. **Great Change in England.**—The same events

Costumes of the Revolution.

produced a great change in England. Burke, Fox, and many others in Parliament demanded that the Americans should be declared free at once. The king adjourned Parliament to prevent the spread of these sentiments, but sent commissioners to treat for peace, promising pardon for all offenses upon the return of the "colonies" to their allegiance. Congress resolved to hold no conference with the envoys unless the British fleets and armies should be withdrawn, or the independence *of* the United States distinctly acknowledged ; and the war went on.

272. **Philadelphia Regained.**—General Howe resigned his command, and Clinton, who succeeded him, was ordered to quit Philadelphia and make his headquarters in New York. Washington pursued his retreating army, and, but for the failure of General Lee, might have won a great victory. As it was, he rallied Lee's flying

brigades and gained the battle of Monmouth;[14] but the British escaped to New York, leaving several hundreds of dead or wounded on the field.

273. Attack on Newport.—Great preparations were made for a combined attack of the French and American forces upon Newport, Rhode Island, which was in the possession of the British. Count D'Estaing arrived from France with a powerful fleet, and learning soon after that Admiral Howe was awaiting him on the open sea, he sailed out of Narragansett Bay for a fight. A terrible storm arose, however, and both fleets, shattered by the tempest, had to withdraw and put into port for repairs. The American forces, unsurported by the fleet, were now compelled to retire from the island, and during the retreat were attacked by the British. The latter, however, were repulsed, and the Americans withdrew in safety.

274. Massacre at Wyoming.—This summer was signalized by a terrible massacre of old men, women, and children in the valley of Wyoming, on the Susquehanna, by a combined force of British and Seneca Indians. All the strong men were absent in the army, while their wives tilled the fields. The forts in which they had found refuge on the enemy's approach, were taken and burnt. Three hundred old men and boys fought valiantly until they were surrounded and slain. The British leaders could not, if they would, restrain their savage allies; every dwelling was burnt, and the beautiful valley became a solitude.

275. Savages in New York.—The same dreadful scenes were repeated at Cherry Valley in New York, by British and Mohawks (November, 1778). The Six Nations (§24 and Note) had been friendly with the colonists until the preceding year, when the influence of the Johnson family[15] had made them allies of the British. For his victory at Lake George (§182), Sir William Johnson had received an immense estate on the Mohawk, and reigned like a king over his tenants and the neighboring Indians. It is said that the old knight died of apoplexy, occasioned by the mental struggle between loyalty to his king and love of his country. His sons were not troubled by the latter feeling, but let loose all the horrors *of savage* warfare against their countrymen.

276. In the summer of 1779 a stern vengeance was inflicted for these outrages. The towns and villages, orchards and corn-fields of the Six Nations were ravaged, and their chiefs, Red Jacket, Brandt, and Cornplanter[16] were signally defeated. Finding that Great Britain was unable to protect them, they ceased from their ravages and remained neutral during the war.

277. Colonel Clark in the North-west.—Virginia was now the most extensive and powerful of the colonies. All the territory north of the Ohio, south of the Great Lakes, and east of the Mississippi was within her chartered limits. Late in 1776 she had organized the settlements west of the Alleghanies (see §243) as the "County of Kentucky." In 1778 her governor, Patrick Henry, fitted out an expedition, of which he entrusted the command to the representative from that colony, Colonel George Rogers Clark, to capture the British posts north of the Ohio River. Hamilton, the British governor at Detroit, was sending out parties of savages through all that region, offering a reward for every white scalp ; and his cruel emissaries spared neither women nor babes.

278. The County of Illinois.—Clark surprised Kaskaskia and Cahokia, whose inhabitants gladly declared them-selves loyal to the United States. So did the people of Vincennes, who were mostly French ; but the fort, newly -

Attack on Vincennes.

reinforced by Hamilton, offered resistance. After a spirited fight it was taken, Hamilton himself and all his garrison becoming prisoners of war. A convoy of supplies from Detroit was also taken with forty prisoners. Virginia publicly thanked Colonel Clark and his brave officers and men for having gained possession for the state of all the important posts on the Illinois and Wabash, and established republican government in place of the British dominion. Every soldier in the expedition was presented with two hundred acres of land. The whole territory north of the Ohio was organized as the "County of Illinois."

279. Fort Jefferson was built on the Mississippi, five miles below the mouth of the Ohio. Natchez and other British settlements on the lower Mississippi were gained by the United States during the summer of 1778, and the great central valley was now held only by Spain and the new Republic, in more or less declared rivalry with the Shawnees, Miamis, and other savages.

Trace on Map No. 4, the main points in Burgoyne's campaign. The scenes of the Indian massacres. The western campaign of Colonel Clark.

NOTES.

1. Within a few days after lite battle of Princeton, the New Jersey militia successfully attacked small parties of the enemy at Springfield and Somerset Court-house, capturing a number of prisoners and much valuable plunder. A little later the British made a raid upon Peekskill, on the Hudson, where General McDougall, with about 250 men, was in charge of army stores. In April General Tryon, with 2,000 soldiers, attacked Danbury, Conn., and destroyed a great many tents and other American supplies; but on his retreat to the Sound his forces were so vigorously pressed by the troops under generals Arnold, Wooster, and Silliman that they were glad to escape to their boats. General Wooster lost his life, and Arnold had a horse shot under him. The losses in killed and wounded were about equally divided. In May Colonel Meigs made a sudden descent on Long Island from New Haven, and destroyed twelve British vessels and many stores at Sag Harbor. In July Colonel Barton, with a body of the Rhode Island militia, surprised the English General Prescott in camp near Newport, and took him prisoner. He was afterwards exchanged for General Charles Lee (§257).

2. In the battle of Brandywine, September 11th, Washington lost 800 in killed and wounded, besides 10 cannon; the British loss was about 600. La Fayette received a severe wound in the leg, which kept him from the field for two months.

One week later a midnight massacre occurred near Paoli, Penn., in which General Wayne's outposts were surprised and cut to pieces by three regiments of Gray's English infantry. Nearly 200 were killed.

3. Washington's night march to Germantown, and the simultaneous attack on the front and flanks of the enemy at sunrise, October 4th, were skillfully and boldly planned. He hoped to win a decisive victory before General Howe could send reinforcements from Philadelphia; and but for three things—a dense fog, a drunken officer, and the delay caused by the storming of the " Chew-house he would have succeeded. General Wayne was in actual possession of the English camp when his forces were fired upon from the rear by another division of the Americans, who mistook them for the enemy. The two bodies fought each other in the fog for some time before the terrible mistake was discovered. It came to light afterwards that the general who was responsible for the blunder was drunk, and he was dismissed the service. The "Chewhouse" was a strong stone building, which six companies of British troops occupied and barricaded, so that they were able to resist all attacks for over an hour. This delay and the carnage at this point proved fatal. Washington ordered a retreat. His losses were 1,000 men; that of the English about 500.

4. Though Howe held the city of Philadelphia, his communications both by land and sea were cut off by Washington's wise disposition of his forces. The land army intercepted British supplies from the country, and the little garrisons of brave men in forts Mifflin and Mercer, on the Delaware, prevented the ascent of ships. Colonel Donop, with a force of 1,200 Hessians, attacked Fort Mercer, and in less than an hour's time lost his own life and 400 men. An attack on Fort Mifflin by the English fleet, November 19th, was more successful. A gallant resistance was made by the garrison, but after losing more than half their number in killed and wounded, the remainder crossed the river to Fort Mercer. In a short time the Americans were obliged to evacuate this post also; thus, at the close of 1777, General Howe had undisputed possession of the Delaware from Philadelphia to the sea.

5. On the retreat from Fort Ticonderoga to Fort Edward, a body of General St. Clair's forces was repulsed at Hubbardton with a loss of between .300 and 400 men. He was compelled to make a circuit of a hundred miles to avoid another unequal contest with the enemy.

6. This expedition was under the command of Colonel St. Leger; the Mohawk Indians, 1,000 in number, were led by their chief, Joseph Brandt. At Oriskany, August 5th, they encountered the veteran, General Nicholas Herkimer, with 800 militiamen, and a furious battle followed. Herkimer received a mortal wound, but directed the movements of his men until the fight was over. Relief came to the Americans at length from Fort Schuyler, which was not far distant, and St. Leger, with his savage allies, was put to flight. The losses on each side were about 200 killed and wounded.

7. General John Stark, of Dunbarton, N. H., had distinguished himself for bravery at Bunker Hill and Trenton, and his neighboring farmers rallied by hundreds at his call to resist this invasion of the British. At the first sight of the enemy he is said to have exclaimed, "See there, my men! there are the red-coats! Before night they're ours, or Molly Stark's a widow!" This story has been disputed on the apparently plausible ground that Mrs. Stark was named Elizabeth; but a paper recently discovered proves that the General had his own preference — in which historians need not oppose him — for calling her Molly. The story, therefore, rests on stronger evidence than before.

8. **General Horatio Gates** had been in command before General Schuyler, and was superseded by him. Schuyler's loss of Forts Ticonderoga and Edward was the cause of Gates being reinstated. Both were brave soldiers: they had served with honor in the "French and Indian War." Indiscreet friends of General Gates afterwards attempted to secure his promotion above General Washington, and his own correspondence shows that he was covetous of the chief command ; but, happily, that change was never made.

9. This is variously called the **first battle of Saratoga**, battle of Bemus's Heights, Stillwater, and Freeman's Farm. It was a hotly contested fight, lasting from noon until dark. The British lost 650 men, the Americans 325.

The losses in the **second battle** (October 7) on the same field were 150 in General Gates's army and 400 in General Burgoyne's. The death of General Frazer on that day was a severe blow to the British. Arnold was promoted to the rank of major-general for his bravery in this fight. The two battles of Saratoga rank among the decisive battles of history ; for they forced the surrender of Burgoyne's army, which, up to that time, was to the Americans the most brilliant victory of the war.

10. **The most serious plot** against Washington, at this time, is known as the "Conway Cabal." Conway was an Irishman by birth, but had come to America with the French allies, and gained rapid promotion. He was at the head of the movement to depose Washington from the chief command of the army, and to appoint General Gates in his stead. When the intrigue became generally known the people condemned it loudly, and suspicion ever afterwards attached to all who were found to have been in any way connected with the plot.

11. Baron Steuben was born in a Prussian fortress, A. D, 17.30, passed his childhood in the camps of soldiers, and entered the army at the age of fourteen. He received wounds at Prague and Kunersdorf, was taken prisoner in Poland, and was the hero of many European battlefields. He displaced Conway as inspector-general of the American army, and by his superior tactics soon converted the raw recruits into efficient, well drilled soldiers. Steuben served to the close of the Revolution, received a pension and tracts of land from the government, settled in Oneida County, N. Y., in 1789, and died there in 1794.

12. Frederic II. of Prussia was the greatest, general of his age. He well knew what it was to fight under tremendous difficulties, for at one time all Europe was combined against him. He said of Washington's movements in New Jersey, at the end of 1776, that they were the most brilliant in the annals of war. Of the American soldiers he said, "I like those brave fellows, and can not help secretly hoping for their success." "The British Parliament," said Frederic, "have acted like an infuriated fool in the American business."

13. Arthur Lee (*b*. 1740, *d*. 1792) rendered important service to his country not only at the court of France, but also in those of Spain, Prussia, and Holland. He was the efficient agent of the Massachusetts colony at London for a time ; and afterwards of his native state, Virginia, at Paris, for the negotiation of loans and the obtaining of arms. He proved a skillful diplomatist. Attractive in person and energetic in action, Arthur Lee has been truly called "the scholar, the writer, the philosopher, and negotiator." In all these capacities he won distinction.

14. During the fury of this battle a young cannoneer was shot down, and his piece was about to be taken by the enemy when his wife — Molly Pitcher — who had been carrying water to the soldiers, bravely seized the rammer, reloaded the cannon, and fired it with fatal effect upon the advancing foe. Washington gave her a sergeant's commission for her heroic conduct. She afterwards went by the name of "Captain Molly."

15. The Johnsons were leading Tories in the region where they lived. The secret of their influence over the Indians was that a sister of Joseph Brandt, the most powerful chief of the Six Nations, was the Indian wife of Sir William Johnson.

16. Red Jacket and Cornplanter were chiefs of the Seneca tribe.

CHAPTER XVIII.
EVENTS OF 1779-1781.

280. War in the South.—The main action was now transferred to the South. Savannah, with all its cannon and stores, was taken by a British force, December, 1778, after a brave but ineffectual resistance. Many people accepted the British protection, but those who were true to American freedom took refuge in the highlands and in Carolina. Georgia became for three years a royal province.

281. Major-general Lincoln[1] was appointed to command the American forces in the South. Port Royal having been taken by the British, was gallantly recaptured by Colonel Moultrie. Charleston was threatened, but not then taken, for upon the approach of Lincoln the enemy hastily retreated. Thenceforth the British general contented himself with ravage and robbery, which only provoked the patriots to sterner efforts, while they ruined the royal cause in the esteem of all right-minded people.

282. Recapture of Stony Point.—The enemy were now in possession of the forts on the lower Hudson which guarded the communication between New York and New Jersey. In July, 1779, General Wayne [2]—"Mad Anthony" he was called—was intrusted by Washington with the recapture of Stony Point.[3] With a small number of chosen men he surprised the guard at the foot of the hill, climbed the rugged height surrounded on three sides by the river, and seized the fort. Though seriously wounded, he was carried at the head of the storming party. Six hundred British were either killed or captured. As Washington had not a force sufficient to hold the fort, the stores were all removed and the works demolished. At Paulus Hook, Major Lee,[4] called "Light-Horse Harry," captured what is Jersey City, almost under the guns of the British in New York.

283. The infant **Navy of the United States** made up in boldness and swiftness of movement what it lacked in size, even entering the British harbors in the West Indies, burning ships at the wharves, and carrying off powder and other stores. A swarm of privateers, commissioned by Congress, captured in three years five hundred English vessels. Captain Paul Jones,[5] on the *"Bon Homme Richard,"*[6] is said to have taken sixteen prizes in six weeks. Among his most famous sea-fights was that with the British frigate *" Scrapis."*

Paul Jones.

With his own hands he lashed the two vessels together, and fought so desperately that the *" Scrapis "* struck her colors just as his own ship was sinking. Both vessels had been on fire many times during their two hours' combat. Jones had barely time to remove his men to the captured vessel, which he sailed into a Dutch port.

284. Winter at Morristown.—The winter of 1779-80 was the coldest in the eighteenth century, and Washington's army at Morristown suffered, if possible, more than a year before at Valley Forge. The longer the war lasted, the more bare of all supplies the country became. Bands of British and Tories ravaged all the coasts, penetrating the James, Potomac, Hudson, and Connecticut rivers, and burning houses, barns, and boats.

285. Fall of Charleston.—During the autumn, the French fleet of D'Estaing had joined with the land forces under General Lincoln in attempting to retake Savannah, but without success. In this siege the brave Pulaski charged with his "legion" upon the fortifications, and fell mortally wounded. His loss was a grievous one to the patriot army. Count D'Estaing, also, received two slight wounds. A thousand brave men lost their lives, among them Sergeant Jasper, who died clasping to his heart the colors presented to his regiment at Fort Moultrie (see Note, p. 142). In March, 1780, Clinton appeared befo*re Charleston with a fleet and army. On the 12th of May the city was compelled to surrender. The whole state was overrun by marauders; all men were ordered into the king's army, and many who refused were murdered in the presence of their wives and children.

286. **Sumter, Marion, and Pickens,**[7] with their spirited and devoted followers, gave the British little peace in their regained province. Knowing all the paths through woods and marshes, shrinking from no hardship and delighting in danger, they sprang upon the invaders at unexpected moments, and often captured numbers greatly superior to their own.[8] Meanwhile the women of the South were equally resolute in maintaining their share of the defense. One lady, whose house had been seized and garrisoned by a British force, suggested to the American officers the plan of setting it on fire, and brought with her own hands the bow and arrows with which firebrands were to be conveyed to the wooden roof. Then she stood watching the flames that were devouring her home until the enemy were forced to surrender themselves as prisoners.

287. **Marion as a Host.**—It is said that a British officer, sent to arrange some matters of business with Marion, was invited by him to dinner. Already charmed by the grace and dignity of his host, he gladly accepted the

Marion's Dinner.

invitation, but was amazed to find that the meal consisted only of baked potatoes served on bark. No apology was made, but the guest could not help saying, "Surely, General, this is not your ordinary fare?" "Indeed it is," replied Marion, "but having to-day the honor of your company, we are so happy as to have more than our usual allowance." The officer returned to Charleston and resigned his commission, saying that America would never be conquered while served by such men.

288. Gates and Greene.—Gates was this year appointed to command in the South, and came with much bluster about "Burgoyning Cornwallis," who was now the British chief. Gates was terribly defeated, however, at Camden,[9] (August, 1780), and his "grand army" was scattered. The brave Baron De Kalb, whose invincible firmness had enabled the Continental troops to stand fast even after the militia gave way, fell at last, covered with wounds. He had been a comrade of La Fayette, and his death was bitterly lamented. The British lost not more than three hundredmen. General Greene[10] was soon afterward appointed to succeed Gates, and found only a tattered and demoralized troop of 2,000 men with which to retrieve the fortunes of the new Republic.

General Greene.

289. In the **battle of the Cowpens** the American militia at first gave way, and the regulars fell back to a better position. The British, supposing that they had gained an uncommonly easy victory, rushed forward, when they were surprised by the sudden facing about of the Continentals, who poured upon them so deadly a fire that they had to run in their turn. They were pursued twenty miles by Colonel Washington,[11] and lost eight hundred men, with all their arms and cannon, while the Americans lost only twelve killed and sixty wounded. This "most extraordinary victory of the war" was due to the spirit and ability of General Morgan,[11] who was bravely supported by his officers and men.

290. A Chase by Cornwallis.—When Cornwallis heard of this reverse he burned his baggage and pursued Morgan, who was now joined by Greene and the main army. The Americans had just crossed the Catawba when the British came in sight, but night and a heavy rain checked the pursuers. Next morning the river was too deep to ford, and Cornwallis was delayed three days.

Greene pushed on to the Yadkin and secured all its boats. Cornwallis followed and again came in sight of the Americans just as they had crossed the stream. Again sudden and violent rains came to their rescue and his discomfiture. Two days later a similar race was begun for the fords of the Dan, and a third time America was saved by the interposition of Providence. In spite of poverty, suffering, and the frightful odds that were yet to be encountered, the brave people took heart again, and believed that their country was destined to be free.

291. Southern States Recovered.—Greene's army being rested and reinforced by troops from Virginia and North Carolina, turned and gave battle near *Guilford Courthouse.* He was defeated, but Cornwallis was so much weakened by his losses in the battle and the previous pursuit, that he abandoned Carolina and withdrew into Virginia.

General Greene, though suffering several defeats, man- aged to keep all his positions, and at *Eutaw Springs* he gained a brilliant victory. In pursuing the British after this battle, great losses were sustained; but in nine months Georgia and the two Carolinas had been recovered, with the exception of the three cities of Savannah, Charleston, and Wilmington.

Where was Stony Point? Paulus Hook (now Jersey City)? On Map No. 4, point out Savannah. Charleston. Camden. Battle-field of the Cowpens. Guilford Courthouse. Eutaw Springs. Trace Cornwallis's pursuit of Morgan and Greene.

Read Simms's "Life of Marion;" Moultrie's "Memoirs of the Revolution;" Henry Lee's "Memoirs of the War in the Southern States;" Cooper's "History of the American Navy;" Mackenzie's "Life of Paul Jones."

NOTES.

1. Major-general Benjamin Lincoln (*b*. 1733, *d*. 1810) was born and died in Hingham, Mass. He was a sturdy farmer,—member of the legislature and of the provincial Congress. Early in the war he showed military ability, and gained rapid promotion. He distinguished himself at White Plains for bravery, and on Bemus's Heights received a wound that kept him for a year out of active service. After his capture at Charleston (§ 285) he was allowed to go home on parole, but was not exchanged for nearly a year. He then hastened to the front, and held important commands until the close of the war (§304). His later years were divided between public office and retirement on his farm.

2. General Anthony Wayne, by reason of his many brilliant feats at arms, became the popular hero of the Revolution. He was born in Chester County, Pennsylvania, 1745, and died at Presque Isle (now Erie, Pa.), 1796, while on his return from a successful expedition against the western Indians. By profession he was a surveyor, and he was long an intimate friend of Franklin. For his heroism at Stony Point, Congress gave him a vote of thanks and a gold medal.

3. "After a careful reconnoissance in person, General Wayne divided his force into two columns and moved forward. The men were to depend upon the bayonet alone, and an order was issued that the nearest officer should Instantly cut down any soldier who took his gun from his shoulder before the word was given. That they might distinguish each other in the darkness, a bit of white paper was fastened to their hats, and they were to shout, ' The fort 's our own ! ' as they entered the works." — Bryant.

4. Major Lee—afterwards General Henry Lee—was one of the leading spirits in the southern department. He was a brave soldier and a skillful officer. He died in 1816. General Robert E. Lee (§523) was his son.

5. John Paul Jones was born in the south of Scotland, 1747. As a boy he was daring and fond of adventure. He became a ship's apprentice at twelve years of age, and made his first voyage to Virginia, where he had a brother. For a time he was mate of a slave-ship, but soon recoiled from the horrors of the business and came to America to live. In 1775 he was appointed lieutenant in the navy, and was the first man to hoist the newly adopted "stars and stripes." The capture of the Serapis was his last sea fight for the Americans, but his successes during the previous three years had been numerous and brilliant. In 1788 Jones was made rear-admiral of the Russian navy, and fought against the Turks. He died at Paris in 1792.

6. The name of Jones's ship is an odd memorial of the circumstances in which he obtained it. While waiting at Boulogne, wearied with the delay of the French officials to answer his application for a command in their navy, he happened to open "Poor Richard's Almanac" (§204) at the sentence, "If you would have your business done, go; if not, send." He took the hint, hastened to Paris, got his ship assigned him, and asked leave to call it "Bon Homme Richard;" i. e., Goodman Richard, in gratitude to the author of his success. His uniform good fortune as a commander was, perhaps, another fruit of his obedience to Franklin's advice.

7. **Sumter, Marion**, and **Pickens** were South Carolinians by birth or adoption; they were among the bravest of the patriot commanders; and their campaigns amid the tangled swamps of the south, leading their motley bands of determined, ragged, and half-armed exiles, present some of the most thrilling episodes of the war. Cornwallis wrote, " Sumter certainly has been our greatest plague in this country;" and of Marion he said, " He has so wrought on the minds of the people that there is scarcely an inhabitant between the Pedee and the Santee that is not in arms against us."

8. "The fate of immense and fertile regions was decided by armies consisting of a few regiments only, and by engagements which in the bloody annals of modern European warfare would be regarded as scarcely more than skirmishes. But the importance of battles does not depend upon the forces engaged, or on the numbers of killed and wounded. In this point of view, the incidents of the southern campaigns become worthy of particular attention." — Hildreth.

9. The loss of the Americans at the **battle of Camden** was nearly two thousand in killed and wounded. "Every corps was scattered; men and officers, separated from each other, tied in small parties, or singly, through the woods. All the baggage and artillery fell into the hands of the enemy. The road for miles was strewed with the killed and wounded, overtaken and cut down by the British cavalry."

10. **Major-general Nathanael Greene** was born of Quaker parentage, in Warwick, Rhode Island, 1742, and died from sunstroke, near Savannah, 1786. Before his appointment to the chief command of

the southern department he had taken an important part iu northern campaigns. He led a division at Trenton, at Princeton, and at Brandywine; and commanded a wing of the army at Germantown and at Monmouth. His military conduct was always brave and skillful. When driven out of South Carolina by Cornwallis, General Greene solemnly recorded a vow that he "would recover that state or die iu the attempt."

11. General Daniel Morgan was a native of Virginia, and died there in 1799. In Braddock's campaign of 1755 he was severely wounded, and was taken prisoner at Quebec the next year. He rendered valiant service in the New Jersey campaigns of 1776 and 1777; but his crowning laurels were won at "the Cowpens," for which brilliant achievement Congress voted him a gold medal.

The gallant **Colonel William Augustine Washington** received a silver medal for his conduct in the same engagement. In several previous battles — Long Island, Trenton, Princeton — he had proved his bravery. He was taken prisoner at Eutaw Springs (§291), and was held by the British until the war closed. He was born in Virginia, 1752, and after the war settled in Charleston, S. C., where lie died, 1810.

CHAPTER XIX.
END OF THE WAR.

West Point.

292. Arnold's Treason.—The summer of 1780 was marked in the north by a strange and disgraceful event. Benedict Arnold had borne his full share in the hardships of the war, and at Quebec and Saratoga had won the admiration of all by his headlong bravery. But his honesty was not equal to his valor. He had made money by speculating in the stores provided for the starving army, and lost it by gambling and luxurious living. He complained that other officers had been promoted to his disadvantage, and that his sacrifices to his country had not been recognized by Congress.

293. After the retreat of Clinton he was placed in command at

Philadelphia, and here he was tried by court-martial for dishonesty, and was sentenced to be publicly reprimanded by the commander-in-chief. Washington performed the painful duty with perfect gentleness, giving to Arnold full credit for his great services, and sparing his feelings as much as possible.

Nevertheless, Arnold — to mend his ruined fortunes and avenge what he chose to consider an injury—made known to Clinton his wish to enter the British service. He obtained from Washington the command of West Point, then the most important post in the country, as controlling the whole line of the Hudson, and soon afterward agreed with the British general to surrender it into his hands. For fourteen months the shameful bargaining had gone on, Arnold trying to secure the highest price for his treason before he took the last fatal step. At length a meeting took place at midnight among the bushes at the foot of the "Long Clove Mountain," below Haverstraw, where Clinton was represented by his adjutant-general, Major André, a brilliant young officer. It was agreed that the British should attack West Point in force, and Arnold promised so to man the defenses that they must fall without a blow.

294. Capture of André.—The wicked plot was foiled by three honest countrymen, Paulding, Williams, and Van Wart,[1] who, in spite of Arnold's pass, arrested André[2] at Tarrytown, on his return to New York. They found in his stockmgs plans of the works at West Point, minutes of the garrison, cannon, and stores,

Capture of André.

and an engineer's report concerning the attack and defense of the place. Refusing Major André's offers of immense rewards for his release, they led him to the nearest American post.

295. André's Death and Arnold's Reward. — André was tried by a court-martial of fourteen general officers, including La Fayette and Steuben. Time and opportunity were afforded him to prepare his defense, but he was found guilty and sentenced to be hung as a spy, October 2, 1780. Arnold escaped, and received his promised reward from the British, together with their undisguised contempt. The next year he appeared with a marauding force of British and Tories in the Chesapeake, burnt Richmond, and ravaged the Virginian coasts. His native state of Connecticut suffered the same treatment when New London was plundered and burnt. But Englishmen of honor were unwilling to serve with a traitor. Arnold soon repaired to England, where he died, twenty years after, in poverty and disgrace.

296. The greatest peril now arose from the want of a central government strong enough to provide for the common defense. The paper money issued by Congress had become so nearly worthless that a dollar was worth scarcely more than two cents in coin. Brave as they were, the soldiers of Washington could not live without food, nor escape disease and death while they must sleep in winter upon the frozen ground without straw or blankets.

297. Mutiny in the Army.—In January, 1781, the Pennsylvania troops at Morristown revolted and marched to Princeton, dragging with them six small cannon. They had had no pay for a year, and had been kept in service after their time, as they understood it, had expired. Hearing of the mutiny, General Clinton hastened with British troops to its aid, sending his agents secretly among the disaffected, and offering them good pay and comforts if they would enter his army. Angry at being regarded as traitors and deserters, the troops at Princeton gave up the agents to their officers to be hanged as spies. The state of Pennsylvania then came to the rescue of its suffering men, and provided pay and clothing for all who would continue in the service.

298. Articles of a closer confederation had already been signed by twelve states. Maryland refused to join them excepting on the condition that the lands north-west of the Ohio River should become the common property of all. But these lands were included in the chartered limits of Massachusetts, Connecticut, New York, and Virginia, and had lately been conquered from the British by Virginian troops (§278)[3]. New York, moreover, had bought from the Six Nations all the lands between the Cumberland Mountains and Lake Erie. Not only were these claims irreconcilable, but union was impossible while the smaller states were at such disadvantage compared with their rich and powerful neighbors. Maryland, especially, saw that all her present and possible settlers would be drawn to Virginia by the cheap lands and light taxes which that great commonwealth could afford.

To promote union, New York set the example of ceding all her western territory to Congress for the general good. Maryland then signed the articles of union. The other three states soon afterward yielded up their claims to the government of the western territory, but Connecticut reserved the ownership of certain lands in Ohio (§129) partly to repay her citizens who had suffered losses by Tory raids during the Revolution (§§284, 295), and partly to create a school-fund which still forms a large share of her provision for public education. Georgia and the Carolinas followed the example of their northern sister-states by ceding their lands beyond the mountains to the general government.

299. The new confederation was far from being a strong and efficient government, but it was a step toward a better union, and it inspired greater confidence in foreign nations than Congress alone had been able to command. Spain had already declared war against Great Britain at the bidding of France, but she bitterly opposed the independence of the United States, lest their example should prove too tempting to her own colonies in America (See §404).

300. The States of Holland had sympathized from the first with the new Republic, whose struggle for freedom recalled their own, but their chief magistrate was so controlled by England that they could never venture upon an American

Surrender of Cornwallis.

alliance. Their governor at St. Eustatius, one of the West India islands, was nevertheless the first foreign power to salute the flag of the United States. England haughtily demanded an apology, and the governor was recalled.

Capture of St. Eustatius. — In February, 1781, without a declaration of war, a British fleet suddenly appeared off the island and demanded its surrender. The new governor was unable to resist ; and the fort and all the shipping, besides merchandise worth fifteen millions of dollars, fell into the hands of the superior power. The Dutch flag was still kept flying until seventeen more vessels had been dishonorably decoyed into the harbor. All the Dutch settlements in South America were captured during the same year, but St. Eustatius was retaken by a French fleet and restored to the Dutch Republic.

301. Armed Neutrality.—Early in 1780 the remaining European powers had joined, under the influence of Catherine the Great, Empress of Russia, in proclaiming an "armed neutrality." Its principles were of great importance as providing for the security of commerce in time of war, and it deprived England of allies in her contest with France, Spain, Holland, and America.

302. The end of the war was now near. After a series of plundering raids through Virginia, Cornwallis intrenched himself at Yorktown, on the peninsula which separates the York from the James River. Here he was soon surrounded by the combined French and American armies under Washington and Rochambeau,[4] and a French fleet commanded by Count de Grasse.[5] The latter inflicted such damage upon the English fleet which came to the rescue that it sailed away to New York.

303. Siege of Yorktown.—To the last moment before marching southward, Washington had beguiled Clinton into the belief that he was going to attack New York, and had thus prevented his sending any aid to Cornwallis. Night and day the fleet and army kept up the bombardment of Yorktown. Washington was every-where, sustaining and encouraging his men by his example, and French as well as Americans were proud to serve under such a leader.

304. Surrender of Cornwallis.—On the 19th of October, 1781, Cornwallis found himself compelled to surrender his 8,000 men, with all his artillery and stores. The scene was one to be remembered. On one side of the road the French forces extended more than a mile in a brilliant line; on the other were Washington and his Continentals. Between these lines marched the British and Hessians with slow and sullen step. Cornwallis did not appear, but sent his sword by a subordinate. General Lincoln was appointed by Washington to receive it,—a delicate way of consoling that officer for having been forced to surrender his own sword at Charleston (§285).

305. Effect of the News.—Philadelphians first learned the good news from their watchman's cry, "Past two o'clock, and Cornwallis is taken!" Early in the morning Congress went in solemn procession to church, to render thanks to God for the deliverance of the nation. In England as well as in America it was felt that the question of independence was decided. Lord North[6] received the news as if it had been "a cannon-ball in his breast." The House of Commons voted, March 4, 1782, that whoever should advise a continuance of the war was an enemy to the king and country.

306. **Carleton in New York.**—Bands of Tories still continued their ravages in the South, robbing, burning, and shooting at their will, without regard to any authority. In New York Clinton was superseded by Sir Guy Carleton, a humane officer, who, when governor of Canada, had refused to execute the king's designs by setting his savage allies upon the defenseless farms and dwellings of the "rebels," and who had offered to receive the sick soldiers of Montgomery and Arnold into his hospitals with free permission to depart as soon as they were well (§247). He now provided, at the king's expense, for the return of refugees who had been sent to the West Indies in violation of the terms of surrender of Charleston, and tried by many kind attentions to make them forget the unjust treatment which they had suffered.

307. **Preliminaries of Peace.**—On the nth of July, 1782, Savannah was evacuated by the British, and Charleston during the following December. Preliminaries of peace were signed at Versailles, near Paris, on the 30th of November.[7] On the eighth anniversary of the battle of Lexington, April 19, 1783, Washington disbanded his army, and the war-worn patriots were at length free to return to their homes.

308. **Departure of the British.**—The final treaty of peace [8] was signed September 3d, 1783, and on the 25th of November all the British troops in America,—now collected in New York,—embarked from the Battery, while General Knox[9] entered the city on the north. On the 4th of December Washington took leave of his comrades[10] in so many

perils and sufferings ; and a few days later he resigned his commission to Congress in a speech full of wisdom and earnest devotion to the interests of his country. Then he retired to well-earned repose upon his farm at Mount Vernon.

Read Sargent's "Life of Andre;" Spark's "Life of Arnold;" Raymond's "Women of the South ; " Sabine's " Loyalists of the American Revolution ; " Washington's Farewell Address to Congress.

NOTES.

1. Each of these patriots was pensioned for life by Congress, and awarded a medal of honor, for their refusal of the bribes offered.

2. **Major John Andre**, born in London, 1751, was adjutant-general of the British forces in America, a brave soldier and an accomplished gentleman. His conduct under trial was manly, and he frankly acknowledged the height of his offense. His only petition was that he might be shot instead of hanged. His remains were taken to England, in 1821, and interred in Westminster Abbey.

3. "Virginia, by virtue of conquests of her militia, asserted title as far north as Takes Erie and Michigan, but due recognition of the ancient charter boundaries of the colony of Connecticut places the northern limit of the cession on the forty-first parallel of north latitude, and permits it to comprise only those parts of the states of Ohio, Indiana, and Illinois, situated south of that parallel." — S. W. Stocking, U. S. Patent Office. (See Map No. 9.)

4. When Count D'Estaing returned to France, in 1780, he urged the government to send a large body of troops to the immediate help of the Americans. **The Count de Rochambeau** was selected to command, and sailed in July with 6,000 men. On his arrival at Newport he assured the General Assembly of Rhode Island that, "as brethren, not only my life, but the lives of my soldiers, are entirely devoted to the service of the Americans" in their struggle for liberty. Rochambeau rendered valuable aid to Washington in the last campaigns of the war. During the Reign of Terror in France he was imprisoned, and narrowly escaped the guillotine. Bonaparte appointed him grand officer of the Legion of Honor. His death occurred in 1807.

5. **Count de Grasse**, at the early age of eleven years, served with the Knights of Malta against the Moors and Turks. He entered the French

navy in 1749, and at the time of his death, 1788, had attained the high rank of naval lieutenant-general. The coöperation of De Grasse with Washington and La Fayette, at the siege of Yorktown, greatly hastened the surrender of Cornwallis. Afterwards he sailed with his fleet to the West Indies, and gained some important victories over the British.

6. An irate English writer, in reviewing the mistakes committed by Lord North in regard to American affairs, says of his ministry: "Such a bunch of imbecility never disgraced the country." Bancroft adds: "Posterity has been towards Lord North more lenient and less just. America gained, through his mismanagement, independence, and can bear him no grudge. In England no party claimed him as their representative, or saw fit to bring him to judgment; so that his scholarship, his unruffled temper, the purity of his private life, and good words from Burns, from Gibbon, and from Macaulay have retained for him among his countrymen a better repute as minister than he deserved."

7. The American commissioners were Jay, Franklin, Adams, and Laurens; the English were Strachey, Oswald, and Fitzherbert. When the articles were signed, many friends surrounded Franklin to offer him congratulations. Rochefoucauld threw his arms around his neck and kissed him. Franklin was overcome with joy, and exclaimed, "My friend, could I have hoped at such an age to have enjoyed so great happiness?"

8. This treaty was signed at Fontainebleau, nearly forty miles from Paris, and was merely a ratification of the preliminary treaty made at Versailles.

9. **Major-general Henry Knox** (born in Boston, 1750, and died in Thomaston, Maine, 1806) was the most noted artillerist of the Revolution. He was aid to General Ward in the battle of Bunker Hill, where his bravery was conspicuous. At Princeton, Brandywine, Germantown, Monmouth, and many other of the hottest battles of the war, Knox directed the American artillery with wonderful effect. He was in the heaviest cannonading to the last at Yorktown. In 1785 he was appointed Secretary of War (§321), and remained a member of the cabinet for ten years, when he retired from public life to the quiet of a farm in Maine.

10. **Washington's words** on this occasion were few, but full of feeling and affection. He said to his fellow-officers: " With a heart full of love and gratitude I now take leave of you. 1 most devoutly wish that

your latter days may be as prosperous and happy as your former ones have been glorious and honorable. I can not come to each of you to take my leave, but shall be obliged to you if each will come and take me by the hand." Tears moistened the cheeks of many of these strong men. General Knox was the first to grasp the great commander's hand. All the others followed; and Washington, according to the custom of the times, kissed each brave soldier in turn as he came to bid adieu.

Before separating, the officers formed themselves into a friendly society called the Cincinnati, in memory of the noble Roman, Cineinnatus, who quitted his plow to serve his country in war, and returned to his peaceful pursuits as soon as the victory was won.

QUESTIONS FOR REVIEW.—Part III.

		Section
1.	Name some of the causes of the American Revolution.	215-224
2.	What resistance was made to the Navigation Laws?	225, 226
3.	Describe the causes and effects of the Boston Tea Party.	227-229
4.	Name the several steps toward union of the colonies.	97, 140, 146, 230, 298
5.	What was done by the First Continental Congress?	230, 231
6.	What by the Second?	234, 235
7.	Describe the first battle of the Revolution.	232, 233
8.	What did Englishmen think of the war?	236
9.	Describe the battle of Bunker Hill.	238-240
10.	Describe Washington's army.	241
11.	What were the "Mecklenburg Resolutions?"	242
12.	How was Kentucky founded?	243
13.	How did King George III. prepare for war?	244
14.	What was done by Americans to prevent Canadian attacks?	237, 245-247
15.	How was Boston relieved and Charleston defended?	248, 249
16.	By what acts were the colonies separated from England?	250
17.	What changes were made in the several colonies?	251
18.	What occurred near and in New York?	252-257
19.	What in the Jerseys?	258-260
20.	What foreigners enlisted under Washington?	261, 269
21.	Describe Burgoyne's campaign in 1777.	262-266
22.	Describe Washington's winter at Valley Forge.	267, 268
23.	What led to the French alliance?	270
24.	How long was Philadelphia held by the British?	263, 272
25.	Describe the attack on Newport.	273
26.	Describe the Indian massacres of 1778, and their	274-276

		Section
	punishment.	
27.	Describe Clarke's campaign in the West.	277-279
28.	What was done in Carolina and Georgia?	280, 281
29.	What posts on the Hudson were retaken in 1779?	282
30.	Tell something of Captain Paul Jones.	283
31.	Describe the campaign of 1780 in the South.	285-291
32.	Tell the story of Arnold's treason.	292-295
33.	What induced the colonies to make a closer union?	296-299
34.	What part did European nations take toward England?	299-301
35.	Describe the last campaign of Cornwallis in America.	302-305
36.	What can you say of Carleton?	306
37.	What were the terms of peace?	307, 308
38.	Name, in review, the principal battles of the Revolution.	232, 239, 249, 253, 259, 263, 265, 266, 272, 278, 282, 285, 288, 289, 291, 303.
39.	What British generals were successively in chief command?	232, 240, 272, 288, 306.
40.	Who were the principal American commanders?	241, 257, 265, 281, 282, 286, 288.
41.	What representatives were sent by the United States to France?	270
42.	What can you say of the naval actions of the Revolution?	273, 283, 302
43.	What states had claims to western lands, and what disposal was made of those claims?	298

PART IV.—GROWTH OF THE UNITED STATES.
CHAPTER XX.
ADOPTION OF THE CONSTITUTION.

309. By the terms of the Treaty of Versailles the United States extended from the Atlantic to the Mississippi, being bounded on the north by the Great Lakes and the St. Lawrence, on the east by the St. Croix River, and on the south by Florida.

The difficulties and dangers which followed the return of peace, were almost as great as those of the war. The nation, as such, was penniless and loaded with debt; its armies were unpaid for the services to which it owed its very existence ; and though there was immense wealth in the soil and mines, years of peaceful industry were needed to bring it to light.

310. There was no general government, for the Articles of Confederation (§298) had proved inadequate to the purpose for which they were framed. The several states had adopted republican constitutions; but whether these thirteen republics were to exist as so many separate nations, or to be united under a monarchy or in a federal league, no man knew. In the summer of 1782 the unpaid soldiers had listened to the proposal of some ambitious officers that they should set up Washington as their king. The great general crushed the plot as soon as it came to his knowledge, and proved his hold upon the affection of his men by keeping them in order and obedience during the trying year, while he was urging upon Congress their just demands. Instead of the half-pay for life, to which officers were entitled, he secured to them a sum equal to five years' full pay,— a necessary provision for those whose private fortunes had been ruined by the war.

311. The Indians were still hostile along the western border.

Among the first acts of the United States as an independent power was a treaty at Fort Pitt with the Delawares, admitting their just claim to their lands until they chose to sell them. In 1784 peace was made with the Iroquois by a grand council at Fort Stanwix, now Rome, New York, and within six years similar treaties were arranged with all the tribes to the southward. Mutual forgiveness of injuries was promised, and peace was restored.

312. The "treaty rights" thus conceded have been the basis of all official dealings with the natives of the far west; but, unhappily, Indian agents have sometimes cared more for their own gains than for the honor of their government, and some private citizens have acted toward the barbarians with reckless cruelty and fraud.

313. **Movements toward Union.**—The jealousies already existing among the states grew deeper and more violent with every year of their separate existence. At length the legislature of Virginia invited all the other states to join her in a convention to agree upon a much-needed system of commercial intercourse. Only five states accepted the invitation, but their delegates at Annapolis, in 1786, advised Congress to call a general assembly to revise the Articles of Confederation.

314. **The Constituent Convention.**—This body met in Philadelphia, May 25, 1787, and was found to comprise delegates from all the states excepting Rhode Island. Never was more important work committed to human hands. Other nations have had their constitutions gradually shaped by circumstances through a course of centuries: — for the first time in the world's history four millions of people were, by their representatives, to choose a government for themselves.

315. **Washington was President of the Convention**, and with him sat some of the wisest and best statesmen that America or the world has known. There was Franklin, now more than eighty years old, who had done invaluable service to his country in England and France, and whose practical wisdom made him one of the ablest

founders of the Constitution; there was Robert Morris,[1] the financier who had supplied the sinews of war by his own unquestioned credit; there were Jefferson, and Livingston,[2] and Jay,[3] who by their profound study of English law had learned to apply universal principles of truth and justice to the needs of a free people.

316. **Differences of Opinion.**—It was soon found that there were *two parties* in the convention. One desired to merge all the states in one indivisible republic, the other to keep the mutual independence of the thirteen, only uniting them in a league for commerce and other special purposes.

317. **The Constitution of the United States**, as reported after four months earnest discussion, sought to reconcile these two extremes. It recognized the sovereignty of each state over its own local affairs, but committed to the Federal government the care of all matters which concerned the nation as a whole, such as coinage, postal service, the maintenance of army and navy, forts, arsenals, and magazines for the common defense, and the making of war, peace, or alliances with foreign powers. (See p. 363.)

The law-making power was vested in a Congress consisting of a Senate and a House of Representatives. Every state is entitled to two senators appointed by its own legislature: the number of representatives from each state depends upon its population, and they are chosen directly by the voters.

The executive power was intrusted to a President, chosen by electors in all the states, for a term of four years. He, with the concurrence of the Senate, appoints embassadors, consuls, judges of the Supreme Court, and the members of his own Cabinet, and gives commissions to officers in the army and navy.

The judical power was vested in a Supreme Court and such inferior courts as Congress might establish.

318. **Opinions of the Constitution.**—A great English statesman of our own time (Mr. Gladstone[4]) has pronounced the Constitution of

the United States to be "the most wonderful work ever struck off at a given time by the brain and purpose of man." Washington wrote of it: "It appears to me little short of a miracle that the delegates from so many states, different from each other in their manners, circumstances, and prejudices, should unite in forming a system of national government so little liable to well-founded objections. . . . It is provided with more checks and barriers against the introduction of tyranny than any government hitherto instituted among mortals." Should it "be found less perfect than it can be made, a constitutional door is left open for its amelioration."

319. Adopted by the States. — The constitution thus framed by the convention was submitted to the people, who in each state chose delegates to consider and pronounce upon it. After severe discussion[5] it was accepted ultimately by all the states. On the first Wednesday in January, 1789, the first general election was held under the Constitution. A month later the electors met, and *George Washington*[6] was chosen to be the first President of the United States without one dissenting voice. *John Adams,* of Massachusetts,

Inauguration of Washington.

received the greatest number of votes at the second balloting, and was declared Vice-president.

320. **Washington's Inauguration.**—Washington's journey to New York, then the seat of government, was like a triumphal progress. Crowds attended him; young girls clothed in white scattered flowers along his way. The oath of office was administered by Chancellor Livingston,[7] of New York, on the balcony of the senate-house, in the presence of throngs of people, who filled the street, the windows, and the roofs of surrounding buildings. And when Washington's voice was heard in acceptance of the pledge to "preserve, protect, and defend the Constitution of the United States," every one felt that the new Republic was safe.

NOTES.

1. Robert Morris (*b.* 1734, *d.* 1806), "the patriot financier," was an Englishman by birth. He emigrated to Philadelphia when thirteen years old, and there commenced a wonderfully successful business career. He was a man of immense fortune at the breaking out of the Revolution, and his credit was better than that of Congress. In 1781 he was made superintendent of finance, and during that year he supplied all the wants of the army in the expedition against Cornwallis. To do this Morris was compelled to give his own notes, which were all paid, to the amount of $1,400,000. He superintended the affairs of the navy, and sent out many privateers on his own account, which proved very efficient. In 1781 he established the "Bank of North America," which helped in a large measure to relieve the embarrassments of the government. During the hard winter at Valley Forge, he sent as a gift to the army a ship-load of clothing and provisions.

When quite an old man Morris lost all his large fortune in a land speculation, and passed the last years of his life a prisoner for debt.

2. William Livingston (*b.* 1723, *d.* 1790) was one of the large family which has contributed a number of celebrities to American history. He was born in New York and educated at Yale College. He studied law, and soon became eminent in his profession. In 1776 he was made governor of New Jersey, and held the position until his death.

3. John Jay (*b.* 1745, *d.* 1829) was one of the most celebrated statesmen of his time. He was of French descent, and was born in New York. In 1764 he graduated at King's (Columbia) College, and then commenced the study of law, pursuing his profession until the disturbances with the mother-country, when he became deeply interested in the questions at issue. He was very moderate in his views as to resistance, but his counsel was usually wise, and he soon became prominent as a politician. In the provincial congress of New York, and in both continental congresses, he took an active part, and was a member of most of the important committees appointed. The constitution of the state of New York is mainly his work. In 1778 he was president of the national congress, and the following year he was appointed minister to Spain. At the close of the Revolution he was one of five commissioners appointed to negotiate the treaty with Great Britain, but the entire work fell upon Jay and Franklin. After his return to America he was appointed secretary of foreign affairs. Washington, when elected president, offered him his choice of office, and Jay chose that of Chief-justice of the United States, being the first to hold the position. Although Jay's treaty of 1794 (§331) with England created such excitement in this country, yet time proved the wisdom of its conditions. On his return from negotiating this treaty he was elected governor of New York, and held the office for six years. He was urged to stand for another term but declined to do so ; he also refused the appointment to his previous position of chief-justice, and retired to his estate in Westchester County, where he quietly passed the remaining twenty-eight years of his life.

4. William Ewart Gladstone is the most prominent statesman of England at the present day. He is the son of a wealthy merchant, and was born at Liverpool in 1809. He took the highest possible honor at Christ Church College, Oxford, where he graduated in 1831, and shortly after this he entered Parliament. He has several times been made premier, and holds that position at present (1881).

5. Patrick Henry (§230 and Note) objected mainly to the first three words, "We, the People," insisting that the convention was called only to form an alliance of states. Virginia ratified the constitution, however, with the full understanding that it united all the people of all the states under one government.

6. George Washington (*b.* February 22d, 1732, *d.* December 14th, 1799). Little or nothing is actually known of Washington's ancestors in England. His great-grandfather, John Washington, emigrated to Virginia in 1657, and served as a colonel in the early Indian wars. George's father died when he was eleven years old, so that his education and training devolved upon his mother. She was a woman of noble character, and, as events proved, was fully equal to the task. All through Washington's life we note the deep love and respect that he bore her, and to her influence, no doubt, is due the development of many of his admirable characteristics.

As a boy Washington was very fond of out-door sports, and it was his great delight to organize his boy friends into a soldier company and drill them. His attendance at school was from necessity quite limited: however, he was a good mathematician, and at the age of sixteen had thoroughly fitted himself as a practical surveyor. One of Washington's early friends was Lord Fairfax, an eccentric Englishman, who owned an immense estate in Virginia. He employed Washington to survey this land, and while engaged in this work, shut off from civilization and compelled to undergo numerous hardships, he learned many lessons that afterward proved useful to him.

When Governor Dinwiddie arrived in Virginia he appointed Washington, with the rank of major, over one of the four military districts into which he divided the colony. It was at this time, and when only twenty- one years of age, that Washington was dispatched on his mission to Venango (§ 176). The soundness of his judgment was shown on that expedition, and disregard of his advice was followed by disaster to Braddock's expedition.

When called upon to take command of the army of the United States, he replied with his usual modesty: "Though I am truly sensible of the high honor done me in this appointment, yet I feel great distress from a consciousness that my abilities and military experience may not be equal to the extensive and important trust." His generosity and devoted patriotism are also shown in another passage of this same reply: "As to pay, sir, I beg leave to assure Congress that as no pecuniary consideration could have tempted me to accept the arduous employment at the expense of my domestic ease and happiness, I do not wish to make any profit from it. I will keep an exact account of my expenses. Those, I doubt not, they will discharge, and that is all I desire." At this time Washington was forty-three years old. He had married Mrs. Martha Custis, a wealthy young widow, in 1759, and being heir himself to large estates, he had devoted himself to agriculture and the improvement of his property. He was naturally domestic, but at his country's eall cheerfully gave up his home eirele, and risked his property and his life. His success is remarkable when we consider the material and resources at his command as compared with those of the enemy, and his own lack of experience in handling large bodies of troops. More wonderful, however, was his indomitable courage and perseverance in the face of every discouragement, on the part of the people, congress, and jealous generals.

At the close of the war Washington looked eagerly for a renewal of his domestic life, but again heroically sacrificed his private desires for his country's good in accepting the presidency. As a president Washington was frequently criticised for his aristocratic tendencies, but he earnestly defended himself from cavils which in the light of the present day seem beneath his notice.

Retiring at the close of his second administration, he onee more resumed the quiet round of plantation life. Mount Vernon had now grown to an estate of eight thousand acres, half of which was under cultivation, and was worked by some two hundred and fifty slaves. When at home Washington personally superintended his affairs and kept his own books. During his entire absence he had an exact report of each week's transactions sent to him by mail.

Virginia presented Washington with canal stock valued at $60,000 in return for his services to the state and nation. This he accepted, but only to endow two institutions of learning,—a college at Lexington, Va., now called the "Washington and Lee University," and a university at the capital of the United States.

In appearance Washington was of commanding presence. He was six feet and two inches tall, broad shouldered, and muscular. His face was unusually calm and dignified in expression, and his manner was formal. In private, however, he was gracious, and even genial, especially with the young.

While taking his usual ride over the plantation, during the morning of the fourteenth of December, 1799, he was caught in a cold storm of rain and sleet. Returning home after two or three hours' exposure to this weather, lie sat down to dine without changing his clothes. The second day following he was attacked with "acute laryngitis," a disease of the throat not then understood, and died within twenty-four hours. Europe vied with America in mourning his loss and eulogizing his name. General Henry Lee, of Virginia, at the request of Congress, pronounced his funeral oration, using the memorable words, "First in war, first in peace, and first in the hearts of his countrymen."

7. **Robert R. Livingston** (*b.* 1746, *d.* 1813) was a cousin of William Livingston, mentioned above. He graduated at King's College, and adopted the profession of law. When a delegate to the second continental congress he was appointed one of the committee of five to draft the Declaration of Independence. He held many important political offices, and was the first chancellor of the state of New York. Through him as minister-plenipotentiary the territory of Louisiana was purchased from France. He did much for the improvement of agriculture in New York, and assisted Fulton in his early experiments in steam navigation (§363).

CHAPTER XXI.
FIRST AND SECOND ADMINISTRATIONS, A. D. 1789–1797.

George Washington, President.   *John Adams, Vice-president.*

321. Washington's Cabinet consisted of Thomas Jefferson, Secretary of State; Alexander Hamilton,[1] Secretary of the Treasury; Henry Knox, Secretary of War; and Edmund Randolph,[2] Attorney-general. John Jay was appointed Chief-justice of the United States.

322. Hamilton's great financial ability soon established confidence and prosperity in commercial affairs. The general government assumed the war debts of the several states, and declared its intention to redeem all the continental paper money at its full value. This was a severe test of public honor, for the greater part of this paper was in the hands of speculators, who had bought it for almost nothing from the starving veterans of the Revolution; and Congress had been forced to issue immensely greater quantities of this currency than would have been needed if it had been worth its nominal value. Nevertheless the new nation was not to begin its existence by breaking its promises.

323. The Bank of the United States was established at Philadelphia, and there, also, the national mint was set up. Taxes were imposed on imports of foreign goods, and on the manufacture of distilled liquors.

In 1790 the **seat of government** was placed for ten years at Philadelphia, and a tract of land ten miles square on either side of the Potomac, which was ceded to the United States by Maryland and Virginia, was adopted by Congress as the site of the future capital. Washington himself selected a site for the city which was to bear his name, and laid the cornerstone of the Capitol in 1793.

Crossing the Alleghanies.

324. The North-western Territory. — The most important act of the last Continental Congress had been the organizing of a settled government for the territory north of the Ohio River. It was, in fact, "the most notable law ever enacted by representatives of the American people," and, to insure its perpetual enforcement, it was not left as a mere act of Congress, which could be repealed at a subsequent session, but its six main provisions were made articles of a solemn compact between the inhabitants of the territory, present and to come, and the people of the thirteen states. No man was to be restricted of his liberty excepting as a punishment for crime; life, property, and religious freedom were protected by just and equal laws. A clause, which several western states have copied in their constitutions, declared that "Religion, morality, and knowledge being necessary to good government, schools and the means of education shall forever be encouraged."

To this end one section in every township was set apart for the support of common schools, and two entire townships for the establishment of a university. Ohio University, at Athens, arose from this foundation, and was the first college west of the Alleghanies.

325. The Ohio Company.—In consequence of this liberal constitution, which was partly suggested by himself, Doctor Cutler,[3] of Massachusetts, as agent of the new "Ohio Company," bought of Congress a million and a half acres of land on the Ohio and Scioto rivers. For other adventurers Doctor Cutler purchased four millions of acres more. The whole vast territory was then known as "The Wilderness," and contained no white inhabitants excepting a few French settlers on its western and northern borders. Attracted by the fertile soil and the assurance of good government, industrious emigrants soon thronged to the new country, and the five states[4] formed from the North-western Territory now contain one fourth of all the population of the United States. General St. Clair,[5] who was President of Congress at the time of the passing of the ordinance, became the first governor of the territory, and took up his residence at *Marietta*, the first town on the Ohio.

326. The Indians on the Miami and Wabash rivers made frequent attacks upon the white settlements, being supplied with powder and guns from forts which the British still held, contrary to treaty, in the heart of the country. Several expeditions against these tribes were repulsed with great slaughter ; even the one led in person by Governor St. Clair ended in surprise and disgrace. General Wayne,—the "Mad Anthony" of the Revolution,—had better success. Having defeated the savages on the Maumee, be so laid waste their country that they were glad to buy peace by retiring west of the Wabash.

327. Whisky Rebellion.—The whisky tax created great discontent in the Monongahela Valley, where the article was largely manufactured, and the spirit of revolt was increased by artful men who wished to overthrow all laws. The rebellion made such headway that the President called out 15,000 militia to suppress it, and himself conducted the citizen-army as far as Fort Cumberland. There he gave the command to General Lee,—formerly "Light Horse Harry," now governor of Virginia,—who marched into the western counties of Pennsylvania. But no fighting was needed; overawed by this spirited policy, the rioters laid down their arms and asked pardon from the government.

328. During the storm of the **French Revolution**, which was now in progress, Washington and his advisers had a most difficult part to play. La Fayette, one of the first and warmest friends of American freedom, was for a little time a leader of the popular movement in France. Our people were strongly inclined to sympathize with the French in their resistance to a despotism far more galling than that of England to her colonies; and when Great Britain, with other European nations, took up arms to force the restoration of kings in France, some ardent spirits in America were eager to plunge into war and pay our debt of gratitude by helping to gain for our comrades in arms the same blessings which we were enjoying.

329. But when the **Reign of Terror** in France had destroyed the very freedom whose name it invoked, and shed torrents of innocent blood, wiser people were alarmed, and thought even tyranny more endurable than such mad violence. Besides, we had England on our north and east, Spain on our south and west, stirring up the Indians to fierce warfare, while English ships commanded our eastern ports. Beside all these foes, the pirate states of the Mediterranean were preying upon all the commerce of Christendom, and hundreds of American citizens were toiling as slaves under the burning sun of Algiers and Morocco.

330. **Great Britain** still held Mackinaw, Detroit, Niagara, Oswego, and several other forts on our frontier, and gave still greater offense during her war with France by seizing American ships and

forcing their sailors to serve on board her own vessels. On the other hand English merchants complained that they could not collect debts due them in America. In some cases many years' interest was claimed on money due before the Revolution, while Congress insisted that the British government, having made payment impossible, was responsible for the delay.

331. Jay's Treaty. — To arrange all these matters John Jay was sent as minister to London, and there negotiated a treaty which settled most of the points in dispute excepting the "right of search." King George agreed to pay for the losses inflicted on American merchant-ships by his privateers, and to vacate the western forts (§326) which, with or without authority from him, had kept alive Indian hostilities against our pioneers in the new territory. On the other hand, Congress provided for the payment of our English debts. The treaty was received with a storm of opposition by those Americans who cherished a bitter hatred against England, and wished success to the French Revolution, which she was fighting to put down. The greatest abuse fell upon Washington himself, who was even accused of overdrawing his salary[6] as President, and threatened with impeachment! Nevertheless, he persevered in what seemed to him the course of duty, and in concurrence with a majority of the Senate ratified Mr. Jay's agreements.

332. Citizen Genet.[7] — Presuming upon the gratitude and affection of our countrymen toward France, her envoy, "Citizen Genet," who had landed at Charleston, enlisted troops and fitted out privateers from the southern states before even presenting himself at the seat of government. A large party of American citizens sustained him, and demanded a declaration of war against Great Britain. Washington firmly resisted this wild policy, and soon Genet was recalled. He chose, however, to remain in this country, and became a citizen of the United States.

333. Two political parties now became clearly divided. The Federalists, with Washington at their head, stood by the treaty with England, and desired a strong central government for the sake of commanding respect abroad and security at home. The *Republicans,* — or Democrats, as they were often called, the two names having nearly the same meaning, — were friends to France, and to the independent sovereignty of our states, while they violently opposed Jay's treaty, the United States Bank, and the payment of state debts by the general government. They constantly sounded the alarm of "monarchy" when any new power was exerted by Congress or the President; and perhaps some of them really feared that Washington might become "king of America," though this apprehension was certainly not felt by the leaders, nor by the more intelligent members of the party. Alexander Hamilton and John Adams were leading Federalists; Jefferson, Madison, and Monroe were the chief Republicans.

334. A treaty with Spain, in 1795, settled the boundaries between the United States on one side, and Florida and Louisiana on the other. The navigation of the Mississippi was secured to American citizens, and they were permitted to use New Orleans for ten years as a place of deposit. This treaty removed a great danger; for the growing products of the West needed this natural outlet, and

Algerine Pirates

some bold spirits had even plotted to seize New Orleans by force,—a movement which must certainly have occasioned war. On the other hand, the Spanish authorities in that city were said to be sending spies and emissaries through the south-western country, hoping to separate that rich territory from the Union, with a view to make it subject at last to Spain.

335. Treaty with Algiers.—During the same year a treaty was made with the pirate government of Algiers, on terms which were humiliating but necessary, as we had no navy. $800,000 were paid to the Dey for the release of American seamen whom he held as slaves, and an annual tribute of $23,000 was promised in return for his engagement to leave our merchant-ships unmolested.

During Washington's two terms of office *Vermont, Kentucky,* and *Tennessee* were organized as states and admitted into the Federal Union (§§223, 243).

336. As his second term of office drew near its close, Washington declined a re-election, in an address to his fellow-citizens, which he caused to be published in a Philadelphia paper. In his last speech to Congress he recommended the establishment of a military academy, a national university, an institution for the improvement of agriculture, and the increase of the navy.

His eight years of chief magistracy had been, if possible, a yet greater service to his country than his eight years' command of her armies. No character was probably ever more free from selfish aims : none could have held together so many discordant interests until they had time to become harmonious.

337. Washington's plea for union may be given in his own words: "The *North* . . . finds in the productions of the South great additional resources of maritime and commercial enterprise, and precious materials of manufacturing industry. The *South,* in the same intercourse, benefiting by the agency of the North, sees its agriculture grow and its commerce expand. . . . The *East,* in a like intercourse with the West, already finds,—and in the progressive improvement of interior communications by land and water, will more and more find,—a valuable vent for the commodities which it brings from abroad or manufactures at home. The *West* derives from the East supplies requisite to its growth and comfort, and . . . must owe the secure enjoyment of indispensable outlets for its own productions to the weight, influence, and future maritime strength of the Atlantic side of the Union."

338. The Republican Court.—Washington had maintained the dignity of the Republic by his grave and stately manners, and the style of his appearance in public. His own tastes were very simple; but some of his advisers doubted whether the people would respect and obey a government which was destitute *of* the pomps and ceremonies that made an essential part of Old World customs. There were others who ridiculed Washington's coach of state and his formal receptions, as "aping the manners of royalty." We shall see that later presidents found it possible to adopt simpler manners, but we may be sure that Washington did nothing from vanity.

339. Results of the First Administration. — Under his faithful care, an era of great prosperity had begun. The honor of the government had been sustained by a secure provision for the payments of its debts, confidence and order were established, commerce flourished, and the products of the soil had become a source of wealth. In spite of the complaints of restless politicians, the people loved their government, for they found it well fitted to secure their peace and happiness.

Read Volume V. of Irving's "Life of Washington;" Life of Hamilton; Griswold's "Court of Washington;" Goodrich's "Republican Court."

NOTES.

1. **Alexander Hamilton** (*b*. 1757. *d*. 1804), born in the West Indies, was one of the most remarkable characters of the Revolution. His mother died when he was a child, and his father being in destitute circumstances Hamilton was taken charge of by his mother's relatives. They placed him in a commercial house when twelve years of age, and although the life was very distasteful to him, he applied himself faithfully to the discharge of his duties. A newspaper article, written when he was but fifteen years old, was so remarkable that his friends determined to give him the benefit of a good education, and he was accordingly sent to New York, where he graduated at King's College. He became much interested in politics, and a speech made by him at a public meeting, in 1774, attracted general attention to him. Soon after this he wrote a number of political pamphlets that at once gave him a high position in the community. When nineteen years old he obtained a commission as captain of artillery, and in this capacity he first attracted the attention of Washington, to whom he finally became aid-de-camp. So implicit was Washington's confidence in this stripling of twenty that he intrusted to him the sole management of his most delicate correspondence with the British commanders and others. After the war he studied law, in which profession he at once rose to eminence, but polities continued to absorb much of his time. He was a member of the Constitutional Convention (§314), and wrote the majority of a series of papers called "The Federalist," which appeared in à New York paper, in defense of the Constitution, and no doubt had much weight in causing its adoption by the several states. Party feeling now ran very high, and

Hamilton's great ability and untiring energy won him many strong friends among the Federalists, and many bitter enemies in the opposite party. As Washington's first Secretary of the Treasury, Hamilton's career was brilliant and sue- cessful, and he readily refuted all the charges brought against him for mismanagement and dishonesty by the Democrats. A split occurring in the Federalist party, Hamilton, by his opposition, gave deep offense to Aaron Burr, who finally challenged him to a duel and shot him.

Hamilton is described as being under the medium height and slight in figure. His complexion was fair and delicate, and his manners were most engaging.

2. **Edmund Randolph** (*b*. 1753, *d*. 1813) was the son of a Virginia royalist, and had been disinherited on account of his political principles. He served on Washington's staff during the Revolution, but was more active as a statesman than as a warrior. He was a member of the Constitutional Convention (§314) where his conduct was rather inconsistent. He refused to sign the constitution, and yet he afterwards worked for its adoption in the Virginia convention. In 1788 he was made governor of Virginia. In the cabinet he pretended to hold a neutral position, but when any issue arose he usually sided with Jefferson against Hamilton and Knox. Upon Jefferson's withdrawal from the cabinet in 1794 Randolph was made Secretary of State, but in the following year resigned his position, having been accused of an intrigue with the French envoy.

3. **Dr. Manasseh Cutler** (*b*. 1742, *d*. 1823) was a highly educated New Englander. After graduating at Yale College he studied successively the three professions of law, theology, and medicine, and also became eminent as a scientist. During the Revolution he served as a chaplain. The "Ohio Company," of which he was a member, was formed by army officers who wished to have their bounty lands located together. Dr. Cutler had built the first emigrant wagon that penetrated the forests of Ohio; and bis son, Jarvis, cut down the first tree in the clearing made at Marietta.

4. **The five states** formed out of the North-west Territory are Ohio, Indiana, Illinois, Michigan, and Wisconsin.

5. **General Arthur St. Clair** (*b*. 1734, *d*. 1818) was of Scotch birth. He had served faithfully in the French and Indian War, and also under Washington during the Revolution. Having been appointed commander-

in-chief of the army sent against the Miamis, he keenly felt the failure of the expedition, and, on Washington's refusal of the investigation which lie demanded, immediately resigned his command. Later, Congress ordered the investigation, and General St. Clair was acquitted of all blame.

6. It was answered by the Secretary of the Treasury that Washington never even touched the sum allowed him by the government, which was drawn and disbursed by the gentleman who had charge of the expenses of his household.

7. Edmond Charles Genet (or Genest) was born at Versailles in 1765, and although his immediate family were prominent royalists, he early avowed republican principles. He represented the French Republic at St. Petersburg, but was soon dismissed from that court and returned to France. He was then appointed embassador to Holland, but before leaving for that country was made minister to the United States. After settling in this country he married the daughter of Mr. George Clinton, then governor of New York.

CHAPTER XXII.
THIRD ADMINISTRATION, A. D. 1797-1801.

John Adams, President. *Thomas Jefferson, Vice-president.*

340. The Second President.—*John Adams*,[1] of Massachusetts, was the second President of the United States, and Thomas Jefferson, of Virginia, having received only three votes less from the electoral college,[2] became Vice-president. These two great men were leaders of opposite parties, and during their four years of office the country was disturbed by a violent conflict of opinions. The inconvenience of such a division of sentiments in the administration led, a few years later, to a change in the mode of election, —a distinct ballot being held for the Vice-president, who has ever since been of the same political party with his chief.

341. Abuse of Privileges.—It had been found that the welcome which the United States offered to refugees of all nations was greatly abused. Men who had been expelled, sometimes for crime, from their native land, found homes and prosperity in America, and used their freedom in misrepresenting and embarrassing the government which protected them. The true interest of our nation was peace and friendship with all others, but this was endangered by the rival partisans of France and England.

342. Alien and Sedition Laws.—In these circumstances Congress passed an *Alien Law*, empowering the president to send out of the country, at short notice, any person whom he might consider dangerous, and lengthening the time requisite for becoming citizens of the United States to fourteen years. It was followed by a *Sedition Law*, which limited the freedom of the press to criticise the government. Under this act it was a crime to "write, print, utter, or publish any false, scandalous, or malicious statement" against either Congress or the President. These laws were violently opposed,—as indeed they were contrary to the spirit of our Constitution,—and in the next administration they were repealed. The great republic accepted the dangers with the blessings of perfect freedom, and rested her hope of security on the virtue and good sense of a majority of her people.

John Adams.

343. Difficulties with France grew very serious. French men-of-war seized American merchant vessels on the high seas, and demanded "enrollment papers" describing the nationality of every sailor. When, as usual, these were not found, — no American law requiring them,—the ship was confiscated and sold for the benefit of her captors.

344. Our minister to the French Republic was insultingly dismissed; and when three special envoys[3] were sent to re-open communications between the governments, they were refused all recognition in their public character, though they were privately informed that a large loan to France, and liberal gratuities to high French officials, would probably open the doors. "Millions for defense, not a cent for tribute," was the spirited reply, and the sister-republics seemed to be drifting into war.

345. War Measures.— Commercial intercourse with France was suspended; our army and navy were increased and reorganized, and Washington was called again to the head of the army. Though war had not been declared, six new frigates put to sea and captured several French prizes in the West Indies. But in 1799 Napoleon Bonaparte came to the head of the French government, and one of his earliest acts was a friendly settlement with the United States.

346. Death of Washington.—Scarcely had Washington retired to his home, in good hope of a peaceful and vigorous old age, when a sudden illness of two days ended his grand and useful life. The whole country mourned him as a father, and those who had been his opponents were most sincere in doing him honor. The British fleet lowered all its flags at receiving news of his death, and Bonaparte, in announcing the event to the French armies, ordered that tokens of mourning should drape all the standards in the public service for ten days.

347. The City of Washington.—The next summer, 1800, the government was removed to its "palace in the wilderness," on the banks of the Potomac. There was little yet to indicate that a beautiful and stately city was to occupy the site chosen by Washington. Mrs. Adams,[4] the President's wife, on her journey from Baltimore to her new home, was actually lost in the woods, and, with her escort, "wandered two hours without finding a guide or path." She adds, "But woods are all you see from Baltimore until you reach this city, which is so only in name."

348. The rich resources of the country were scarcely dreamed of. Anthracite coal had been discovered in Pennsylvania, but its value was so little understood that it was used for mending roads. Cotton had been introduced into Georgia in 1786, and the south-eastern states were found to contain the finest cotton lands in the World, but the separation of a single pound of cotton from its seeds required a Whole day, and the woven fabric was more costly than linen. In 1793 *Eli Whitney*,[5] of Massachusetts, while visiting in Georgia, invented a cotton-gin which could do the work of hundreds of men in clearing the fiber from the seed. *Arkwright,* in England, had already perfected his machine for spinning cotton, and *James Watt* his steam- engine. These three inventions revolutionized the manufactures of England and America. With the wonderful power of steam, England was now able to weave clothing for the world, and America was prepared to furnish all the raw material that English looms required. Cotton became one of the most important products of the United States, and a source of enormous wealth to the South. The. first American cotton mill was set up in Rhode Island by *Slater,* a pupil of Arkwright, and the building mm vet be seen.

349. In February, 180 **Ohio,** of five states formed from the North-warrior admitted to the Union. Though both It and n had held trading posts on the rivers first to belle and the Jesuits (§§156, 158), to permanent settlement was at Marietta, where : senior of the whole territory resided (§ 325). Fort Washington and the village of Columbia, near the junction of the Little Miami and the Ohio, were the foundations of greater city of *Cincinnati,* which took its name from to military society formed by Revolutionary officers (Note . 178).

Read life Works of John Adams; Hildreth's "History of the United state after Adoption of Federal Constitution, Vol. I.

NOTES.

1. John Adams was born at Braintree, Mass., in October, 1735. He was a graduate of Harvard College in the class of 17.55, and was admitted to the bar three years later. In 1764 he was married. He was an active and influential member of both the first and second Continental congresses, and by his energy and eloquence did more, perhaps, than any other man to crystallize the American sentiment in favor of independence. Jefferson drew up the immortal "Declaration," but it was Adams who persuaded congress to adopt it. He was the most distinguished signer. Jefferson himself said that "he [Adams] was the pillar of its support; its ablest advocate and defender." The appointment of Washington to the chief command of the army was at the suggestion of John Adams. In after years he criticised him severely, but lived to see and to acknowledge the injustice of his criticism. During the first two years of the war his labors were incessant and overwhelming. Besides being chairman of the Board of War and of Appeals, he was at the head of twenty-five important congressional committees. As commissioner to France and Holland, and as "minister plenipotentiary to negotiate a treaty with Great Britain," the diplomacy and practical wisdom of John Adams accomplished great results. He secured loans of large amounts, and influenced leading European powers to make treaties of amity and commerce with the new American republic. With Jay and Franklin he framed the preliminary treaty of Versailles. After the declaration of peace Adams was appointed minister to the English court, which position he filled until 1788. Congress passed a resolution thanking him for the "patriotism, perseverance, integrity, and diligence" displayed during his career abroad. Bancroft, in summing up the character of President Adams, says: "His nature was robust and manly, his convictions were clear, his will fixed. His overweening self-esteem was his chief blemish; and if he compared himself with his great fellow-workers, there was some point on which he was superior to any one of them. He had more learning than Washington or any other American statesman of his age; clearer insight into the constructive elements of government than Franklin; more power in debate than Jefferson; more force in motion than Jay; so that, by varying and defining his comparisons, he could easily fancy himself the greatest of them all. . . . His vanity, however, did not reach beyond the surface; it impaired the luster, not the hardy integrity of his character. He was humane and frank, generous and clement. . . . His courage was unflinching every where; he never knew what fear was."

One of John Adams's grandsons writes of him : "Nobody could see him intimately without admiring the simplicity and truth which shone in all his actions, and standing in some awe of the power and energy of his will. His nature was too susceptible to emotions of sympathy and kindness, for it tempted him to trust more than was prudent to the professions of some who proved unworthy of his confidence. Ambitious in one sense he certainly was, but it was not the mere aspiration for place or power. It was a desire to excel in the minds of men by the development of high qualities, — the love, in short, of an honorable fame, that stirred him to exult in the rewards of popular favor."

Many of the acts of President Adams were violently denounced by his partisan opponents, and the press was very bitter in its criticism ; but the sober judgment of later years has approved most of his public measures. He and Jefferson became widely alienated for a time; but before their death, which by a singular coincidence occurred on the same day—the fiftieth anniversary of the Declaration of Independence—a happy reconciliation had taken place.

2. The second clause of Section I, Article II, of the United States Constitution, begins thus; "Each state shall appoint, in such manner as the legislature thereof may direct, a number of Electors equal to the whole number of Senators and Representatives to which the state may be entitled in the Congress." These Electors meet in their respective states at a specified time after a presidential election, and vote by ballot for President and Vice-president. These bodies of Electors, taken together, are known as the **Electoral College.**

3. The minister was Charles Cotesworth Pinckney, and the special envoys were Pinckney, John Marshall, and Elbridge Gerry.

4. Abigail Adams was a woman of strong character, sterling good sense, and marked intellectual ability. She shared her husband's tastes for books, sympathized with his high aims, made his home bright and happy, and won the esteem of all with whom she was associated. She died in 1818. The published "Letters" between John Adams and his wife are among the most valuable literary contributions of their time.

5. Before the invention of Whitney's cotton-gin the cleaning of a single pound of green-seed cotton was a day's work for a southern field-hand. The state of South Carolina paid Whitney $50,000 for the use of his invention, and North Carolina a fixed percentage on each machine. But a succession of lawsuits for infringements of his patent, the burning of his factory, and other misfortunes took away all his profits; and lie retrieved his fortunes by the manufacture of fire-arms for the government, at Whitneyville, Conn. He died at New Haven in 1825.

CHAPTER XXIII.
FOURTH AND FIFTH ADMINISTRATIONS, A. D. 1801-1809.

Thomas Jefferson, President.   *Aaron Burr, George Clinton, Vice-presidents.*

350.   **The Third President.**—In the year 1800 parties were so evenly balanced that no president could be chosen by the electors. By a provision of the constitution the choice, therefore, devolved upon the House of Representatives. After a close ballot *Thomas Jefferson*[1] was declared to be President-elect, and *Aaron Burr*,[2] of New York, Vice-president.

Thomas Jefferson.

351.   Jefferson may be considered as the founder of the *Democratic Party*, which, from the beginning, claimed for the several states all powers which were not expressly conferred upon the general government; aimed at the greatest possible simplicity and economy in the administration of public affairs; and insisted that all material improvements, such as bridges and the clearing of river-beds, should be made at the expense of the district to which they belonged.

352.   Jefferson was deeply versed in English law, while as the

framer of the Declaration of Independence he was, perhaps, of all men then living, most familiar with the principies of the American constitution. Seven years' residence in France had filled him with dread and hatred of absolute governments, and with zeal for the universal rights of man.

353. In his **style and demeanor** as president he cultivated the extreme of republican simplicity, even receiving the British embassador in dressing-gown and slippers. On the occasion of his first address to Congress, he rode alone to the Capitol, tied his horse to the paling which then surrounded it, and entered unattended. The formality of an address was afterwards dispensed with, a written message taking its piace. Jefferson called about him a cabinet distinguished for high talents and education. James Madison was Secretary of State, and Albert Gallatin,³ a Swiss by birth, was in charge of the treasury.

354. The Treasury.—Distrusting the Federalists, and especially Alexander Hamilton, their leader, Jefferson requested his new Secretary of the Treasury to look sharply into the records of his office, thinking that occasion might be found for charges against its late chief. Gallatin was no less keenly opposed to his predecessor on political grounds, but after severe examination he reported to the President that no improvement was possible in the management of the treasury, for that Hamilton had "made no blunders and committed no frauds."

355. Indian Policy.—The difficult question of a policy toward the Indians was settled during this administration nearly as it has always remained. The leading points were to purchase their lands, excepting what they would themselves cultivate, to lead them to agriculture instead of war and hunting, and to remove them west of the Mississippi as soon as it could be peacefully and justly done.

356. **The greatest event** of Jefferson's term of office was the purchase of the vast territory west of the Mississippi, lately ceded by Spain to France. Robert Livingston and James Monroe were the agents of the United States. Great anxiety was felt, for, after a short and treacherous peace, France and England were again on the eve of war; and the latter, with her superior power on the sea, might easily have wrested from France all her remaining possessions in America. In that case the United States could scarcely have maintained their dearly bought independence.

357. For the **Territory of Louisiana** the commissioners agreed to pay fifteen millions of dollars, of which one fourth was due from the French government to American citizens for depredations upon their commerce (§343). These claims were assumed by Congress and paid from the purchase-money. Upon signing the treaty, Bonaparte remarked: "This accession of territory strengthens forever the power of the United States, and I have given to England a maritime rival that will humble her pride." Livingston said: "We have lived long, but this is the noblest work of our whole lives. This treaty will change vast solitudes into flourishing districts. . . and will prepare ages of happiness for innumerable generations of human creatures."

358. **Lewis and Clarke's Expedition.**—Captains Lewis and Clarke[4] were commissioned to explore the northern part of the acquired territory, which extended from the upper Mississippi westward to the Pacific Ocean. Ascending the Missouri to its sources, they penetrated a wilderness inhabited chiefly by wolves and bears. Crossing a portage of only thirty-six miles to the head-waters of the Columbia River, they threaded the primeval solitudes to its mouth. The story of their travel during two years and three months is full of wild adventure.

359. **The Territory of Orleans** was organized within the present limits of the state of Louisiana; the remainder of the new possession was known for some years as *Louisiana Territory*.

Lewis and Clarke's Expedition.

360. The humiliating[5] treaty with Algiers (§335) had not hindered the attacks upon American ships by pirates from Tripoli, another of the Barbary states. In the seaports of New England it was no uncommon occurrence on a Sunday to hear a letter read in church from some honored citizen, now a slave on the northern coast of Africa, begging his old neighbors to advance money for his ransom.

In 1801 the Pasha of Tripoli declared war against the United States, and Commodores Preble and Morris[6] were sent to bombard his capital and bring him to terms. During the blockade the frigate *"Philadelphia"* was captured by the enemy and taken into port. Lieutenant Decatur sailed into the harbor by night, with seventy-six men in a small vessel, surprised and recaptured the frigate, and burned her to the water's edge under the guns of the Pasha's castle. In 1805 that dignitary was glad to obtain peace by promises of better behavior.

361. The death of Alexander Hamilton in a private combat with Vice-president Burr in 1804, horrified the nation, and went far to put an end to the murderous custom of dueling. Hamilton disapproved the practice, but when challenged by Burr, on account of some political offense, he imagined that honor compelled him to accept. He purposely fired into the air, and at the same moment received a mortal wound.

362. Jefferson was re-elected the following autumn to the head of the government, but with George Clinton,[7] of New York, as Vice-president. Burr's reckless spirit drove him into the wilderness, where he plotted the formation of a new and rival state from the southwestern territory of the Union. He succeeded in ruining one[8] at least of his accomplices, but he was betrayed by another,[9] and his scheme came to nought. He was tried for treason at Richmond, Ya. This crime was not proved, and he was released; but the career which his brilliant talents might have made honorable and useful, was wrecked, and his old age was dismally unhappy.

363. The year 1807 is memorable for the earliest success of **steam navigation.** Several ingenious men had been experimenting on the application of Watt's invention to modes of travel; but to Robert Fulton,[10] a native of Pennsylvania, is due the credit of having persevered until all obstacles Avere overcome. He was liberally aided by Chancellor Livingston of New York. His first boat, the "*Clermont,*"ascended the Hudson from New York to Albany in 1807. Five years later he built at Pittsburgh the first Mississippi steamer, which, descending the Ohio and Mississippi rivers, reached New Orleans in December, 1812.

364. The furious **war now raging between France and England** seemed destined to engulf the infant commerce of the United States. Each nation desired to prevent supplies reaching its rival; neutral vessels were forbidden to enter any European port; and thus the American carrying trade was cut off at a blow. Equally vexatious was the pretended "right of search." In June, 1807, the British ship *"Leopard"* fired into the American frigate *"Chesapeake,"* near Fortress Monroe, killed three men, wounded eighteen, and carried off four, under the pretense that they were British subjects. The king's government expressed "regrets," but re-affirmed the right of search.

365. Congress retaliated by an **Embargo Act**, prohibiting the sailing of all vessels for any foreign port. This was injurious to British commerce, but it occasioned yet greater suffering in America. In New England, which was more dependent upon trade than the rest of the country, it met with determined opposition. Jefferson always believed that if the Embargo Act could have been faithfully observed by the whole people, the war which marked his successor's administration might have been prevented. But the opposing interests were too strong, and after fourteen months it was repealed.

Read Tucker's " Life of Jefferson," and Lord Brougham's review of it in "Edinburgh Review," 1837 ; Lewis and Clarke's Journal; Jefferson's Autobiography.

NOTES.

1. Thomas Jefferson (born at Shadwell, Va., 1743, died at Monticello, 1826). "Just thirty-three years old, married, and happy in his family, affluent, with a bright career before him, he was no rash innovator by his character or his position ; if his convictions drove him to demand independence, it was only because he could no longer live with honor under the British 'constitution which he still acknowledged to be better than all that bad preceded it.' . . . No man of his century had more trust in the collective reason and conscience of his fellow-men or better knew how to take their counsel ; and in return he came to be a ruler over the willing in the world of opinion. Born to an independent fortune, he had from his youth been an indefatigable student. Of a hopeful temperament and a tranquil, philosophic cast of mind, always temperate in his mode of life and decorous in his manners, lie was a perfect master of his liassions. He was of a delicate organization, and fond of elegance ; his tastes were refined ; laborious in his application to business or the pursuit of knowledge, music was his favorite recreation. He was a skillful horseman, and took a never-failing delight in the varied beauty of rural life. The range of his studies was very wide; he was not unfamiliar with the literature of Greece and Rome; had an aptitude for mathematics and mechanics, and loved especially the natural sciences. . . . Jefferson was a hater of superstition and bigotry and intolerance; he was an idealist in his habits of thought and life. . . .

In his profession, the law, he was methodical, painstaking, and successful. Whatever he had to do, it was his custom to prepare himself for it carefully ; and in public life, when others were at fault, they often found that he had already hewed out the way; so that in council men willingly gave him the lead, which he never appeared to claim, and was always able to undertake. . . . The nursling of his country, the offspring of his time, he set about the work of a practical statesman, and his measures grew so naturally out of previous law and the facts of the past that they struck deep root and have endured." — Bancroft.

2. **Aaron Burr** was born at Newark, N. J., 1756, and died on Staten Island, 1.836. His father and his grandfather, the distinguished Jonathan Edwards (§202), were both presidents of Princeton College, of which institution Burr was a graduate. Before he was three years of age both of his parents died, and Aaron was left to the care of relatives. He was a great reader in his youth, and an industrious student. He commenced reading theology, but soon abandoned it and turned to the profession of law. Soon after the battle of Lexington he enlisted in the patriot army, and rose from a sick-bed io join Arnold's expedition to Quebec (§ 246), and valiantly led a forlorn hope in the assault on that citadel (§247). Owing to ill health he resigned his commission in the army in 1779, and commenced the practice of law at Albany in 17S2. As a lawyer Aaron Burr ranked among the foremost of his day: it is claimed he never lost a case. His political life began in the New York legislature in 1784. He was subsequently attorney-general of the state, and in 1791 was sent to the United States Senate. His political honors culminated in the Vice-presidency. Alexander Hamilton had vehemently opposed him from his first entrance into politics. He believed Burr to be a dangerous man to place in office. It was his repeated utterances to this effect which provoked the fatal challenge. After the duel Burr was disfranchised from New York state, and lost social caste and political influence. He plunged into the wild scheme of subjugating Mexico and uniting it to a portion of the southwestern states, over which he was to rule supreme, and at his death his idolized daughter, Theodosia, was to become queen ! His plots were pronounced treasonable, and in 1.806 President Jefferson proclaimed against him and authorized his capture. After his trial at Richmond he went to Europe and wandered aimlessly, from city to city, under constant surveillance, and at times in the depths of poverty. Yet with all his troubles and disappointments he never seemed despondent. He returned to New York in 1812, and resumed the practice of law with

success; but his old friends and admirers, except a very few, shunned him. When seventy-eight he married Madame Jumel, a wealthy widow, to obtain a home during the few years he had yet to live; but they soon had trouble and separated, and Burr's last sickness was in humble lodgings provided by one of his life-long friends. He was buried at Princeton by the side of his father and grandfather.

3. **Albert Gallatin** was born in Geneva, Switzerland, in 1761, and died at Astoria, N. Y., 1849. In 1779 he graduated with honors from the University of Geneva, and the next summer left home and friends and brilliant prospects to try his fortunes in America. He married in 1789, but his wife lived only a few months. To drown his grief Gallatin plunged into politics, and soon became a leader of the anti-Federalists. Both political parties in Pennsylvania united upon Albert Gallatin for United States Senator in 1793, but he was prevented from taking his seat by a flaw in his naturalization papers. Serving three years in the Pennsylvania legislature he entered Congress in 1795, and by his ability assumed the leadership of the Republicans. From 1801 he was for twelve years Secretary of the Treasury, and his able administration stamped him as one of the foremost financiers of his time. Owing to his wise statesmanship he was frequently selected as commissioner to negotiate important treaties with foreign powers. He was United States minister to France from 1816 to 1823, and to England in 1826-7. In 1824 he was nominated for Vice-president, bnt withdrew from the candidacy. Gallatin's subsequent business career was successful, and his numerous financial and historical writings added greatly to his reputation. " His eminent and manifold services to his adopted country, his great abilities and upright character assure him of a high position in the history of the United States."

4. **Meriwether Lewis and William Clarke** were of Virginia birth, and both had abundant experience in Indian warfare, so that the perils of their long expedition merely added zest to the enterprise. Their return to St. Louis, September, 1806, was nearly two and a half years after their departure from that point. Lewis was made governor of Missouri territory, and died near Nashville in 1809. Clarke also became governor of Missouri territory; and, later, Superintendent of Indian Affairs. He died at St. Louis in 1838.

Many of the Indians met with on this journey were as much surprised at seeing white men as the savages who greeted the landing of Columbus more than three hundred years before. In the history of their expedition, referring to this point they say: " They [the Indians] had, indeed, abundant sources of surprise in all they saw. The appearance of the men, their arms, their clothing, the canoes, the strange looks of the negro, and the sagacity of our dog, — all in turn shared their admiration, which was raised to astonishment by a shot from the air-gun : this operation was instantly considered as a great ' medicine,' by which they, as well as the other Indians, mean something emanating directly from the Great Spirit, or produced by his invisible and incomprehensible agency."

5. When Commodore Bainbridge presented himself on one occasion with the yearly tribute at Algiers, he was commanded by the Dey to proceed on some business of his to Constantinople. Upon his replying that such were not his orders, the Dey remarked : " You are under my orders ; your people are my subjects, else why do they pay me tribute?" The Commodore suggested to his government that tribute should be paid henceforth from the cannon's mouth.

6. **Commodore Edward Preble and Commodore Charles Morris** were both born in New England, and rank among the distinguished officers of the American navy. Preble died at Portland, Die., in 1807. During the war of 1812 Commodore Morris did conspicuous service. He was severely wounded in the fight between the "Constitution" and the "Guerrière" (§ 372). He died at Washington, D. C., 1856.

7. "**George Clinton** (*b.* 1739, *d.* 1812) was the undisputed leader of the popular party. He had been governor of New York since 1777, and was re-elected every other year to that office for eighteen years. . . . Able, tough, wary, a self-willed man, wielding with unusual tact the entire patronage of the state, and dear to the affections of the great mass of the people, he is an imposing figure in the politics of the time, and must ever be regarded as the Chief Dian of the state of New York during the earlier years of its independent existence." — James Parton.

8. This refers to **Harman Blennerhasset**, an Irishman of good birth and education, who brought to America considerable wealth, and built an elegant home on an island in the Ohio River below Marietta. On his way west Burr stopped at Blennerhasset's house, and, by his glowing representations and pleasant promises, easily won the Irish gentleman's support in his wicked schemes. When Burr became emperor of the southwest, Blennerhasset was to be made a duke and given the principal foreign ministry! His money and all his estates were lost in the fatal enterprise, and he died a broken-hearted old man, on the island of

Guernsey, 1831.

9. General James Wilkinson, then governor of Louisiana, is the person alluded to. He was believed by many to have been at first a sharer with Aaron Burr in his treasonable designs, but was acquitted of such complicity in a trial held in 1811. After Jefferson's proclamation, General Wilkinson used every means to arrest Burr and to defeat his plans.

10. Robert Fulton (*b*. 1765, *d*. 1815) was in his earlier years more of an artist than a mechanic, and he went to London to perfect himself in portrait-painting under the famous Benjamin West. While there he met Earl Stanhope, James Watt, and others engaged in finding practical uses for the recently invented steam-engine, and his mind was directed to the solution of the same problem. His first application of steam-power for propelling boats was on the Seine, in 1803, but the experiment was not very successful. After the success of the "Clermont," Fulton's reputation was world-wide. He built many river steamboats, and constructed the first United States steam war-vessel—named "Fulton the First." Among his inventions were an improvement in canal-locks, a submarine torpedo, and machines for marble-sawing, flax-spinning, and rope-making.

CHAPTER XXIV.
SIXTH ADMINISTRATION, A. D. 1809-1813.

James Madison, President.   *George Clinton, Vice-president.*

366. The Fourth President.—Jefferson, having followed the example of Washington in declining a third term of office, was succeeded by *James Madison,*[1] of Virginia, who was inaugurated March 4, 1809. *George Clinton,* of New York, was re-elected as Vice-president. The same principles continued to control the government, and the same harmony was visible in the cabinet.

James Madison.

367. The difficulties with England grew worse. Our harbors were blockaded by British vessels which boarded every American ship entering or leaving, and forced seamen, who were supposed to be British subjects, into their own service. Their doctrine was, "Once an Englishman, always an Englishman;" while the United States held then, as now, that a foreigner can, if he will, renounce his allegiance to his sovereign and become a citizen of the Republic.

368. At least six thousand of our seamen had been thus forced into the British navy, and nine hundred American

Impressment of Seamen.

vessels had been boarded within eight years. President Madison made every effort to maintain peace between the two countries, but in vain. War was declared by the United States in June, 1812.

The Indians of the North-west were now united in a strong confederacy under the Shawnee chief, Tecumseh,[2] and their ravages upon our frontier settlements for a year past were supposed to have been incited by British emissaries. General Harrison, having been sent to subdue them during the autumn of the preceding year, had been surprised by a night attack near the Tippecanoe; but he received it with such spirit, and his men fought so bravely, that the assailants were routed with great slaughter.

369. The first movement against the British was attended by the greatest disgrace that has ever befallen American arms. Marching from Dayton, Ohio, General Hull and 1,500 men toiled for a month through dense forests to Lake Erie, and thence to Detroit. An invasion of Canada was the object; and after a brief pause for refreshment Hull crossed the river, but learning that Mackinaw had been taken, and that a force of British and Indians was approaching, he hastily retreated.

370. Hull's Surrender.—He was soon followed by General Brock, governor of Canada, and Tecumseh, with their respective forces. The Americans were eager for a fight, but to their amazement and grief Hull raised a white flag over the fort without firing a single cannon. Not only Detroit, but all Michigan Territory was surrendered to the British. Fort Dearborn, on the present site of Chicago, was taken by Indians about the same time, and its garrison were either tomahawked or made prisoners. General Hull was tried by court-martial and sentenced to be shot as a coward, but the President spared his life.

371. The invasion of Canada by General Van Rensselaer's command was less humiliating, though scarcely more successful. Crossing Niagara River, his men drove the enemy from their position on Queenstown Heights; but the commander of the New York militia refused to leave that state to reinforce him, and though Colonel Scott[3] and his men fought bravely, they were forced to surrender themselves as prisoners of war. General Brock fell in the first action.

372. Naval Victories.—These losses on land were compensated by brilliant victories on the sea. The American navy had for years been so neglected that it could hardly be said to exist. But what was wanting in material was made up by spirit and energy. Three days after the surrender of Detroit, Captain Isaac Hull,[4] a nephew of the disgraced general, attacked the British frigate *Guerrière,*and in an action of two hours so demolished her that she could not be taken into port. Her crew and stores were removed to the victorious *Constitution*, better known by her nickname as "Old Ironsides."

373. Soon afterward the American sloop-of-war *Wasp* captured the British *Frolic*, which was convoying a fleet of merchantmen. So fierce was the forty-five minutes' battle that there was not a man on the *Frolic* able to pull down her flag. Before the *Wasp* could be put into a condition to make sail, both she and her shattered prize were taken by a seventy-four gun ship of the enemy.

These are only two of many brilliant actions that might be narrated. The President gave letters of marque to a host of **privateersmen**, which scoured every ocean and captured in seven months three hundred British merchant vessels with 3,000 prisoners. These successes gave the more surprise because Englishmen had been supposed invincible on the sea.

374. **The campaign of 1813** was arranged on nearly the same plan as that of the preceding year, but with different officers. General Dearborn, commander-in-chief of all the forces, was with the army of the center on *Niagara River;* General Harrison in the *North-west*, and General Hampton on *Lake Champlain*. As before, the only successes of any consequence were on water ; the actions of the eastern and central divisions of the army were so indecisive that they need not be recorded.

375. In the west **General Harrison** undertook the recovery of the ground which Hull had lost. A part of his forces captured Frenchtown, on Raisin River, but were defeated a. few days later by the British and Indians. The latter treated their prisoners with the usual savage brutalities, and General Proctor, who had pledged his word for the safety of the surrendered, so far from checking them, drew *off* his white troops, leaving his allies maddened by liquor and excited to butchery by the bounty which he had offered for every scalp. A few Kentuckians were dragged as prisoners to Detroit and offered for sale from door to door. Tecumseh himself reproached Proctor as unfit to be a general, and used his own influence for the protection of the captives.

376. General Harrison was twice besieged in Fort Meigs, on the Maumee, by Proctor and Tecumseh. The enemy, twice repulsed, turned to attack Fort Stephenson, on the lower Sandusky, commanded by Major Croghan, with only one hundred and fifty men; but here they were still more summarily defeated, and retired into Canada.

377. What the World thought of Americans.— During the first busy years when our new Republic was repairing the wastes of its war of independence, and obtaining a foothold among the nations, the taunting remark was often heard that Americans cared only for money-making, and had lost the spirit which had won their freedom. The gallantry with which the national honor was maintained upon the sea inspired both surprise and admiration ; and among the heroes who regained for America the world's respect, none was braver than James Lawrence.[5]

378. In command of the *Hornet* he vanquished the British brig *Peacock* in a fifteen minutes' fight *off* Guiana. Re-

"Don't give up the Ship."

turning home he was transferred to the *Chesapeake*, then undergoing repairs in Boston Harbor. Here he was challenged by the British flagship *Shannon* to come out and fight. The *Chesapeake* was only partly manned and unready for action, but following his first brave impulse he put to sea. He was mortally wounded early in the action, but as he was carried below he cried with dying breath, "Don't give up the ship!" That order could not be obeyed, but the spirit of it inspired many a future victory.

379. The United States brig *Argus*, after taking twenty merchantmen, was herself captured by the *Pelican* in August, 1813. Captain David Porter, of the *Essex*, passing around Cape Horn into the Pacific Ocean, made prizes of twelve English ships and several hundreds of sailors, many of whom were glad to take service as

Americans. A little fleet was thus formed which protected the American whaling ships in the Pacific. The *Essex* was finally taken when in a friendly harbor, and Captain Porter wrote home, ' ' We are unfortunate, but not disgraced.

380. The Great Lakes were still controlled by the British, who possessed Michigan and threatened Ohio. Captain Oliver H. Perry[6] was commissioned to dispute that control. He had first to create a fleet from the forests on Lake Erie, while sailors were brought overland in stage-coaches. Scarcely were his nine ships ready for action when the British fleet bore down upon him near Put-in Bay. Perry's flag-ship, the *Lawrence*, bore at her mast-head a pennon inscribed, "Don't give up the ship!"

381. Battle of Lake Erie.—The battle was severe, and the *Lawrence*, having fought two of the British squadron at once, was riddled and shattered. Perry, seizing his flag, sprang into a boat and was rowed to the *Niagara*, whence he ordered a fresh onset upon the enemy's line. He won a complete victory, and went back to the sinking *Lawrence* to receive the surrender upon her deck. Then he wrote to General Harrison: " We have met the enemy and they are ours,—two ships, two brigs, one schooner, and one sloop."

382. It was the first time that a whole British squadron had surrendered, and the news was received with pride and joy throughout the country. In fact, it virtually ended the war, for it led to the breaking up of the Indian confederacy and the recovery of all the land lost by Hull's surrender.

383. Harrison crossed into Canada and hotly pursued the British, whom he overtook near the River Thames. The Kentuckians rushed into the battle crying, " Remember the Raisin ! " Proctor fled. His men laid down their arms, and were spared. Tecumseh spurred on his warriors with his war-whoop, resounding above the roar of musketry, but suddenly it ceased. Then the savages knew that their leader was dead, and they sought refuge in the Canadian forests.

In 1812 the Territory of Orleans (§359) was organized into the state of *Louisiana,* and was admitted into the American Union.

NOTES.

1. **James Madison** (*b.* 1751, *d.* 1836) was born at King George, Va., of English descent. He had unusual educational advantages from his earliest years, and after graduating at Princeton, when twenty years of age, he pursued au extensive course of study, embracing law, theology, philosophy, and general literature. At this period of his life he permanently impaired his bodily vigor by over-study, and by allowing himself only three or four hours' sleep each day. He interested himself at once in politics, and in 1776 was elected a member of the Virginia Convention. On the return of Jefferson from France, Madison was offered that mission, but declined it. He also refused the position of Secretary of State when Jefferson vacated it, feeling that he would create a discord in Washington's cabinet. At the time of the Constituent Convention he was an ardent Federalist, but later changed his views, and was before long recognized as the leader of the Democratic party. When Jefferson was elected President, Madison became Secretary of State, and retained the office eight years.

Madison's contributions to the " Federalist," and his state papers generally, are considered among the most able productions of American statesmen. His writings have been purchased and published by the general government. Thomas Jefferson, in his Autobiography, has left the following estimate of his successor:

" Mr. Madison came into the House in 1776, a new member and young; which circumstances, concurring with his extreme modesty, prevented his venturing himself in debate before his removal to the Council of State in November, '77. From thence he went to Congress, then consisting of few members. Trained in these successive schools, he acquired a habit of self-possession which placed at ready command the rich resources of his luminous and discriminating mind, and of his extensive information, and rendered him the first of every assembly afterwards of which he was a member. Never wandering from his subject into vain declamation, but pursuing it closely, in language pure, classical, and copious, soothing always the feelings of his adversaries by civilities and softness of expression, he rose to the eminent station which he held in the great National Convention of 17S7 (§314) ; and in that of Virginia which followed, he sustained the new Constitution in all its parts, bearing off the palm against the logic of George Mason, and the fervid declamation of Mr. Henry. With these consummate powers were united a pure and spotless virtue which no calumny has ever attempted to sully. Of the powers and polish of his pen, and of the wisdom of his administration in the highest office of the nation I need say nothing. They have spoken, and will forever speak for themselves."

At the. close of his presidential career Madison retired to his farm of " Montpelier," in Virginia, and devoted himself to the agricultural interests of the county. For a long period he acted as visitor and rector of the University of Virginia. Madison's last public service was in 1829, when he was a member of the Virginia Convention to remodel the state constitution. His presence produced a great sensation, but from his age and infirmities he was unable to take part in the debate.

2. Tecumseh was born near the present town of Springfield, Ohio, about 1768. He and his brother, who assumed to be a prophet, endeavored, in 1805, to unite all the western tribes into one nation against the whites. They had partially succeeded, when the defeat of the prophet at Tippecanoe, in 1811, prevented further steps in that direction.

3. This was Winfield Scott, who afterwards became a celebrated general. See Note 4, page 259.

4. Isaac Hull (*b.* 1775, *d.* 184.3), the son of a Revolutionary officer, was born at Derby, Conn., and when nineteen years old became master of a merchant vessel. When troubles with France arose, in 1798, he entered the navy as a lieutenant, and distinguished himself by several daring exploits. His defeat and capture of the " Guerrière " was felt to be of the greatest importance, as it was the first naval action of the war.

5. James Lawrence (*b.* 1781, *d.* 1813) was born in Burlington, N. J., and entered the navy as a midshipman when seventeen years old. In the war with Tripoli' he served with distinction, and took part in the destruction of the "Philadelphia" (§360). Congress rewarded him with a gold medal for his capture of the " Peacock."

6. Oliver Hazard Perry (*b.* 1785, *d.* 1819) was born in Newport, R. I., and in 1799 first saw active service in the navy as a midshipman on the frigate " General Greene," under the command of his father. The battle of Lake Erie was his greatest achievement, although he did good service throughout the war. In 1819, while cruising on the Columbia coast, South America, he contracted yellow fever, and died just as his vessel reached Port Spain, on the island of Trinidad.

CHAPTER XXV.
SEVENTH ADMINISTRATION, A. D. 1813-1817.

James Madison, President.   Elbridge Gerry, Vice-president.

384. **The southern Indians** had this summer surprised Fort Mimms, in Alabama, and murdered men, women, and children to the number of nearly four hundred. The volunteer troops of Georgia, Mississippi, and Tennessee mustered to avenge the massacre, and among them General Jackson gained confidence by his quick, decisive movements. Several victories were won in the autumn of 1813, and in spite of hardships,—the men having sometimes no food but acorns,— Jackson resolved to hold the country all winter. In March the last battle was fought at Horse-shoe Bend, where a thousand Creek warriors, with many women and children of their tribe, were slain without pity. The Holy Ground of the Creeks, which they had thought could never be taken, passed into the possession of their conquerors.

385. Burning of Washington. — During these two years the British visited the coasts of Maryland, Virginia, and the Carolinas, more in the character of pirates and plunderers than of honorable warriors,—burning villages and farm buildings, robbing churches, and even murdering the sick in their beds. Meeting very little opposition, General Ross, in 1814, marched to Washington and destroyed most of the buildings and records belonging to the government, together with much private property.[1]

386. Bombardment of Baltimore.—Both fleet and army then advanced upon Baltimore, but the city was well defended by the Maryland militia, while Fort McHenry withstood a storm of balls and bombs, which lasted from sunrise until after midnight, without the slightest apparent injury. It was during this bombardment that Francis S. Key, an American patriot, detained on board the British fleet, wrote the "Star Spangled Banner." Failing of their purpose, the enemy withdrew. It is only fair to say that Admiral Cockburn,[2] the chief marauder, was denounced by some of the best people in his own country as a disgrace to the British navy.

387. The New England States suffered even more than the Southern, for their commerce and fisheries were broken up by a strict blockade. The light-houses were kept in darkness, as they served only as guides to the enemy. Owing to a temporary peace in Europe, the British were largely reinforced in 1814, and American operations were mainly defensive.

Oswego was attacked in May by a force from Canada, and Colonel Mitchell, unable to defend it, withdrew his garrison. The enemy burned the barracks, dismantled the works, and retired. The spirit of the Americans rose with difficulties. On the third of July they captured Fort Erie, opposite Buffalo, and two days later defeated General Riall at Chippewa, after a hard-fought battle.

388. Lundy's Lane.—Three weeks later Generals Brown[3] and Scott gained a brilliant victory at Lundy's Lane, near Niagara Falls, where General Riall was made a prisoner. Seeing that a hill crowned with cannon was the key to the British position, General Brown said to Colonel James Miller,[4] "Colonel, take your regiment, storm that work, and take it." "I'll try, sir," was the reply, and marching steadily up the hill, he took it.

389. The British made repeated attempts to regain Fort Erie. Early in August they commenced a regular siege

Battle of Lundy's Lane.

which lasted more than six weeks; but on the 17th of September a spirited sortie was made by the garrison, resulting, after a severe contest, in the capture of all the British works. Quitting the siege in disgust, General Drummond marched away, and the attempt was not renewed. In November the fort was demolished, and the American army retired to winter-quarters at Buffalo and Black Rock.

390. **War unpopular in New England.**—From the beginning the war had been unpopular in New England, where the Federalists were most numerous. The English thought it possible to separate the eastern from the southern states, and even to win them back to their old obedience. To this end they planned in the campaign of 1814 to repeat the movement of Burgoyne (§262). An army of 14,000 men and a fleet of gun-boats entered the state of New York by way of Lake Champlain.

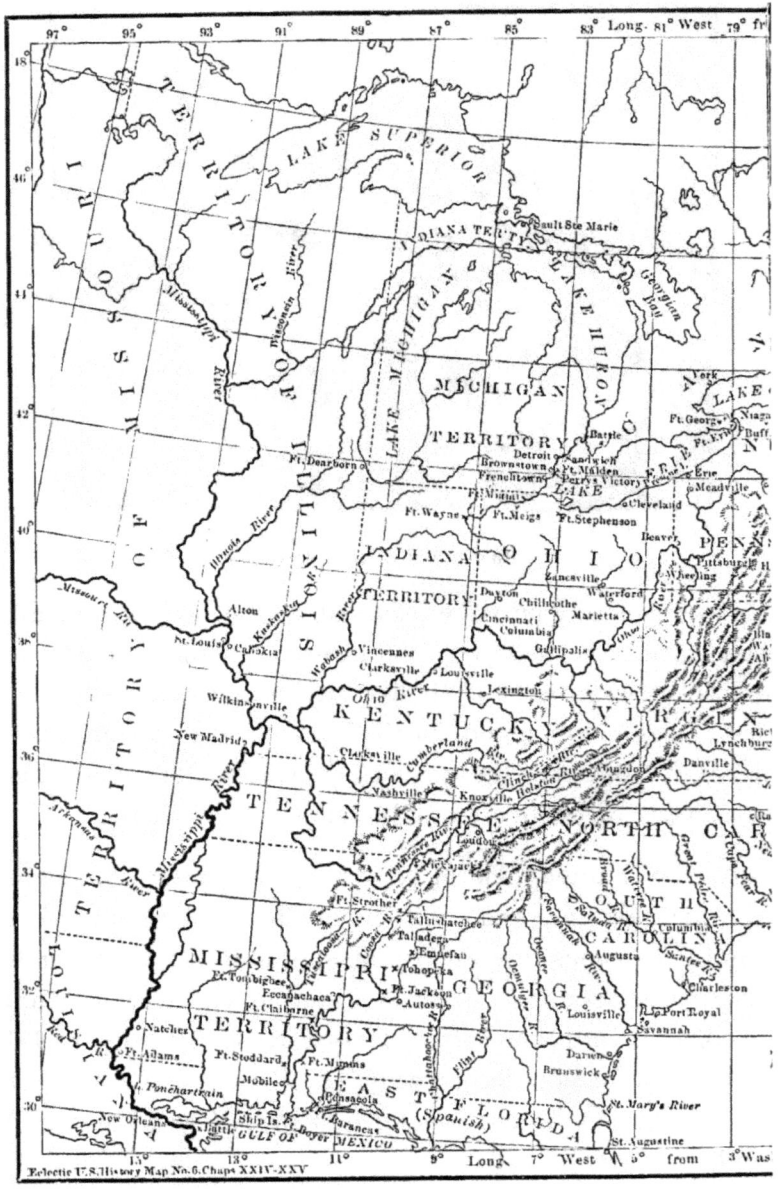

391. Battle of Plattsburgh. — They were met near Plattsburgh by Commodore McDonough[5] on the lake and by General Macomb[6] on land. The naval battle lasted only two hours, but the American victory was complete. The British commodore was killed ; his larger vessels were captured. The combat on land was equally severe, but it ended in success for the Americans, and the invading forces marched back into Canada.

392. The Hartford Convention. — The opposition in New England to a continuance of the war had now reached its height. In December some of the leading Federalists held a convention at Hartford. Its consultations were secret, and its enemies considered them disloyal. In the joy of the success at Plattsburgh, most people had become better affected toward the war, and the Federal party lost much ground in consequence of the Hartford Convention.

393. Treaty of Ghent. — Before its sessions were ended peace had been signed at Ghent by the commissioners of the United States and Great Britain. But as ocean steamers and telegraphs were not yet in existence. a needless battle was fought below New Orleans before the news arrived in America.

394. Learning that the British were about to attack the city, **General Andrew Jackson** marched thither with the same forces that had subdued the Creeks (§384). Nine miles below New Orleans he formed a breastwork, chiefly of cotton-bales and sand-bags. Here he was attacked, January 8, by General Pakenham and his veteran army of 12,000 men, most of whom had been trained in the wars with Napoleon. To oppose them Jackson had less than half that number of undisciplined troops, but among these were the sharp-shooters of Kentucky and Tennessee.

395. Battle of New Orleans. — The British advanced in splendid order under the fire of the American cannon, but as soon as they came within rifle-range they wavered, and their brilliant columns were strewn upon the plain. They were rallied, but only to break again, and fall under the deadly aim of the marksmen. Pakenham was killed, and his two next officers were severely wounded. The British captured one important battery, but they could not follow up their success, and the American victory was one of the most complete of the war. After a loss of more than 2,000 men the invaders withdrew to Lake Borgne, and soon afterward embarked for Jamaica.

396. The news of peace was hailed with irrepressible joy by the whole nation. Bells rang merrily; bonfires blazed ; messengers on fleet horses spurred to inland villages, shouting the glad tidings as they rode. The "Second War of American Independence" had commanded the respect of other nations, and though the "right of search" was not mentioned in the treaty of Ghent, it was never again asserted by Great Britain.

397. The Barbary States had taken advantage of the war to renew their attacks upon vessels of the United States. Commodore Decatur[7] was sent with a squadron to mend their behavior. Having captured two of the largest Algerine frigates, he sailed successively into the harbors of Algiers, Tunis, and Tripoli, where he obtained the release of all American prisoners, and payment for some, at least, of the losses inflicted by the pirates, and put an end forever to claims of tribute from the United States.

398. Great distress followed the war. While cut off from all trade with Europe, Americans had employed their money in manufactures, which for a few years were very prosperous. As soon as the war was over, and the superior but cheaper fabrics of France and England began to flood our markets, home manufactures were ruined. To protect our rising industries, and at the same time meet the interest of a war debt of a hundred millions, duties were imposed on foreign goods entering our ports. This "American System," as it was called, of protection for home industries, found favor with the Federalist party and the manufacturing states; while the agricultural states and the Democratic party have usually favored free trade.

399. In 1816 *Indiana* became the nineteenth state in the Union. *Michigan* had been organized as a separate *Territory* in 1805, and *Illinois,* including Wisconsin, in 1809.

Read Jefferson's Works, Vol. I.; Benton's "Thirty Years in the United States Senate," Vol. I. ; Hildreth's " History of the United States;" Cooper's "History of the American Navy;" Lossing's "Field Book of the War of 1812; " Life of Madison in "National Gallery of Distinguished Americans," Vol. II.

NOTES.

1. The British force numbered 4,000. The news of their approach created a panic, and the undisciplined and inexperienced militia, hurriedly gathered to oppose them, tied at the first lire. "Such," says Hildreth, "was the famous battle of Bladensburg, in which very few Americans had the honor to be either killed or wounded, not more than fifty in all ; and yet, according to the evidence subsequently given before a congressional committee of investigation, every body behaved with wonderful courage and coolness, and nobody retired except by orders or for want of orders."

2. This was Sir George Cockburn (*b.* 1772, *d.* 1853), who afterwards rose to the highest rank in the English navy, and served in several important official positions. In 1815 he carried out the sentence of Napoleon, conveying him to St. Helena on board his ship.

3. General Jacob Brown (*b.* 1775, *d.* 1828) was of Quaker origin, and was born in Pennsylvania, but at the time of the war of 1812 was a resident of the state of New York. Throughout the war he maintained a reputation for great bravery and military skill, and at its close he received a gold medal and a vote of thanks from Congress. He remained in the regular army after peace was declared, and finally attained the chief command. Brownsville, on the site of his estate in Jefferson County, New York, is named after him.

4. James Miller was born at Peterborough, New Hampshire, in 1776, and was educated for the profession of law; but finding it distasteful, he entered the United States army, in 1808, with the commission of major. He was distinguished throughout the War of 1812 for his remarkable bravery, and this exploit at Lundy's Lane won for him the rank of brevet brigadier-general and a gold medal from Congress bearing the motto, "I'll try." This battle was fought on a dim moonlight night, and Miller's command succeeded in creeping up the hill in the shadow of an old rail-fence undiscovered by the British until almost upon them. Miller resigned his commission in 1819 to accept the governorship of Arkansas; he held this position six years, and was then made collector of the port at Salem, Mass. He held the latter office until 1849, when he was disabled by paralysis, and in 1851 a second stroke of the disease killed him.

5. **Commodore Thomas McDonough** (*b.* 1783, *d.* 1825) was born in New Castle County, Delaware, and entered the navy as a midshipman when sixteen years of age. He was one of the officers of the "Philadelphia," and only eseaped capture by the Algerines through having been left with a prize at Gibraltar. He afterwards assisted, under Decatur, in recapturing and burning his old vessel (§ 360). His victory on Lake Champlain was rewarded by Congress with a gold medal, and by various cities and towns with civic honors. The state of Vermont presented him with a tract of land overlooking the seene of his victory, lie died on board a vessel sent to bring him home from his command of the Mediterranean squadron, to which he had been appointed after the War of 1812.

6. **General Alexander Macomb** (*b.* 1782, d. 1841), a native of Detroit, was an officer of the United States army from his seventeenth year until his death, beginning as a cornet of cavalry and ending as major-general in command of the army. The battle of Plattsburgh was his greatest achievement, and won him a vote of thanks and gold medal from Congress, as well as his brevet as major-general.

7. **Commodore Stephen Decatur** was the son of a naval officer of the Revolution, and was born at Sinncpnxcnt, Maryland, in 1779. When twenty years old he entered the navy, and a few years later brought himself prominently into notice by recapturing and burning the "Philadelphia " (§360). For this exploit he was at once promoted to a captainey, and served with distinction in succeeding actions during the Tripolitan War. His greatest victory in the War of 1812 was the capture of the "Macedonian," an English frigate, after a stubborn tight of an hour and a half. For this action Congress voted a gold medal to Deeatur, and a silver one to each commissioned officer under him. In 1820 he had a correspondence with Commodore Barron in reference to the affair of the "Chesapeake" and "Leopard," § 364 (Barron having commanded the former vessel), which resulted in a duel between the two officers: both fell at the first fire. Decatur was wounded mortally, and died within twenty-four hours. Barron recovered.

CHAPTER XXVI.
EIGHTH AND NINTH ADMINISTRATIONS, A. D. 1817-1825.

James Monroe, President. *Daniel D. Tompkins, Vice-president.*

400. The Fifth President.—*James Monroe,*[1] *of* Virginia, the fifth President of the United States, had a happy and popular administration. The country speedily recovered from the disasters occasioned by the war; the fame of its rich, unoccupied lands drew a tide of immigrants from Europe, whose labor helped to develop the natural wealth of the country, and, by making roads, bridges, and canals, to supply outlets for its productions.

James Monroe.

401. Slavery.—In colonial times negroes had been held as slaves in the North as well as the South (§148); but while corn and most of the northern products could be more profitably raised by free laborers,—cotton, rice, sugar, and tobacco, the four chief staples of the South, were supposed to require the labor of slaves (§135). Notwithstanding this there had been opposition to the introduction and extension of slavery by the South itself from the earliest colonial times (§§152, 148). The Federal Constitution did not mention slaves, but left to each state existing at the time of its adoption, the duty of making or modifying laws concerning them. The territories being under the direct government of Congress, this question had to be decided for them and for all states to be formed from them.

Henry Clay.

402. The Missouri Compromise.—Thomas Jefferson, a slave owner, made the first proposition in Congress to restrict slavery in 1784. It then failed to pass, but when the North-west Territory was organized, in 1787, slavery was there prohibited by a unanimous vote of Congress, and the act was approved by Washington. One northern state after another emancipated its slaves, and the boundary line of slavery separating the North and the South became more strictly defined. In 1817 the state of *Mississippi* was admitted to the Union; *Illinois* followed in 1818, *Alabama* in 1819, and *Mame* in 1820. Upon the application of *Missouri* for leave to form a state constitution, the important question arose in Congress whether any more slave-states should be admitted. After long discussion it was supposed to be settled by the *Missouri Compromise,* which admitted that state with its slaves, but prohibited the extension of slavery into any territory of the United States north of 36° 30' north latitude.

Henry Clay,[2] of Kentucky, was the chief advocate of the compromise, and he used all his eloquence in calming the angry passions which the discussion had excited, and in promoting peace and brotherly confidence.

403. Events of 1819, — *The first ocean steamer* crossed the Atlantic, from Savannah to Liverpool, in 1819. The same year a treaty was made by which *Spain ceded Florida, of* which she had again obtained possession (§ 193), to the United States, the latter undertaking to pay five millions of dollars due from the former power to American citizens. Florida became a territory under the control of Congress, and the President appointed General Jackson to be its governor.

404. The Monroe Doctrine. — A ten years' revolution had now resulted in the separation of most of the Spanish colonies from their mother-country (§299). In recognizing Mexico and five South American republics as independent states, President Monroe announced the principle of his foreign policy: "The American continents, by the free and independent position which they have assumed and maintained, are not to be considered as subject to future colonization by any foreign power." "Friendship with all, entangling alliances with none," has been the spirit of international relations founded upon the "Monroe Doctrine."

La Fayette.

At the close of his first term **Mr. Monroe was reelected** by the votes of every state.

405. Visit of La Fayette.—In 1824 La Fayette, then an old man, revisited the country which in his youth he had aided to make free. Every-where he was welcomed by tokens of the gratitude and love of the people. He stood with reverent affection at the tomb of Washington; he laid the corner-stone of Bunker Hill Monument on the spot where Warren had fallen fifty years before; and when he returned home, it was in a national frigate, named *The Brandywine* in honor of his first battle in the cause of American freedom.

406. Removal of Indians.—In 1825 Mr. Monroe recommended to Congress the removal of all Indian tribes to the country west of the Mississippi, far beyond the limits of the states and territories then existing. The Creeks and Cherokees of Georgia had so improved their lands that they were unwilling to remove. At last, however, terms were agreed upon,—a large sum of money to be paid by the United States, with a guarantee of undisturbed possession of lands in the *Indian Territory*,—and under the two following presidents the removal was effected.

407. The Cherokees, owning immense numbers of cattle, horses, hogs, and sheep, were the most civilized of all the tribes. Mills, salt works, churches, schools, and well- ordered farms soon rewarded their industry in their western homes. Native merchants sold the cotton and other products of their lands for merchandise. Spinning, weaving, and other mechanical arts found place among them, though planting and cattle-raising are their chief employments. Many of their men are highly educated, and their government is carried on under written laws with a dignity and propriety not always to be found among people longer civilized.

408. The Creeks are less united, each chief having his own village and retainers; but they, too, are peaceful cultivators of the soil, and export great quantities of grain. They are less given to manufactures than the Cherokees.

Read Monroe's "Tour of Observation through the North-eastern and North-western states in 1817;" Life of Monroe in "National Portrait Gallery of Distinguished Americans," Vol. II.

NOTES.

1. **James Monroe** (*b*.1758, *d*. 1831) was a Virginian by birth, and was educated at William and Mary College. During the Revolution he fought as a subordinate officer at Trenton, Brandywine, Germantown, and Monmouth, and after the war took a prominent part in politics, both in the Virginia Assembly and in Congress. He appreciated the weakness and inefficiency of the general government under the tirst articles of confederation, and the Constituent Convention (§ 314) was the ultimate result of his motion in Congress to invest that body with the power to regulate trade between the states. However, in the Virginia Convention he strongly opposed the adoption of the Constitution as submitted, thinking it conferred too much power on the general government. His conduct as minister plenipotentiary to France, to which office lie was appointed in 1794, greatly offended the administration, whose policy he opposed, and he was recalled. From 1799 to 1802 he was governor of Virginia, and was then sent by Jefferson to negotiate for the purchase of Louisiana. In 1811 he was again elected governor of Virginia, and during the same year was appointed by Madison as his Secretary of State. He also held the position of Secretary of War at the same time, and finding the treasury empty, he pledged his own means in order to secure the defense of New Orleans. Under Monroe's administration party lines disappeared, and the period came to be known as " the era of good feeling." He was a man of sterling character, and worked earnestly for the good of the whole country. His administration gave new life to every branch of the publie service, and the resources of the country were developed in an unprecedented manner. He died in New York City July 4th, 1831, and was buried there ; but in 1858 his remains were removed in state to Richmond, Virginia, and there re-interred in the Hollywood Cemetery.

2. **Henry Clay** (*b*. 1777, *d*. 1852) was born near Richmond, Va. His father, a Baptist preacher, died when Henry was five years old. His mother married a second time, and removed to Kentucky, leaving Henry at work as clerk in a retail store in Richmond. He soon abandoned this

position, however, and became a copyist in a law office. Licensed as a lawyer in 1797, he removed to Lexington, Ky., and soon established a flourishing practice through his remarkable power of influencing juries. He took a prominent part in the discussion over the constitution drawn up for the state of Kentucky, and in 1803 was chosen a member of the state legislature. In 1806, although hardly of legal age, Clay was chosen to till a vacancy in the United States Senate. Here he made an Impression by warmly advocating the policy of internal improvement. The following year he was again elected to the legislature of Kentucky and was appointed speaker. While in this office he was accused as a demagogue by Mr. Humphrey Marshall; a duel ensued, in which both parties were wounded. Clay's popularity continuing, he was sent to the House of Representatives in 1811, and at his first appearance was made speaker, an honor unprecedented since the meeting of the first Congress. He was a strong advocate for the war against Great Britain, and, in fact, may be said to have forced Madison into his declaration ; at its close he was sent to negotiate the peace of Ghent (§ 393). Clay's weighty speeches also brought about the recognition of the South American states (§ 404). In 1824 five candidates were nominated for the presidency, Clay being one of them. As no one received the requisite number of votes, Congress had to choose among the three highest candidates, Andrew Jackson, John Quincy Adams, and William H. Crawford. Clay and his friends voted for Adams, who was elected, and when the latter appointed Clay his Secretary of State the cry of "Bargain!" was immediately raised. This charge occasioned a duel between Clay and John Randolph, in which neither was hurt. Clay had retired from public life in 1842, but in 1848 he was again sent to the Senate, where he struggled hard to avert the great battle on the slavery question. Unfortunately his health gave way, and in 1851 he was compelled to retire to private life, and in the following year, on the twenty-ninth of July, he died. Congress adjourned on the news of his death, and the following day eulogies were delivered in both Senate and House. New York and the chief cities of Kentucky honored the day of his funeral.

CHAPTER XXVII.
TENTH ADMINISTRATION, A. D. 1825-1829.

John Quincy Adams, President.   *John C. Calhoun, Vice-president.*

409. **The Sixth President.**—Among four candidates for the presidency in the autumn of 1824, the electors failed to make a choice; the decision, therefore, devolved again (§ 350) upon the House of Representatives, and *John Quincy Adams*,[1] of Massachusetts, son of the second President (§ 340), received the highest office in the gift of the people. *John C. Calhoun*,[2] of South Carolina, was Vice-president, and Henry Clay became Secretary of State.

410. **Character of the Younger Adams.**—Trained from his childhood in the service of his country, the new President was a statesman of great ability and of upright character. He had filled several important foreign missions, and had been at different times senator and Secretary of State. Nevertheless his administration, though peaceful and prosperous, was not altogether popular. With the multiplication of industries the conflict of interests became more violent.

411. **Public Improvements.**—One party desired that Congress should appropriate money for great public works which were needed to develop the resources of the country; the other insisted that each section must take care of itself. The greatest of these works then in progress was the Erie Canal, which connects the waters of Lake Erie with Hudson River, and the grain-fields of the West with the markets of Europe. It was formally opened in October, 1825, when the Governor of New York and many guests sailed from Buffalo to the city of New York, in a state-barge attended by music and the roar of cannon.

412. Within a few years the *first steam locomotive* in the United

States was put in service on the "Dela-ware and Hudson Canal Railroad." Steam was soon introduced on the "Baltimore and Ohio" and the "Albany and Schenectady" railroads, and on that of South Carolina from Charleston to Hamburg. Gradually the iron network overspread the whole country, and the remotest corners of the land were brought into Swift and constant communication with the great cities of the coast.

John Quincy Adams.

413.   The semi-centennial of American Independence was celebrated with joy and gratitude, July 4, 1826. On that day the President's venerable father and Thomas Jefferson died at their widely separated homes, in Massachusetts and Virginia. Fifty years before both had set their names to the Declaration which gave their country her rightful place among the nations; both bad served her in missions abroad and in the highest office at home.

414.   The President absolutely refused to employ the influence of the government to secure his re-election: he was opposed by many of his own officers, and *General Andrew Jackson* received the greatest number of votes. Soon after his retirement from the presidency, Mr. Adams returned to Washington as representative from Massachusetts. He served his native state in that office until 1848, when he died at his post in the Capitol. He had been in high public service fifty-three years.

NOTES.

1. **John Quincy Adams** was born at Braintree, Mass., July, 1767. As a boy he was very precocious, and attracted attention wherever he went for his vigor of mind and body. At the age of eleven he accompanied his father to France, and was placed at school in Paris. In the summer of 1780 he went with his father to Holland and entered the University of Leyden. For fourteen months he was private secretary to the American minister to Russia, and after this service he made the tour of Sweden, Norway, the Netherlands, France, and England. He was a youth of keen powers of observation, and kept a faithful record of all that he saw and heard in these foreign lauds. Returning to America, young Adams entered the junior class at Harvard College, and graduated in 1788. Three years later lie was admitted to the Boston bar. A series of trenchant political letters which he contributed to the newspapers about this time drew attention to Adams as a man of more than ordinary power. President Washington appointed him minister to The Hague, and later to Portugal. In 1797 he was married to Miss Johnson, and was transferred by his father — then President — to Berlin. In 1803 he was chosen United States senator by the Federalists. In 1809 he was appointed minister to Russia. He negotiated commercial treaties with Prussia, Sweden, and Great Britain, and was the most conspicuous of the American commissioners in the important treaty of Ghent, 1814. He was President Monroe's Secretary of State during the eight years of his administration, which position he filled with signal ability. In the presidential election of 1824 the three candidates besides John Quincy Adams were Andrew Jackson, Henry Clay, and William H. Crawford — all four belonging to the same political party. Jackson received ninety-nine electoral votes, Adams eighty-four, Crawford forty-one, and Clay thirty-seven. Henry Clay threw his influence in favor of Adams, which secured his election. The friends of the other two defeated candidates formed a coalition against the new President which made his office very uncomfortable, and insured his defeat for a second term. He entered Congress in 1831, and ably represented his district for seventeen years, until stricken with death on the floor of the House of Representatives February 21st, 1848. "John Quincy Adams," says the Hon. George S. Hilliard, " had more learning, perhaps, but John Adams had much more genius. In energy, spirit, firmness, and indomitable courage, John Q. Adams was his father's equal; in selfcommand, in political prudence, and even, perhaps, in capacity for hard work, his superior. In some

respects the son was far more fortunate than the father. The brilliant period of his career was towards its close. The longer he lived the higher he rose, and he died as such men prefer to die, still an admired and trusted champion, with harness on his back and spear in hand." Adams's strength in debate while in Congress gained for him the title of "the old man eloquent."

2. **John Caldwell Calhoun** (*b*. 1782, *d*. 1850). This great statesman, and champion of southern rights and opinions, was born in Abbeville District, South Carolina. His ancestors on both sides were Irish Presbyterians. In youth he was very studious, and made the best use of such opportunities for education as the frontier settlement afforded. He graduated at Yale College in 1801, and studied law at Litchfield, Connecticut. In 1808 he was elected to the legislature of South Carolina; and, three years later, he was chosen to the national House of Representatives. During the six years that he remained In the House, he took an active and prominent part in the stirring events of the time. In 1817 he was appointed Secretary of War, and held the office seven years. From 1825 to 1832 he was Vice-president of the United States. He then resigned this office, and took his seat as senator from South Carolina. In 1844 President Tyler called him to his cabinet as Secretary of State ; and, in 1845, he returned to the Senate, where he remained till his death. During all his public life Mr. Calhoun was active and out-spoken. His earnestness and logical force commanded the respect of those who differed most widely from him in opinion. He took the most advanced ground in favor of "State Rights," and defended slavery as neither morally nor politically wrong. His foes generally conceded his honesty, and respected his ability; while his friends regarded him as little less than an oracle.

CHAPTER XXVIII.
ELEVENTH AND TWELFTH ADMINISTRATIONS, A. D. 1829-1837.

Andrew Jackson, Pres.   *John C. Calhoun, Martin Van Buren, Vice-pres.*

415. The Seventh President. — President Jackson[1] differed from his predecessor in his lack of education and early advantages; but he was a successful and popular general, and no man doubted his courage, honesty, or energy of will. He began by making a clean sweep of all public offices, dismissing ten times more men in one year than all former presidents had removed since the adoption of the Constitution. Their places were filled by his political friends. The '' system of rotation," thus begun, has ever since prevailed, on the principle that "the spoils of the enemy belong to the victor."

Andrew Jackson.

416. Violent debates arose in Congress on questions concerning the public lands and the raising of a revenue for the government. The opposing interests of the North and the South now became more fiercely clamorous. Daniel Webster,[2] of Massachusetts, and Robert Hayne,[3] of South Carolina, argued with great eloquence, the one for "Liberty and Union, now find forever," the other for "State

Rights" of nullification or secession.

417. In 1832 additional duties were imposed by Congress upon foreign goods. A convention in South Carolina declared the act to be null, and prepared to resist at Charleston the collection of the duties. The legislature of that state even threatened to secede and place Mr. Calhoun, then Vice-president of the United States, at the head of a "Southern Confederacy" in case the government should attempt to enforce its laws. But the prompt appearance of war vessels and an army under General Scott proved the sincerity and the power of the government. Mr. Clay exerted his peacemaking influence in another compromise bill, providing for a gradual reduction of duties, and the excitement was allayed.

John C. Calhoun.

418. Several Indian disturbances occurred during this administration. The *Sacs* and *Foxes* of Illinois had sold their lands to the United States; but they refused to remove, and, in concert with the *Winnebagoes* of Wisconsin, attacked the miners who were now congregating in the rich lead region about Galena. The Indians were defeated in several battles by government troops, and in 1832 their noted chief, Black Hawk, with others, was taken as a captive to Washington. Having witnessed the power and wealth of the United

States as displayed in the eastern cities, the chiefs returned and counseled their people to lay down their arms. The Winnebagoes, as well as the Sacs and Foxes, now exchanged their lands for tracts west of the Mississippi, with yearly supplies of money and provisions.

419. The Seminole war was longer and more obstinate. The everglades of Florida afforded refuge to many fugitive slaves, who, marrying Seminoles, became closely allied with them in interests, and increased their power. A daughter of one of these marriages was the wife of *Osceola,* a famous and powerful chief. Nevertheless, in visiting with her husband a United States fort, she was seized and carried away as the slave of a family from whom her mother had escaped. Her husband, expressing his rage, was thrown into irons.

Daniel Webster.

420. Osceola's Vengeance. — Meanwhile a treaty had been made with certain chiefs for the removal of the Seminoles to lands west of the Mississippi. Osceola pretended to consent, and was released ; but it was only to plot a terrible vengeance against the whites. General Thompson, who had so grossly ill-used him, was surprised and killed; a hundred men under Major Dade were massacred the same day in Wahoo Swamp. The war was relentless on both sides. Osceola was taken at length by treachery, and died of fever in Fort Moultrie. His people kept up their resistance for seven years, in impenetrable marshes, whose noxious vapors fought for them, destroying thousands of lives among their assailants. Generals Scott and Taylor at length completed the work which Jackson had begun, and the Avar ended in 1842, after a cost of thirty millions of dollars and innumerable lives.

421. No President has ever made so unsparing use of his *veto power* as did Jackson. Congress having passed an act renewing the charter of the United States Bank, which was to expire in 1836, he refused his signature, and proceeded of his own authority against the advice of his cabinet, to remove the public funds deposited in its vaults.

422. Prosperous Times.—These funds were distributed among eighty-nine banks of deposit in various states, which lent them out on easy terms to merchants and farmers, and thus increased the mania for wild speculations which had taken possession of every class. Public lands were bought to the amount of $24,000,000 in a year. Villages and even cities were laid out by hundreds; great works were projected, and state debts were incurred for their completion. Foreign goods were imported in greater quantities than ever before. Foreign immigrants thronged to the fertile lands of the North-west. Foreign capital, disturbed by revolutions in Europe, sought investments here. Proud of its great, rich territory, and of its rapid growth in wealth, the "universal Yankee nation" doubtless offended the taste of its less fortunate contemporaries, and acquired a reputation for conceit which it has not even yet lived down.

423. A Full Treasury.—The government was not only out of debt, but had in the banks a surplus of $37,000,000 beyond all needful reserves. This was distributed among the several states for public uses, the principal to be returned when called for. The Middle and Western states used this additional income in the improvement of thoroughfares and the perfecting of their systems of public schools; the

Southern States, largely, in increasing the area of cotton production; for the improved mill machinery of England demanded, at good prices, all the cotton that American fields could furnish.

424. The Specie Circular.—While the banks were embarrassed by the withdrawal of the government money, President Jackson issued his famous *Specie Circular,* requiring all payments for public lands to be made in coin. This was only a reasonable precaution, for such a multitude of banks had been founded for mere speculation that their notes might easily become worthless, but in the excited state of the money market it hastened a crisis of which we shall learn in the next chapter.

425. Troubles with France.—The President's foreign policy was equally energetic and decisive. The king of France had agreed in 1831 to pay $5,000,000 for damage done to American commerce during the wars of Napoleon. Payment being delayed, President Jackson proposed to make reprisals on French merchant ships. England then intervened as mediator; France paid her debts, and war was averted.

426. At the autumn election of 1836 *Martin Van Buren,* of New York, was chosen to be President. The electors failed to unite upon a Vice-president, and the Senate chose for it's presiding officer Colonel Richard M. Johnson, of Kentucky. *Arkansas* was admitted as a state in June, 1836; *Michigan* in the following January.

Read "Lives" of Jackson by Eaton, Cobbett, or Kendall. Account of his administration in Williams's and Lossing's "National History of the United States."

NOTES.

1. Andrew Jackson was born at the waxhaw settlement, North Carolina, March 15, 1767. His father had died a short time before, and the hapless orphan's lot at first seemed an unpromising one. At the age of thirteen he volunteered under General Sumter, and was taken prisoner the next year. After the Revolution he supported himself by working at saddlery and teaching school,—his spare hours being employed in the study of law. Admitted to the bar in 1786, he removed to Nashville two years later; and, when Tennessee became a territory, President Washington appointed young Jackson district attorney. His law practice at this period was large and lucrative. His popularity was such that he was chosen, in 1796, as the first Representative in Congress from the new state of Tennessee. The next year he was made United States Senator, but soon resigned to accept a supreme judgeship in his own state. This position he filled until 1804, when he retired from the bench, went into trade, and settled on his plantation—" the Hermitage"—near Nashville. Jack- son's violent temper, and his quickness to resent an injury, involved him in many personal quarrels. In a duel with Charles Dickinson, in 1806, he was severely wounded, and his opponent was killed. When Aaron Burr came west in 1805, and again in 1806, he was the guest of Jackson ; and the Tennessee politician at first entered warmly into his plans, believing them to mean simply war against Spain. But when Jackson discovered the treasonable designs of Burr he at once denounced him, and informed President Jefferson of his suspicions.

Andrew Jaekson's military career may be said to have begun in the Creek War of 1813. In May, 1814, he was made a major-general in the United States army, and marched without orders upon Mobile and Pensacola. He next moved upon New Orleans, and by skillful maneuvering and great generalship won his famous victory of January 8, 1815 (§395). The Seminole War was his next opportunity for the display of military skill. In 1823 Jackson was again sent to the Senate, and in 1824 received fifteen more electoral votes for President than John Quincy Adams, but the decision of the House gave to Adams the high office. In the election of 1828, however, Jackson received one hundred and seventy-eight votes, while but eighty-three were cast for Adams. At his second election Andrew Jackson received the votes of all bnt seven states. His strong common sense, unswerving honesty, indomitable energy, and shining patriotism made amends for the lack of softer and more refined traits; marked his administration with deeds of moral courage; and stamped it as a political and social era in the history of our country. His foreign policy was highly creditable. The nullification movement, the bank war, the Indian troubles, and the hot debates on the currency, tariff, and slavery questions—all together made Jackson's term of office an exciting one. He was glad to retire to the quiet scenes of his "Hermitage," where he died of dropsy, June, 1815.

2. **Daniel Webster** born in Salisbury, N. H., 1782, died at

Marshfield, Mass., 1852) had as a boy no educational advantages beyond the home instruction of his father and mother, and a few terms in the district schools of the neighborhood. He passed nine months of diligent study at Phillips Exeter Academy, and finished his preparation for college in the family of a minister at Boscawen. He graduated from Dartmouth, with high honors, in 1801. During his college course he had shown special proficiency in the classics, in English literature and history, in vigor of writing, and power in debate. At this period he is described by his friend, George T. Curtis, as having "a faculty for labor something prodigious, a memory disciplined by methods not taught him by others, and an intellect expanded far beyond his years. He was abstemious, religions, of the highest sense of honor, and of the most elevated deportment. His manners were genial, his affections warm, his conversation was brilliant and instructive, his temperament cheerful, his gayety overflowing. He was beloved, admired, and courted by all who knew him." In 1805 Daniel Webster was admitted to the bar in Boston, and located in Portsmouth, N. H., in 1807; in 1808 he was married to Miss Grace Fletcher; in 1812 he was elected to Congress by the Federalists, and was a prominent member of the House for two terms. Then he removed to Boston, and, during the busy practice of his profession for the next seven years attained the reputation of the greatest lawyer of his time. In 1823 Webster was again sent to the national House of Representatives, and was twice re-elected; but, in 1827, he was transferred to the Senate, of which body he was, perhaps, the most conspicuous figure during the next twelve years. Webster married a second time in 1829. As Secretary of State under Harrison and Tyler, and again under Fillmore, he managed the foreign affairs of the nation with consummate skill. He was returned to the United States Senate in 1845, where he continued until he entered Fillmore's cabinet in 1850. In May, 1852, he was thrown from a earriage and severely injured. This accident, no doubt, hastened his death.

    3. Robert Young Hayne (*b*. 1791, *d*. 1840) entered the United States Senate in 1823, and served two terms. He was educated for the law, fought in the War of 1812, was speaker of the house in the South Carolina legislature, and attorney-general for the state before coming to Washington. Before his senatorial term was ended he was chosen governor of South Carolina, and boldly defied President Jackson to enforce his proclamation in regard to the nullification acts.

    Hayue possessed brilliant talents, and was especially strong in debate.

CHAPTER XXIX.
THIRTEENTH ADMINISTRATION, A. D. 1837-1841.

Martin Van Buren, President.   *Richard M. Johnson, Vice-president.*

427. The Eighth President. — President Van Buren[1] was of the same political party with his predecessor, under whom he had been Vice-president the last four years. His term began with panic and ruin in the commercial world, owing partly to the reaction that must always follow extravagant speculation, partly to bad harvests and high prices of food, partly to a check in the demand for cotton, and partly to abrupt money movements under Jackson's administration.

Martin Van Buren.

428. Commercial Disasters.—A great firm in New Orleans failed on the day of Van Buren's inauguration ; within two months New York merchants had failed to the amount of one hundred millions, and those of New Orleans to half that sum. Every part of the country shared the distress. Banks failed; public works and manufactures ceased; hundreds of thousands of people were thrown out of employment, and multitudes lacked bread. Eight states were bankrupt, and even the general government had to delay the payment of interest on its bonds.

The Charlotte.

429. **The Bank of the United States** had been re-chartered by the state of Pennsylvania. It failed in 1841 for the third and last time, but all its debts were ultimately paid in full. So were those of the Union and of all the states excepting Mississippi and Florida ; but it was long before American bonds ceased to be a name of reproach in the money-markets of Europe.

430. **The Sub-treasury Law.** — To prevent similar disasters in future, the President proposed an act requiring all public moneys to be kept, not in banks, but in the treasury at Washington, or in sub-treasuries at other cities. Banks were required to limit and secure their

operations by depositing funds with the government. The "Sub-treasury Bill" was unpopular, and defeated the re-election of the President; but it finally became a law in 1839, and though repealed in 1841 it was re-enacted in 1846, and circumstances have proved its wisdom.

431. In 1837 **Canada** was in rebellion against England, and many people on our northern border wished her success. But when good wishes took the shape of arms and war material for the insurgents, the President ordered all citizens to abstain from hostilities under penalty of forfeiting the protection of their government, and General Scott was sent to the frontier to preserve the peace. The steamer Charlotte, which had been fitted out with supplies for the Canadians, was seized by a British party, and, having been set on fire, was allowed to drift over Niagara Falls. The boundary line between Maine and New Brunswick was additional cause of trouble, and there was great excitement among restless spirits who were eager for a fight, but happily good sense prevailed; the President's proclamation was regarded, and the danger of war passed by.

432. **The Democratic party** had now been in power forty years, with the exception of the four years of the second Adams's administration. The *Whigs,* who had lately assumed that name in memory of revolutionary times (§248 and Note) comprised all that were left of the Federalists, with those who for various reasons had become dissatisfied with Democratic policy.

433. **General William Henry Harrison** was the Whig candidate in 1840. Memories of his victories at Tippecanoe and the Thames (§§368, 383), together with the affection inspired by his benevolent and upright character, made the campaign a very enthusiastic one. Harrison's simple frontier life was ridiculed by his opponents in the nick-names "Log Cabin Candidate" and "Hard Cider Campaign;" but these were caught up by his partisans and made their rallying cries.

Harrison was elected by an immense majority, with John Tyler, of Virginia, as Vice-president.

NOTES.

1. **Martin Van Buren** (*b*. 1782, *d*. 1862) was born at Kinderhook, N. Y., and alter being educated as a lawyer entered on his political career at the early age of eighteen, when he was sent as a delegate to the nominating convention of the Democratic party. In 1812, and again in 1816, he was elected to the state senate, and from 1815 to 1819 he was attorney-general of New York. Not being entirely satisfied with some of the Democratic principles, he reorganized the party in his own state in 1818, and this new faction held control of public affairs there for twenty years. In 1821 Van Buren was elected a member of the convention called to revise the New York state constitution, and took a prominent part in the discussions of that body. During the same year he was elected to the United States Senate, and was re-elected in 1827. He, however, resigned in 1828 to accept the office of governor of New York. President Jackson made Van Buren his Secretary of State in 1829, but the latter resigned in 1831, and a few months later was sent as minister to England. After his arrival in that country the Senate refused to confirm his nomination, claiming that as Secretary of State he had pursued a weak course toward England in reference to questions of trade between her West Indian colonies and America. In return for this piece of " party persecution," the Democrats elected Van Buren Vice-president in 1832 over the very Senate that had refused to confirm him. In January, 1837, the electoral vote for President stood : Martin Van Buren, 170; William H. Harrison, 73; Hugh L. White, 26; Daniel Webster, 14 ; W. P. Mangum, 11 ; and the following March Van Buren took his seat.

Although defeated in 1840 by such a sweeping majority, Van Buren's friends tried to effect his renomination for the presidency in 1844, but they failed in their object through his openly avowed opposition to the annexation of Texas. Van Buren and his followers withdrew from the Democratic party in 1848, disagreeing on the question of slavery in newly acquired territories, and formed a new party known as the "Free Democrats." Van Buren was nominated by them for Vice-president but was defeated. He then retired permanently from politics, passing his remaining days in the pleasures of European travel and in the quiet seclusion of his estate at Kinderhook.

CHAPTER XXX.
FOURTEENTH ADMINISTRATION, A. D. 1841-1845.

William H. Harrison, President. *John Tyler, Vice-president.*

434. The Ninth and Tenth Presidents. — President Harrison[1] lived only one month after his inauguration. "Killed by office-seekers" would probably be the true verdict; for, anxious to do justice to all men, he gave to the throng of applicants time which he needed for repose. He died April 4, 1841. **John Tyler,**[2] of Virginia, became President, retaining the same cabinet which Harrison had appointed and the Senate had confirmed.

435. National Bank Question. — On the question of re-chartering a National Bank, President Tyler was in violent opposition to his party. Twice a bill for that purpose was passed by Congress, and twice it was vetoed by the President. All his cabinet resigned, excepting Mr. Webster, Secretary of State, who was engaged in negotiating an important treaty with Great Britain.

William H. Harrison.

436. This **"Webster and Ashburton Treaty"** disposed of two long vexed questions between the two countries. The north-eastern boundary-line of the United States was fixed where it still remains; the "right of search" was formally renounced by Lord Ashburton on the part of Great Britain ; and it was now agreed that the navies of the two nations should unite in the suppression of the slave-trade.

437. Dorr's Rebellion.—Domestic peace was interrupted by "Dorr's Rebellion" in Rhode Island. The constitution of that state was no other than the old colonial charter granted by Charles IL, which allowed only property owners to vote, and in other respects was unsuited to the altered conditions of the times. All parties agreed that there must be a change, but in choosing the manner of it the "suffrage party," with Thomas Dorr[3] at its head, was opposed to that of "law and order." Dorr and his partisans attempted to seize the state arsenal, but were repulsed by the militia and afterwards dispersed by United States forces. The "law and order party " prevailed, and a new constitution was adopted in 1843.

John Tyler.

438. The Mormons.—Far more serious difficulty arose with the Mormons, a sect founded in 1830 at Manchester, N. Y., by Joseph Smith,[4] who pretended to have received a revelation from Heaven. As the new religion promised freedom from restraints, its followers were many; but for the same reason they were not wanted as neighbors. It must be said, however, that they were more orderly than a large part of the community about them. Being expelled from Ohio by the citizens in 1838, and from Missouri by the state militia in 1839, they built a new city and a splendid temple at Nauvoo, in Illinois.

439.   Brigham Young in Utah.—Here again they came into collision with the laws; their prophet and his brother were imprisoned, and were killed by a band of ruffians who broke open the jail. At length the Mormons, under their new leader, Brigham Young,[5] went beyond the Rocky Mountains to the valley of the Great Salt Lake. Here their industry soon transformed the arid plains (§15) into blooming gardens. Recruits flocked in from all parts of the world, chiefly from Great Britain and northern Europe. In 1850 Utah was organized as a territory of the United States, and Brigham Young was appointed by Congress to be its governor. His opposition to judges and other officers of the United States caused him to be superseded the next year, but he continued to be the prophet and absolute chief of the Mormons until his death in 1877.

440.   Texas.—The most exciting question of Tyler's administration concerned the fate of Texas. Until 1836 that great country was part of the republic of Mexico, though the most powerful party among its citizens, both for numbers and energy, had of late been emigrants from the United States. Under their leadership[6] Texas declared her independence in 1835, and secured it the next year by the decisive battle of San Jacinto.[6] She then asked admission to the United States, but was refused. The application was renewed in 1844, the Democrats strongly favoring acceptance and the Whigs opposing it.

441.   Annexation of Texas.—Mr. Calhoun frankly declared that the purpose in annexing Texas was "to extend the influence of slavery, and secure its perpetual duration." This was not desired by the northern people, who also objected to the burden of the Texan debt, which the United States were to assume, and to the war with Mexico, which must grow out of the unsettled dispute as to boundaries. Henry Clay was the candidate of the Whig party; *James K. Polk,* of Tennessee, that of the Democrats. The latter was elected, and as the question of annexation was thus decided by popular vote, *Texas* was admitted before his inauguration. *Florida* was also made a state on the last day of Tyler's term of office.

442. The electro-magnetic telegraph, invented by Professor Samuel F. B. Morse, was now first put to practical use. Congress appropriated $30,000 to test the invention, and a line was built from Washington to Baltimore. The first public dispatch ever sent over the wires was the announcement of Polk's nomination, May 29th, 1844.

NOTES.

1. William Henry Harrison (*b.* 1773, *d.* 1841) was the son of Benjamin Harrison, a signer of the Declaration of Independence and, later, governor of Virginia. At the age of nineteen he entered the army as an ensign, and served in the expeditions against the Indians conducted by Governor St. Clair and " Mad Anthony " (§ 326). He thus became experienced at an early age in Indian warfare, and prepared the foundations of his later renown. At the age of twenty-two he was made a captain, and commanded Fort Washington on the site of Cincinnati; two years later he resigned in order to accept the position of secretary of the North-west Territory. He held this office two years, and then was sent to represent the people of that district as their delegate to Congress. In 1801 the Northwest Territory was divided, and Harrison was appointed governor of the "Territory of Indiana," which included the present states of Indiana, Illinois, Michigan, and Wisconsin. During his governorship he made several important treaties with the Indians, and fought the celebrated battle of Tippecanoe (§368, and Note). Harrison's part in the War of 1812 has been described in the text (§§375, 376, 383). After the war he turned his attention to polities, and served in both branches of Congress and in the Ohio state senate. Under John Quincy Adams he was sent as minister plenipotentiary to Colombia, S. A., bnt being recalled immediately after Jackson was elected, Harrison retired from politics, and during the next seven years led a quiet and peaceful life on his farm near Cincinnati. In 1836 he again entered the political arena, and was defeated for the Presidency by Van Buren; but, four years later, the nomination of the same candidates gave rise to one of the most exciting campaigns our country has witnessed. As stated in the text, Harrison's success cost him his life.

    2. John Tyler (*b.* 1790, *d.* 1862) was born in Charles City Co., Virginia. His father was a Revolutionary patriot, and for some years was governor of the state. Tyler graduated at William and Diary College, studied law, and shortly after being admitted to the bar was elected to the legislature. This was the beginning of a long political career, during which he served at various times in the House and Senate, in his state legislature, as governor of Virginia, and finally as Vice-president and President of the United States. His course as President was condemned by his own party, the Whigs, while it gained him no support among the Democrats; and, although nominated for a second term by a convention held in Baltimore, lie found himself so unpopular that lie was compelled to withdraw from the contest. When the Southern States seceded, in 1861, Tyler was sent as a delegate from Virginia to the Peace Convention at Washington, of which lie was president. This convention failed of its purpose, and, returning to his native state, he espoused the Southern cause. At the time of his death lie was a member of the Confederate Congress.

    3. Thomas William Dorr, the leader of the suffrage party, was tried and convicted of treason. He was sentenced to imprisonment for life, but was released in 1847.

    4. Joseph Smith was of Scotch descent, and was born in Sharon, Vermont, in 1805. He led a dissolute life when young, and was very ignorant. When twenty-one years of age he pretended to have received from an angel tablets of gold upon which was written the "Book of Mormon." He deciphered the hieroglyphics of this book by means of a pair of wonderful spectacles provided by the angel, and dictated its contents to his secretary to write in English. This secretary and two other persons bore witness to the actual existence of the golden tablets, and to their mysterious disappearance as soon as they were transcribed. Unfortunately for the new religion Smith quarreled with these witnesses shortly after, and they denounced the whole story as a hoax. Smith attempted to introduce polygamy into the Mormon belief when they settled at Nauvoo, Illinois, but was strongly resisted by certain of the community, who established a press and published opposition articles. Smith headed a mob which demolished this press, but this act cost the "prophet" his liberty, and ultimately his life, as narrated in the text.

5. Brigham Young was born at Whitingham, Vermont, in 1801, and was a man of limited education. He first joined the Mormons while they were located at Kirtland, Ohio, and soon became a prominent leader among them through his eloquent preaching and strong personal influence. After Smith's death Young was the successful candidate for presidency of the church against three competitors. In 1852 he introduced polygamy as "the celestial law of marriage" into the Mormou belief, declaring that it had been revealed to Smith nine years before. Young died in 1877, and the Mormons are rapidly losing control of Utah.

6. The most prominent American in the Texan revolt was General Samuel Houston, one of the most remarkable characters in American history. He was born near Lexington, Virginia, in 1793. His mother, a poor widow, removed to Tennessee in 1807, but her son shortly left her, and went to live with the Cherokee Indians in Arkansas, where he made many strong friends among the chiefs. Three years later he returned, and after teaching school for a time enlisted as a private in Jackson's campaign against the Creeks (§ 384). Retiring at the close of the war with the rank of lieutenant, he commenced the study of law, and was soon a prominent politician. After holding several minor offices he was elected to Congress, and kept his seat there for four years, when he was elected governor of Tennessee, at the age of thirty-fonr. Two years later he married, but almost immediately separated from his wife, resigned from the governorship, and went to live with his old friends the Cherokees.

In 1832 Houston went to Texas and took a prominent part in the revolutionary movement. After Texas declared her independence, Houston was made commander-in-chief of her army. Santa Anna, the Mexican general, butchered two American forces that had surrendered to him, in cold blood, and then attacked Houston, who had but 783 men, with a force of 1,600 men. This was the famous battle of San Jacinto, in which 630 Mexicans were killed, and nearly all the rest were captured; among the latter was Santa Anna. The American loss was eight killed and twenty-five wounded. Houston worked earnestly for the annexation of Texas to the United States, and after it was accomplished was elected United States Senator. In 1859 he was elected governor of Texas, but being opposed to secession he resigned his office when that state went out of the Uuion, and retired to private life. He died July 25th, 1863.

CHAPTER XXXI.
FIFTEENTH ADMINISTRATION, A. D. 1845-1849.

James K. Polk, President.   *George M. Dallas, Vice-president.*

443. The Eleventh President.—Early in Mr. Polk's[1] term of office the northern boundary of **Oregon** was settled by treaty with Great Britain. Columbia River had been first visited and named by an American sea-captain[2] in 1792. After its exploration by Lewis and Clarke (§358) the colony of Astoria was founded on its southern bank by John Jacob Astor,[3] of New York, as a depot of the fur trade. British subjects meanwhile settled on the northern branch of the Columbia and on the Fraser River.

James K. Polk.

444. Boundary of Oregon and British America.—So long as the fur trade was the only object, the two nations could agree to occupy the land together. But in 1834 the Willamette Valley began to be settled by American citizens, who desired the protection of their own government. Others were for claiming the whole coast to latitude 54° 40', and "Fifty-four forty, or fight," was a party cry in the election of 1844. But in 1846, after several years' negotiation, the boundary was drawn at 49°, and there it still remains. *Oregon Territory* was organized in 1848.

In 1859 the state of *Oregon* and the territories of *Washington* and *Idaho* were formed from the same lands.

445. The south-western boundary was not so peaceably settled. Mexico claimed the Nueces River, Texas the Rio Grande, as the dividing line; and the United States had now undertaken the Texan quarrel. General Taylor, with an "Army of Occupation," entered the disputed territory, and in April, 1846, built Fort Brown, on the Rio Grande.

446. War with Mexico.—The Mexicans began hostilities by surprising and killing or capturing a party of United States dragoons. Soon afterward they attempted to cut off General Taylor himself, who had gone for supplies to Point Isabel, but they were defeated in a hard-fought battle at *Palo Alto,* and still more decisively the next day at the ravine of *Resaca de la Palma.* War was now formally declared, and fifty thousand volunteers were called for. Three hundred thousand pressed forward, eager for adventure. Crossing the Rio Grande, Taylor captured Matamoras and several other Mexican towns.

447. Three plans comprised the campaigns of 1846 and 1847: (1) General Taylor, as before, was to hold the *line of the Rio Grande.* (2) General Kearney, with the Army of the West, was to cross the Rocky Mountains and conquer *New Mexico and California.* (3) General Scott,[4] commander-in- chief, was to advance from Vera Cruz to the *City of Mexico.*

448. Capture of Monterey.— In September, 1846, General Taylor moved upon Monterey. The city was defended by the mountain gorges which obstructed approach, and by strong works manned by 10,000 Mexicans. It was taken, however, in four days, and the Americans fought their way from house to house, until all had surrendered.

449. General Santa Anna[5] was now President of the Mexican Republic and at the head of her forces. With a fine army of 20,000 men he marched to attack Taylor in the mountain-pass of Buena Vista. The Americans numbered less than 5,000, but they fought furiously, and at every charge the Mexicans were repulsed. At length these fled to the southward, and General Taylor remained in undisturbed possession of the valley of the Rio Grande.

450. Capture of Vera Cruz.—He had already sent the greater part of his forces to the aid of General Scott, who landed in March with 12,000 men before Vera Cruz. This place was defended by the strong castle of San Juan de Ulloa, but after a heavy cannonade of four days both castle and city were surrendered.

451. Advance on the Capital.—The main army then commenced its march to the capital, which lies 7,500 feet above the sea-level. On the heights of *Cerro Gordo* Santa Anna was found strongly posted with 15,000 men. His positions were all stormed and carried; 3,000 Mexicans were made prisoners, and the invading army pressed on. *Pueblo,* a city of 80,000 people, was taken without resistance, and here General Scott waited three months for additional forces.

452. Arriving in August at the summit of the Cordilleras, the American army could look down upon the *City of Mexico,* lying in its beautiful valley studded with lakes and encircled by lofty mountains. But all the roads thither were guarded by strong works and defended by Santa Anna with 30,000 Mexicans. Choosing a difficult route to the southward, Generals Pillow and Twiggs forced the strongly intrenched camp at *Contreras,* in a spirited fight of only seventeen minutes, and the same day captured the heights of *Churubusco, w*hile General Worth stormed *San Antonio.*

453. Surrender of Mexico.—The way was now open to the gates of the capital, for the reserve forces of Santa

Invasion of Mexico.

Anna were routed by Generals Shields and Pierce, and the city government sent to ask a truce. On the 7th of September the army was again in motion; the great fortress of *Chapultepec,* commanding the city, was taken by storm; Santa Anna and his officers fled; and on the 4th the flag of the United States floated over the imperial palace of the Montezumas.[6]

454. Other Movements.—Meanwhile General Kearney had captured *Santa Fé* (§48) and dispatched Colonel Doniphan with a thousand men to conquer the province and city of *Chihuahua.* He defeated the Mexicans in two battles, and completely accomplished his mission.

Gold Digging.

Kearney, with only 400 dragoons, proceeded to the conquest of *California*. This, however, was achieved before his arrival.

455.   Captain John C. Fremont, with a party of engineers, was exploring the region of the Rocky Mountains for a new route to Oregon, when he heard that the Mexican commander in California was about to expel all Americans from his province. At the same time Fremont received orders from his own government to protect the interests of its citizens as far as was possible.

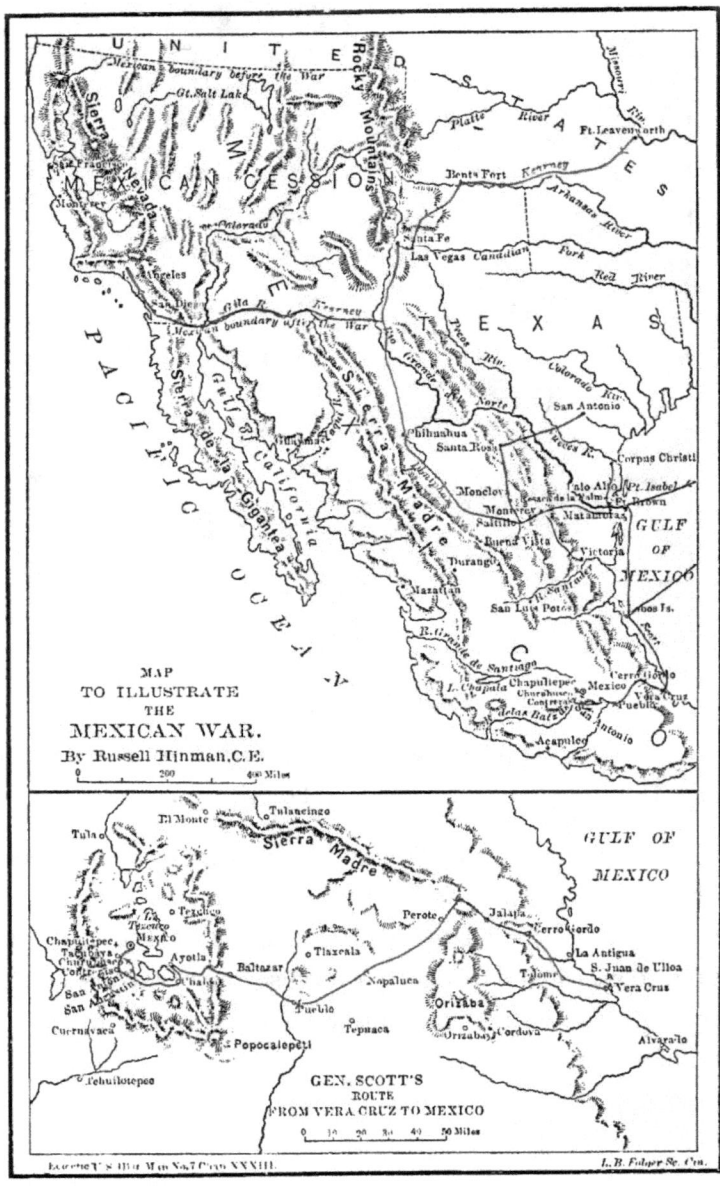

456. California Independent. — Raising a force of volunteers among the Americans who were in California for purposes of trade, Fremont many times defeated the Mexicans in the Sacramento Valley, and in concert with Commodore Stockton, who was cruising with an American fleet off the Pacific coast, completely gained control of the country. California declared her independence of Mexico, July 5, 1846.

457. Treaty of Guadalupe Hidalgo. — With the surrender of her capital the power of Mexico was broken. By the treaty of *Guadalupe Hidalgo,* Upper California, with Nevada, Utah, Arizona, and New Mexico, was ceded to the United States. The latter agreed to pay fifteen millions of dollars for these territories, and to assume the debts due to American citizens from the Mexican government. The other captured places were restored.

458. Gold Discovered. — Scarcely was this treaty signed when news came that gold had been discovered on the American Fork of Sacramento River. The report spread around the world, and from every country a throng of excited adventurers rushed toward the "diggings." Ships were deserted, while officers and men joined in the scramble for sudden wealth. From the Atlantic States thousands embarked for the long voyage around Cape Horn; others crossed the fever-haunted Isthmus; while multitudes journeyed overland, many of whom died of hunger and hardship on the desolate plains.

459. San Francisco, from a sleepy Spanish "mission" (§48), surrounded by a village of mud cabins, became in a year a busy town of 15,000 people. At first the rough and reckless crowd had its own way, and the worst disorders prevailed; but at length the best citizens formed themselves into "vigilance committees," and succeeded in enforcing justice; so that society became as peaceful as in older states. As the gold fever subsided, mining continued to be an important and regular industry of California, while the inexhaustible wealth of her soil and the wonderful equability and healthfulness of her climate drew thousands of new citizens.

460. The Wilmot Proviso.—On the question of governing the great, rich countries acquired from Mexico, violent contests arose. As early as 1846 David Wilmot[7] had introduced into Congress a bill for excluding slavery from all future territories of the United States. This "Proviso" was defeated, but in the election of 1848 both Whigs and Democrats were opposed by a "Free Soil Party." It was not strong enough to secure even one electoral vote, but its principle—that of limiting slave-labor to the states it already occupied—was gaining ground.

461. New States.—During Polk's administration *Iowa* (1846) and *Wisconsin* (1848) were admitted to the Union. Iowa was first occupied by a Frenchman named Dubuque, who carried on trade with the Indians from a fort and factory near the town which bears his name. The towns of Burlington and Dubuque were founded in 1833 by emigrants from Illinois. French missions and trading stations were also the first white settlements in Wisconsin, whose name means "the gathering-place of waters." In later years many industrious people from Norway, Sweden, Denmark, and northern Germany have found homes in the state.

Point out on Map No. 9, the Columbia River. The northern boundary of the United States, from the Lake of the Woods to the Pacific Ocean. On Map No. 7, the south-western boundary as claimed by Mexico in 1845; as claimed by Texas. General Taylor's first position in 1846. The sites of his principal victories. The march of General Scott from the coast to the capital of Mexico. The route of General Kearney. The boundaries of the lands ceded by Mexico in the Treaty of Guadalupe Hidalgo. San Francisco.

Read Jay's "Mexican War" and Ripley's "War with Mexico;" Dawson's "American Battle Fields."

NOTES.

1. James Knox Polk (*b.* 1795, *d.* 1849) was born in Mecklenburg County, North Carolina, his grand-uncle having been one of the promoters of the Mecklenburg Resolutions (§242). The family moved to Tennessee in 1806, and Polk received his education at the University of

Nashville. After graduating he studied law, and in 1823 commenced his political career as a member of the state legislature. From 1824 to 1839 he was a member of Congress, where he distinguished himself in his opposition to the administration of John Quincy Adams, and later by his support of Jackson. He was elected governor of Tennessee in 1839, but failed in his attempt for reelection two years later. As President, Polk displayed ability in his administration of public affairs, although he was not a man of remarkable gifts or attainments. In character lie was amiable, little given to display, grave in manner, and irreproachable in his private life. Three months after his successor took the presidential chair, Polk died, after a very short illness, at his home in Nashville, Tenn.

    2. This was Captain Robert Gray, of Boston, Mass., who entered the river on the 11th of May, in his vessel, "Columbia Rediviva," after which the stream was named.

    3. John Jacob Astor (*b.* 1763, *d.* 1848) was the son of a German peasant, and was born near Heidelberg. When sixteen years of age he went to London and joined his brother, a maker of musical instruments. He worked at that trade until the close of the American Revolution, when he started for Baltimore with some musical instruments, which lie proposed to sell on commission. During the passage lie became acquainted with a fur trader, who revealed the profit to be made in furs; and Astor, acting on this, exchanged his instruments for furs ou his arrival, and thus began a business which, before long, assumed colossal proportions.

    4. Winfield Scott (*b.* 1786, *d.* 1866) was born at Petersburgh, Va. After graduating at William and Mary College he adopted the profession of law, but almost immediately abandoned it, entering the army as a captain in 1808. His brilliant career in the War of 1812, the Creek War, and the war with Mexico, has made him one of the most renowned of American generals, while the tact and judgment displayed in managing the delicate questions of the tariff trouble in South Carolina, and the Canadian agitation of 1837 (§431), marked him as a skillful diplomate. He was retired in 1861 on full pay and rank, and passed his remaining days at West Point. He has left behind him several military works, a few letters, and a book of memoirs of his life.

    5. Antonio Lopez de Santa Anna was one of the most prominent characters in Mexico during the revolutionary times which existed there from 1810 to 1870. He commenced his military career in 1821, when only twenty-three years of age, and during his life, besides holding prominent military commands, was three times elected president and twice made dictator. He was banished or compelled to flee the country no less than five times; and on one occasion, being convicted of treason, his vast landed estates were confiscated. They were never returned to him, and he died at Vera Cruz in comparative poverty and obscurity, in 1876.

6. **The Montezumas** were emperors of ancient Mexico.

7. **David Wilmot** (*b.* 1814, *d.* 1868) was born at Bethany, Pa., and was a member of Congress from 1845 to 1851. The "Proviso" which has made his name celebrated was an amendment to a bill appropriating $2,000,000 for the purchase of Mexican territory, and was simply a repetition of the language of the Ordinance of 1787 by which the Northwest Territory was organized (§324). It provided that "neither slavery nor involuntary servitude shall ever exist in any part of said territory, except for crime, whereof the party shall first be duly convicted."

CHAPTER XXXII.
SIXTEENTH ADMINISTRATION, A. D. 1849-1853.

Zachary Taylor, President. *Millard Fillmore, Vice-president.*

462. The Twelfth President.—*General Zachary Taylor,*[1] of Louisiana, a popular hero of the Mexican War, was elected by the Whig party, and became President of the United States in 1849. Soon afterward **California**, having adopted a state constitution, asked for admission to the Union. This aroused all the sectional disputes, for the Californians had decided to have no slaves. The South opposed the admission of a free state as contrary to the Missouri Compromise (§402). The North replied that the Compromise applied only to the Louisiana purchase; that a large part of California was north of 36° 30' north latitude; and that, moreover, the people of the new state had a right to choose for themselves.[2]

Zachary Taylor.

463. The Compromise of 1850.—Henry Clay acted the part of peace-maker, as he had done before, but the effect of his compromise was only to delay for ten years the appeal to arms. Six things were proposed in his "Omnibus Bill:"[3] (1) California to be admitted as a free state; (2) The admission of new states legally formed by the division of Texas; (3) Utah and New Mexico to be organized as territories without mention of slavery; (4) The claims of Texas to New Mexico to be bought by the United States for ten millions of dollars; (5) The slave-trade to be forbidden in the District of Columbia; and (6) Slaves escaping to free states to be arrested and returned to their owners. After long debate, in which Clay and Webster bore a distinguished part, the bill was passed.

Millard Fillmore.

464. The Thirteenth President. — While it was under discussion, President Taylor died, after only sixteen months of office. Public duties, amid the intense excitement of the time, had weighed the more heavily upon him because he was unused to political life. His last words were, "I have tried to do my duty; I am not afraid to die." *Millard Fillmore,*[4] of New York, the Vice-president, now came to the head of the government. Daniel Webster was appointed Secretary of State. Part of the duties of that office were devolved upon the new "Department of the Interior," which has charge of the public lands, of dealings with the Indians, and of issuing patents.

465. The Gadsden Purchase. — By peaceful agreement with Mexico, a large tract of land south of the River Gila was added to the territory of Arizona. Twenty millions of dollars were paid by the

United States for this "Gadsden Purchase," so called because it was negotiated by Senator Gadsden of South Carolina.

466. Within less than three years **three public men** died who were unsurpassed by any of their countrymen in eloquence or in their control of the destinies of the nation. Calhoun died in March, 1850; Clay in June, 1852; and Webster in the following October. Though often strongly opposed on questions of policy, each thoroughly respected the personal character of his opponents. All had been unsuccessful candidates for the highest office. Clay had resigned his hopes and his favorite policy in the effort to make peace between extreme parties, replying to his friends who remonstrated: "I would rather be right than be President." Many think that Webster made a similar sacrifice in his famous "Seventh of March Oration" in New York, where he strove to conciliate the Southern interests at the expense of his influence in New England.

467. The Fugitive Slave Law.—All party questions were now absorbed in the overwhelming excitement concerning slavery. "The Fugitive Slave Law," a part of the "Omnibus Bill," was bitterly resented in the Northern States. Most northern people had been content to feel that slaveholding, whether right or wrong, was no concern of theirs, and to leave the responsibility to those who had assumed it. It was a different matter to see fugitives hunted by officers of the United States in the streets of Boston, and to be even required to assist in the pursuit. On the other hand, the South felt that northern men were willing to accept a large share in the profits of slave-labor, while refusing their support to the system, and even assuming to censure those who were directly involved in it.

468. Personal Liberty Laws.—Several of the states enacted "Personal Liberty Laws,"[5] practically annulling the obnoxious decree. While the excitement was at its height the election of 1852 resulted in the elevation of *Franklin Pierce,* of New Hampshire, to the Presidency, by the Democratic party, which commanded the entire suffrage of the South.

NOTES.

1. Zachary Taylor (*b*.1784, *d*. 1850) was of Virginian birth; his father, a Revolutionary officer, removed to a plantation near Louisville, Ky., when Zachary was still a baby, and became one of the prominent politicians of the state. Zachary lived on the plantation until twenty-four years of age, and had but ineager opportunities for education. He then entered the army as a lieutenant, and two years later distinguished himself by the brave defense of a fort on the Wabash, under his command, against a much superior force of Indians. This was at the opening of the War of 1812, and established Taylor's reputation as an Indian fighter. He was accordingly almost constantly employed on the western frontier and in Florida, either fighting or as an Indian agent, until the opening of the Mexican War, when he had risen to the rank of brigadier-general.

His soldiers were devoted to him. They called him " Old Rough-and-Ready," and this name became the rallying cry of the party which elected him President. While Taylor declared himself willing to accept the nomination for President, he at the same time expressed his doubts as to his fitness for the position, and insisted upon entire freedom from party pledges. He was conservative in his views; and although an advocate of slavery, was strongly opposed to the Secession party, which began to gain power in the South during his term of office.

One of his daughters married Jefferson Davis, and his son. General Richard Taylor, was one of the last Confederate generals to surrender to the United States.

2. This principle came to he known as "Squatter sovereignty." A little later (§473) we shall see its advocates and opponents changing sides.

3. Called the " Omnibus Bill " from its including so many widely different provisions. Before passage it was divided into separate bills.

4. Millard Fillmore (*b*. 1800, *d*.1874) was born in Cayuga County, N. Y., which at that time was very sparsely settled, and the young boy had the simplest of rudimentary education. He was apprenticed to a trade when fourteen, but being ambitious he studied hard during spare hours, and finally obtaining a release from his master he entered a law office as a clerk. After two years of drudgery there he went to Buffalo, and although at first almost penniless and an entire stranger he succeeded in making a living, and in winning friends who secured his admission to the bar. His abilities soon made him known, and his rise was rapid.

His political life commenced in 1828, when he was elected to the state legislature. In 1832 he was first elected to Congress, and served one term. He was reëlected in 1836, and held his seat until 1842, when he declined a renomination. In doctrine he was a staunch Whig,-and took an active part in the debates in Congress. He was appointed chairman of the committee of ways and means, a most important post, and took the leading part in drawing up the tariff of 1842. After retiring from Congress, Mr. Fillmore was a candidate for Vice-president, but failed to secure the nomination. He was also defeated as the Whig nominee for governor of New York in 1844 ; but in 1847 he was elected comptroller of the state, and displayed great ability in that office.

As President, Fillmore won the sincere admiration of his cabinet. His messages to Congress contained many suggestions of great value to the country, but none of them were carried out owing to purely political reasons. Fillmore signed the various acts comprised in Mr. Clay's compromise measures, being convinced of their constitutionality; but the Fugitive Slave Law, which was included, wasso offensive to the Abolition Party that when Mr. Fillmore was again nominated for President in 1856 by the "American" party, he was unable to secure the electoral vote of a single northern state. He then retired to private life in Buffalo, N. Y., where he died in 1874, of paralysis.

5. These laws aimed to secure the liberty of escaped slaves who might enter the several free states, and were at once denounced as contrary to the Constitution (Article 4, Section 2).

CHAPTER XXXIII.
SEVENTEENTH ADMINISTRATION, A. D. 1853-1857.

Franklin Pierce, President. *William R. King, Vice-president.*

469. The Fourteenth President.—*Two peaceful events* marked the summer of 1853. Following an example set by London two years before, a "Crystal Palace" was opened at New York in July for an " Exposition of the arts and industries of all nations." Several "World's Fairs" have been held since then ; and it may be hoped that the improved acquaintance with each other's resources, and the mutual interests which may be founded upon them, have done something to promote among all nations unity, peace, and concord.

470. Perry in Japan.—During the same month, July, 1853, Commodore Perry, in command of an American fleet, entered the harbor of Yeddo, and announced the desire of his government to make a treaty with Japan. That interesting empire had kept itself secluded for centuries from all intercourse with other nations, and the doors were now opened only with caution and reserve. But in 1854 a treaty was concluded which admitted American merchants to Japanese ports, and a rich commerce soon sprang up, leading to wonderful changes in the policy and relations of Japan.

471. Pacific Railroad Explorations.—It had now become evident that great advantages would be gained if the rich Pacific coast could be connected with the East by railroads; and, although many deemed the scheme absurd, Congress ordered surveys to be made by a corps of engineers. Accordingly, five different routes were explored during 1853-4, and the possibility of building such roads was ascertained.

Franklin Pierce.

472. The Ostend Manifesto.—Cuba had always been viewed with longing eyes by the United States, but several attempts to purchase it failed, and a filibustering expedition,[1] undertaken in 1851, to seize the island by force, ended in disaster. In 1854 another attempt at purchase was made. The American ministers to England, France, and Spain met at Ostend, Belgium, and published a manifesto which set forth the advantages to be derived by both Spain and the United States from the transfer of Cuba, at a reasonable price, as well as the danger to both nations of allowing it to remain in the possession of Spain. England and France, however, joined Spain in opposing the plan, and after some temporary excitement the matter was dropped.

473. The Kansas-Nebraska Bill.—The great political events of Pierce's[2] administration arose from a bill introduced into Congress by Senator Stephen A. Douglas,[3] of Illinois, "to organize the territories of Kansas and Nebraska." Disregarding the Missouri Compromise (§402) this bill left to the majority of people in each territory the choice whether to enter the Union as a slave or a free state. It became a law after five months of violent debate. Then began a rush for the first possession of the land.

474. Kansas was the immediate object. Missourians were earliest on the ground, and, guarding the nearest approaches, forced emigrants from New England to take a circuitous route through Iowa. In 1856 a convention at Lecompton framed a state constitution admitting slavery. Another convention at Topeka declared the first to be illegal, as the ballot had been controlled by armed voters from Missouri, and proceeded to organize Kansas as a free state. Two capitals and two legislatures claimed to be the lawful centers of government.

475. **Civil war** broke out. Lawrence, which had been settled by Massachusetts people, was plundered and burnt. Murder and all kinds of violence were unrestrained. Congress refused a seat to the delegate from Kansas, and sent a committee to investigate the manner of his election. It was made evident that there had been no true expression of the will of the majority. Governor Geary[4] was appointed with a military force sufficient to secure order.

476. **The Republican Party** was now organized on the principle of resistance to the extension of the slave-holding interest. It comprised the greater number of Whigs, all the Free-soilers, and those Democrats who opposed the extension of slavery in the territories. Fremont[5] was the Republican candidate for the Presidency in 1856, and received the electoral votes of eleven states. One state voted for Fillmore, who had been nominated by the American or "Know-Nothing" party. The remaining nineteen states gave their votes to *James Buchanan,* the Democratic candidate, who became the fifteenth President of the United States.

NOTES.

1. The " Filibusters," as they were called, were a lawless set who, after the Mexican War, organized expeditions within the United States against Cuba and Central America. The expedition against Cuba consisted of 500 men, commanded by a Cuban named Lopez. They were defeated and imprisoned, and Lopez was executed.

2. **Franklin Pierce**, of New Hampshire, was born 1804, and died, 1869. He graduated at Bowdoin College in the class of 1824, and was admitted to the bar three years later. He was very successful as a lawyer.

His political life began in the legislature of his state, from which, in 1833, he was transferred to the lower house of Congress. In 1837 he was chosen United States Senator. Twice Mr. Pierce refused cabinet appointments by President Polk, and once'declined the nomination of his party for governor of New Hampshire. He favored the annexation of Texas, and was among the first to volunteer for the Mexican War (§ 453). For bravery in action he rapidly rose from the ranks to a brigadier-generalship, and was commissioned by General Scott to arrange an armistice after the battle of Churubusco. When made President, in 1852, he received 254 electoral votes to 42 east for Winfield Scott. Pierce's entire administration was one of intense political excitement. Party feeling ran high in all parts of the country. The President was an advocate of the doctrine of "State Kights," and opposed every anti-slavery movement. After the expiration of his term of office Mr. Pierce made an extended European tour, and then settled down in his quiet New Hampshire home.

3. **Stephen Arnold Douglas** was born in Brandon, Vt., 1813, and died at Chicago, 1861. He emigrated to the West in 1833, and a year later commenced the practice of law in Jacksonville, 111. He showed such ability in his profession that at the youthful age of 22 years he was chosen attorney-general of the state. In 1840 be was appointed secretary of state, and the same year a judge on the supreme bench of Illinois. Douglas first became a candidate for Congress in 1837, but was defeated. Again nominated by the Democrats in 1813, he was more successful. He was re-ëlected to the House of Representatives the two following terms, and in 1847 was promoted to the Senate. He was an acknowledged leader in this high body for the remainder of his life. During his long congressional career Mr. Douglas took part ably in the discussion of every important political question before the nation. He was a master of constitutional law, a powerful debater, and exerted a strong personal influence over his audiences. He was a man of large frame, though not tall, and was popularly styled "the little giant." His Kansas-Nebraska bill, which embodied the doctrine of " squatter sovereignty " (as termed by the papers of the day) was the cause of exciting controversy throughout the land, and led to the formation of the Republican party. At the Baltimore Convention, in 1852, Mr. Douglas received 92 votes as candidate for the Presidency; and at Cincinnati, in 1856, 121 votes. In 1860 he was the nominee of the northern wing of the Democratic party, and received a very large popular vote. He greatly deplored the Civil

War, and strongly denounced the doctrine of secession.

4. John W. Geary (ft. 1819, cl. 1873) was a well known Pennsylvania politician and soldier. He served with valor in the Mexican War; went to California in 1849, where he held several important offices; accepted the governorship of Kansas during the stormy times of 1856, but was compelled to yield to the stronger faction ; recruited a regiment of Pennsylvania volunteers in 1861, and fought gallantly till the close of the Civil War, having been promoted to the rank of major-general. After the war he was twice elected governor of his native state.

5. John Charles Fremont is of French descent, and was born in Savannah, Georgia, 1813. To him more than to any other man are Americans indebted for the early exploration and first intelligent survey of the vast territory between the Mississippi River and the Pacific Ocean. He was a tine mathematician and a good civil engineer. His proposal to the government to explore the unknown region of the Rocky Mountains was accepted, and in 1842 he set out on his first expedition. Much valuable information was gained, and soon after his return Fremont fitted out a second exploring party much larger than the first. During the next half dozen years be crossed the continent many times, often suffering the most extreme dangers from cold, and hunger, and the Indians. He became known as "the pathfinder." Under Fremont's leadership upper California was taken from the Mexicans. The American settlers on the Pacific slope elected him governor of California in 1846, and the next January he dictated the terms of surrender to the Mexican forces. President Taylor commissioned Fremont to run the boundary line between Mexico and the United States. In 1850 he was sent as United States Senator from the new state of California.

In the presidential election of 1856 he received 114 electoral votes to Buchanan's 174. During the Civil War he was a major-general in the Union army: his campaigns were in Missouri and Virginia. In 1878 President Hayes appointed John C. Fremont governor of Arizona Territory.

CHAPTER XXXIV.
EIGHTEENTH ADMINISTRATION, A. D. 1857-1861.

James Buchanan, President.   *John C. Breckenridge, Vice-president.*

477. The Fifteenth President.—Early in Mr. Buchanan's administration two northern states were added: *Minnesota* in 1857, and *Oregon* in 1859, making thirty-three in all. The new President [1] desired to appease ali strife, but the conflict of principles was now too serious to yield to persuasion. The Chief-justice [2] of the United States declared that slaves might be carried by their masters into any state of the Union. But this was contrary to the laws of several states and to the Ordinance of 1787 (§ 324), which prohibited slavery in the North-west Territory.

James Buchanan.

478. The excitement became greater when *John Brown*,[3] formerly of Kansas, actually invaded the state of Virginia with a party of about twenty men, for the purpose of liberating slaves. He gained possession of the arsenal at Harper's Ferry, thinking to arm the negroes whom he expected to join him. He was easily captured,—his party being either killed or dispersed,—and was tried, convicted, and put to death under the laws of Virginia. Though this rash movement had no support, the news of it excited a rage of resentment throughout the South, where it was considered as an expression of universal Northern feeling.

479.   The Democratic Party itself, in convention at Charleston, became divided on the question of slavery in the territories. The seceding minority formed a new convention at Richmond, and nominated John C. Breckenridge,[4] of Kentucky, to be the next President. The majority adjourned to Baltimore and nominated Stephen A. Douglas, of Illinois. A third party named John Bell,[5] of Tennessee, and Edward Everett,[6] of Massachusetts, for President and Vice-president. The Republicans meanwhile nominated *Abraham Lincoln,* of Illinois, and Hannibal Hamlin, of Maine.

Jefferson Davis.

480.   By dividing its forces, the Democratic Party lost the power which it had held for twelve out of fifteen presidential terms since the accession of Jefferson. Mr. Lincoln was therefore elected by a plurality of votes. He was a native of Kentucky. He had educated himself, in spite of poverty and adverse circumstances, to be a successful lawyer and a popular representative in Congress, and had fairly won the confidence of his fellow-citizens by his energetic and upright character.

481. Secession. — Immediately after the election of Lincoln, the political leaders of South Carolina put in operation their plan of withdrawing from the Union. A convention, called for that purpose, passed an ordinance of secession, which was ratified by the state legislature, December 20, 1860. Within a few weeks Georgia and all the Gulf States had followed the example.

482. The Star of the West. — In Charleston Harbor Major Anderson, commanding the government troops in Fort Moultrie, removed by night to Fort Sumter, — a much stronger position. But his supplies were low, and his men were few; he could not long withstand an attack from the batteries which had been erected on the land. Early in January, 1861, President Buchanan determined to secretly send reinforcements and provisions to the beleaguered national fort. To this end, he ordered the steamer "Star of the West" to Charleston Harbor with men and supplies. But news of her coming reached South Carolina before the vessel; and, on attempting to approach Fort steamer was fired upon from Morris Island, and struck several times. She was obliged to put back to New York without accomplishing the mission of the President. This was the opening act of the Civil War.

Kansas was admitted to the Union as a free state on the 29th of this month, and took an active part in succeeding events.

483. Confederate States of America. — A convention of delegates from six of the seven seceding states met at Montgomery, Alabama, in February, 1861, and organized a new government under the title of the "Confederate States of America." The main features of its constitution were modeled upon those of the United States, but the sovereign rights of each state were recognized ; the favor of foreign nations was sought by pledges of free trade; and slavery was guaranteed protection not only in existing states but in territories yet to be acquired.

Jefferson Davis,[7] of Mississippi, and *Alexander H. Stephens,*[8] of

Georgia, were elected President and Vice-president of the new Confederacy.

484. Washington itself was the **headquarters of secession** during the winter of 1860-'61. Many leaders of the movement were in the cabinet of Mr. Buchanan and in the Senate of the United States. The national government was paralyzed. Its navy was scattered to the most distant seas, and a great part of its cannon, rifles, and military stores were in southern forts and arsenals, which were taken almost without exception by the authorities of the Confederate States. Many southern officers in the army and navy, believing their obedience due to their native states rather than to the Union, resigned their commissions and offered their services to the Confederate government.

485. *Fort Pickens,* near Pensacola, and *Fort Sumter,* in Charleston Harbor, were still held for the United States; and *Fortress Monroe,* the strongest work on the coast, was never lost, but served as a base of operations at sea.

NOTES.

1. James Buchanan, of Pennsylvania, was born 1791 ; graduated at Dickinson college, 1809; was admitted to the bar, 1812 ; elected to the lower branch of Congress, 1828; appointed minister to Russia, 1831; was United States Senator from 1833 to 1845; became Secretary of State under Polk, and minister to England under Pierce. He was nominated for President by the Democrats in convention at Cincinnati, in the summer of 1856. His administration covered the stormy political period just before the outbreak of the Civil War. He was blamed by the Unionists for not taking measures to prevent secession, but after his retirement from the Presidential chair he wrote a book explaining and defending his policy while in office. Buchanan was never married; he died in 1868.

2. Roger Brooke Taney (*b.* 1777, *d.* 1864) of Maryland was the Chief-justice who made this decision. The case is known as "the Dred Scott case." Taney was appointed Chief-justice by President Jackson in 1835, and took his seat upon the Supreme bench in 1837.

3. John Brown was born in the year 1800 at Torrington, Conn. When a boy he moved to northern Ohio. Going to Kansas in 1855, he and four grown sons were prominent in their armed opposition to the pro-slavery party. Their home was near the town of Ossawotomie, from which the father became known as "Ossawotomie Brown." His invasion of Virginia with so small a number of followers would seem to indiente his insanity at the time. Even his enemies credit him with undaunted bravery.

4. **John Cabell Breckenridge** (*b.* 1821, *d.* 1875) was of an excellent Kentucky family, received a good education, and took a prominent part in national politics. He was a major in the Mexican War, and afterwards was elected to his state legislature. In 1851, and again in 1853. he was sent to the United States House of Representatives. He was Buchanan's Vice- president, and in 1860 was made United States Senator. He defended the Southern Confederacy on the floor of the Senate, and then joined the Confederate army. He was created a major-general, and took part in several of the most important conflicts of the war. He was appointed Confederate Secretary of War in 1865, and after the close of the struggle went to Europe, where he remained for a few years. He died at his home in Kentucky.

5. **John Bell** (*b.* 1797, *d.* 1869) was a statesman upon whom his native state conferred many political honors. First elected a member of the United States House of Representatives in 1827, he was returned for seven consecutive terms; in 1834 he was chosen Speaker of the House. President Harrison selected Mr. Bell as his Secretary of War. In 1847 lie was elected to the United States Senate, and again in 1853. His nomination for the Presidency was by the "Constitutional Union" party.

6. **Edward Everett** (*b.* 1794, *d.* 1865) was a distinguished American statesman, orator, and writer. Robert C. Winthrop, of Massachusetts, sums up Everett's character thus: "He was an ardent and gifted scholar, an accomplished and devoted professor, a cautious and conservative statesman, a sincere and earnest patriot, an exhaustless and consummate rhetorician. He was a true man, an ever-obliging and faithful friend, a good citizen. . . . The annals of our country to the day of his death will be searched in vain for another so ready, prolific, and brilliant a writer and speaker, or for one who has done more both to adorn American literature, and to advocate and advance every public interest and patriotic cause."

7. **Jefferson Davis** was born in Kentucky, 1808; graduated from the United States Military Academy, West Point, 1828; was employed for a

time in arduous frontier service, and fought bravely in the Mexican War. He was severely wounded at the battle of Buena Vista. He first entered Congress—the lower house—in 1845, and was promoted to the Senate in 1S17. During President Picree's administration, Davis was his Secretary of War. Afterwards he returned to the Senate, and was one of the most prominent Democratic leaders until the outbreak of the Civil War. His fortunes in the Confederacy are related in the text.

8. **Alexander Hamilton Stephens** was born near Crawfordville, Ga., 1812. He was a graduate of the State University at the age of 20; was admitted to the bar in 1834; and entered the state legislature two years later. Since that date he has been actively engaged in political life most of the time. He was sent to the United States House of Representatives in 1843, where he remained for sixteen years—a statesman whose ability was recognized by all parties. After the Civil War the Georgia general assembly elected Mr. Stephens to the United States Senate; but, the state not having been fully restored to the Union under the reconstruction requirements, lie was not permitted to take his seat. Since 1872, however, he has been a member of the United States House of Representatives.

QUESTIONS FOR REVIEW. —PART IV.

Section

1. Describe the condition of the states at the close of the Revolution. — 309, 310
2. What arrangements were made with the Indians? — 311, 312
3. Describe the formation and adoption of the Constitution. — 313-319
4. Name the first President and his cabinet. — 320, 321
5. What was their policy in money matters? — 322
6. What four causes of disturbance in Washington's time? — 326-330
7. What three foreign treaties were made? — 331, 334, 335
8. What did Washington say of the advantages of union? — 337
9. Describe his character and habits as President. — 336, 338, 339
10. Describe the two political parties and their principles. — 333, 340, 351, 390, 392, 398
11. What three cities have been seats of the Federal Government? — 320, 323, 347
12. What occasioned the Alien and Sedition laws, and why were they repealed? — 341, 342
13. What troubles with France during Adams's administration? — 343-345
14. How did cotton become profitable? — 348
15. Describe the beginning of Ohio. — 324, 325, 349
16. What can you tell of Jefferson, his policy and character? — 351-353
17. How was Louisiana acquired, and what was done with it? — 356-359
18. Describe the successive dealings of the government with the Barbary States. — 329, 335, 360, 397
19. Tell the story of Aaron Burr. — 350, 361, 362

	Section
20. What caused the War of 1812?	364-36S
21. Describe the first campaign on land.	368-371
22. What was done by the American navy?	372, 373, 377-382
23. What was done by General Harrison?	375, 376, 383
24. Describe two campaigns of Jackson.	384, 394, 395
25. Describe the war on the coast.	385, 386
26. What was the cause of the Hartford Convention?	387, 390, 392
27. What occurred in 1814 in northern New York?	390, 391
28. Describe the return of peace.	393, 396, 398, 400
29. What seven states were admitted A.D. 1812-1820?	383, 399, 402
30. Describe the progress of slavery.	62, 135, 148, 152, 251, 401, 402, 441
31. Describe the progress of steam navigation.	363, 403
32. What is the "Monroe Doctrine?"	404
33. What was Mr. Monroe's Indian policy?	406
34. Describe J. Q. Adams's administration.	409-414
35. Describe the policy of Jackson.	415, 421-425
36. What was the subject of Webster's and Hayne's debate?	416, 417
37. Describe Indian affairs during Jackson's administration.	418-420
38. Describe the financial condition and policy of the Government.	422-424
39. What changes during Van Buren's term?	427-430
40. Describe Harrison's election and time of service.	433, 434
41. Describe Tyler's policy.	435
42. What happened in Rhode Island?	437
43. Tell the story of the Mormons.	438, 439

	Section
44. What treaties were made with Great Britain in 1842 and 1846?	436, 443, 444
45. What occasioned a war with Mexico ?	440, 441, 445
46. Describe its main events.	446-456
47. What were the terms of peace ?	457
48. Consequences of the gold discovery?	458, 459
49. What was the Wilmot Proviso ?	460
50. How were Iowa and Wisconsin first settled?	461
51. Describe Taylor's administration. That of Fillmore.	51. 462-468
52. Foreign treaties made and attempted.	470, 472
53. Pacific Railroad explorations.	471
54. Consequences of the Kansas-Nebraska Bill.	473-476
55. What were the great events of Buchanan's term ?	477-485

PART V.—the war of the states.

CHAPTER XXXV.
NINETEENTH ADMINISTRATION, A. D. 1861-1865.

Abraham Lincoln, President.   Hannibal Hamlin, Vice-president.

The First Gun,—Battery Stevens.

486. The Sixteenth President.—No President since Washington had taken upon him so heavy a burden with the oath to "preserve, protect, and defend the Constitution of the United States." That Constitution had secured great happiness to the people during seventy-two years of seldom-broken peace : it was yet to be seen whether it would bear the strain of civil war,—such a war as the world had not known in nineteen hundred years.

487. In his inaugural address Mr. Lincoln[1] declared that he had neither the right nor the wish to interfere with Southern institutions, but designed to hold and defend the property of the United States against any who should assail it. He threw upon the politicians of the South the whole responsibility of the calamities which must follow the destruction of the Union, assuring them that there could be no conflict unless they themselves should choose to begin it.

Abraham Lincoln.

488. Miscalculations.— No one, probably, imagined the horrible magnitude of the struggle then commencing. Mr. Seward,[2] then Secretary of State, predicted that the war,—if there was a war,—would not last more than ninety days. The South, on the other hand, relied upon the great number of her sympathizers in the North to prevent any energetic action on the part of the Government. Moreover, she believed that if her cotton was withheld from European factories, France and England would combine to put an end to the war and procure the needed supply.

489. Fall of Fort Sumter.— Before daylight of the 12th of April, 1861, the first cannon-ball from a Confederate battery struck the wall of Fort Sumter. The bombardment was kept up for thirty-four hours, until at midnight of the 13th Major Anderson found that longer resistance was impossible. By the terms of surrender he marched out with his eighty men, with all the honors of war, and spent the remnant of his powder in a last salute to the stars and stripes.

490. The news flew along the electric wires and aroused both divisions of the country to more decided action. Virginia, Arkansas,

North Carolina, and Tennessee, which had wavered, renounced the Union and joined their fortunes with the Confederate States. On the other hand, Missouri, Kentucky, Maryland, and Delaware refused to secede. The navy-yard at Norfolk, with its 2,000 cannon and immense stores of war materials were seized by Virginia troops. The United States arsenal at Harper's Ferry was burned by order of the Government.

491. Formation of Armies.—Both presidents called for volunteers, and both calls were answered with enthusiasm. For the defense of the national capital, which was in immediate danger, militia regiments hastened from Massachusetts, Rhode Island, and New York. The "Sixth Massachusetts" was attacked in its passage through Baltimore, and several men were killed. It was the eightysixth anniversary of the battle of Lexington, where their great-grandfathers had shed the first blood in the struggle for freedom (§232). Even then it was felt to be unnatural and degrading that men of the same English race should destroy each other. The present strife was more unnatural, and all who were not maddened by excitement felt that victory on either side must be mingled with regret.

Sketch of Charleston Harbor.

492. In the east **the main field of war** was Virginia; in the west, at first, Missouri. Though the latter state had voted against secession, it contained a strong Confederate party, and sixty battles were fought upon its soil within a year. In the part of Virginia west of the Alleghanies a majority of the people were attached to the Union. In 1861-62 the necessary steps for organization were taken, and the separate state of **West Virginia** was admitted to the United States in June, 1863. Meanwhile General McClellan, with his Union army, gained repeated victories over the Confederate generals Garnett, Floyd, and Lee, who sought to retain West Virginia by force.

493. **Richmond**, the capital of old Virginia, was also the capital of the Confederate States. The Southern cry, "On to Washington!" was echoed by the Northern shout, "On to Richmond ! " The most serious battle of the year took place at *Bull Run*, on Sunday, July 21. General Beauregard[3] commanded the Confederate army of 40,000 men; General McDowell's forces consisted of a nearly equal number of volunteers for ninety days. For six hours the Northern men stood their ground, and kept or regained all their positions. The Confederates were once broken and driven a mile and a half from the field; but they were rallied by "Stonewall" Jackson, whose inflexible bravery and noble character made him one of the great heroes of the war.

494. **A Southern Victory.**—At the moment when the Confederate cause seemed lost, suddenly General Kirby Smith arrived with fresh forces for their relief. The Union troops, exhausted by intense heat and furious fighting, were thrown into confusion, and battle was changed to flight. A confused throng of fugitives filled all the roads to Washington, and never rested until they were safely over the Long Bridge across the Potomac. Later in the evening Colonel Einstein, of Pennsylvania, returned to the battle-field and brought off six cannon.

495. According to Mr. Pollard, the Southern historian, the victory at Bull Run was a misfortune to the Confederacy, for it led to ill-grounded confidence. Southern volunteers left the army in crowds, thinking that the war was over. The National Government was roused to more serious effort. Congress voted five hundred millions of dollars and half a million of men. General George B. McClellan,[4] who had distinguished himself in West Virginia, was called to command the Army of the Potomac; and when, a few months later, General Scott retired from active service, McClellan became commander-in-chief of all the forces of the United States.

George B. McClellan.

496. **Of the national navy** only one war-steamer was on the Atlantic coast, and there was not a gun on the Mississippi or any of its branches. With wonderful energy the Government created a great steam-navy to blockade the Southern ports, and a fleet of gun-boats to patrol the Mississippi.[5] Though European governments declared that a blockade of so long a coast-line could never be enforced, they acknowledged within a few months that it was complete and effective.

497. **The Blockade.**—The South had been used to receive all manufactured articles from Europe in exchange for her cotton and other agricultural products. Now that she was cut off from intercourse with the civilized world, cotton could not go out and cannon could not come in; and though she had begun the war with abundant supplies of money and material (§484), its continuance must depend on breaking or "running" the blockade.

498. Many a spirited chase occurred between the national steamers and the low, light, neutral-colored craft which swarmed in bays and sounds, and slipped out at night, bound for the West Indies or for Europe. President Davis issued "letters of marque" to privateers who made reprisals upon Northern commerce. Captain Semmes,[6] of the *Sumter,* had many successes; but at length he was blockaded in the port of Gibraltar, until he sold his vessel and traveled to England to buy a new one. This was the far-famed *Alabama,* so called, though she was registered only by her number, 290, on the builder's list. In her cruise of twenty months she almost drove American commerce from the sea, destroying sixty-five vessels and property worth $10,000,000. She was sunk at last in a battle with the United States war-steamer *Kearsarge,* commanded by Captain Winslow, on the coast of France, June, 1864.

499. Messrs. Mason and Slidell, envoys to England and France from the new Confederacy, were taken in the Bahama Channel from the English mail-steamer *Trent,* by Captain Wilkes, of the United States steam sloop-of-war *San Jacinto.* Great wrath was expressed at this "insult to the British flag," and it was predicted that England within twenty days would break the blockade and declare war against the United States.

500. End of the Trent Affair.—Mr. Lincoln's government, however, promptly disavowed the act of Captain Wilkes, and set the envoys at liberty, having no mind to assert a "right of search" which had been so justly resented when exercised by Great Britain before 1812 (§367). France, England, and Spain had proclaimed neutrality toward both "belligerent powers," thus recognizing the Confederacy as on nearly the same footing as the United States. The neutrality was infringed in England by the fitting out of vessels in the Confederate interests, but the damage thence resulting was made good by the payment of $15,500,000 after the war.

501. Before **the end of 1861** the National Government had regained a considerable part of the Atlantic coast by the capture of the forts at Hatteras Inlet and Port Royal Entrance,[7] and the occupation of Tybee Island, near the mouth of Savannah River. The army, which had numbered 16,000 at the beginning of the year, had risen to 600,000 by the first of December, and the Secretary of War announced that the Government was able not only to protect itself, but to attack any foreign power which should meddle with our domestic affairs.

NOTES.

1. Abraham Lincoln (*b*. 1809, *d*.1865) was born in Hardin (now Larue) County, Ky. His father could neither read nor write, and when his son was in his eighth year he migrated to the backwoods of Indiana. Here Abraham grew to manhood as a farm laborer and store clerk, with but little time or opportunity for education. In 1828 he was hired by a flat-boatman, and made a trip to New Orleans. After his return his family removed to Illinois, and he was employed for some time in assisting his father to split rails for the fences. In the succeeding years we find him employed variously as a flatboatman, clerk, surveyor, postmaster, and river pilot. During the Black Hawk War (§ 418) he served as captain, and on his return, becoming interested in polities, he was elected to the Illinois state legislature in 1834. In the midst of his varied occupations he managed to study law, and was admitted to the bar in 1837. He settled at Springfield, Illinois, where lie. attained great reputation as a lawyer. He took a prominent part in the Presidential campaigns of 1840 and 1844, and was elected to the House of Representatives in 1846. From this time he was not prominent in politics until the repeal of the Missouri Compromise (§402), when he was called upon to reply to a speech made by Stephen A. Douglas at Springfield, Ill., in support of the Kansas-Nebraska bill. Lincoln's speech ou this occasion is considered the most effective ever made by him. It carried the audience by storm, and at once stamped Lincoln as the proper candidate to pit against Douglas. The contest between these two for the United States Senatorship resulted in Douglas's favor, but brought Lincoln prominently before the country, and led to his nomination in I860 for the Presidency.

In appearance, as in character, Lincoln was a most remarkable man. He was six feet four inches high, gaunt and rugged, a fitting type of the class from which he. sprang. But the rougit exterior covered a noble mind and a heart that bore "malice toward none, with charity for all." In his death the South felt that it had lost its best friend; the North, its grandest President ; and the colored people, their emancipator. His name is fitly coupled with that of Washington, and "The Martyred President " will ever remain sacred in the memory of the American people.

2. **William Henry Seward** (*b.* 1801, *d.* 1872) was born in Florida, Orange County, N. Y., and after graduating at Union College commenced the practice of law. He was soon drawn into politics, and before he was thirty years of age was elected to the state senate. From this time forward we find him prominent in the councils of both state and nation. Twenty-four years of his life were spent in the three important posts of governor of New York, Senator in Congress, and Secretary of State. Iu the latter position he had the most difficult office to fill in Lincoln's cabinet, owing to the great importance at that time attached to our foreign relations. His keen, far-seeing judgment and prompt, decisive action justified the President's selection. Mr. Seward was a man of indomitable perseverance and courage. " Few public men of any note have been subjected to more sudden and desperate reverses, and none ever bore them with more fortitude or set to work more energetically to recover from them." While these qualities made him respected and admired of his friends, they also roused the most bitter feelings in his opponents; and during the latter part of his political career, as an adherent of Andrew Johnson, he was repeatedly subject to savage attacks even by his own political party ; but Seward remained unconquered to the end, and, though broken in health, spent the declining years of his life iu a trip around the world. This was followed on his return by the publication of a book describing his travels, and full of keen observations on all that he had seen. He died at Auburn, New York, in the seventy-second year of his age.

3. **General Pierre Gustave Toutant Beauregard**, one of the most prominent and efficient generals of the South, was born near New Orleans, in 1818, and was educated at West Point, where he graduated in 1838. He was twice breveted for gallant service in the Mexican War, first as a captain and afterward as a major. At the close of that war he was made a member of a special board of engineers for the improvement of harbors and rivers, and the erection of defenses on the Gulf of Mexico. Later he had charge of the construction of the custom-house, quarantine warehouses, and marine hospital at New Orleans. In January, 1861, he was appointed superintendent of West Point, but almost immediately

resigned the position and entered the army of the Confederacy with the rank of brigadier-general. At the time of the surrender he had attained the highest possible rank. He then retired to private life in New Orleans.

4. General George Brinton McClellan was born in Philadelphia in 1826, and graduated at West Point with high honors. He saw his first active service in the war with Mexico, where he distinguished himself for gallant conduct, and was breveted first lieutenant and captain. As an engineer, he accompanied exploring expeditions up the Red River and over the route of the Northern Pacific Railroad. The Government appointed him on a commission to visit the seat of the Crimean War in 1855, and on his return published his official report on the "Organization of European Annies, and Operations in the Crimea." He has also written and translated other works of a military nature. In 18.57 he resigned from the army, and interested himself in various railroad enterprises until the breaking out of the Civil War. Much dissatisfaction was felt at his apparently dilatory conduct of the war in Virginia, and he was finally ordered on November 7, 1862, to proceed to Trenton, N. J., and there await further orders. He took no further part in the war, and resigned his position in the army on November 8th, 1864, the day he was defeated as the Democratic nominee for President. For the three years succeeding January 1, 1878, he was governor of New Jersey.

5. This was due to the energy and ability of Mr. G. V. Fox, Assistant Secretary of the Navy. "For four years his ardent mind, practical and full of resources, effectively controlled the department, and at the expiration of those memorable four years he retired without aspiring to any other reward than the satisfaction of having served his country well."

6. **Raphael Semmes** was the Paul Jones of the Civil War (§283). He was born in Charles County, Maryland, in 1809, and entered the navy as a midshipman in 1826. He gained his first experience in the Mexican War, where he served both on hoard ship and on shore. He has published several works giving accounts of the Mexican War, and the exploits of the "Sumter" and "Alabama."

7. The bombardment of Fort Walker, one of the forts guarding Port Royal, was so severe that the garrison was compelled to evacuate it, excepting three brave men, who remained, and for half an hour continued to load and fire the only gun that replied to the enemy.

CHAPTER XXXVI.
NINETEENTH ADMINISTRATION EVENTS OF 1862.

Abraham Lincoln, President.   Hannibal Hamlin, Vice-president.

502. Three objects were now kept steadily in view by the Union generals: (1) The opening of the Mississippi River; (2) The recovery of the coast; and (3) The capture of Richmond.

The first was accomplished by a severe and continuous struggle of eighteen months. General Albert Sidney Johnston [1] commanded the Confederate forces in the West. His main task was to protect the "Memphis and Charleston Railroad," which connected the country west of the Mississippi with Richmond and the coast, and conveyed supplies of Texan beef to the Southern army. His line of defense extended from Columbus to Bowling Green in Kentucky; and its strongest points were near the center of the line, at Fort Henry, on the Tennessee, and Fort Donelson, on the Cumberland River.

503. Fort Henry was first attacked by the Union gunboats under Commodore Foote,[2] and was taken after an hour's fighting; but the garrison made good their retreat to the stronger works of *Fort Donelson*. This was besieged by General Grant with a Union army, in concert with the gun-boats which arrived two days later up the Cumberland. An attack was made, but a heavy cannonade from the fort repulsed the gun-boats, and Commodore Foote received a serious wound. Early the next morning the garrison attempted to break through the besieging lines and escape to Nashville ; but though the fight was desperate, they were defeated and driven within their trenches. The national soldiers lay three nights on the frozen ground, pelted by storms of sleet and snow.

504. Surrender of Donelson.—Before daylight of February 15, General Buckner, then commanding the fort,—as his superiors, Floyd and Pillow, had consulted their own interests by retiring,—sent to ask what terms of capitulation would be accepted. Grant replied, "None, but unconditional surrender;" and added, "I propose to move immediately upon your works." Fort Donelson was surrendered with 15,000 men, and the line of defense thus broken was necessarily abandoned. Nashville, Columbus, and Bowling Green were occupied by Union troops, and the Mississippi was open as far as to Arkansas.

505. **Grant** was placed in command of the new military department of *Western Tennessee,* and the field of conflict was removed to the southern border of that state. The "Memphis and Charleston Railroad" was now the object of attack, especially at Corinth, where it crosses the " Mobile and Ohio Railroad." Ascending the Tennessee River, Grant posted himself near Pittsburg Landing, at Shiloh, awaiting reinforcements from Buell.

506. Battle of Shiloh.—Here he was attacked by Generals Johnston and Beauregard with a fine Confederate army of 40,000 men. The battle raged all day mainly to the advantage of the assailants, who captured the Union camp, with thirty flags, 3,000 prisoners, and an immense quantity of war materials. They were compelled to fall back, however, with the loss of their general-in-chief, while Generals Grant and Sherman rallied the Union forces, many of whom had never been in battle before, and saved the first day's engagement from being an utter rout.

507. The next morning the fight was renewed. Buell's fresh forces had arrived upon the field, and the tide turned. The second day's battle continued from before sunrise until late in the afternoon. At last the Confederates retreated in good order toward Corinth, and Grant remained in possession of the field. Island Number Ten was surrendered on the same day, after a three weeks' bombardment, and its garrison of 5,000 men became prisoners of war.

508. A battle on the Mississippi between the Union gun-boats and the Confederate ironclads, resulted in victory to the former. Fort

Pillow was abandoned, Memphis was taken, and the great river was open to the Union forces as far south as Vicksburg. Beauregard abandoned Corinth, and fell back on his third line of defense, extending through central Mississippi to Alabama.

During this grand campaign for the Mississippi and the railway connections in the South, the war in Missouri had been virtually ended by the expulsion of General Price and the defeat of his army, — now transferred to General McCulloch, — at Pea Ridge, in Arkansas. The Confederates had increased their numbers by several thousands of Indians; but these were thrown into confusion by the terrific roar and fatal effects of the Federal artillery, so that they only contributed to the defeat of their allies.

509. A Double Movement.—"The war was in truth a vast siege," but the South was unwilling to have it so. A double movement was now made to break through the besieging lines and carry the conflict into the North. On the same day, Lee moved into Maryland and Bragg[3] into Kentucky, hoping to secure those border states, — whose people were almost equally divided in sympathy between the Union and the Confederacy, — and then march on to dictate terms of peace in Philadelphia or New York. We will follow the western movement first.

510. The Campaign in Kentucky.—Bragg marched from Chattanooga to Frankfort, pursued by Buell, whose force was increased by all the men whom Grant could spare. General Kirby Smith defeated a Union army at Richmond, Kentucky, and threatened Cincinnati. The first object of both Confederate generals was Louisville; but this was saved by the arrival of Buell a few hours in advance, and the invasion of the North was abandoned. Bragg and Smith set up a provisional government at Frankfort, and urged all the people of Kentucky to join the cause of the Confederacy.

511. But while the Confederate generals were offering peace and brotherhood, their foragers were stripping farms of live-stock, and mercantile houses of clothing and provisions, paying only in worthless Confederate scrip (§579). Assuming that Kentucky was now in the Confederacy, they even drafted men into their ranks according to the law in force in the South. Their losses by desertion were greater, however, than their gains by conscription, and though many refugees accompanied their retreating army, taking with them their slaves, whom they were afraid of losing by the success of the North, the mass of the plundered Kentuckians felt less disposed than ever to break their connection with the Union.

512. National Victories.—Though defeated at *Perryville,* Kentucky, Bragg effected the retreat of his "wagon-train forty miles long " to Chattanooga. While Grant's army in Mississippi was weakened (§510) by Buell's detachments, the Confederates attacked *Iuka* and *Corinth*. They were defeated at both places,—at the latter with immense loss.

513. Murfreesborough.—Neither government was satisfied with the campaign in Kentucky. Buell was superseded by Rosecrans, and Bragg was ordered northward again to finish his work. On the last day of 1862 the two armies met before *Murfreesborough,* in Tennessee. At first the Confederates were victorious; but Sheridan's bold and prompt action saved the Union cause. The carnage was frightful; and during New Year's Day, 1863, "the two armies, breathless with their death struggle, stood looking at each other." The fight was renewed January 2d,—the next day. Bragg retreated, and another costly victory had been won for the nation.

514. On the lower Mississippi, meanwhile, yet more important events had occurred. Early in April Captain Farragut,[4] with a fleet of armed steamers and mortar-boats, in concert with a land force under General Butler, undertook the capture of New Orleans. This largest and richest city of the Confederacy was defended by two great forts seventy miles down the river; below these a strong iron chain stretched from bank to bank ; and the river was guarded by gun-boats, fire-rafts, and a floating battery.

515. Surrender of New Orleans.—A heavy cannonade from the fleet produced no effect upon the forts, and Farragut determined to pass them. Protecting his gun-boats with iron chains and bags of sand suspended over their sides, he steamed boldly up the river, encountered and destroyed twelve out of thirteen of the Confederate armed steamers, and advanced to the city. Confiding in the river defenses, the commandant at New Orleans had sent a large detachment of his troops to reinforce Beauregard and Bragg. As soon as the Union fleet came in sight, fire was set to the immense stores of cotton, ships, gun-boats, steamers, and docks. General Butler took military possession of the city. The forts and fleet below were soon afterward surrendered. Farragut, ascending the river, captured Baton Rouge and Natchez, and, passing the guns of Vicksburg, joined the Union fleet above.

NOTES.

1. Albert Sidney Johnston (*b.* 1803, *d.* 1862) was born in Mason County, Kentucky. He graduated at West Point in 1826, and had seen active service in frontier duty and in the Black Hawk War. He then resigned and went to Texas, where he attained chief command of the Texan forces. He also served as a volunteer in the war between the United States and Mexico, and in 1849 re-entered the regular army with the rank of major. At the breaking out of the Civil War he had attained the rank of brevet brigadier-general, bestowed for meritorious service in Utah. He would doubtless have borne a more conspicuous part in the war but for his early fall at Shiloh.

2. Andrew Hull Foote (*b.* 1806, *d.* 1863) was born in New Haven, Connecticut, and entered the Navy, 1822. In 1861 he was made flag officer of the Western naval fleet, and personally conducted the building of the gun-boats to be used.

Through neglecting his wound received at Fort Donelson he nearly lost his life, and was compelled for a time to retire from active service. He was made a rear-admiral, and in May, 1863, was ordered to take command of the South Atlantic Squadron, but while on his way to do so he was taken suddenly ill in New York, and died.

Admiral Foote was a man of great moral as well as physical courage, and did much to improve the morals of those under his command. He commanded the respect and admiration of the entire Navy and his loss was keenly felt.

3. General Braxton Bragg (*b*. 1817, *d*. 1876) was born in Warren County, North Carolina, and was educated at West Point. In the Mexican War he was breveted on three separate occasions for gallant conduct. He resigned troni the army in 1856, and settled on a plantation at Thibodeaux, La. At the opening of the Civil War he was made a brigadier-general in the Confederate army, and on the death of A. S. Johnston at Shiloh succeeded him in command, with the full rank of general. After the battle of Perryville he was relieved of his command and placed under arrest by the Confederate authorities. He was almost immediately released, however, and restored to his former rank. He was again relieved after defeat at Mission Ridge, and was called to Richmond as military adviser to the Confederate president, with whom he was a great favorite. At the close of the Civil War he was engaged as chief engineer in the improvements in Mobile Bay.

4. David Glascoe Farragut (*b*. 1801, *d*. 1870) was the most illustrious naval officer of the Union in the Civil War. His naval career began at the early age of eleven, when he served on board the "Fssex" in the War of 1812 (§379). He then received the highest praise from Commodore Porter in his official report of a battle with the British " Argus," and would have been promoted in rank had he been old enough to allow of it. Aside from an attack and capture of a pirate stronghold in Cuba, in 1823, Farragut saw no active service until the war broke out in 1861, when he had advanced to the rank of captain. He received the thanks of Congress for his gallant capture of New Orleans, and was placed first on the list of rear-admirals. After the capture of Mobile (§560) Farragut again received the thanks of Congress, and a new grade of rank, that of vice- admiral was created for him : this was followed in July, 1S66, by the creation of the still higher rank of Admiral, which was conferred on him as a mark of most distinguished honor. The following year Farragut joined the European squadron, to the command of which he had been appointed, and every-where received marks of the highest respect from the foreign powers. After his return from this command his health began to fail, and, while on a journey for its improvement, he died at the Portsmouth navy-yard.

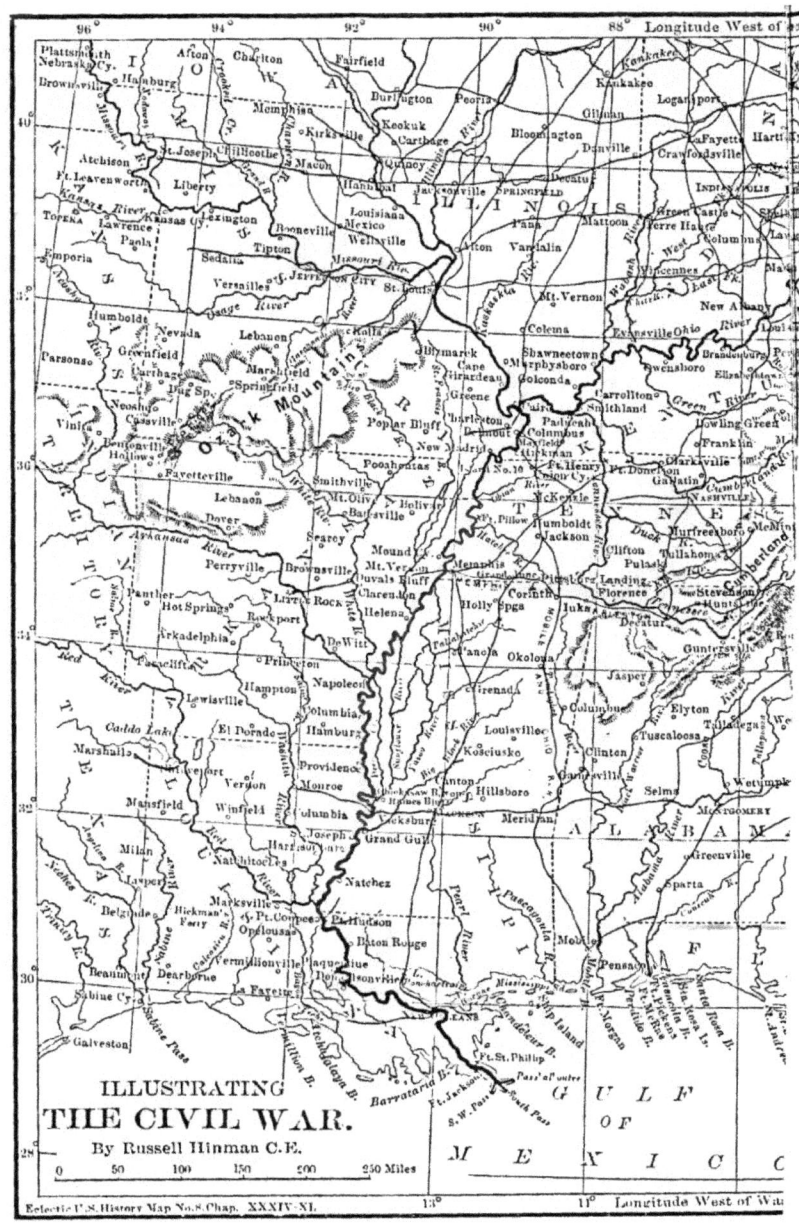

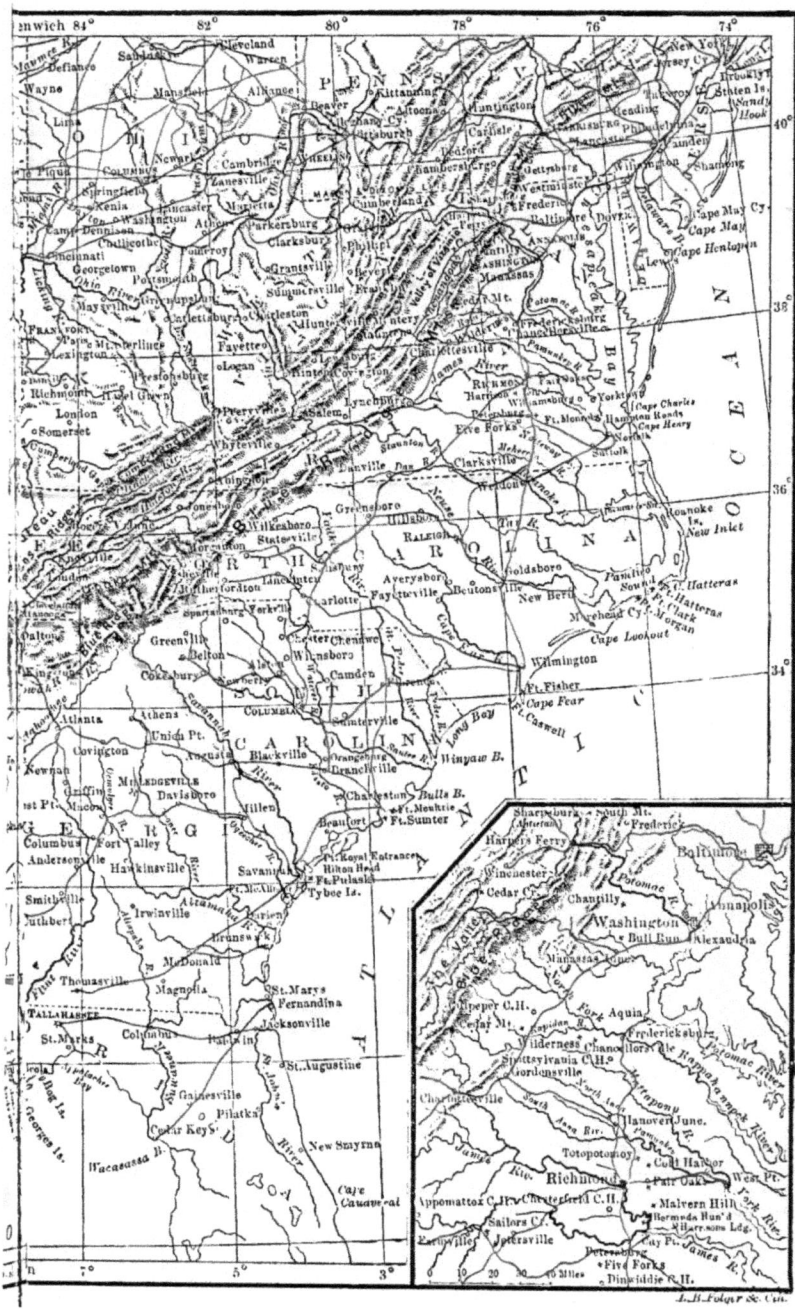

CHAPTER XXXVII.
NINETEENTH ADMINISTRATION—EVENTS OF 1862 (Continued).

Abraham Lincoln, President.   *Hannibal Hamlin, Vice-president.*

516. On the 8th of March, 1862, a strange-looking craft appeared in Hampton Roads. It was the old United States steamer *Merrimac*, now in Confederate service, cut down to the water's edge and fitted with a sharp steel prow and a sloping iron-plated roof. Steering directly for the sloop-of-war *Cumberland*, it so disabled her by one blow of her steel beak that she sank, with her flag flying and with all her men on board.[1]

517. The United States frigate *Congress* was next attacked. She was run ashore, but the *Merrimac* poured into her such a storm of shot and shell that she was forced to surrender. The new sea-monster then retired to Norfolk, intending to complete its work of destruction the next day. Early in the morning it steamed out again, and approached the steam frigate *Minnesota*; but before it had fired a gun a new champion appeared upon the scene.

518. It was the iron-clad *Monitor* of Captain Ericsson,[2] which had arrived from New York during the night, just in time for its first trial of strength. Its deck near the surface of the water was protected by a heavy iron sheathing; it was surmounted by an iron tower, which, slowly revolving, turned its two enormous guns in every direction. The duel between these odd antagonists was not unlike David fighting Goliath, for the *Monitor* was less than one fifth the burden of the *Merrimac*. But the shot and shells of the latter rolled harmlessly off the iron sheathing of her little opponent, while her huge beak passed above the deck and could not reach the tower. The *Monitor* glided nimbly away from every charge, and found out every weak spot in the *Merrimac's* armor, where a heavy ball from her guns could make a leak.

Monitor and Merrimac.

519. At length, unable either to silence her assailant or to engage any other vessel while she was present, the *Merrimac* withdrew to Norfolk for repairs. She was blown up by the Confederates two months later, on the surrender of Norfolk to the United States. The national government immediately contracted with Captain Ericsson for a fleet of "Monitors," which effectually defended the coast, and made the United States for a time the greatest naval power in the world.

520. The movement toward Richmond by the Union forces was attended with tremendous difficulties and losses, and no favorable result. A second march to Manassas was rewarded by the capture of Quaker guns[3] and an empty camp. The Army of the Potomac was then removed to Fortress Monroe, and spent a month and more in digging intrenchments — and graves — in the deep mud of the peninsula which had witnessed the surrender of Cornwallis (§302).

When, at length, the Federals were ready to assault Yorktown, the Confederates again gave them the slip, and retreated towards Richmond.

521. A battle at Williamsburg resulted in loss to both and gain to neither party, except that the Confederate general succeeded in covering the retreat of his baggage-train. The Federals kept the hard-won field, and buried their dead. McClellan then slowly advanced, and after two weeks saw the spires and roofs of Richmond. The Confederate Congress hastily adjourned, and a mass of retreating fugitives clogged all the roads to the southward.

522. Defense of Richmond.—But while McClellan awaited reinforcements, J. E. Johnston, the Confederate commander-in-chief, warded off his intended blow by sending "Stonewall" Jackson up the Shenandoah Valley to threaten Washington. This brilliant dash was successful in preventing McDowell's march to the aid of McClellan, and the attack upon Richmond.

523. A two days' **battle at Fair Oaks** would probably have ended in victory to the Confederates but for the disabling of their chief by a serious wound. General Robert E. Lee,[4] who succeeded him, had time to raise immense numbers of recruits and strengthen the defenses of Richmond; and by severing McClellan from his supplies, forced him to move his army to the James. This difficult movement was only accomplished with seven days' tremendous fighting, usually successful, but fearfully costly of life. The Federal army, still outnumbering its enemy, then posted itself at Harrison's Landing below Richmond.

524. Washington was now seriously threatened. General Pope, commanding the Union forces in northern Virginia, was defeated at *Cedar Mountain,* and three weeks later had to encounter the whole army of Lee on the old battle-field of *Bull Run.* Two days' fighting ended in a severe defeat of the Federals; and, after another sharp conflict at *Chantilly*, Pope retreated to Washington and resigned his command.

Robert E. Lee.

525. **Lee crossed the Potomac** and invaded Maryland, pursued by McClellan, who had restored the Union army to perfect condition after its ruinous campaign. Stonewall Jackson seized Harper's Ferry with its arsenal of cannon and small arms, and twelve thousand Union prisoners; but on the same day Lee was defeated at *South Mountain*, and his northward march was arrested.

526. Battle of Antietam.—At Sharpsburg, in the beautiful valley of *Antietam*, one of the most terrific battles of the war was fought, on the 17th of September. For fourteen hours the mountains echoed to the roar of five hundred cannon and mortars, and when night came 25,000 men lay dead or wounded upon the field ; but neither side could claim a victory. Lee retreated into Virginia, followed at a distance by McClellan, who was soon afterward relieved of command by General Burnside, of Rhode Island.

527. Battle of Fredericksburg.—Burnside advanced in December to attack the strong Confederate works in the rear of Fredericksburg on the Rappahannock. The assault was made with splendid courage and steadiness, and was five times renewed under a storm of cannon-balls, but it was repulsed with a loss of twelve thousand Union men.

528. General Results.—The year had been, on the whole, *disastrous to the national interests in the East,* though the control of the Atlantic coast had been extended by the recovery of Norfolk in Virginia, of Roanoke Island and several points in North Carolina, of Fort Pulaski near Savannah, and of the eastern ports of Florida.

On the other hand the year had been marked by *great successes in the West,* and only two posts on the Mississippi,— Vicksburg and Port Hudson,—were held by the Confederacy. The operations against Vicksburg were checked for a time by the destruction of Grant's magazines of supplies at *Holly Springs,* in Mississippi, by General Van Dorn and his cavalry. Fifteen hundred prisoners were taken, and the property destroyed was variously valued at from one to four millions of dollars.

NOTES.

1. "Through the hole she had made, large enough for a man to enter, the water poured in. In vain Lieutenant Morris, who commanded the "Cumberland," worked the pumps to keep her afloat a few moments more, hoping that a lucky shot might find some weaker place. He only abandoned his guns, as, one after another, the settling of the sinking ship swamped them in the water. The last shot was fired by Matthew Tenney from a gun on a level with the water. That brave man then attempted to escape through the port-hole, but was borne back by the incoming rush, and went down with the ship. With him went down nearly one hundred dead, sick, and wounded, and those who, like him, could not extricate themselves. The "Cumberland" sank in fifty-four feet of water. The commander of her assailant saw the flag of the unconquered but sunken ship still flying above the surface." —*Draper.*

2. **John Ericsson** was born, in 1803, in the province of Vermeland, Sweden; and at an early age displayed great mechanical ability. After serving some years as an engineer in the Swedish army, he went to England, where he introduced several important inventions which attracted great attention and gained the inventor several medals and

prizes. His invention of the propeller not being well received, however, he came to the United States in 1839, and two years later built a war steamer, the "Princeton," for the Government, which was the first steamship ever built with the propeller machinery. This vessel Was also furnished with numerous other ingenious inventions of Ericsson's which have since come into common use. The revolving turret, however, is the most important of Ericsson's inventions, and has caused a complete change in the naval architecture of the world.

3. **"Quaker guns"** are wooden imitations of cannon, frequently used to deceive an enemy as to the strength of a position.

4. **Robert Edward Lee** (*b.* 1807, *d.* 1870) was one of the ablest generals, and one of the most noble characters brought into prominence by the Civil War. He was born at Stafford House, Westmoreland County, Va., and graduated, second in his class, at West Point in 1829. He displayed his great ability, and was employed in the most responsible positions even during the times of peace, and when war was declared with Mexico he was appointed chief engineer. The professional ability and personal bravery there displayed added new laurels to his fame, and rapidly won him the brevets of major, lieutenant-colonel, and colonel. At the close of the war he was recognized by the army as the fitting successor of General Seott whenever the latter should retire from the head of the army.

A letter writ ten to his sister after the secession of Virginia plainly indicates his feeling in regard to the Civil War, and sets forth his reason for giving his services to the Confederate cause. In it he says: "Now we are in a state of war which will yield to nothing. The whole South is in a state of revolution, into which Virginia, after a long struggle, has been drawn ; and though I recognize no necessity for this state of things, and would have forborne and pleaded to the end for redress of grievances, real or supposed, yet in my own person 1 had to meet the question whether I would take part against my native state. With all my devotion to the Union, and the feeling of loyalty and duty of an American citizen, I have not been able to make up my mind to raise my hand against my relatives, my children, and my home. I have therefore resigned my commission in the army, and, save in the defense of my native state, with the hope that my poof services will never be needed, I hope I may never be called on to draw my sword."

During the first year of the war, although one of five generals appointed by the Confederate Congress, Lee was kept in the background, but on his appointment as commander-in-chief, in 1862, new life was infused into the armies under him, and that energy which never flagged to the bitter end began to make itself felt. Although outnumbered,—sometimes by more than two to one,—he kept up the unequal fight for three years, and in the battles during that period usually inflicted far heavier losses than he received. Probably not even Napoleon was so devotedly loved by his soldiers as was Lee, and under his command they were almost invincible. He has been charged with grave mistakes in several instances, such as the invasion of Pennsylvania, which led to the defeat at Gettysburg, and the defense of Petersburg: but in these two, at least, the only error that can be assigned him is in giving way, against his own judgment and advice, to a higher political authority.

The war left him homeless and penniless, and he gladly accepted the presidency of what is now called the " Washington and Lee University," at Lexington, Va. Here, after a quiet, useful life of five years, he died. It is worthy of record that during these last years he used all his influence, in a quiet way, to remove the bitter sectional feelings induced by the war.

CHAPTER XXXVIII.
NINETEENTH ADMINISTRATION EVENTS OF 1863.

Abraham Lincoln, President.   Hannibal Hamlin, Vice-president.

A Truce in the Trenches.

529. The year 1863 opened with **the greatest event of the war.** Until July of 1862 the President had acted in all sincerity upon his avowed intention to leave slavery unmolested in the states where it existed, though his party was pledged to prevent its extension into new states and territories. General Butler had indeed confiscated the negroes whom he found employed upon the Confederate earthworks near Fortress Monroe, considering them as "contraband of (-95) war," and they had been fed and protected as Union refugees. But when Fremont, in Missouri, and other generals, had undertaken to liberate the slaves of those who were fighting against the Government, the President had disapproved and reversed their action.

530. The South, on the other hand, had declared one chief object of secession to be the founding of a republic, of which African slavery should be the corner-stone. If the war was ever to end, this corner-stone must be removed. On the 22d of September, 1862, five days after the battle of Antietam, President Lincoln issued a proclamation declaring that after one hundred days "all persons held as slaves within any state or designated part of a state, the people whereof shall be in rebellion against the United States, shall be then, thenceforward, and forever free."

531. The Emancipation became effective on the first day of January, 1863. Freedmen were invited to enter the service of the United States, and regiments of colored troops were organized in South Carolina and Kansas. Free negroes had already been armed and drilled for Confederate service, and General Butler, commanding at New Orleans, had received several such regiments into the armies of the United States. Within the year more than fifty thousand colored men had enlisted as soldiers and sailors, and they contributed much to the final victories of the Union on the Mississippi.

532. Chancellorsville. — In January, 1863, General Hooker[1] succeeded to the command of the Army of the Potomac. He found it greatly demoralized: 80,000 men and 3,000 officers were absent from their posts. His rigorous discipline soon made it the "finest army on the planet." It was defeated, however, in a two days' battle at *Chancellorsville,* with a loss of 17,000 men. To the South the joy of victory was clouded by the loss of "Stonewall" Jackson,[2] whose impetuous charge with 25,000 men upon the Union right had decided the fortunes of the day. He was returning in the evening to his camp, when he was fired upon through a blunder of some of his own men, and was mortally wounded.

533. New York Riots. — The Southern leaders were now ready for a vigorous invasion of the North, and their cause seemed about to triumph. The Union armies were weakened by the expiration of terms of enlistment, and a riot broke out in New York in resistance to a draft. For three days the disorders continued; a colored orphan asylum and an armory were plundered and burned ; negroes Avere assaulted and even killed by the mob.

Stonewall Jackson.

The peace party had gained strength by the long continuance of the war, with its ruinous cost in blood and treasure; and the force of the Government was correspondingly diminished.

534. Invasion of the North.—Perhaps nothing could so effectually have reunited and nerved the Northern people as the actual invasion of their soil. Lee advanced to Chambersburg, in Pennsylvania, and on the 1st of July met the Army of the Potomac at Gettysburg. General Meade[3] was in command, having superseded Hooker only two days before. The armies were equal in numbers, each counting eighty thousand men, but the Union forces had greatly the advantage in a strong natural position along the crest of Cemetery Ridge.

535. Battle of Gettysburg.—Three days the battle raged which was deciding the fate of a continent. On either side men admired the magnificent valor and steadiness of their opponents. Finally, on the afternoon of July 3d, the flower of the Confederate army, 18,000 strong, made a desperate charge upon the center of the Union line, and in the face of a terrible fire forced their way into the very intrenchments. Here fierce hand-to-hand fighting lasted a few minutes, and then the assailants gave way. The Southern loss is said to have been 36,000 men; that of the North, 23.000. The battle-field was afterwards consecrated as a national cemetery.

536. The retreat of Lee and the surrender of Vicksburg occurred at the same hour, and the result of the war was no longer doubtful. The great stronghold of the Mississippi had been invested by the Federal armies on the 19th of May. Their terrific bombardment on the three following days failed to take the place, and a regular siege began. Citizens refused to leave the town, but dug caves in the damp earth of the hill-sides to avoid the storm of mortarshells exploding in their streets.

537. The Confederate soldiers, who had been sadly demoralized by five severe defeats within twenty days, recovered themselves within the strong works of Vicksburg. Often their pickets were posted within ten yards of those of the Federals ; and, laying aside their arms by mutual consent, the men would spend the night-watches in friendly chat, regardless of the fact that they might be ordered to become each other's murderers before another sun should set. But these informal truces never made either party less brave or less obedient when the stern command was given.

538. End of the Siege. — The outworks of Vicksburg, — Haines's Bluff and Chickasaw Landing, — were soon gained by the Federals, and the latter became their base of sup- plies. Both parties suffered from want of water and from the poisonous vapors of the swamps during the burning days and chilly nights of June. The Confederates, besides, were pinched with hunger, and exhausted by forty-seven days and nights of unrelieved duty in the trenches, when on the 3d of July General Pemberton proposed a surrender. It took place on the 4th, — 15 generals, 31,600 men, and 172 cannon, — the greatest surrender of men and material that had then ever been made in war, and only surpassed since in the capture of Metz and Paris by the Germans.

539. Port Hudson, which had been enduring a similar siege by General Banks, surrendered four days later than Vicksburg. The war was ended on the Mississippi; the divided members of the Confederacy were never reunited; and the great river flowed, unvexed by hostile craft, from Minnesota to the Gulf.

540. Morgan's Raid.—During this eventful month of July the Confederate General Morgan made a dash into Indiana and Ohio with 4,000 cavalry. He entered the former state at Brandenburg, and, after scouring the country around Cincinnati, thought to leave Ohio at Parkersburg. Here, however, his retreat was cut off by the Federal gun-boats in the Ohio River, and he was overtaken by the state militia. Most of his men were captured, and he spent four months in the penitentiary at Columbus.

541. Autumn of 1863.—The most important events of the autumn were in the mountain region of eastern Tennessee and northern Georgia. Throughout the South the people of the mountainous regions were ready to aid and support the National cause; and the Government desired to protect them, as well as to hold the great natural barriers between the Atlantic slope and the Mississippi Valley.

542. The cliff, which the Indians had named *Chattanooga*, or Eagle's Nest, rises like a wall two thousand feet from the

Lookout Mountain.

banks of the Tennessee. Its English name is Lookout Mountain, while the Indian name of the cliff has been applied to the town near its base. This was and is a great railway center, through which the whole interior of the cotton region is connected with the North. Missionary Ridge, on the east and south, was the boundary of the Cherokee Nation before its removal to the westward ; and here, two hundred years ago, the French missionaries held their schools of native children.

543. Siege of Chattanooga.—General Rosecrans, during the summer of 1863, gained all Tennessee for the Union cause; but in September he was severely defeated on the *Chickamauga River*, nine miles from Chattanooga, and was closely besieged for two months in the town by General Bragg. At this point Rosecrans was relieved of command; and the three military departments of the Ohio, the Tennessee, and the Cumberland were united under General Grant. He arrived at Chattanooga, October 23, and in five days threw open the road to Nashville, by which abundant supplies reached the starving National troops. As the first provision train steamed into the station, soldiers, sick with hunger, thronged to embrace the very locomotive as if it had been a living friend.

544. Their health and spirits were suddenly restored. General Thomas,[4] who had saved the battle on the Chickamauga from being a rout, commanded the Army of the Cumberland. General Hooker arrived from Virginia with 23,000 men ; Sherman, with four divisions of his victorious army of the Tennessee, came to have part in the decisive battle which was now to be fought for the possession of the gate-way to the South.

545. Battle of Lookout Mountain.—On the 23d of November Thomas seized and fortified *Orchard Knob,* advancing the National line one mile beyond that which the Confederates had occupied a few hours before. Here Grant stationed himself to watch the great battle-field thirteen miles in length. The next day Hooker charged up *Lookout Mountain* above the river mists which settled densely in the valley. All the morning the battle raged "above the clouds;" but the victory was complete. The next day Hooker descended the north-eastern slope and advanced to the Rossville Gap in Missionary Ridge, while Sherman carried the northern end of the same range, and forced Bragg to weaken his center to save his extreme right.

546. Battle of Missionary Ridge.—While the Confederates were making this difficult movement, the decisive blow was struck by the Army of the Cumberland, which, dashing over the plain at a full run, with their bayonets held in a dazzling, wavering line, charged up Missionary Ridge under a plunging fire from the Confederate guns. Fifty- five minutes from their first movement they were in full possession of the ridge; and the cannon at the summit had not cooled when they Avere wheeled about and fired against their late masters.

Sheridan pursued and captured most of the artillery which Bragg had removed.

Joseph Hooker.

547. Sherman immediately pushed northward to the relief of Burnside, who was shut up in *Knoxville* by General Longstreet.³ The latter, with superior numbers, attacked him as soon as he heard of the Confederate defeat at Chattanooga. Burnside's men fought bravely, though weakened by short rations, and the attack was repulsed.

NOTES.

1. Joseph Hooker (*b.* 1814, *d.* 1879) wasborn al Hadley, Mass., and graduated al West Point in 1837. His first active service was in the war against the Seminoles. In the Mexican War he was distinguished by three successive brevets, rising to the rank of lieutenant-colonel. In 1853 he resigned from the army, and engaged in farming in California. At the outbreak of the war in 1861 he tendered his services to the United States, and was appointed brigadier-general of volunteers. Throughout the war be was noted for his personal bravery, and came to be known as "Fighting Joe." He retired in 1868 on the full rank of major-general.

2. Jonathan Thomas Jackson was born in 1824 at Clarksburg, Harrison County, in what is now West Virginia. He graduated at west Point in 1846, but after gallant service in the Mexican War he resigned from the army, having accepted an appointment to a chair in the Virginia State Military Institute at Lexington. Here he remained in comparative obscurity until 1861, when he at once tendered his services to the Southern Confederacy. He was exactly two years in its service, being placed in command of Harper's Ferry, May 2d, 1861, and falling at Chancellorsville, Mav2d, 1863. His firm stand at Bull Run changed the fortunes of the day, and gained for him and his brigade the undying name of "Stonewall." In his "Valley Campaigns," with a comparatively petty force, he struck blow after blow with a rapidity and secrecy that were marvellous, and managed to neutralize a Federal force aggregating 70,000 men. He thus ruined McClellan's general plans, and inspired the gravest fears in the North for the safety of Washington. In the history of Chancellorsville, by Hotchkiss and Allan, Jackson is thus spoken of:

He was the most remarkable man produced by our Civil War. His previous comparative obscurity, his rapid rise to power and fame, his wonderful achievements with means always limited, and success almost unbroken, the mighty enthusiasm with which he inspired soldiers and people, gave to his career the character of romance, and seem rather the fancied story of some knight of old than the history of a simple, unpretending citizen." .... "He fell ere his victory was completed, but enough had been done to till up the full measure of his fame."

3. George Gordon Meade was born at Cadiz, Spain, in 1815, where his father was at that time United States naval agent. Meade graduated at West Point in 1835, and served with distinction against the Seminoles and throughout the Mexican War. On his return from the latter the citizens of Philadelphia presented him with a sword. He was in many of the hardest fought battles of the war, and at Antietam was slightly wounded and had two horses shot under him. For his hard-won victory at Gettysburg he received the thanks of Congress, and after the war closed many honors were bestowed upon him. The citizens of Philadelphia presented his wife with a house, and, after his death in 1872, subscribed a fund of $100,000 for his family.

4. George Henry Thomas (*b.* 1816, *d.* 1870) was born in Southampton County, Va., and graduated at West Point in 1840. The next year he was breveted for gallantry in the war with the Seminoles, and during the Mexican War he was advanced to the rank of brevet major. During the live years immediately preceding the Civil War, Thomas, as major of the Second Cavalry, was stationed in Texas. Of this regiment A.S. Johnston was colonel, Robert E. Lee lieutenant-colonel, W. J. Hardee senior major, with Kirby Smith, Fitz Hugh Lee, Hood, and others, as subordinate officers, who afterwards became prominent on the

Southern side during the war. Considering this faet, his surroundings, and the place of his birth, Thomas's adherence to the Union is remarkable. Few generals on either side did better service or so commanded the love and esteem of their subordinates. His stand at Chickamauga after the rout of the right and center, was one of the most heroic events of the war. When peace was declared Thomas had attained the rank of major-general of the regular army, and it is characteristic of the man that he refused the rank of lieutenant-general, tendered him in 1868, on the ground that he had done nothing since the war to deserve such promotion. Upon his death, Congress passed resolutions of sympathy, and military honors accompanied his burial at Troy, N. Y.

5. **General James Longstreet** was born in South Carolina in 1820. but removed with his family during his childhood to Alabama, from which state be received his appointment to West Point. Here he graduated in 1842, and in the Mexican War, which soon followed, he was advanced for gallant conduct to the rank of brevet major.

He resigned his commission in 1861 to join the Confederate army, in which he bore a conspicuous part from the battle of Bull Run, where he commanded a brigade, to the close of the war, when he had attained the rank of lieutenant-general. He possessed something of Stonewall Jackson's ability to draw out to the fullest extent the fighting qualities of the men in his command. It was he that covered the retreat of Lee to Richmond after the battle of Williamsburg § 521). At Fair Oaks (§ 523) his troops bore the brunt of the battle, and during the seven days lighting that followed, were reduced in numbers nearly one half. Again, at Fredericksburg, in Virginia, and at Chickamauga, in Tennessee, it was Longstreet's command that carried the day for the Confederates. After being driven from Knoxville by Sherman he joined Lee in Virginia, and was severely wounded in the battle of the Wilderness by his own troops.

Since the war General Longstreet, accepting the situation, has done his utmost to restore harmony of feeling between the divided sections of his country. In 1880 he was appointed U. S. minister to Constantinople.

CHAPTER XXXIX.
NINETEENTH ADMINISTRATION EVENTS OF 1864.

Abraham Lincoln, President.   Hannibal Hamlin, Vice-president.

548. The main military movement of the early months was the " Meridian raid" of part of Sherman's army. They destroyed all the railroads centering at Meridian, Mississippi, with their bridges and trestle-works, and made it impossible for the Confederates either to draw supplies from the state or to move large bodies of troops within it.

549. Lieutenant-general Grant.— Congress revived the grade of lieutenant-general, hitherto borne only by Washington and Scott, and in March General Grant was placed at the head of all the armies of the United States. Henceforth there was no scattering of forces. Grant in the East, and Sherman in the West, acted upon one plan, which they had formed together in an interview at Cincinnati.

550. Battles in the Wilderness.— The fortunes of the Confederacy now depended upon two armies : that of General Lee, in Virginia, and that of General J. E. Johnston, in Georgia. Grant crossed the Rapidan and commenced his march to Richmond. All the obstacles that the highest military genius could invent, and that perfect valor and discipline could execute, were thrown in his way. Dense woods blocked his advance, and a two days' battle in this gloomy "Wilderness" cost 20,000 of his brave men; but acknowledging no defeat, he pressed on, intending to turn the Confederate right flank and cut their line of connection with Richmond.

551. Lee perceived the plan, and checked it by placing a division of his army upon Grant's road to *Spottsylvania Court-house.* Five days' severe fighting resulted in immense losses to both parties and no decided gain to either. Still Grant telegraphed, "I propose to fight it out on this line, if it takes all summer." He relied upon the superior resources of the North in men and means; and thought that, the campaign once begun, the interest of all parties required him to push it through to the speediest possible conclusion.

Philip H. Sheridan.

552. Sheridan's Raid. —Of three side-movements which he had planned, only one succeeded. General Sigel was severely defeated in the Shenandoah Valley, and General Butler on the James. General Sheridan,[1] however, made a brilliant cavalry dash around the rear of the Confederate army, destroyed miles of railroad on which it depended for supplies, and even captured some of the outer defenses of Richmond.

553. The Confederate General Early, meanwhile, with 20,000 men, dashed down the *Shenandoah Valley*, crossed into Maryland and Pennsylvania, and threatened Washington. It was saved, however, by the timely advance of National troops, and Early retreated. In October he was met by Sheridan, who defeated him twice, and drove him up the Valley. In a battle at *Cedar Creek*, the Confederates seemed likely to regain all that they had lost, for the Federals were driven four miles from their position; but Sheridan, hearing the roar of cannon thirteen miles away, galloped to the field just in time to rally his disordered lines and lead them back to victory. Washington was never again threatened by the Confederates. The beautiful Shenandoah Valley was left bare of every thing that could feed or tempt an army.

554. Disaster at Petersburg.—Grant was still pushing his advance, resisted at every step. Crossing the James, he besieged both Richmond and Petersburg. At the latter place a mine was sprung under a Confederate fort, and the Union troops pressed forward over theruins; but they were met by a storm of shot and shell which destroyed four thousand lives in a few minutes.

Joseph E. Johnston.

A first attempt upon the *Weldon Railroad* failed with immense loss; but in August that important line was secured by the National troops, and Richmond was cut off from the South. The siege continued until April of 1865.

555. Campaign in Georgia.—Sherman moved from Chattanooga toward Atlanta three days later than Grant entered upon his campaign in the Wilderness. His forces were nearly double those of Johnston,[2] who conducted a masterly retreat among the woods and mountains of northern Georgia. Avoiding a battle, Johnston intrenched himself in the strongest positions where, if attacked, he always repulsed his enemy; but Sherman, by a skillful flank movement, always managed to seize his lines of supply and force him to fall back.

556. In this way the two armies arrived near *Atlanta*, where Johnston was superseded by General Hood, and more active operations commenced. Johnston's cautious tactics, though they had displeased his superiors, were fully justified by the results. Hood was three times defeated within nine days, with a loss of 20,000 men. Sherman broke up the railroads to the west and south of Atlanta, and managed to throw himself between two divisions of Hood's army, so that he could crush them both in succession.

William T. Sherman.

557. Destruction of Atlanta.—Thus out-generaled and cut off from supplies, Hood destroyed what he could of the mills, foundries, and stores in Atlanta, and abandoned

558. Sherman's March to the Sea.—Hood pushed northward into Tennessee, expecting that Sherman would follow him. But this was no part of the Federal plan. Leaving Generals Schofield and Thomas to complete the destruction of Hood's army, Sherman[3] burned Atlanta, and moved rapidly toward the sea, with his army of 60,000 men. Moving in four columns, living upon the country as they went, tearing up and twisting iron rails so as utterly to destroy railway connections, the conquering army left a track of desolation sixty miles in width behind it. No effective resistance was encountered, for all able-bodied men were in Confederate camps. The South had put forth her last efforts, and the Confederacy was indeed "an empty shell."

559. The city of Savannah was abandoned, after Fort McAllister had been taken by storm, and it was occupied by General Sherman, December 21.

General Butler's attempt upon Fort Fisher, which guarded *Wilmington,* in North Carolina, failed a few days later: but Commodore Porter[4] maintained his position with his gunboats, and upon the arrival of fresh troops the fort was taken, January 15, 1865. The last port of the Confederacy was now closed.

560. Mobile Bay.—The forts and floating defenses of *Mobile* harbor had been taken in August, by Admiral Farragut, in one of the most remarkable naval actions of the war. The approaches from the Gulf were well guarded, not only by forts and batteries on shore, but by sunken torpedoes, and by a powerful fleet, commanded by the highest officer of the Confederate navy. The fourteen Federal vessels that were outside the bar advanced, "two abreast and lashed together," delivering their broadsides of heavy shot with perfect precision as they passed the forts. Four Federal iron-clads already within the bar joined in the battle, which was kept up for three hours with great spirit and resolution on both sides. The severest conflict was with the Confederate ram *Tennessee,* which engaged five Union vessels at once, but at length surrendered. Mobile Bay was restored to the nation, and blockade-running ceased in the Gulf. *Charleston* had been besieged since June of 1863 by Admiral Dahlgren and General Gillmore.

561. Re-election of Lincoln.—At the autumn election of 1864 Abraham Lincoln was chosen President by an immense majority in the loyal states, *Andrew Johnson,* of Tennessee, being Vice-president. Congress voted an amendment[5] to the Constitution, declaring that "neither slavery nor involuntary servitude, except as a punishment for crime, shall exist within the United States, or in any place subject to their jurisdiction." In due time this amendment was ratified by the legislatures of more than two thirds of the states, and became a fundamental law of the land.

NOTES.

1. **Philip Henry Sheridan** was born in Somerset, Perry County, Ohio, in 1831, and received his education at West Point. Until the breaking ont of the Civil War he was stationed most of the time in Texas and on the Pacific coast. He was then made chief quartermaster to the army of South-western Missouri, and it was not until May of 1862 that he was transferred to a cavalry command. He immediately began to show that ability and energy which afterwards caused him to be recognized as the most able cavalry leader of the war. For defeating a superior cavalry force at Booneville, Miss., on July 1st, 1862, he was made brigadier-general, and, the following December, was advanced to the rank of major-general for gallant action at Murfreesborough. At Chickamauga he again distinguished himself: and, at the head of his division, fearlessly led the charge up Missionary Ridge. When Grant was made lieutenant-general of the United States armies in 1864, he had Sheridan transferred to the East, and gave him command of the cavalry in the Army of the Potomac. The many brilliant raids and hard-won victories which followed, increased his fame; and the decisive battle of Five Forks, conducted by Sheridan with rare skill, compelled Lee to evacuate Petersburg.

Sheridan's rank is now lieutenant-general of the regular army, and his head-quarters are at Chicago, Illinois.

2. **Joseph Eccleston Johnston** was born in Prince Edward County, Va., in 1807, and graduated at West Point in 1829. Of all the Southern generals, he had held the senior rank in the United States army, and, notwithstanding a great deal of unjust criticism, he probably did more for the Confederate cause than any general except Lee.

He had had extensive experience on the western frontier, against the Florida Indians, and in the Mexican War. During the latter he was twice wounded, and for his gallantry was three times breveted, rising to the rank of colonel. In 1860 he had attained the rank of brigadier-general of staff, and held this position when he resigned his commission April 22d,

1861, and cast his lot with the Confederacy. After the surrender of his army to General Sherman, he addressed the following order to his troops:

"Comrades: In terminating our official relations, I earnestly exhort yon to observe faithfully the terms of pacification agreed upon : and to discharge the obligations of good and peaceful citizens, as well as you have performed the duties of thorough soldiers in the field. By such a course you will best secure the comfort of your families and kindred, and restore tranquillity to our country."

3. **William Tecumseh Sherman** was born in Lancaster, Ohio, in 1820. When he was nine years of age his father died, and the Hon. Thomas Ewing took Sherman into his family. After graduating at West Point in 1840, Sherman saw active service in the Seminole War, but took no part in the Mexican War which followed. At that time he was stationed on the Pacific coast, where he remained until 18.50. He then was sent to New York as bearer of dispatches, and while there was married to Ellen Ewing, daughter of his benefactor. He resigned from the army in 1853, and engaged in banking in San Francisco and New York. During 1858 and 1859 he practiced law in Leavenworth, and on January 1, I860, he assumed the duties of superintendent of the "Louisiana State Seminary of Learning, and Military Academy" at Alexandria. When it seemed probable that the stale would join in the secession movement, Sherman demanded his release from the governor of the state. His request was granted, and in February of 1861 Sherman removed to St. Louis. Being appointed colonel in the regular army, he embarked in the war, commanding a division at the memorable battle of Bull Run. After that battle, he was made brigadier-general of volunteers and transferred to the West. His action there soon stamped him as an able commander, and in his official report of the battle of Shiloh General Grant said, "I am indebted to General Sherman for the success of the battle." His gallant service during the siege of Vicksburg was rewarded by the rank of brigadier- general in the regular army. When Grant was made lieutenant-general, he had Sherman appointed as his successor in chief command of the Western armies of the Union, and the latter immediately began to prepare for that " March to the Sea," which is one of the most celebrated events in our history.

After Grant's resignation of the office, Sherman was appointed General of the army, and still holds that position, with head-quarters at Washington.

4. David Dixon Porter was born in Philadelphia in 1813. His father was David Porter, who did such gallant service in the War of 1812 (§379). Both father and son entered the service of Mexico in her war with Spain, and when the latter was only fourteen years of age he was engaged in a very bloody sea-fight with a much superior Spanish vessel. That war closing, young Porter entered the United States Navy, and after a long interval of peace, during which he served in the Mediterranean squadron, and on the coast survey at home, the Mexican War gave him an opportunity of adding fresh laurels to an already famous name. His first service in the Civil War was the relief of Fort Pickens, and he then immediately began the construction and organization of the mortar flotilla which did such effective work in the reduction of New Orleans and Vicksburg. Porter's aid in capturing the last point won him the rank of rear-admiral, and he was given command of all the naval forces on the western rivers above New Orleans. Being transferred to the North Atlantic blockading squadron, Porter crowned his valuable services to the Union by the capture of Fort Fisher at Wilmington, N. C. He was made vice-admiral in 1866, and for the four succeeding years had charge of the naval school at Annapolis. In 1870, on the death of Farragut, he succeeded to the highest rank, as Admiral of the Navy of the United States.

5. It will be noticed that the wording of this amendment is identical, in part, with that of the act establishing the North-west Territory (§324), and with the language of the Wilmot Proviso (§ 460, Note).

CHAPTER XL.
TWENTIETH ADMINISTRATION EVENTS OF 1865.

Abraham Lincoln, President. *Andrew Johnson, Vice-president.*

562. **Sherman in South Carolina.**—After a month's rest in Savannah, Sherman pursued his "grand march" through the Carolinas. Columbia was taken, February 17, after its stores of cotton had been set on fire. The flames spread to dwellings, and a great part of the city was consumed. General Hardee found it necessary to abandon Charleston. The immense magazines of cotton were kindled by his orders; unhappily the fire reached a mass of powder, and two hundred lives were destroyed by the explosion.[1] Though every effort was made to arrest the flames, the fair city became a scene of ruin and desolation.

563. **Passing into North Carolina**, Sherman was met by Johnston, who had been again placed in command. The latter was defeated at *Averysboro* and *Bentonville,* and, April 13, Sherman took possession of *Raleigh.* The forces of the Confederacy now consisted of the remnant of Johnston's troops and Lee's army of 40,000 men, which lay behind the earth-works of Richmond and Petersburg, hemmed in by Grant's 100,000 veterans.

564. **The Last Effort.**—To disguise his plan of moving southward to join Johnston, Lee attacked and took Fort Steedman, but it was almost immediately recaptured. Three thousand men were lost in the vain assault, and Grant made no movement to relax his hold upon the Southern roads. On the first of April Sheridan advanced to *Five Forks,* twelve miles in the rear of Lee's position, and captured its garrison of 5,000 men.

565. **Advance upon Richmond.**—The next morning the Union

army advanced upon Richmond. Resistance was no longer possible. President Davis was in church when the news reached him that the lines were broken and that Lee was forced to retire from the capital. Measures were immediately taken for removing the papers and other property of the Confederate government. Citizens took the alarm, and soon the streets were clogged with wagons carrying household goods and valuables. The confusion increased all night. The city authorities ordered the destruction of all intoxicating liquors; but some soldiers managed to secure a portion, and added the horrors of a mad carousal to those inseparable from the abandonment of the city.

566. Burning of Richmond.—Four great store-houses of tobacco were set on fire by General Ewell's order; ironclads were blown up; bridges burnt; the flames "leaped from street to street," and the roar of the conflagration was heard above the rumbling of wheels and all the other sounds of flight. On Monday morning, the 3d of April, the National forces occupied the Confederate capital.

567. Lee's Surrender.—Lee retreated westward, closely pursued by Grant. His men had nothing to eat but the shoots of trees, and were so worn out that their progress was very slow. Arms were thrown away, and hundreds deserted at a time. Sheridan, with his cavalry, hung on his flanks, and captured thousands of prisoners. Finally, on the 9th, Lee surrendered his entire command, then consisting of less than 28,000 men, at Appomattox Court-house, Virginia. Officers and men, having given their word of honor to fight no more against the United States, "until properly exchanged," were dismissed to their homes. Johnston surrendered [2] on similar terms to Sherman, April 26th, and the few scattered forces of the Confederacy followed the example.

Fortress Monroe.

568. President Davis, after a feeble attempt to keep up the forms of a government at Danville, escaped to the southward. He was arrested by Union forces near Irwinsville, Georgia, and was held for two years a prisoner at Fortress Monroe. Then he was released on bail, and the proposed trial for treason never took place.

569. Mr. Lincoln's second Inaugural Address, on the 4th of March, 1865, fairly stated the positions of the two parties in the Civil War: "Both read the same Bible, and pray to the same God ; and each invokes His aid against the other. . . . The prayers of both could not be answered. That of neither has been answered fully. The Almighty has his own purposes. . . . With malice towards none, with charity for all, with firmness in the right, as God gives us to see the right, let us strive on to finish the work we are in, to bind up the Nation's wounds, ... to do all which may achieve and cherish a just and lasting peace among ourselves and with all nations."

It was believed that the same just and manly spirit which had guided the nation through the tempest of civil war would best preside over its interests in the restoration of peace. But so it was not to be.

570. Thanksgiving Day.—The fourth anniversary of the surrender of Sumter was appointed by the President as a day of thanksgiving for *the close of the war*. By his invitation a party of distinguished civilians repaired to Charleston, and witnessed the raising of the stars and stripes above the ruined fort.[3] He remained at his post in Washington. In the evening, learning that the people would be disappointed if he failed to appear at the theater, he went thither accompanied by his wife. A half-mad actor, named John Wilkes Booth, who had been nerving himself to the horrid deed by draughts of brandy, entered the President's private box and shot him through the head; then, leaping to the stage, escaped, took horse, and spurred away into the darkness. At the same time another murderer visited the house of Mr. Seward, who was ill in bed, and stabbed him several times, but not mortally.

571. Death of the President.—Mr. Lincoln lingered until the next morning in unconsciousness, and then died. The horror and indignation excited by the wicked plot was not confined to the North. It was found, however, that only a few persons of no great reputation were concerned in it.[4] Booth was overtaken and shot, as he refused to surrender; four of his accomplices were hanged, and three Avere imprisoned for life.

As the funeral escort of the dead President passed through the northern cities to his old home in Springfield, Illinois, it was attended by many tokens of the love and grief of the people.

572. The Seventeenth President.—Vice-president *Andrew Johnson* took the oath of the highest office on the day of Mr. Lincoln's death, and became the seventeenth President of the United States.

573. Nevada was the third state formed (1864) from the lands acquired from Mexico. Its rich silver mines, discovered in 1859, have drawn a crowd of adventurers; and in no state have such sudden and immense fortunes been made. *Carson City* and *Virginia City* are centers of mining interests.

Several territories were divided during this period, and *Dakota, Arizona, Idaho,* and *Montana* received regular territorial governments.

Read histories of the Civil War by Greeley, Draper, Stephens, Pollard, and Lossing : Moore's "Rebellion Record;" Badeau's " Life of Grant;" Johnston's "Narrative of Military Operations."

NOTES.

1. "Some boys had discovered powder at the depot of the "Northwestern Railway,"and amused themselves by throwing some of it on the burning eotton in the street. The powder dropping from their hands soon formed a train, along which tire ran to the large quantity stored at the depot. A terrible explosion followed, by which the city was shaken to its foundations"–*Lossing.*

2. Terms of surrender were first agreed upon between Sherman and Johnston on the 18th of April. But the terms were considered too liberal by the Government, and were refused.

3. On this occasion a well-deserved compliment was paid to Anderson, then a major-general. With his own hands he raised the identical flag that he had been compelled to lower four years before.

4. It was at first supposed that Jefferson Davis and a number of leading Confederates were implicated in the plot, and President Johnson accordingly offered rewards for their capture : $100,000 for Davis, $25,000 each for four others, and $10,000 for another.

CHAPTER XLI.
RESULTS OF THE CIVIL WAR.

574. The war once over, all reasonable men were ready to join in repairing its wastes and forgetting its enmities. Doubtless there were selfish Northern adventurers, who cared only to make their own fortunes out of the poverty of the exhausted South and the ignorance of the freedmen ; while there were disappointed politicians, who, having failed to destroy the Government, used every opportunity to obstruct its action. Both these classes presented obstacles to the thorough restoration of peace, but their influence could not be lasting.

575. The strength and the clemency of the great Republic were equally proved by the circumstances attending the close of the war. The hopes of its enemies were disappointed. It had been said that the peaceful, industrious pursuits of the majority of the people had unfitted them for war; and that, used as they were to personal independence, they would never submit to the needful discipline of the army. But it was found that men will fight most cheerfully and bravely for a government that represents their will and promotes their prosperity, and that happy home-life, so far from destroying courage, is a strong incentive to it.

576. Great anxiety was expressed, at the close of the war, lest the letting loose of more than a million of men, used to the rough disorders of camp-life, might endanger the security of the country. The very persons who had said "Americans will never fight," now predicted that they would never cease from fighting. But the disbanded citizensoldiers gladly and peaceably returned to their homes, and public order was not seriously disturbed.

577. The National debt had increased to more than twenty-seven hundred millions of dollars. If to this be added the expenses of states, counties, and towns, the cost of the war was at least

$4,000,000,000. Part of the sum was raised by the issue of "greenbacks;" *i. e.*, the Government's promises to pay certain amounts to the bearer; and these fell in value until $2.90 in paper had to be paid for $1.00 in gold. Gold and silver coin disappeared, and, until the Government provided a fractional paper currency, postage-stamps did duty as small change.

578. **Prosperity and Public Credit.**—At the same time, the immense contracts given out by the Government afforded work to multitudes of people, and never were wages higher nor the appearances of prosperity greater than during the early years of the war. Though the war expenses toward the end of the great conflict exceeded in one year the whole cost of the Government from Washington to Buchanan, yet public credit was unshaken, and the loan called for in March, 1865, was taken to the amount of $530,000,000 in five months.

579. **The Confederate paper money** was only a promise to pay certain sums, two or six months after the conclusion of peace between the Confederate States and the United States. As the hope of such a peace vanished, the currency became worthless, and was found scattered about the streets of Nashville and Atlanta like waste paper. The bonds of the Confederacy, of course, could never be paid.

580. **The loss of life** during the war was not far from 600,000 on both sides. It is impossible to number the lingering deaths of those whose health was ruined by exposure on battle-fields and in camps. Some idea of the maiming effects of war may be obtained from the fact that the United States provided more than seven thousand artificial limbs for disabled soldiers.

581. **If we ask what was gained** by all this suffering and expenditure of life and treasure, we find that the South, before the war was over, gave up the two principles for which it was ostensibly made. The right of secession was indeed a principle which no government could admit, and, notwithstanding its assertion of state sovereignty,

the Confederacy was from the very beginning more strongly centralized than the Union had ever been. Its leaders found, just as their fathers had found in Revolutionary times (§234), that a rope of sand is not strong enough to bear the strain of war. One flag, one uniform, were seen all through the South, and one will at Richmond controlled all movements.

582. Abandonment of Slavery.—The other principle was far more reluctantly abandoned; but before Lee's surrender the Confederate government, like that of the Union two years before, had come to the resolution to arm the negroes, and thus in the end to set them free. The two purposes of the war being thus given up, it might seem that the conflict itself should have ceased; and so it would, at an earlier date, if the people had been as well informed as its government.

583. No one can hear without the warmest admiration of the sacrifices and sufferings of the Southern people. Cut off from their usual means of communication with the outer world, they were deluded by false rumors of success and false reports of the character of their opponents. Naturally, bitter prejudices prevailed; and it was long before the people found that their Northern fellow-countrymen Avere human like themselves, and that the real interests of all were the same. Before the end of the Avar, every man between the ages of seventeen and fifty-five had been called to the ranks; property every-where was seized by the Confederate government at its own prices. 100,000 soldiers deserted within a few weeks, not from cowardice, for no men Avere ever braver, but because their families were starving.

584. The conduct of the war on both sides proved *the progress of science*. During some great battles, all the National major-generals were in council, though hundreds of miles apart, by the aid of electric wires. Fifteen thousand miles of military telegraph were sold when the war was over. The antiquated cannon and small arms with which the conflict began were replaced by Dahlgrens, columbiads, and the most improved rifles, and in naval architecture America surpassed all nations.

585. Sanitary Commissions.—Never had science and human sympathy gained such victories over the horrid brutalities of war. The *United States Sanitary Commission* dispensed twelve millions of dollars in money and supplies for the relief of the sick and wounded, and the *Western. Sanitary Commission,* three millions more. But money could not measure the service rendered : the home comforts added to the rough necessaries of the military hospital; the "feedingstations " and night lodgings for soldiers returning home on sick-leave; the strength imparted by the assurance that their sufferings were gratefully remembered.

586. The Christian Commission, also, shared the hardships of the march, the trench, the battle-field; and cared for both bodies and souls. It cheered the sick, comforted the dying, buried the dead. It supplied $5,000,000 in money and material. Both Commissions continued their kind offices after the war was over, providing homes for disabled soldiers and employment for those who needed it.

587. Foreign Results of the War.—One sixth part of all the people in England depended for their daily bread upon the cotton manufacture, and suffered severely from the blockade (§497) which deprived them of their material for work. Lancashire weavers were starving; and neither Egypt nor India could supply cotton enough to give them employment. Moreover, English manufacturers were injured by the high tariff (§398) which excluded their goods from American markets, and a very strong and bitter feeling against the Union prevailed. The British government, however, resisted all pressure which would have carried it into interference in the Avar.

588. Napoleon III., Emperor of the French, believing that the Union was already destroyed, sent an army to Mexico, thinking to establish an empire of the "Latin Race " in America, and perhaps to regain part of the great territory which France had sold (§§356, 357).

But the Union victories, and the firm remonstrances of the Government, led him to abandon his Mexican plans. The Emperor Maximilian, whom he had placed upon a tottering throne, was betrayed and shot ; his poor wife, crazed with grief, vainly besought help from the governments which had led him to his destruction. Mexico continued to be a republic, on friendly terms with the United States.

QUESTIONS FOR REVIEW.—Part V.

		Section
1.	With what views and expectations did the North and the South go to war?	487, 488
2.	Describe the beginning of hostilities.	489
3.	What Southern states refused to secede?	490
4.	Name the eleven seceding states.	481, 490
5.	What preparations were made on both sides?	491
6.	What changes occurred in Virginia?	492
7.	Describe the first great battle and its effects.	493-495
8.	The blockade and attempts to break it.	496-498
9.	The affair with the British steamer Trent,	499, 500
10.	What was accomplished during 1861 ?	501
11.	What three objects comprised the Federal plan of the war ?	502
12.	Sketch the campaign in which forts Henry and Donelson were taken.	502-504
13.	Describe the battle of Shiloh, or Pittsburg Landing.	505-507
14.	What occurred meanwhile on the Mississippi and in Missouri ?	508
15.	What was the Confederate plan for the autumn of 1862?	509
16.	Describe the campaign in Kentucky.	510-513
17.	What was done on the lower Mississippi?	514, 515
18.	Describe the doings of the Merrimac and the first Monitor.	516-519
19.	What was done in 1862 by the Army of the Potomac?	520-524
20.	What resulted from Lee's first invasion of Maryland?	525, 526
21.	What was the general result of 1862?	528
22.	What were the causes and effects of the Emancipation Proclamation ?	529-531
23.	What changes and disasters to the Army of the Potomac, January to May, 1863?	532

	Section
24. Describe Lee's second invasion of the North.	533-535
25. The siege and surrender of Vicksburg and Port Hudson.	536-539
26. General Morgan's movement north of the Ohio.	540
27. The objects, scenes, and events of the Chattanooga campaign.	541-547
28. Grant's campaign in the Wilderness.	549-554
29. Sherman's movements in Georgia.	555-559
30. What three cities were besieged by the U. S. Navy?	559, 560
31. What was done by Sherman in the Carolinas?	562, 563
32. Describe the surrender of Richmond, of Lee's army, and of the Confederate president.	564-568
33. The second inauguration and the death of Lincoln.	569-571
34. Sum up the effects of the Civil War at home and abroad.	574-582, 587, 588
35. What scientific improvements were of use during the war?	584
36. What was done by the Sanitary and Christian Commissions?	585, 586

PART VI.—THE UNION RESTORED.

CHAPTER XLII.
Johnson's administration, a. d. 1865-1869.

589. An important question had now to be settled. Were the lately seceded states out of the Union or in it? The President [1] held that they had never been out ; a majority in Congress, though denying the privilege of secession, insisted that they had forfeited their state rights and must be dealt with as territories. The difference of policy between Congress and the President grew wider, and three important laws were passed over his veto. One established a *Freedmen's Bureau* to protect and provide for the lately emancipated slaves; a second guaranteed their *civil rights :* a third made it illegal for the President to *remove any civil officer* without the consent of the Senate.

Andrew Johnson.

590. Impeachment of Andrew Johnson.—The last, —called the "Tenure of Office Bill," —was infringed by the President's dismissal of Edwin M. Stanton,[2] Secretary of War. Thereupon the House of Representatives impeached Andrew Johnson before the bar of the Senate, March, t868.

Chief-justice Salmon P. Chase[3] presiding. The trial lasted more than two months. The President was acquitted, as one vote was lacking of the two thirds required for his condemnation.

591. The work of Reconstruction went on. The principle of the Civil Rights Bill was embodied in a Fourteenth Amendment to the Constitution, which was promptly accepted by Tennessee, and ultimately by the other states. In time all the new state governments annulled the ordinances of secession, repudiated the Confederate war-debts, and were admitted to representation in Congress. One source of bitterness remained. Candidates for office were required to take the "iron-clad oath," as it was called, declaring that they had no part in the war for secession. Few of the intelligent class in the South could take this oath,, though many frankly accepted the results of the war, and were ready in good faith to resume their allegiance to the United States. The consequence was that public offices often fell into the hands of Northern immigrants and freed negroes.

592. Submarine Telegraph.—The year 1866 was signalized by the successful completion of a submarine telegraph connecting Europe and America. The hero of the enterprise was Mr. Cyrus W. Field,[4] of New York, who, during twelve years of costly experiments, never lost heart, even under disastrous failure; but, crossing the ocean fifty times, succeeded in imparting his own courage to English and American capitalists. The first transatlantic cable was laid in 1858 from Heart's Content, in Newfoundland, to Valencia Bay, in Ireland. It transmitted four hundred messages, but ceased to work within a month.

593. Many ridiculed the idea of renewing the attempt, but Mr. Field soon formed a new company with a capital

Sitka.

of three millions of dollars; a greatly improved cable was constructed, and in June, 1865, the *Great Eastern* began to lay it on the ocean bed. Half her task was completed, when the cable broke and was lost beneath the waves. A new company was promptly formed, a new cable made, and in the following summer the two hemispheres were connected by lines of instant communication. Repairing to the scene of her former failure, the *Great Eastern* picked up the lost cable, joined the severed strands, and successfully laid it. Afterwards a cable was laid from Brest, in France, to Duxbury, in Massachusetts.

594.   The purchase of all Russian America for $7,200,000, in 1867, greatly enlarged the territory of the United States. From its southwestern peninsula, the whole country is called *Alaska*. Sitka, its chief town, is said to be the rainiest settlement on the globe. The wealth of the region consists in its pine and cedar timber, its seal-skins and other valuable furs, and its mineral deposits, including gold. The Yukon, one of the great rivers of the world, flows for 2,000 miles through the territory. Its waters abound in fish.

Nebraska was admitted as the thirty-seventh state in the Union during the year of the Alaska purchase. *Wyoming Territory* was organized in 1868, having been formed from parts of Dakota, Idaho, and Utah.

595. The Burlingame Embassy.—One notable event of 1868 was the arrival of an embassy from China, the first ever sent by that exclusive empire to any foreign power. Its head was Honorable Anson Burlingame, an American citizen, and lately his country's representative in China. He had so commanded the confidence of the Chinese government that the emperor had induced him to undertake this important mission, not only to the United States but to several European courts. The Chinese had begun to cross the Pacific in great numbers, to find employment in California and the inland mining states. A treaty, now concluded between the Asiatic Empire and the American Republic, guaranteed security of life, liberty, and property to the people of either nation while in the territory of the other.

NOTES.

1. **Andrew Johnson's** career is a striking example of the self-made man. He was born in 1808 at Raleigh, N. C,, where his father at different times pursued the calling of bank porter, constable, and church sexton. The family were so poor that young Johnson received no schooling whatever, and at the age of ten was apprenticed to a tailor. Soon after this he had his ambition aroused by a charitable gentleman, who used to read to the men in the shop, and diligently employed his leisure hours in learning to read. After residing for a short period at Laurens C. H., South Carolina, he removed to Greenville, Tennessee, in 1826, and there married. Under his wife's instruction Johnson rapidly extended his education, and. becoming interested in local politics, was twice elected alderman and twice mayor of the city. He was three times elected to the state legislature, and finally made his appearance as a representative in Congress in 1843. He retained his seat there until 1853, when he was elected governor of Tennessee. Johnson was a Democrat in principle, and in 1860 was an adherent of the Breckinridge party; but when the question of secession arose, Johnson, who was then a United Stales Senator, took a firm stand for the Union. This aroused a storm of

indignation in the secession party in his native state, and on his return there in May, 1S61, a moli entered the cars for the purpose of lynching him. He, however, met them boldly, pistol in hand, and the mob retired.

Lincoln appointed Johnson military governor of Tennessee in 1862, when his bold, energetic management of affairs attracted general attention throughout the North, and marked him as a fitting complement for the presidential ticket of 1865.

Johnson's course as President was a great surprise and disappointment to the party that elected him, but probably no President could have carried out a pian of reconstruction that would have been effective and at the same time acceptable to those still burning with the angry passions of civil war.

The President attempted to secure the Democratic nomination for reelection but failed. He was also defeated as candidate for United States Senator in 1870, and for Representative in 1872. Finally, in 1875, he was elected to the Senate, but his health failed, and on the 31st of July of that year he died.

2. **Edwin McMasters** Stanton (b. 1814, d. 1869) was born at Steubenville, Ohio, and received his education at Kenyon College in that state. Being admitted to the bar in 1836, he commenced practice at Cadiz, Ohio, but afterwards removed to Steubenville. In 1847, although retaining his office in the latter city, he removed to Pittsburgh, and afew years later acquired a national reputation as counsel for the state of Pennsylvania against the Wheeling & Belmont Bridge Co., tried before the Supreme Court of the United States. His business before this court became so continuous and important that in 1856 he removed to Washington. Two years later he was sent as United States counsel to the Pacific Coast in some land cases involving millions of money. He was successful in these cases, and while employed thus collected Mexican archives which were scattered far and wide through California in the hands of unauthorized parties. These archives aided in the detection of false claims to land and mines, and were of incalculable value.

In 1860 Mr. Stanton was suddenly appointed Attorney-general of the United States by President Buchanan. The office had not been sought, but was accepted at the cost of a lucrative law practice. when Buchanan's term expired Mr. Stanton resumed the practice of law; but in 1862 Lincoln appointed him Secretary of War. This office, like the preceding one, was unsought, and the appointment was made on the urgent solicitation of prominent citizens. "The characteristics of Mr. Stanton's administration were integrity, energy, determination, singleness of purpose, and the power to comprehend the magnitude of the rebellion and the labor and cost in blood and treasure involved in suppressing it."

In 1869 Grant appointed Mr. Stanton as an associate justice of the United States Supreme Court. The Senate immediately confirmed the appointment, but before he could take his seat he died after a brief illness, having worn himself out in the service of his country.

3. Salmon Portland Chase (*b.* 1808, *d.* 1873) was born at Cornish, N. H. His father died when Chase was but nine years old, and the latter's uncle, then an Episcopal bishop in Ohio, undertook his education. After a collegiate training, first at Cincinnati College and then at Dartmouth, he went to Washington, where he taught school while studying law. In 1830 he removed to Cincinnati to practice, and there employed his leisure time in preparing an edition of the "Statutes of Ohio," which at once gave him reputation, and has since superseded all other editions.

Chase was a warm advocate of anti-slavery principles, and may be considered virtually the originator and leader of what has since become the Republican party. In 1849 he was elected United States Senator, and took a prominent part in all the exciting debates over the slavery question which occurred during his term (§§ 463, 467, 468, 473-476). He was elected governor of Ohio in 1855, and re-elected in 1857 by a larger majority than had ever been given a governor in that state. He was returned to the United States Senate in 1860, but President Lincoln almost immediately made him Secretary of the Treasury, and he bore one of the most arduous positions during the Avar, evolving and carrying out financial schemes with wonderful judgment and skill. As a foundation to work upon he had an empty treasury and a poor National credit; yet he rapidly repaired both evils, and by the National banking system, which was purely his invention, placed the finances of the country on a sounder basis than ever before known.

Mr. Chase resigned from this office in June, 1864, only to accept, in the following December, the still more responsible position of Chief-justice of the United States. The grave questions raised immediately succeeding the war, which involved the constitutionality of certain acts of Congress and the President, the reconstruction of the South, and other matters of equal importance were dealt with by him in a manner to excite the admiration of all.

In 1870 a paralytic stroke ruined his physical health, and although still able to perform the duties of his office with the usual clearness and greatness of mind, he gradually wasted away and finally died at New York in the sixty-sixth year of his age.

4. Cyrus W. Field was born at Stockbridge, Mass., in 1819, and, after an ordinary education in his native town, went to New York when fifteen years old, and rapidly worked his way from a clerkship to the head of a large and prosperous mercantile house. At the age of thirty-four he retired, and for six months traveled in South America. Shortly after his return, lie was applied to for aid in establishing a telegraph line across Newfoundland to connect with a fast line of ocean steamers. He became interested in the project, and conceived the idea of extending the telegraph line across the ocean. The undertaking seemed almost preposterous, but Mr. Field went to work with his usual energy, never ceasing in his endeavors nor losing hope until success finally crowned his efforts. Not content with this wonderful achievement, Dlr. Field endeavored to organize a company to establish a submarine cable from San Francisco to Japan, and thus complete the telegraphic circuit of the globe. He did not succeed, however, and for the present the undertaking has been abandoned.

CHAPTER XLIII.
TWENTY-FIRST AND TWENTY-SECOND ADMINISTRATIONS, A. D. 1869-1877.

Ulysses S. Grant, President.   Schuyler Colfax, Henry Wilsor, Vice-presidents

Crossing the Prairies.

596. The Eighteenth President. By the elections in the autumn of 1868 *General Ulysses S. Grant* [1] became the eighteenth President, and *Schuyler Colfax*, of Indiana, Vice-president of the United States.

597. The Pacific Railroad was completed in May, 1869. For six years the great work had been in progress, at once from San Francisco in the west, and Omaha, Nebraska, in the east. The two construction-trains met at Ogden, in Utah, one party having completed 882 miles of road, the other 1032. The great continent, of which Columbus and his fellow discoverers saw only the eastern edge, no longer blocked the way to India, but afforded the speediest passage to it even for Europeans.

598. The first few months of 1870 saw **the restoration of the**

South to all her abandoned rights. The senators and representatives of Texas, last of all the seceded states, resumed their seats in Congress March 30. On the same day the President proclaimed the Fifteenth Amendment,—already adopted by Congress and ratified by two thirds of the states,—as part of the Constitution. It prevented the legal denial of his right to vote to any citizen of the United States on account of race, color, or previous condition of servitude.

599. **Unsettled war claims**, arising from the mischief done by Confederate cruisers under the British flag, occasioned some anxiety both in England and America. But neither government was unwise enough to plunge the two nations into war for matters which could be settled by reason. A "Joint High Commission," consisting of five English and five American statesmen, met at Washington, and, after a fair discussion, agreed that all claims of either nation against the other should be decided by three modes of arbitration :

600. (1) The **"Alabama Claims,"**—including demands for injury done by several other English-built Confederate cruisers,—were submitted to a board of commissioners from five friendly nations. This board met at Geneva, Switzerland, in the summer of 1872, and, having heard the lawyers on both sides, decreed that Great Britain should pay to the United States fifteen and a half millions of dollars. To the lasting praise of the British government, the amount was paid without demur.

601. (2) A question concerning the **boundary between Washington Territory and British Columbia** was referred to the Emperor of Germany, and his decision was accepted by both parties. (3) Some years later three commissioners, one English, one American, and one chosen by the first two, met at Boston to settle **claims arising from the fisheries** near the coasts of Nova Scotia and Newfoundland. In consequence of their award, the United States paid to Great Britain five millions of dollars. Lovers of peace rejoice that a step has thus been made toward the good time coming,—though doubtless yet too far away,—when cannon-law between nations shall be esteemed as

obsolete and brutal as "fist-law" between individual men.

Ulysses S. Grant.

602. **The Chicago Fire.**—The years 1871 and 1872 were marked by several dreadful fires. For two days Chicago was burning,—solid masses of stone, iron, and brick making scarcely more resistance to the fierce heat than the lightest wooden buildings. Nearly 100,000 persons were deprived of homes; and the property destroyed was worth $200,000,000. About the same time the great lumber-lands of Wisconsin and Michigan were visited by immense conflagrations. The flames spread from forests to villages; people plunged into lakes or rivers to escape them, but uncounted hundreds perished.

603. **Boston** was visited in November, 1872, by a similar disaster, though with less loss of life and property. More than sixty acres, covered with magnificent structures of granite and brick, were laid in ashes. The disaster was greater from an epidemic which had disabled all the horses in Boston, so that the heavy fire- engines had to be drawn by men. With wonderful energy both Chicago and Boston recovered from their great calamities; so that within a year or two "the burnt districts" were only to be known by more splendid and massive buildings than those which the flames had destroyed.

604. **Horace Greeley,**[2] founder and editor of the "New York

Tribune," was proposed for the presidency, in the autumn of 1872, both by the Liberal branch of the Republican party and by the Democrats. He loved peace, and at the first movement toward secession in 1860 had even advocated a friendly separation of the states rather than war. He soon changed his views, and favored the "short, sharp, and decisive" conflict which might lead to settled peace. His name was on the bond which released the ex-president of the Confederacy from prison; and many thought his election would hasten the return of good feeling between different sections of the country. Grant, however, was re-elected with *Henry Wilson,* of Massachusetts, as Vice-president; and Greeley, broken down by labor, excitement, and domestic sorrow, died within the month.

Horace Greeley.

605. Grant's Indian Policy.—The President had a new and hopeful plan for preventing trouble with the Indians. This was to civilize and win them by every possible means to the pursuits of peace. To this end he proposed schools, model farms, premiums for success in cattle-raising, etc.; and, as Quaker policy toward the Indians was the only one that had ever succeeded (§120), he committed all questions concerning them to a board consisting mainly of "Friends," while an educated Indian, who had served on his staff during the war, was a prominent member. But this humane scheme could not immediately efface the memory of many wrongs.

606.   The Modocs had been ordered from their lands in Oregon to a new reservation in the Indian Territory. They refused to go, and, intrenching themselves upon their "lava-beds," defied the Government to remove them. Their leader was " Captain Jack," whose father had been killed by the order of a United States officer, when under a flag of truce. The Modocs were soon surrounded and overpowered; but to avoid bloodshed a truce was agreed upon, during which General Canby and six commissioners met the chiefs in council. Revenge and treachery won the day. The General and a kind-hearted clergyman were murdered in the presence of the council; another commissioner was shot but not killed. War was then prosecuted until the whole band surrendered, and their chiefs, having been tried by court-martial, were put to death.

607.   Effects of Paper Money.—The unsettling of values by the Civil War (§§577, 578) still kept the money- markets in an excited and unhealthy state. There was great seeming prosperity; hundreds of millions of the public debt were paid; but eight years went by without any serious attempt to redeem the Government's promises on the greenbacks, and the frequent rise and fall of their value gave every opportunity to wild speculation.

608.   Railways and Money Panics.—More railroads were begun than the country needed or could pay for. Chief of these was the "Northern Pacific," from Duluth, on Lake Superior, to Puget Sound. Its stock was largely held and sold by a banking firm in Philadelphia. The failure of this firm in 1873 gave a shock to the commercial world, and in the panic many banks and other establishments were forced to suspend payments. Public works ceased; multitudes of the poor were without employment. "Hard times" were most keenly felt by those who had no share in causing them.

609.   Worst of all was the destruction of confidence. No one knew whom to trust. So many enormous fortunes had been made by fraudulent contracts or by scarcely less fraudulent speculation, that men were tempted to despise the moderate rewards of honest employments, and to join in the rush for sudden wealth. Reproach fell even upon Senators and Representatives at Washington. A long series of investigations resulted in the clearing of a few names, but left others deeply shadowed.

610. Ring Robberies.—The management of New York and other great cities fell into the hands of thieves, who robbed the public treasury and bribed voters to keep themselves and their tools in power. Tax-payers were too busy to look after their own interests. Suddenly their eyes were opened, and then the movement toward reform was as swift and thorough as the current of crime and corruption had been. So many frauds were brought to light that "at first sight it seemed as if the world had suddenly grown worse; on second reflection it was clear that it was growing better."

611. The Specie Resumption Act, passed by Congress in 1876, provided for the redemption in coin of all legal tender notes on and after January 1, 1879.

Colorado, the thirty-eighth state, was admitted to the Union in 1876. The wonderful dryness of its air makes it the paradise of pilgrims in search of health; while its metallic wealth affords abundant attraction to miners and adventurers.

612. The Centennial Year.—The year 1876 completed a century of American Independence. The great Republic had surpassed the hopes of her friends and disappointed the wishes of her enemies. Though assailed by foes within, she had proved strong enough not only to conquer but to forgive. The Centennial was celebrated by a great International Exposition at Philadelphia. More than two hundred buildings were erected in Fairmount Park, where a magnificent display of the products of all the zones delighted increasing throngs of visitors for six months.

613.   Dom Pedro II., the energetic and enlightened Emperor of Brazil, was present, with President Grant, at the opening, and afterwards pursued his journey through the states, inquiring into every thing that could be of use to his great undeveloped empire.

614.   The war with the Sioux more sadly signalized the Centennial summer. Instead of confining themselves to the extensive lands in Dakota which they had accepted by treaty with the United States, these savages were committing robberies and murders in Montana and Wyoming. A large detachment of the regular army was sent to subdue them. General Custer, with the Seventh Cavalry, was reconnoitering near the Little Horn River, when he suddenly came upon the Indians in force. A fierce battle followed, in which the General, with every man of his command, was slain.

This great disaster led, of course, to a stern following up of the war. The savages were defeated many times during the summer, autumn, and winter, until a remnant of their number, under the chiefs Sitting Bull and Crazy Horse, escaped into British territory.

615.   The Republican party had now been in power sixteen years, the most exciting and momentous years in the history of our country. Violent differences of opinion had arisen in those years concerning finance, reconstruction, and other questions occasioned by the war; and the presidential canvass of 1876 was the most closely contested that had

Custer's Last Fight.

ever been held. "Returning Boards" had been appointed in some of the Southern states with the power of declaring the result of elections. Their decision in favor of the Republican party in Florida and Louisiana was immediately denounced by the Democratic party as fraudulent; the Republicans firmly disputed the accusation, and serious trouble seemed imminent.

616.   **The Joint High Commission.** — When Congress met, there was a long debate. It was agreed at last that a Commission consisting of five Judges of the Supreme Court, five Senators, and five Representatives should hear the evidence and decide. Their conclusion was reached two days before the end of General Grant's term. It was to the effect that the Republicans had cast one hundred and eighty-five

electoral votes for *Rutherford B. Hayes,* of Ohio; the Democrats had cast one hundred and eighty-four for Samuel J. Tilden, of New York. So the vexed question was settled, and President Hayes was inaugurated (the 4th being Sunday) on the 5th of March, 1877.

NOTES.

1. **Ulysses S. Grant** was born in 1822 at Point Pleasant, Clermont Co., Ohio, and passed his boyhood in the neighboring village of Georgetown. At the age of seventeen he entered West Point, where he graduated four years later without having distinguished himself, being twenty-first in a class of thirty-nine. As a second lieutenant he was stationed or the frontier until the breaking out of the Mexican War. He was in every important battle of the latter except that of Buena Vista, and received the warmest praise from his superior officers for gallant conduct. He was rewarded by brevets on two occasions. He resigned his commission as captain in 1854, and attempted farming near St. Louis. Not meeting with much success, however, he accepted a position in his father's tannery at Galena, Illinois. Here he lived in comparative obscurity, and at the breaking out of the Civil War was entirely unknown to the public. When President Lincoln issued his call for volunteers Grant organized and drilled a company at Galena, and at the same time offered his services by letter to the Adjutant-general, but was ignored. Marching his company to Springfield, Illinois, he was appointed by the governor to muster the state volunteers, and five weeks later was made colonel of a regiment. He first reported to General Pope, in Missouri, and shortly after, having been appointed brigadier-general of volunteers, he was placed in command of the district of South-east Missouri. His first act of importance was the seizure of Paducah, which had great influence in keeping Kentucky in the Union ; and the capture of Fort Donelson, which followed soon after, gave him a National reputation and won him his commission of major-general of volunteers. His career was now a series of brilliant successes, and his generalship at Chattanooga is considered by military authorities as the masterpiece of the War. He has been severely criticised tor recklessly sacrificing the lives of bis soldiers, but without just cause; for although the battles during his advance on Richmond were unusually severe and costly to the Union side, yet Grant felt that he was pursuing the shortest and best course to put an end to the horrors of civil war, and the result proved the correctness of his judgment.

Grant was included in the plot of the conspirators who murdered Lincoln, and probably escaped death through declining the latter's invitation to join the party at the theater.

Alter his second term as President had expired, he made a tour of the globe, and no individual in the world's history ever received such a continuous series of ovations. The erowned heads of Europe vied with the common people in paying him marked attention, and his reception on his return home by the country at large was no less enthusiastic.

2. Horace Greeley (*b* 1811, *d*. 1872) was born at Amherst, New Hampshire, and was a remarkably precocious child. He could read when only two years old, and at the age of seven had read all the books upon which he could lay his hands within a radius of seven miles from his father's farm-house. When Horace was ten years of age his father moved to Vermont, and in this state the son took his first step in the profession of journalism, being apprenticed to a printer. The newspaper on which he worked as a compositor was discontinued in 1830, and Greeley went west to visit his parents, who had in the meantime removed to Erie County, Pa. He worked at his trade there for a short time, but wages being very low he determined to go to New York, where lie arrived August 17th, 1831, with but ten dollars in money and a small bundle of clothing. After working as a compositor for about a year and a half he embarked in successive ventures as a journalist, but with poor success financially, until finally, April 10th, 1841, lie issued the first number of the "New York Tribune," which has since made the name of Horace Greeley celebrated throughout the English-speaking world. He was justly proud of his success in his chosen profession; and in his autobiography says, " I cherish the hope that the journal I projected and established will live and flourish long after 1 shall have moldered into forgotten dust, being guided by a larger wisdom, a more unerring sagacity to discern the right, though not by a more unfaltering readiness to embrace and defend it at whatever personal cost; and that the stone which covers my ashes may bear to future eyes the still intelligible inscription, ' Founder of the New York Tribune.' "

Mr. Greeley's peculiar political position, as well as his personal eccentricities made him the butt of numberless caricatures during the campaign in which he was defeated, and in addition to the harassing political strain, he suffered the private grief occasioned by his wife's death. The result was an attack of inflammation of the brain, which ended his life ina very short time. His funeral was public and most impressive. The body lay in state in the New York City Hall, and was visited by an immense throng of people, among whom were the President, Vice-president, and Chief-justice of the United States.

CHAPTER XLIV.
TWENTY-THIRD ADMINISTRATION, A. D. 1877-1881.

Rutherford B. Hayes, President. *William A. Wheeler, Vice-president.*

617. The Nineteenth President.—Among President Hayes's[1] first measures was the withdrawal of National troops from the Southern states. Governor Wade Hampton, of South Carolina, and other officials, assured him that their presence only promoted irritation, and was not needed for the preservation of order. The President desired to do all that the most generous confidence could dictate toward soothing all feelings of bitterness and establishing peace and friendship.

618. Civil Service Reform was the next object. Ever since Jackson's administration the rule had been that "to the victors belong the spoils" after an election (§415). Postmasters and other officials had been appointed upon the recommendation of members of Congress, not always with a view to the fitness of the candidate, but rather as payment for political services. President Hayes was pledged to consult the service of the public rather than of the politicians, and to regulate both his appointments and dismissals by questions of personal worth.

619. The "Grangers."—The immense power and wealth of certain railway companies had for several years attracted attention. During the war an association, called the "Patrons of Husbandry," was formed to protect the interests of Western farmers against exorbitant charges for transportation on the part of the railroads, and in general to oppose all oppressive monopolies. In 1874 there were twenty thousand " Granges," or local associations, and a membership of a million and a half.

620. Railway Riots.—In the summer of 1877 railway interests were threatened in a less orderly way. Brakemen and other train-hands on the "Baltimore and Ohio Railroad" "struck" at Martinsburg, in West Virginia, in consequence of a reduction in their wages. The business of the whole road was suspended. The example was quickly followed upon other roads. Buildings and rolling- stock were burnt; and from opposition to the companies the movement became rebellion against the states and even the Government at Washington, which sent troops to put down the insurgents.

Rutherford B. Hayes.

621. Pittsburgh, in Pennsylvania, was the scene of the greatest violence. The mob numbered 20,000 men, and for two days had entire control of the city. 100 lives were destroyed; 125 locomotives and 2,500 freight and express cars were burnt. Riots occurred at Chicago, St. Louis, and even at San Francisco; but here it was not railway capitalists, but the employers of Chinese laborers, who were attacked.

622. Communism.—The alarming fact was that the leaders in all these places were not railway hands, but restless "communists." who were traveling from place to place exciting workmen against their employers. While the men were "striking," their families too often were starving. The railway riots were put down within a fortnight; but the great question of employers and employed remained to tax the best energies of thoughtful minds for many years to come.

623. The Chinese Question.—The large immigration of Chinese laborers makes the problem more difficult. They already number more than 150,000 in America, of whom 60,000 are in the state of California alone. They cross the Pacific often in large companies under the direction of contractors, and find employment in the mines, in factories, in market-gardening, and domestic service. On the one hand, fear has arisen lest the relations of "coolies" with the contractors may abridge the personal liberty which the Government wishes to guarantee to every inhabitant of the country; on the other, lest the habits of heathenism, which the immigrants have brought with them, may prove injurious to the morals of the community. It can not be said, however, that the noisiest opponents of the Chinese are the most orderly or most Christian part of the population; while the "heathen" very often set a worthy example of quiet industry and obedience to law.

624. In the early months of 1879 a bill passed both houses of Congress setting aside part of the Burlingame treaty (§ 595), and putting a check on further immigration from China. President Hayes vetoed the bill, considering the faith of the United States pledged to the fulfillment of the treaty until both governments can agree to change it. Moreover, it was argued that our republic has always taken the risks of free immigration, hoping by schools and other elevating influences to make useful citizens of the newcomers and their children.

625. What no one fears or regrets is the presence of one hundred and four Chinese youth in our academies and colleges. Since the opening of the great Asiatic empire to intercourse with other nations, boys of good birth and talents have been sent to be educated in the United States at the expense of their own government. Their superintendent here is Yung Wing, a Chinese mandarin, who is himself a graduate of Yale College, and lately minister of China at Washington. The government of Japan has sent not only boys to American colleges, but young women to fit themselves for teachers of girls at home.

James A. Garfield.

626. Cost and Credit of the Government.— On the first day of 1879 payments in gold were resumed by the Treasury and the national banks; and thus, after eighteen years, the disturbing effects of the Civil War upon the currency were ended. The war debt, though diminished by over nine hundred millions of dollars since 1866, still occasions by far the greatest item of public expense. The cost of the Government, as such, *i. e., of* the civil service, army, and navy, is comparatively small, and is met by duties on foreign goods. The interest and sinking fund of the public debt are provided for by the internal revenue, which is levied mainly on tobacco, whisky, and malt liquors. All surplus revenue, from whatever source, is devoted to the reduction of the National debt.

627. The four years' term of Mr. Hayes was chiefly remarkable as a period of peace and prosperity. Bounteous harvests supplied an enormous export of grain to European markets. Immigrants arrived at our ports in greater numbers than ever before, and an unusual proportion of these were industrious people, who were likely to be an advantage rather than a burden to the country. The census taken in June, 1880, showed the population of the United States to be more than fifty millions.

The election in the following November resulted in the choice of *James A. Garfield*,[2] of Ohio, to be the twentieth President of the United States, and of *Chester A. Arthur*, of New York, to be Vice-president. The Democratic candidate for the Presidency was Winfield S. Hancock, U. S. A.

NOTES.

1. **Rutherford Birchard** Hayes was born at Delaware, Ohio, in 1822. He graduated at Kenyon College, in that state, and after taking his degree at the Harvard Law School commenced the practice of law at Fremont, Ohio. In 1849 he moved to Cincinnati, and soon established a flourishing practice. He was made major of the Twenty-third Ohio Volunteers in 1861, and served throughout the war. He was badly wounded at South Mountain (§525), and shortly after was promoted to a colonelcy. Gallant service in many of the hardest battles of the Army of the Potomac was rewarded by successive advances in rank, and at the close of the war Hayes was a brevet major-general. After the battle of Cedar Creek (§553), in which he took part, Hayes was notified of his election to Congress from the second district of Ohio. He resigned from the army in June, 1865, and the following December took his seat in Congress. He was re-elected in 1866, but resigned his seat to accept the governorship of Ohio: the latter office was held for two successive terms, when lie again became a candidate for Congress and was defeated. In 1875 he received an unprecedented honor in his native state, being elected governor for the third time. His popularity in Ohio, and the stand taken by him on the issues at stake in his last contest for the governorship, brought him prominently before the country, and resulted in his nomination for the presidency in 1876.

2. James A. Garfield is of New England descent, and was born in Cuyahoga County, Ohio, in 1831. His father died when James was but two years of age, leaving his widow with four small children to struggle for life in the backwoods. James received a meager education, and at the age of twelve began to aid in supporting the family,—first as a

carpenter, then as a book-keeper, and then as a boatman on the canal. Abandoning the latter occupation on account of sickness, his ambition for a higher education became aroused, and lie secured it in the face of many obstacles. He was so poor that he was compelled to work in the mornings and evenings and Saturdays to help pay his tuition. Thus lie prepared for Hiram College, of which he was first janitor and student, then a teacher, and finally the president. Before attaining the latter positions, however, he had improved his mental attainments by a course at Williams College, where he graduated with high honors in 1856. While president of Hiram College, in 1860, Garfield was admitted to the bar, but lie did not leave his position there until the breaking out of the Civil War, when he was appointed colonel of an Ohio regiment. After the battle of Chickamauga he was brevetted major-general, and then resigned bis commission to accept a seat in the House of Representatives. He was re-elected to the successive Houses until 1879, when he was elected to the Senate. His political life lias been one of constant labor and study, and few politicians have developed sudi breadth of thought and soundness of judgment.

CHAPTER XLV.
PROGRESS OF THE REPUBLIC.

Smithsonian Institution.

628. Territory and Population.—In little more than a century the United States has grown, from a line of scattered colonies on the Atlantic coast, to a continental power bordering two oceans and covering more than three and a half millions of square miles. The summer sun never sets upon its whole extent, for a new day dawns upon the forests of Maine before its predecessor has quitted the westernmost island of Alaska. The population has multiplied in the same time from less than three to nearly fifty millions. About one half of the whole territory, including Alaska (§594), is still public land, at the disposal of Congress and the President. This includes, of course, the least valuable portions of the country west of the Mississippi (§15);

but there are yet unoccupied fertile lands capable of maintaining hundreds of millions of human beings.

629. Railroads and Telegraphs.—Fifty years ago there were twenty-three miles of railroad in the United States; now there are more than ninety thousand miles. The magnetic telegraph was then unknown ; now telegraphic lines measure one hundred and ten thousand miles, and use wire enough to go ten times around the globe. These two items give but a slight hint of the improved means of traffic and communication. The fatigue and danger in traveling enormous distances have been reduced almost to nothing, and the cost of freight has been similarly lessened.

The telegraph itself is replaced in some instances by the **telephone**, which transmits the spoken words instead of mere conventional signals. By its means a famous speaker or singer can be heard scores of miles away—while its value in business is beyond calculation.

630. Immigration.—The rapid extension of public works has been owing in great measure to immigrations from Europe. By reason of their fortunate position, with but few neighbors, the United States have been comparatively free from the wastes and burdens of war which afflict most of the European nations. Instead of spending some of the best years of their lives in camps and barracks, men are at liberty to provide comforts for themselves and their families. This and other causes have led to a constant stream of immigration across the Atlantic ever since the end of our War of 1812. Many of the new-comers were skilled mechanics, and brought money enough to establish themselves well in their chosen country. Others could at least dig canals, grade railway-beds, and earn for their children better opportunities than they themselves had enjoyed. Even during our Civil War the high prices of labor drew larger numbers to America than ever had come in the same period before. In the ten years, A. D. 1860-1870, nearly four and one half millions of European immigrants entered the Northern ports.

Louis Agassiz.

631. Beside all the industrial advantages thus derived from the Old World, it ought not to be forgotten that some of the best brains of Europe,—either exiled by political troubles or desiring peace and freedom for the better prosecution of science,—have made America their home. Among the latter class was Professor Louis Agassiz, the Swiss *savant*, who knew more about fishes than almost any other man living, and whose death in 1873 was mourned in two hemispheres. Among the former were Doctor Francis Lieber, of Columbia College, New York; Carl Schurz; and many others.

632. Manufactures.—American cotton mills and the full adoption of the Federal Constitution date from the same year. In 1789 Samuel Slater, a pupil of Arkwright (§348), came to this country and established the first mill for spinning cotton yarn, at Pawtucket, in Rhode Island. England did not then allow the export of machinery, nor even of plans, so that Slater had to set up his wheels and spindles chiefly from memory and with his own hands. His "Old Mill" still exists.

In 1812 Francis Lowell, in like manner, partly invented and set up a power-loom at Waltham, in Massachusetts. He carried on all the processes which convert raw cotton into finished cloth, in one establishment,—the first of its kind in the world. The cotton manufacture has grown from those humble beginnings until it employs 100,000 persons in 1,074 factories; and many flourishing cities, like Lowell and Lawrence, Fall River, Manchester, and Little Falls, owe their wealth to this important industry.

633. **Paper-making** has advanced equally in amount and far more in quality. If we compare the Continental paper-money with the National bank-note currency of the present day, we shall see progress both in the manufacture of material and in the art of engraving. Millions of bales of rags are imported every year to the paper factories of Massachusetts, and fine note-paper is sent to Europe in return. Many new materials, such as wood-fiber, straw, jute, and manilla are used as well as rags,

634. **Vulcanized India Rubber.**—Among the inventions which have wrought the greatest changes is that of vulcanized India Rubber. Mr. Charles Goodyear found, in 1839, that by mixing the native gum with sulphur and white lead, it became practically an *elastic metal* of wonderful tenacity. It serves numberless purposes, such as belting and hose for machinery, springs and wheels for cars, pavements, coating of telegraphic wires, etc. Combined with tar and sulphur, the same gum affords material for jewelry and many small articles, being as black and lustrous as jet.

635. **The sewing machine** is due mainly to the perseverance of an American, Elias Howe, Jr., who in 1846 received a patent for the first really successful instrument of the kind. Singer, Wilson, Grover and many others have invented improvements; but of the millions of machines manufactured in the United States, every one has been indebted to Howe for some essential feature. Germany and Russia, as well as many other countries, use American sewing machines.

636. The inventive genius which the subduing of a great, wild continent first called into action, has been only heightened by prosperity. The soil of South Africa, Australia, and Japan is turned by American plows, and their harvests are gathered by American mowers

and reapers; fires in European cities are extinguished by American steam fire- engines; American palace-cars roll over European railways; and American steam-boats ply on the Rhine, the Danube, and the Bosporus. Great London newspapers are printed on the type-revolving press invented by Richard Hoe of New York. The development of the great mineral wealth of the Pacific states has called for new implements and machinery for mining. The most important is the Stetefeldt Furnace for reducing silver ore, which was invented at Austin, Nevada, in 1867.

637. **Illumination.**—In countless other inventions America only shares the general progress of the age. The streets of cities, which half a century ago were made passable at night only by the glimmer of whale-oil lamps, now blaze with gas; and if present prospects be fulfilled, night will soon rival day by means of electric lights.

The *mail service* is a wonder of cheapness and celerity. A postal card can be sent from Maine to Oregon for one cent, a newspaper for two, and a letter for three cents.

638. **The Weather Department** at Washington, established in 1870, gives notice in advance of the approach of storms, the rise and fall of rivers, and all aërial changes, by means of its telegraphic communications with all parts of the United States, and with more than a dozen stations in distant parts of the globe. Nine tenths of its predictions have proved true. Lives and property have been saved by these timely warnings; and the science of meteorology, on which so many interests depend, has been studied more thoroughly than could ever be done by a smaller scale of observations.

639. **Education.**—The same zeal for knowledge which moved the first colonists in their poverty to establish schools for their children, has occasioned munificent endowments in our times for institutions of learning. Instead of the seven colleges of Revolutionary days, we have three hundred and sixty-six colleges and universities, though Harvard, Yale, and their venerable contemporaries, have never lost their high

rank, but have been enriched by new and generous endowments. Harvard bestows degrees upon women who pass examinations equivalent to those of regular students. For the higher education of women exclusively, Vassar, Wellesley, and Smith colleges, and many others have been endowed by private munificence. Cornell University, at Ithaca, N. Y., is open equally to young men and women. It is so liberally endowed by the state and general governments, by Ezra Cornell, whose name it bears, and by others, that it places the means of the highest education within the reach of rich and poor alike.

640. **The Peabody Fund.**—The grandest endowment ever made for purposes of education was that of George Peabody, for many years banker in London, but a native of Massachusetts. His gifts for schools, colleges, libraries, and museums in the United States amounted to more than five and a quarter millions of dollars. More than three millions went for the support and encouragement of common schools in the Southern states, which, owing to scattered population and other causes, had not yet organized their plans for elementary education.

641. **Public Schools.**—Now there is not a state nor an organized territory without its system of public schools. More than eight millions of children are named on the rollbooks of these schools, and the yearly cost of their education is not less than one hundred millions of dollars. In eleven states attendance at school is required by law: for if even parents are neglectful, the state can not afford to have ignorant voters growing up. Beside the common schools, there are high schools, academies, normal schools for the training of teachers, scientific and professional schools, and special institutions for the blind, the mute, and the feebleminded.

642. **American literature** has shared and aided the general progress. Among essayists. Emerson. Whipple, Dana, and Stedman; among historians. Bancroft. Prescott. Irving. Kirk. Motley, and Parkman: among poets. Bryant. Longfellow. Whittier. Lowell, and Aldrich; among novelists, Cooper. Hawthorne, and Mrs. Stowe, are

known and admired beyond the limits of their own country. Besides, we have had men of both thought and action, who have told the story of their own great deeds. Doctor Kane's record of winters passed in the icy regions of the arctic zone, and Stanley's story of exploration in Central Africa are brilliant additions to the literature of voyages and travels.

643. Advancement of Science.—Americans have contributed their full share to the advancement of science; and the Government has been ever ready, by liberal grants in aid of voyages and researches, to further the general enlightenment. The Smithsonian Institution uses for the same ends the income derived from the bequest of James Smith- son. a son of the English Duke of Northumberland. Dying at Genoa, in 1829. this gentleman—though he had never been in America—bequeathed his whole fortune to the Government of the United States, to found at Washington an institution "for the increase and diffusion of knowledge among men." The Institution began its work in 1846 with a yearly income of $40.000.

644. If in a general review of the rapid progress vast extent, and present prosperity of our country, we are tempted to a moment's pride, we must recollect that duties grow with opportunities. Our forefathers left the comforts of home— in some cases rank and luxury—in Europe. that they might found new states on the broad foundation of equal rights to all. Their sons may expect just as much honor and wealth as their strong, industrious hands, alert and well-stored brains, and sterling characters can win.—no more. In America, more than in any other country on the globe, success depends on personal qualities. Though fraud and pretense may now and then gain a transient advantage, there is only one sure road to high and permanent distinction, and that is—deserve it.

Children of the common schools! in thirty years the great republic will be in your hands to wreck or to save and carryforward to a greatness and glory beyond what even your fathers planned.

QUESTIONS FOR REVIEW. —Part VI.

		Section
1.	What differences of policy between Congress and President Johnson?	589, 590
2.	What amendments were made in the Constitution of the United States?	561, 591, 598
3.	Describe the failures and final success of the transatlantic telegraph.	592, 593
4.	What states and territories were organized between i860 and 1870?	492, 573, 594
5.	Describe our affairs with China since 1868.	595, 623-625
6.	What important railroad was completed in 1869?	597
7.	What settlements have been made with England?	599-601
8.	What great conflagrations in 1871 and 1872?	602, 603
9.	What is said of Horace Greeley?	604
10.	Describe President Grant's policy toward and dealings with the Indians.	605, 606, 614
11.	What changes in money matters during his terms?	607-611
12.	How was the Centennial celebrated?	612, 613
13.	Describe the election of 1876 and its result.	615, 616
14.	Describe the policy of President Hayes.	617, 618
15.	Who were the "Grangers"?	619
16.	Describe the labor riots of 1877.	620-622
17.	What are the chief items of public income and expenditure?	626
18.	Who was elected President in 1880?	627
19.	What progress during a hundred years in extent, population, and means of intercourse?	628, 629
20.	What has occasioned immigration to America?	630, 631
21.	Describe the progress of manufactures	632, 633
22.	Name some important inventions.	634-637
23.	What has been done for education?	639-641
24.	What for science?	638, 643
25.	Name some of the chief American authors.	642

THE ECLECTIC HISTORY OF THE UNITED STATES

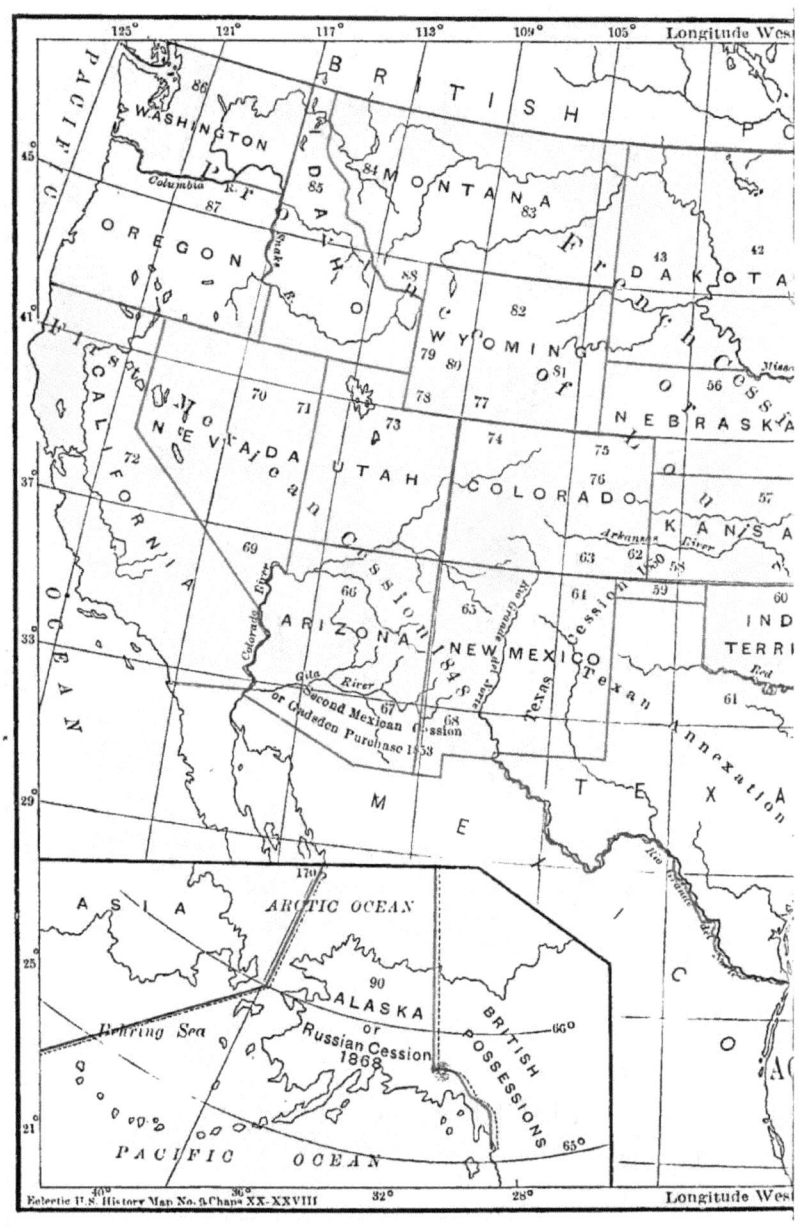

SKETCH SHOWING THE
ACQUISITION AND DISTRIBUTION
OF
TERRITORY.
By Russell Hinman, C.E.

TRANSFERS OF TERRITORY IN THE UNITED STATES.
(Numerals Refer to Map No. 9.)

1 and 2. — Part of original state of Massachusetts erected into state of Maine, 1820.

3. — Part of public land of the United States.

4. — One of original thirteen states.

5. — Formed into state of Vermont in 1791 out of the state of New York.

6. — One of original thirteen states; included 1 and 2, and extended west to the Mississippi River.

7. — One of original thirteen states.

8. — One of original thirteen states; originally extended west to the Mississippi River.

9. — One of original thirteen states; originally including 5; a claim of Massachusetts to portion of territory of southern New York was settled in 1786 by a convention at Hartford.

10. — One of original thirteen states.

11. — One of original thirteen states; in 1792, 89 added.

12. — One of original thirteen states.

13. — One of original thirteen states; originally embraced 13 and 14.

14. — Ceded to the United States for a capital city by Maryland in 1790.

15. — Ceded to the United States for a capital city by Virginia in 1790; retroceded to Virginia by United States in 1846.

16. — One of original thirteen states ; originally embraced 15, 16, 17, 18, 31, 54, and 55.

17. — Formed into state of West Virginia out of Virginia in 1863.

18. — Formed into state of Kentucky, 1792, out of Virginia.

19. — One of original thirteen states; originally embraced 19 and 20.

20. — Ceded to United States by North Carolina in 1790, and with 23, 24, and 28 erected into the Territory south of the Ohio River; admitted as state, 1796.

21. — One of original thirteen states; originally comprised 21, 23, 24, and 28.

22. — One of original thirteen states ; originally comprised 22, 25, 26, 27, and 29.

23. — Ceded by South Carolina to United States in 1787 ; in 1790 transferred to Territory south of Ohio River (23, 24, 28, and 20) ; in 1802 ceded to Georgia.

24. — Ceded by South Carolina to United States in 1787; in 1790 transferred to Territory south of Ohio River; in 1804 to Mississippi territory; in 1817 to Alabama territory, and in 1819 to state of Alabama.

25. — Ceded by Georgia to United States, 1802; transferred to Mississippi territory, 1804 ; to Alabama territory, 1817 ; and to state of

Alabama, 1819.

26.—Erected, with 27, into Mississippi territory, 1798, subject to Georgia's claims, which were ceded to the United States, 1802 ; to Alabama territory 1817 ; to state of Alabama, 1819.

27.—Same as 26 until 1S17, when erected into state of Mississippi.

28.—Ceded to United States by South Carolina, 1787; erected into Territory south of Ohio River, 1790; transferred to Mississippi territory, 1804; and to state of Mississippi, 1817.

29.—Ceded to United States by Georgia, 1802; transferred to Mississippi territory, 1804; and to state of Mississippi, 1817.

30.—Ceded to United States by France, 1803 ; transferred to Mississippi territory, 1812; and to state of Mississippi, 1817.

31.—Ceded to United States by France, 1803; transferred to Mississippi territory, 1812; to Alabama territory, 1817; state of Alabama, 1819.

32.—Ceded to United States by Spain, 1819 ; erected into Florida territory, 1822; into state of Florida, 1845.

33.—Ceded to United States by France, 1803; transferred to state of Louisiana, 1812.

34.—Ceded to United States by France, 1803; erected into territory of Orleans, 1804; admitted as state of Louisiana, 1812.

35.**—Ceded to United States by France, 1803; included in district Louisiana in 1804; in territory Louisiana, 1805; in territory Missouri, 1812; erected into Arkansas territory, 1819; admitted as state of Arkansas, 1836.

36.—Admitted as state of Missouri, 1821.

37.—Added to state of Missouri, 1836.

38.—Annexed to territory of Michigan, 1834 ; to territory Wisconsin, 1836; to territory Iowa, 1838; admitted as part of state of Iowa, 1846.

39.—Same as above to and including admission to territory Iowa ; transferred to state of Iowa, 1846.

40.—Same as 39; transferred from state to territory Iowa, 1846; to territory Minnesota, 1849; to state Minnesota, 1858.

41.—Annexed to territory Michigan, 1834; territory Wisconsin, 1836; tertory Iowa, 1838; territory Minnesota, 1849; state Minnesota, 1858.

42.—As above, to and including territory Minnesota, 1849; included in territory Dakota, 1861.

43.—Transferred from territory Missouri to territory Nebraska, 1854; to territory Dakota, 1861.

44.—Ceded by Great Britain, 1783; included in territory north-west Ohio River, 1787; to territory Indiana, 1800; to territory Illinois, 1809; to

---

* All of the French cession west of the Mississippi River (except 34) was ceded to the United States as the " Province of Louisiana" in 1803; erected into district of Louisiana, 1804 ; into territory of Louisiana, 1805; into territory of Missouri, 1812. The subsequent descriptions of territory within the French cession will be carried on from this point, — and a repetition of these changes common to all, avoided.

territory Michigan, 1818; to territory Wisconsin, 1836; to territory Minnesota, 1849; to state Minnesota, 1858.

45. — As above, to and including territory Wisconsin, 1836; admitted as state Wisconsin 1848.

46. — As 44, to and ineluding territory Michigan, 1818; to state Michigan, 1837.

47. — Ceded by Great Britain, 1783; territory north-west Ohio River, 1787; territory Indiana, 1800; territory Michigan, 1818; territory Wisconsin, 1836 ; state Wisconsin, 1848.

48. — Ceded by Great Britain, 1783 ; transferred to Territory north-west Ohio River, 1787; territory Indiana, 1800; territory Michigan, 1818; state Michigan, 1837.

49. — Ceded by Great Britain, 1783; transferred to Territory north-west Ohio River, 1787; territory Indiana, 1800; territory Michigan, 1805; state Michigan, 1837.

50. — Ceded by Great Britain; transferred to Territory north-west Ohio River, 1787; territory Indiana, 1802; territory Michigan, 1805; state Michigan, 1837.

51. — Ceded by Great Britain, 1783; transferred to Territory north-west Ohio River, 1787 ; to territory Michigan, 1805; to state Ohio, 1836.

52. — Ceded by Great Britain, 1783; transferred to Territory north-west Ohio River, 1787 ; territory Indiana, 1800; territory Michigan, 180.5; to state Indiana, 1816.

53. — North of 41st parallel ceded by Great Britain, 1783; south of same by Virginia, 1784 ; territory north-west Ohio River, 1787 ; admitted as state Ohio, 1803.

54. — North of 41st parallel ceded by Great Britain, 1783; south of same by Virginia, 1784; Territory north-west Ohio River, 1787; territory Indiana, 1800; state Indiana, 1816.

55. — North of 41st parallel ceded by Great Britain, 1783; south of same by Virginia, 1781 ; Territory north-west Ohio River, 1787; territory Indiana, 1800; territory Illinois, 1809; state Illinois, 1818.

56. — Territory Nebraska, 1854; state Nebraska, 1867.

57. — Territory Kansas, 1854; state Kansas, 1861.

58. — Ceded by Texas, 1850; transferred to territory Kansas, 1.854; to state Kansas, 1861.

59. — Ceded by Texas, 1850; never lias been organized.

60. — Ceded by France, 1803; declared "Indian country," 1834.

61. — The independent republic of Texas, admitted as state of Texas, 1845.

62. — Ceded by Texas, 1850; transferred to territory Kansas, 1854 ; territory Colorado, 1861 ; state Colorado, 1876.

63. — Ceded by Texas, 1850; transferred to territory New Mexico, 1850; territory Colorado, 1861 ; state Colorado, 1876.

64. — Ceded by Texas, 18.50; transferred to territory New Mexico, 1850.

65. — Ceded by Mexico, 1848: transferred to territory New Mexico,

18.50.

66. — Ceded by Mexico, 1848; transferred to territory New Mexico, 18.50; territory Arizona, 1863.

67. — Ceded by Mexico, 1853; transferred to territory New Mexico, 1854; to territory Arizona, 1863.

68. — Ceded by Mexico, 1853; transferred to territory New Mexico, 1854.

69. — Ceded by Mexico, 1848; transferred to territory New Mexico, 1850; to territory Arizona, 1863; to state Nevada, 1866.

70. — Ceded by Mexico, 1848; transferred to territory Utah, 18.70; territory Nevada, 1861 ; erected into state Nevada, 1864.

71. — Ceded by Mexico, 1848; transferred to territory Utah, 1850; state Nevada, 1866.

72. — Ceded by Mexico, 1848; admitted as state of California, 1850.

73. — Ceded by Mexico, 1848; territory Utah, 18.70.

74. — Ceded by Mexico, 1848; territory Utah, 1850; territory colorado, 1861 ; state Colorado, 1876.

75. — Ceded by France, 1803 ; territory Missouri to territory Nebraska, 18.54 ; territory Colorado, 1861 ; state Colorado, 1876.

76. — Ceded by France, 1803; territory Missouri to territory Kansas, 1854; to territory Colorado, 1861 ; to state Colorado, 1876.

77. — Ceded by Mexico, 1848; transferred to territory of Utah, 1850; territory Nebraska, 1861 ; territory Idaho, 1863; territory Dakota, 1864; territory Wyoming, 1868.

78. — Ceded by Mexico, 1848; territory Utah, 1850; territory Wyoming, 1868.

79. — Ceded by France, 1803 ; territory Missouri to territory Oregon, 1848; territory Washington, 1853; territory Idaho, 1863; territory Wyoming, 1868.

80. — Ceded by Fiance, 1803; territory Missouri to territory Oregon, 1848; territory Washington, 18.53; territory Nebraska, 1861 ; territory Idaho, 1863 ; territory Dakota, 1864 ; territory Wyoming, 1868.

81. — Coded by France in 1803 (except south-west corner, which was ceded by Mexico in 1848); transferred to territory Nebraska, 1854; territory Idaho, 1861 ; territory Dakota, 1864. territory Wyoming, 1868.

82. — Ceded by France, 1803; transferred to territory Nebraska, l854; territory Dakota, 1861; territory Idaho, 1863; territory Dakota, 1864; territory Wyoming, 1868.

83. — Ceded by France, 1803 ; transferred to territory Nebraska, 1854 ; ter-Dakota, 1861 ; territory Idaho, 1863; territory Montana, 1864.

84. — Ceded by France, 1803 ; transferred to territory Oregon, 1818 ; territory Washington, 1853; territory Idaho, 1863; territory Montana, 1864.

85. — Ceded by France, 1803; transferred to territory Oregon, 1848; territory Washington, 1853; territory Idaho, 1863.

86. — Ceded by France, 1803; transferred to territory Oregon, 1848; territory Washington, 18.53.

87. — Ceded by France, 1803; transferred to territory Oregon, 1848; state Oregon, 1859.

88. — Ceded by France, 1803; transferred to territory Nebraska, 1854; territory Dakota, 1861; territory Idaho, 1863; territory Dakota, 1864 ; territory Montana, 1873.

89. — Ceded by state of New York, 1781, and Massachusetts, 1785, to United States; transferred to Pennsylvania, 1792.

90. — Ceded by Russia, 1867 ; unorganized territory of Alaska.

Synopsis of Twenty-three Administrations.

1, 2.—GEORGE WASHINGTON, 1789-1797. Public credit established by Hamilton—United States Bank and Mint at Philadelphia— Whisky riot and Indian ravages suppressed—Treaties with Great Britain, Spain, and Algiers—Vermont, Kentucky, and Tennessee admitted. §§ 321-339

3.—JOHN ADAMS, 1797-1801. Party strife between Federalists and Republicans—Alien and sedition laws—French republic threatens war, but Bonaparte makes peace—United States Government removed to Washington City, in the district ceded by Maryland and Virginia—Coal and cotton become sources of wealth—Ohio admitted as a state in 1803. §§ 340-349

4, 5.—THOMAS JEFFERSON, 1801-1809. Republican plainness at the White House—Purchase of Louisiana; its northern part explored by Lewis and Clarke—War with Tripoli ends in victory to the United States—Steam navigation on the Hudson—English Right of Search retaliated by the Embargo Act. 350-365

6, 7.—JAMES MADISON, 1809-1817. War with Great Britain—Harrison's victory at Tippecanoe—Hull surrenders Detroit and all Michigan Territory—American victories on ocean and lakes— State of Louisiana admitted—Massacre at Raisin River—Southern Indians surprise Fort Mims, but are subdued by Jackson —British ravage Atlantic coast, burn Washington, bombard Baltimore—Burn Oswego—American victories at Lundy's Lane and Plattsburgh — Hartford Convention opposes the war— Jackson's victory at New Orleans—Peace at Ghent—War against Barbary States puts an end to tribute—Duties imposed for protection of home industries—Indiana organized as a state, Michigan and Illinois as territories. §§ 366-399

8, 9.—JAMES MONROE, 1817-1825. Return of prosperity—Mississippi, Illinois, Alabama, Maine, and Missouri admitted as states— "Missouri Compromise" advocated by Henry Clay—First steamship crosses the Atlantic—Florida is ceded by Spain— Monroe Doctrine enunciated. §§ 400-408

10.—JOHN QUINCY ADAMS,1825-1829. Completion of Erie Canal —First steam locomotives on "Delaware and Hudson Canal Railroad"—Death of John Adams and Thomas Jefferson on semi-centennial of American Independence. §§409-414

11, 12.— ANDREW JACKSON, 1829-1837. Changes in offices under Government—Debates on public lands—"Nullification" in South Carolina—Firmness of the President—Indian disturbances North and South—Seminole War—

The President vetoes rechartering of United States Bank, and removes public funds — Era of prosperity and wild speculations — Surplus in United States Treasury divided among the states — Jackson's Specie Circular — Arkansas and Michigan admitted. §§415-426

13. — MARTIN VAN BUREN, 1837-1841. Commercial failures and panic — Repudiation by two states; bankruptcy of eight — The Sub-Treasury Law — Sympathy with Canada — Rise of the Whig Party. §§427-433

14. — WILLIAM HENRY HARRISON (1841) died after one month in office.

JOHN TYLER, 1841-1845. Refuses to recharter National Bank, and his cabinet resign — Webster-Ashburton Treaty settles boundary of Maine and New Brunswick — Dorr's rebellion in Rhode Island — Removal of Mormons to Utah — Annexation of Texas and admission of Florida — First telegraph established. §§434-442

15. — JAMES KNOX POLK, 1845-1849. North-west boundary settled by treaty with Great Britain — War with Mexico — General Taylor gains battles of Palo Alto, Resaca de la Palma, Monterey, and Buena Vista — General Scott marches from the coast to the capital, which surrenders — General Kearney conquers New Mexico; General Fremont and Commodore Stockton, California — Treaty of Guadalupe Hidalgo transfers to United States upper California, Nevada, Utah, Arizona, and New Mexico — Gold discovered in California — The Wilmot Proviso — States of Iowa and Wisconsin admitted.
§§443-461

16. – ZACHARY TAYLOR, 1S49-1S50. California admitted to the Union by Clay's Omnibus Bill — Death of the President.

MILLARD FILLMORE, 1850-1853. Daniel Webster Secretary of State — Gadsden Purchase secures southern Arizona — Death of Calhoun, Clay, and Webster — Fugitive Slave Law opposed by Personal Liberty laws in several states. §§462-468

17. — FRANKLIN PIERCE, 1853-1857. World's Fair in New York — Perry's expedition to Japan — Explorations for Pacific Railroad —"Ostend Manifesto" by three American ministers, looking to the acquisition of Cuba — Organization of Kansas and Nebraska — Border warfare — Rise of Republican and American, or "Know-Nothing," parties. §§469-476

18. — JAMES BUCHANAN, 1857-1861. Minnesota and Oregon admitted — John Brown's invasion of Virginia — Division of Democratic party — Election of Abraham Lincoln — Ordinances of secession in South Carolina, Georgia, and the Gulf States — Jefferson Davis elected President of the Confederate States — United States forts and arsenals seized by Southern forces. §§477-485

19. — ABRAHAM LINCOLN, 1861-1865. Bombardment and fall of Fort Sumter — Eleven

states in Secession—Separation of West Virginia—Union defeat at Bull Run—McClellan commander-in-chief—Blockade of southern Atlantic coast—The " Trent Affair " set right by United States Government—Recapture of Hatteras Inlet, Port Royal Entrance, and Tybee Island. §§486-501 1862.—Forts Henry and Donelson taken by Grant—Battle of Shiloh—Capture of Island No. 10, Memphis, and Fort Pillow— Federal victory at Pea Ridge—Bragg's campaign in Kentucky— Confederate defeats at Iuka, Corinth, and Murfreesborough— Capture of New Orleans by Farragut and Butler—*Merrimac* and *Monitor* in Hampton Roads—McClellan's march to Richmond— Second defeat at Bull Run—Invasion of Maryland—Battle of Antietam—Union defeat at Fredericksburg. §§ 502-528
1863.—Emancipation of all slaves in seceded states—Enlistment of 50,000 negroes in Federal armies and navies—Union defeat at Chancellorsville; death of "Stonewall" Jackson—Riots in New York—Invasion of Pennsylvania—Confederate defeat at Gettysburg—Surrender of Vicksburg and Port Hudson ends the war on the Mississippi—Morgan's raid in Indiana and Ohio— Campaign of Chattanooga ends in Union victories at Lookout Mountain and Missionary Ridge. §§529-546
1864.—Grant, as Lieutenant-general, at head of United States armies—Battles of the "Wilderness" costly and indecisive— Battle of Cedar Mountain saved by " Sheridan's Ride"—Sieges of Richmond and Petersburg begun—Sherman defeats Hood, burns Atlanta, marches through Georgia to the sea ; captures Savannah—Re-election of President Lincoln. §§547—561
1865.—Burning of Columbia and part of Charleston—Sherman's march through the Carolinas—Abandonment and burning of Richmond—Surrender of Lee's and Johnston's armies—Murder of President Lincoln—Nevada admitted, and territories organized. §§ 562-573

20.—ANDREW JOHNSON, 1865-1869. "Reconstruction Policy" of the President differing from that of Congress, he is impeached, but acquitted—Fourteenth Amendment to the Constitution secures the civil rights of freedmen—Most of the Southern states repeal their ordinances of secession, and are re-admitted to the Union—Submarine telegraph successfully established between Ireland and America, 1866—Purchase of Alaska—Burlingame embassy from China makes a treaty of friendship. §§ 589-595

21, 22.—ULYSSES S. GRANT, 1869—1877. Pacific Railroad completed—Texas, last of the seceded states, resumes place in Congress —Treaty of Washington provides for settlement of all differences between England and the United

States—Alabama claims, fixed by International Board at Geneva, are paid by Great Britain—Fires in Chicago, the north-western forests, and in Boston—Grant's Indian Policy—Murder of General Canby by the Modocs—Commercial panic and distress— Ring robberies in great cities-—Congress passes a Specie Resumption Act—Colorado becomes a state—Centennial Exposition at Philadelphia—War with the Sioux—Massacre of General Custer and his army—Joint High Commission from Senate, Representatives, and Supreme Court decide the results of the Presidential election of 1876. §§596—616

23.—RUTHERFORD B. HAYES, 1877—1881. Pledges of peace and civil service reform—Railway riots suppressed—Chinese Question in California—Act to set aside the Burlingame Treaty passed by Congress but vetoed by the President— Resumption of gold payments January, 1879—Election of James A. Garfield, of Ohio, to be the twentieth President of the United States, November, 1880. §§ 617-627

APPENDIX

THE DECLARATION OF INDEPENDENCE

IN CONGRESS, July 4, 1776.

The Unanimous Declaration of the Thirteen United States of America.

When, in the course of human events, it becomes necessary for one people to dissolve the political bands which have connected them with another, and to assume, among the powers of the earth, the separate and equal station to which the laws of nature and of nature's God entitle them, a decent respect to the opinions of mankind requires that they should declare the causes which impel them to the separation.

We hold these truths to be self-evident : that all men are created equal ; that they are endowed by their Creator with certain unalienable rights ; that among these are life, liberty,and the pursuit of happiness; that, to secure these rights, governments are instituted among men, deriving their just powers from the consent of the governed ; that, whenever any form of government becomes destructive of these ends, it is the right of the people to alter or to abolish it, and to institute a new government, laying its foundation on such principles, and organizing its powers in such form as to them shall seem most likely to effect their safety and happiness. Prudence, indeed, will dictate, that governments long established should not be changed for light and transient causes; and, accordingly, all experience hath shown that mankind are more disposed to suffer, while evils are sufferable, than to right themselves by abolishing the forms to which they are accustomed. But when a long train of abuses and usurpations, pursuing invariably the same object, evinces a design to reduce them under absolute despotism, it is their right, it is their duty, to throw off such a government, and to provide new guards for their future security. Such has been the patient sufferance of these colonies, and such is now the necessity which constrains them to alter their former systems of government. The history of the present King of Great Britain is a history of repeated injuries and usurpations, all having in direct object the establishment of an absolute tyranny over these States. To prove this, let facts be submitted to a candid world.

He has refused his assent to laws the most wholesome and necessary for the public good.

He has forbidden his governors to pass laws of immediate and pressing importance, unless suspended in their operations till his assent should be obtained ; and when so suspended, he has utterly neglected to attend to them.

He has refused to pass other laws for the accommodation of large districts of people, unless those people would relinquish the right of representation in the legislature—a right inestimable to them, and formidable to tyrants only.

He has called together legislative bodies at places unusual, uncomfortable, and distant from the depository of their public records, for the sole purpose of fatiguing them into compliance with his measures.

He has dissolved representative houses repeatedly for opposing, with manly firmness, his invasions on the rights of the people.

He has refused, for a long time after such dissolutions, to cause others to be elected, whereby the legislative powers, incapable of annihilation, have returned to the people at large for their exercise ; the state remaining, in the meantime, exposed to all the dangers of invasions from without and convulsions within.

He lias endeavored to prevent the population of these States; for that purpose obstructing the laws for the naturalization of foreigners; refusing to pass others to encourage their migration hither, and raising the conditions of new appropriations of lands.

He has obstructed the administration of justice by refusing his assent to laws for establishing judiciary powers.

He has made judges dependent on his will alone for the tenure of their offices, and the amount and payment of their salaries.

He has erected a multitude of new offices, and sent hither swarms of officers to harass our people and eat out their substance.

He has kept among us, in times of peace, standing armies, without the consent of our legislatures.

He has affected to render the military independent of, and superior to, the civil power.

He has combined with others to subject us to a jurisdiction foreign to our constitution, and unacknowledged by our laws; giving his assent to their acts of pretended legislation:

For quartering large bodies of armed troops among us ;

For protecting them, by a mock trial, from punishment for any murders which they should commit on the inhabitants of these states;

For cutting off our trade with all parts of the world ;

For imposing taxes on us without our consent ;

For depriving us, in many cases, of the benefits of trial by jury ;

For transporting ns beyond seas to be tried for pretended offenses ;

For abolishing the free system of English laws in a neighboring province, establishing therein an arbitrary government, and enlarging its boundaries, so as to render it at once an example and fit instrument for introducing the same absolute rule into these colonies:

For taking away our charters, abolishing our most valuable laws, and altering, fundamentally, the forms of our governments ;

For suspending our own legislatures, and declaring themselves invested with power to legislate for us in all cases whatsoever.

He has abdicated government here by declaring us out of his protection, and waging war against us.

He has plundered our seas, ravaged our coasts, burned our towns, and destroyed the lives of our people.

He is at this time transporting large armies of foreign mercenaries to complete the works of death, desolation, and tyranny, already begun with circumstances of cruelty and perfidy, scarcely paralleled in the most barbarous ages, and totally unworthy the head of a civilized nation.

He has constrained our fellow-citizens, taken captive on the high seas, to bear arms against their country, to become the executioners of their friends and brethren, or to fall themselves by their hands.

He has excited domestic insurrection among us, and lias endeavored to bring on the inhabitants of our frontiers the merciless Indian savages, whose known rule of warfare is an undistinguished destruction of all ages, sexes, and conditions.

In every stage of these oppressions we have petitioned for redress in the most humble terms : our repeated petitions have been answered only by repeated injury. A prince whose character is thus marked by every act which may define a tyrant, is unfit to be the ruler of a free people.

Nor have we been wanting in attentions to our British brethren. We have warned them, from time to time, of attempts by their legislature to extend an unwarrantable jurisdiction over us. We have reminded them of the circumstances of our emigration and settlement here. We have appealed to their native justice and magnanimity, and we have conjured them, by the ties of our common kindred, to disavow these usurpations, which would inevitably interrupt our connections and correspondence.

They, too, have been deaf to the voice of justice and of consanguinity. We must, therefore, acquiesce in the necessity which denounces our separation, and hold them, as we hold the rest of mankind—enemies in war; in peace, friends.

We, therefore, the representatives of the UNITED STATES OF AMERICA, in General Congress assembled, appealing to the Supreme Judge of the world for the rectitude of our intentions, do, in the name and by the authority of the good people of these colonies, solemnly publish and declare, That these United Colonies are, and of right ought to be, Free and Independent States ; that they are absolved from all allegiance to the British crown, and that all political connection bet ween them aud the state of Great Britain is, and ought to be, totally dissolved ; and that, as Free and Independent States, they have full power to levy war, conclude peace, contract alliances, establish commerce, aud to do all other acts and things which Independent States may of right do. And for the support of this Declaration, with a firm reliance on the protection of DIVINE PROVIDENCE, we mutually pledge to each other our lives, our fortunes, and our sacred honor.

JOHN HANCOCK.

NEW HAMPSHIRE.—Josiah Bartlett, William Whipple, Matthew Thornton.

MASSACHUSETTS BAY.—Samuel Adams, John Adams, Robert Treat Paine, Elbridge Gerry.

RHODE ISLAND, ETC.—Stephen Hopkins, William Ellery.

CONNECTICUT.—Roger Sherman, Samuel Huntington, William Williams, Oliver Wolcott.

NEW YORK.—William Floyd, Philip Livingston, Francis Lewis, Lewis Morris.

NEW JERSEY.—Richard Stockton, John Witherspoon, Francis Hopkinson, John Hart, Abraham Clark.

PENNSYLVANIA.—Robert Morris, Benjamin Rush, Benjamin Franklin, John Morton, George Clymer, James Smith, George Taylor, James Wilson, George Ross.

DELAWARE.—Cæsar Rodney, George Read, Thomas M'Kean.

MARYLAND.—Samuel Chase, William Paca, Thomas Stone, Charles Carroll of Carrollton.

VIRGINIA.—George Wythe, Richard Henry Lee, Thomas Jefferson, Benjamin Harrison, Thomas Nelson, Jr., Francis Lightfoot Lee, Carter

Braxton.

NORTH CAROLINA.—William Hooper, Joseph Hewes, John Penn.

SOUTH CAROLINA.—Edward Rutledge, Thomas Heyward, Jr., Thomas Lynch, Jr., Arthur Middleton.

GEORGIA.—Button Gwinnett, Lyman Hall, George Walton.

CONSTITUTION

OF THE

UNITED STATES OF AMERICA.

WE, the people of the United States, in order to form a more perfect union, establish justice, insure domestic tranquillity, provide for the common defense, promote the general welfare, and secure the blessings of liberty to ourselves and our posterity, do ordain and establish this Constitution for the United States of America.

ARTICLE I.—SECTION 1.

1. All legislative powers herein granted shall be vested in a Congress of the United States, which shall consist of a Senate and House of Representatives.

SECTION 2.

1. The House of Representatives shall he composed of members chosen every second year by the people of the several States ; and the electors in each State shall have the qualifications requisite for electors of the most numerous branch of the State legislature.

2. No person shall lie a Representative who shall not have attained to the age of twenty-five years, and been seven years a citizen of the United States, and who shall not, when elected, be an inhabitant of that State in which he shall be chosen.

3. Representatives and direct taxes sitali be apportioned among the several States which may be included within this Union, according to their respective numbers, which shall be determined by adding to the whole number of free persons, including those bound to service for a term of years, and excluding Indians not taxed, three fifths of all other persons. The actual enumeration shall be made within three years after the first meeting of the Congress of the United States, and within every subsequent term of ten years, in such manner as they shall by law direct. The number of Representatives shall not exceed one for every thirty thousand, but each State shall have at least one Representative; and until such enumeration shall be made, the State of New Hampshire shall be entitled to choose three; Massachusetts, eight ; Rhode Island and Providence Plantations, one; Connecticut, five; New York, six; New Jersey, four; Pennsylvania, eight ; Delaware, one ; Maryland, six ; Virginia, ten ; North Carolina, five; South Carolina, five; and Georgia,

three.

4. When vacancies happen in the representation from any State, the executive authority thereof shall issue writs of election to fill such vacancies.

5. The House of Representatives shall choose their Speaker and other officers, and shall have the sole power of impeachment.

Section 3.

1. The Senate of the United States shall be composed of two Senators from each State, chosen by the legislature thereof, for six years; and each Senator shall have one vote.

2. Immediately after they shall be assembled in consequence of the first election, they shall be divided as equally as may be into three classes. The seats of the Senators of the first class shall be vacated at the expiration of the second year, of the second class at the expiration of the fourth year, and of the third class at the expiration of the sixth year, so that one third may be chosen every second year; and if vacancies happen, by resignation or otherwise, during the recess of the legislature of any State, the Executive thereof may make temporary appointments until the next meeting of the legislature, which shall then till such vacancies.

3. No person shall be a Senator who shall not have attained to the age of thirty years, and been nine years a citizen of the United States, and who shall not, when elected, be an inhabitant of that State for which he shall be chosen.

4. The Vice-president of the United States shall be president of the Senate, but shall have no vote, unless they be equally divided.

5. The Senate shall choose their other officers, and also a president pro- tempore, in the absence of the Vice-president, or when he shall exercise the office of President of the United States.

6. The Senateshall have the sole power to try all impeachments. When sitting for that purpose, they shall be on oath or affirmation. When the President of the United States is tried, the Chief-justice shall preside; and no person shall be convicted without the concurrence of two thirds of the members present.

7. Judgment in eases of impeachment shall not extend further than to removal from office, and disqualification to hold and enjoy any office of honor, trust, or profit, under the United States; but the party

convicted shall nevertheless be liable and subject to indictment, trial, judgment, and punishment, according to law.

SECTION 4.

1. The times, places, and manner of holding elections for Senators and Representatives shall be prescribed in each State by the legislature thereof; but the Congress may, at any time, by law, make or alter such regulations, except as to the places of choosing Senators.

2. The Congress shall assemble at least once in every year, and such meeting shall be on the first Monday in December, unless they shall by law appoint a different day.

SECTION 5.

1. Each house shall be the judge of the elections, returns, and qualifications of its own members, and a majority of each shall constitute a quorum to do business; but a smaller number may adjourn from day to day, and may be authorized to compel the attendance of absent members in such manner and under such penalties as each House may provide.

2. Each House may determine the rules of its proceedings, punish its members for disorderly behavior, and, with the concurrence of two thirds, expel a member.

3. Each House shall keep a journal of its proceedings, and from time to time publish the same, excepting such parts as may in their judgment require secrecy ; and the yeas and nays of the members of either House, on any question, shall, at the desire of one fifth of those present, he entered on the journal.

4. Neither House, during the session of Congress, shall, without the consent of the other, adjourn for more than three days, nor to any other place than that in which the two Houses shall be sitting.

SECTION 6.

1. The Senators and Representatives shall receive a compensation for their services, to be ascertained by law, and paid out of the Treasury of the United States. They shall in all eases, except treason, felony, and breach of the peace, be privileged from arrest during their attendance at the session of their respective Houses, and in going to and returning from the same; and for any speech or debate in either House, they shall not be questioned in any other place.

2. No Senator or Representative shall, during the time for which he

was elected, be appointed to any civil office under the authority of the United States which shall have been created, or the emoluments whereof shall have been increased, during such time; and no person holding any office under the United States shall be a member of either House during his continuance in office.

SECTION 7.

1. All bills for raising revenue shall originate in the House of Representatives; but the Senate may propose or concur with amendments, as on other bills.

2. Every bill which shall have passed the House of Representatives and the Senate, shall, before it become a law, be presented to the President of the United States: if he approve lie shall sign it, but. if not he shall return it with his objections to that House in which it shall have originated, who shall enter the objections at large on their journal, and proceed to reconsider it. If, after such reconsideration, two thirds of that House shall agree to pass the bill, it shall be sent, together with the objections, to the other House, by which it shall likewise he reconsidered, and il approved by two thirds of that House, it shall become a law. But in all such cases the votes of both Houses shall be determined by yeas and nays, and the names of the persons voting for and against the bill shall be entered on the journal of each House respectively. If any bill shall not be returned by the President within ten days (Sundays excepted) after it shall have been presented to him, the same shall be a law, in like manner as if he had signed it, unless the Congress, by their adjournment, prevent its return, in which case it shall not be a law.

3. Every order, resolution, or vote, to which the concurrence of the Senate and House of Representatives may be necessary (except on a question of adjournment) shall be presented to the President of the United States, and before the same shall take effect shall be approved by him, or, being disapproved by him, shall be re-passed by two thirds of the Senate and House of Representatives, according to the rules and limitations prescribed in the case of a bill.

SECTION 8.

The Congress shall have power —

1. To lay and collect taxes, duties, imposts, and excises, to pay the debts and provide for the common defense and general welfare of the

United States; but all duties, imposts, and excises shall be uniform throughout the United States;

2. To borrow money on the credit of the United States;

3. To regulate commerce with foreign nations, and among the several States, and with the Indian tribes;

4. To establish a uniform rule of naturalization, and uniform laws on the subject of bankruptcies throughout the United States;

5. To coin money, regulate the value thereof and of foreign coin, and fix the standard of weights and measures;

6. To provide for the punishment of counterfeiting the securities and current coin of the United States;

7. To establish post-offices and post-roads;

8. To promote the progress of science and useful arts, by securing for limited times to authors and inventors, the exclusive right to their respective writings and discoveries;

9. To constitute tribunals inferior to the Supreme Court;

10. To define and punish piracies and felonies committed on the high seas, and offenses against the law of nations;

11. To declare war, grant letters of marque and reprisal, and make rules concerning captures on land and water;

12. To raise and support armies, but no appropriation of money to that use shall be for a longer term than two years;

13. To provide and maintain a navy;

14. To make rules for the government and regulation of the land and naval forces ;

15. To provide for calling forth the militia to execute the laws of the Union, suppress insurrections, and repel invasions;

16. To provide for organizing, arming, and disciplining the militia, and for governing such part of them as may be employed in the service of the United States, reserving to the States respectively the appointment of the officers and the authority of training the militia according to the discipline prescribed by Congress;

17. To exercise exclusive legislation in all cases whatsoever over such district (not exceeding ten miles square) as may, by cession of particular States and the acceptance of Congress, become the seat of the Government of the United States, and to exercise like authority over all

places purchased by the consent of the legislature of the State in which the same shall be, for the erection of forts, magazines, arsenals, dockyards, and other needful buildings ; and,

18. To make all laws which shall be necessary and proper for carrying into execution the foregoing powers, and all other powers vested by this Constitution in the Government of the United States, or in any department or officer thereof.

SECTION 9.

1. The migration or importation of such persons as any of the States now existing shall think proper to admit, shall not be prohibited by the Congress prior to the year one thousand eight hundred and eight, but a tax or duty may be imposed on such importation, not exceeding ten dollars for each person.

2. The privilege of the writ of habeas corpus shall not be suspended unless when in cases of rebellion or invasion the public safety may require it.

3. No bill of attainder or ex post facto law shall be passed.

4. No capitation or other direct tax shall be laid, unless in proportion to the census or enumeration hereinbefore directed to be taken.

5. No tax or duty shall be laid on articles exported from any State. No preference shall be given by any regulation of commerce or revenue to the ports of one State over those of another ; nor shall vessels bound to or from one State be obliged to enter, clear, or pay duties in another.

6. No money shall be drawn from the treasury but in consequence of appropriation's made by law; and a regular statement and account of the receipts and expenditures of all public money shall be published from time to time.

7. No title of nobility shall be granted by the United States; and no person holding any office of profit or trust under them, shall, without the consent of the Congress, accept of any present, emolument, office, or title, of any kind whatever, from any king, prince, or foreign state.

SECTION 10.

1. No State shall enter into any treaty, alliance, or confederation ; grant letters of marque and reprisal; coin money; emit bills of credit; make any thing but gold and silver coin a tender in payment of debts ; pass any bill of attainder, ex post facto law, or law impairing the

obligation of contracts, or grant any title of nobility.

2. No State shall, without the consent of the Congress, lay any imposts or duties on imports or exports except what may be absolutely necessary for executing its inspection laws: and the net produce of all duties and imposts laid by any State on imports or exports shall be for the use of the treasury of the United States; and all such laws shall be subject to the revision and control of the Congress. No State shall, without the consent of Congress, lay any duty of tonnage, keep troops or ships of war in time of peace, enter into any agreement or compact with another State or with a foreign power, or engage in war, unless actually invaded, or in such imminent danger as will not admit of delay.

ARTICLE II. — SECTION 1.

1. The Executive power shall be vested in a President of the United States of America. He shall hold his office during the term of four years, and, together with the Vice-president, chosen for the same term, be elected as follows :

2. Each State shall appoint in such manner as the legislature thereof may direct, a number of Electors equal to the whole number of Senators and Representatives to which the State may be entitled in the Congress; but no Senator or Representative, or person holding an office of trust or profit under the United States, shall be appointed an Elector.

Clause 3 has been superseded by the 12th Article of Amendments.

4. The Congress may determine the time of choosing the Electors, and the day on which they shall give their votes; which day shall be the same throughout the United States.

5. No person, except a natural-born citizen, or a citizen of the United States at the time of the adoption of this Constitution, shall be eligible to the office of President; neither shall any person be eligible to that office who shall not have attained to the age of thirty-five years, and been fourteen years a resident within the United States.

6. In case of the removal of the President from office, or of his death, resignation, or inability to discharge the powers and duties of the said office, the same shall devolve on the Vice-president; and the Congress may by law provide for the case of removal, death, resignation, or inability, both of the President and Vice-president, declaring what officer shall then act as President, and such officer shall act accordingly, until the disability be removed or a President shall be elected.

7. The President shall, at stated times, receive for bisservices a compensation, which shall neither be increased nor diminished during the period for which he shall have been elected, and he shall not receive within that period any other emolument from the United States or any of them.

8. Before he enter on the execution of his office, he shall take the following oath or affirmation :

" I do solemnly swear (or affirm) that I will faithfully execute the office of President of the United States, and will, to the best of my ability, preserve, protect, and defend the Constitution of the United States."

Section 2.

1. The President shall be commander-in-chief of the army and navy of the United States, and of the militia of the several States when called into the actual service of the United States; he may require the opinion, in writing, of the principal officer in each of the executive departments, upon any subject relating to the duties of their respective offices, and he shall have power to grant reprieves and pardons for offenses against the United States, except in cases of impeachment.

2. He shall have power, by and with the advice and consent of the Senate, to make treaties, provided two thirds of the Senators present concur ; and he shall nominate, and by and with the advice and consent of the Senate, shall appoint ambassadors, other public ministers and Consuls, Judges of the Supreme Court, and all other officers of the United States, whose appointments are not herein otherwise provided for, and which shall be established by law; but the Congress may by law vest the appointment of such inferior officers as they think proper, in the President alone, in the Courts of law, or in the heads of Departments.

3. The President shall have power to fill up all vacancies that may happen during the recess of the Senate, by granting commissions which shall expire at the end of their next session.

Section 3.

He shall, from time to time, give to the Congress information of the state of the Union, and recommend to their consideration such measures as he shall judge necessary and expedient; he may, on extraordinary-occasions, convene both Houses, or either of them, and in case of disagreement between them with respect to the time of adjournment, be may adjourn them to such time as he shall think proper; be shall receive ambassadors and other public ministers ; he shall take care that the laws be faithfully executed, and shall commission all the officers of the United States.

SECTION 4.

The President, Vice-president, and all civil officers of the United States, shall be removed from office on impeachment for, and conviction of, treason, bribery, or other high crimes and misdemeanors.

ARTICLE III. — SECTION 1.

The judicial power of the United States shall be vested in one Supreme Court, and in such inferior Courts as the Congress may from time to time ordain and establish. The Judges, both of the Supreme and inferior Courts, shall hold their offices during good behavior, and shall, at stated times, receive for their services a compensation which shall not be diminished during their continuance in office.

SECTION 2.

1. The judicial power shall extend to all cases in law and equity arising under this Constitution, the laws of the United States, and treaties made, or which shall lie made, under their authority ; to all cases affecting ambassadors, other public ministers, and consuls; to all cases of admiralty and maritime jurisdiction; to controversies to which the United States shall be a party ; to controversies between two or more States ; between a State and citizens of another State ; between citizens of different States; between citizens of the same State claiming lands under grants of different States; and between a State, or the citizens thereof, and foreign States, citizens, or subjects.

2. In all cases affecting ambassadors, other public ministers, and consuls, and those in which a State shall be a party, the Supreme Court shall have original jurisdiction. In all the other cases before mentioned, the Supreme Court shall have appellate jurisdiction, both as to law and fact, with such exceptions and under such regulations as the Congress shall make.

3. The trial of all crimes, except in cases of impeachment, shall be by jury; and such trial shall be held in the State where the said crimes shall have been committed; but when not committed within any State, the trial shall be at such place or places as the Congress may by law have directed.

Section 3.

1. Treason against the United States shall consist only in levying war against them, or in adhering to their enemies, giving them aid and comfort. No person shall be convicted of treason unless on the testimony of two witnesses to the same overt act, or on confession in open court.

2. The Congress shall have power to declare the punishment of treason, but no attainder of treason shall work corruption of blood, or forfeiture, except during the life of the person attainted.

ARTICLE IV — Section 1.

Full faith and credit shall be given in each State to the public acts, records, and judicial proceedings of every other State. And the Congress may, by general laws, prescribe the manner in which such acts, records, and proceedings shall be proved, and the effect thereof.

Section 2.

1. The citizens of each State shall be entitled to all privileges and immunities of citizens in the several States.

2. A person charged in any State with treason, felony, or other crime, who shall flee from justice, and be found in another State, shall, on demand of the executive authority of the State from which he fled, be delivered up, to be removed to the State having jurisdiction of the crime.

3. No person held to service or labor in one State, under the laws thereof, escaping into another, shall, in consequence of any law or regulation therein, be discharged from such service or labor, but shall be delivered up on claim of the party to whom such service or labor may be due.

Section 3.

1. New States may be admitted by the Congress into this Union ; but no new State shall be formed or erected within the jurisdiction of any other State ; nor any State be formed by the junction of two or more States, or parts of States, without the consent of the legislatures of the States concerned as well as of the Congress.

2. The Congress shall have power to dispose of and make all needful rules and regulations respecting the territory or other property belonging to the United States; and nothing in this Constitution shall be so construed as to prejudice any claims of the United States, or of any particular State.

Section 4.

The United States shall guarantee to every state in this Union a republican form of government, and shall protect each of them against invasion ; and, on application of the legislature, or of the Executive (when the legislature can not be convened) against domestic violence.

ARTICLE V.

The Congress, whenever two thirds of both Houses shall deem it necessary, shall propose Amendments to this Constitution, or, on the application of the legislatures of two thirds of the several States, shall call a convention for proposing Amendments, which, in either case, shall be valid to all intents and purposes as part of this Constitution, when ratified by the legislatures of three fourths of the several States, or by conventions in three fourths thereof, as the one or the other mode of ratification may be proposed by the Congress: provided, that no Amendment which may be made prior to the year one thousand eight hundred and eight shall in any manner affect the first and fourth clauses in the ninth section of the first article ; and that no State, without its consent, shall be deprived of its equal suffrage in the Senate.

ARTICLE VI.

1. All debts contracted and engagements entered into, before the adoption of this Constitution, shall be as valid against the United States under this Constitution as under the Confederation.

2. This Constitution, and the laws of the United States which shall be made in pursuance thereof, and all treaties made, or which shall be made, under the authority of the United States, shall he the supreme law of the land; and the judges in every State shall be bound thereby, any thing in the constitution or laws of any State to the contrary notwithstanding.

3. The Senators and Representatives before mentioned, and the members of the several State legislatures, and all executive and judicial officers, both of the United States and of the several States, shall be bound by oath or affirmation to support this Constitution; but no religious test shall ever be required as a qualification to any office or public trust under the United States.

ARTICLE VII.

The ratification of the Conventions of nine States shall be sufficient for the establishment of this Constitution between the States so ratifying the same.

AMENDMENTS TO THE CONSTITUTION.

ARTICLE I.

Congress shall make no law respecting an establishment of religion, or prohibiting the free exercise thereof; or abridging the freedom of speech or of the press; or the right of the people peaceably to assemble, and to petition the government for a redress of grievances.

ARTICLE II.

A well-regulated militia being necessary to the security of a free state, the right of the people to keep and bear arms shall not be infringed.

ARTICLE III.

No soldier shall, in time of peace, be quartered in any house without the consent of the owner, nor in time of war, but in a manner to be prescribed by law.

ARTICLE IV.

The right of the people to be secure in their persons, houses, papers, and effects, against unreasonable searches and seizures, shall not be violated, and no warrants shall issue, but upon probable cause, supported by oath or affirmation, and particularly describing the place to be searched, and the persons or things to be seized.

ARTICLE V.

No person shall be held to answer for a capital or otherwise infamous crime, unless on a presentment or indictment of a grand jury, except in cases arising in the land or naval forces, or in the militia when in actual service in time of war or public danger ; nor shall any person be subject for the same offense to be twice put in jeopardy of life or limb ; nor shall be compelled in any criminal case to be a witness against himself; nor be deprived of life, liberty, or property, without due process of law ; nor shall private property be taken for public use without just compensation.

ARTICLE VI.

In all criminal prosecutions, the accused shall enjoy the right to a speedy and public trial, by an impartial jury of the State and district wherein the crime shall have been committed, which district shall have been previously ascertained by law, and to be informed of the nature and cause of the accusation ; to be confronted with the witnesses against him ; to have compulsory process for obtaining witnesses in his favor, and to have the assistance of counsel for his defense.

ARTICLE VII.

In suits at common law where the value in controversy shall exceed twenty dollars, the right of trial by jury shall be preserved, and no fact tried by a jury shall be otherwise re-examined in any Court of the United States, than according to the rules of the common law.

ARTICLE VIII.

Excessive bail shall not be required, nor excessive fines imposed, nor cruel and unusual punishments inflicted.

ARTICLE IX.

The enumeration in the Constitution of certain rights shall not be construed to deny or disparage others retained by the people.

ARTICLE X.

The powers not delegated to the United States by the Constitution, nor prohibited by it to the States, are reserved to the States respectively, or to the people.

ARTICLE XI.

The judicial power of the United States shall not be construed to extend to any suit in law or equity, commenced or prosecuted against one of the United States by citizens of another State, or by citizens or subjects of any foreign State.

ARTICLE XII.

The Electors shall meet in their respective States, and vote by ballot for President and Vice-president, one of whom, at least, shall not be an inhabitant of the same State with themselves; they shall name in their ballots the person voted for as President, and in distinct ballots the person voted for as Vice-president, and they shall make distinct lists of all persons voted for as President, and of all persons voted for as Vice-president, and of the number of votes for each, which lists they shall sign and certify, and transmit sealed to the seat of the government of the United States, directed to the President of the Senate. The President of the Senate shall, in the presence of the Senate and House of Representatives, open all the certificates, and the votes shall then be counted; the person having the greatest number of votes for President shall be the President, if such number be a majority of the whole number of Electors appointed; and if no person have such majority, then from the persons having the highest numbers, not exceeding three, on the list of those voted for as President, the House of Representatives shall choose immediately, by ballot, the President. But in choosing the President, the votes shall be taken by States, the representation from each State having one. vote; a quorum for this purpose shall consist of a member or members from two thirds of the States, and a majority of ail the States shall be necessary to a choice. And if the House of Representatives shall not choose a President, whenever the right of choice shall devolve upon them, before the fourth day of Diarch next following, then the Vice-president shall act as President, as in the case of the death or other constitutional disability of the President. The person having the greatest number of votes as Vice-president shall he the Vice-president, if such number be a majority of the whole number of Electors appointed, and if no person have a majority, then from the two highest numbers on the list the Senate shall choose the Vice-president; a quorum for the purpose shall consist of two thirds of the whole number of Senators, and a majority of the whole number shall be necessary to a choice. But no person constitutionally ineligible to the office of President shall be eligible to that of D ice-president of the United States.

ARTICLE XIII.

1. Neither Slavery nor involuntary servitude, except as a punishment, for crime, whereof the party shall have been duly convicted, shall exist within the United States, or any place subject to their jurisdiction.

2. Congress shall have power to enforce this article by appropriate legislation.

ARTICLE XIV.

1. All persons born or naturalized in the United States, and subject to the jurisdiction thereof, are citizens of the United States and of the State wherein they reside. No State shall make or enforce any law which shall abridge the privileges or immunities of citizens of the United States; nor shall any State deprive any person of life, liberty, or property, without due process of law, nor deny to any person within its jurisdiction the equal protection of the laws.

2. Representatives shall be apportioned among the several States according to their respective numbers, counting the whole number of

persons in each State, excluding Indians not taxed. But when the right to vote at any election for the choice of electors for President and Vice-president of the United States, Representatives in Congress the executive and judicial officers of a State, or the members of the legislature thereof, is denied to any of the male inhabitants of such State, being twenty-one years of age, and citizens of the United States, or in any way abridged, except for participation in rebellion or other crime, the basis of representation therein shall be reduced in the proportion which the number of such male citizens shall bear to the whole number of male citizens twenty-one years of age in such State.

3. No person shall be a Senator or Representative in Congress, or elector of President and Vice-president, or hold any office, civil or military, under the United States, or under any State, who, having previously taken an oath, as a member of Congress, or as an officer of the United States, or as a member of any State legislature, or as an executive or judicial officer of any State, to support the Constitution of the United States, shall have engaged in insurrection or rebellion against the same, or given aid or comfort to the enemies thereof. But Congress may, by a Vote of two thirds of each House, remove such disability.

4. The validity of the public debt of the United States, authorized by law, including debts incurred for payment of pensions and bounties for services in suppressing insurrection or rebellion, shall not be questioned. But neither the United States nor any State shall assume or pay any debt or obligation incurred in aid of insurrection or rebellion against the United States, or any claim for the loss or emancipation of any slave; but all such debts, obligations, and claims shall be held illegal and void.

5. The Congress shall have power to enforce, by appropriate legislation, the provisions of this article.

ARTICLE XV.

1. The right of citizens of the United States to vote shall not be denied or abridged by the United States, or by any State, on account of race, color, or previous condition of servitude.

2. The Congress shall have power to enforce this article by appropriate legislation.

QUESTIONS ON THE CONSTITUTION OF THE UNITED STATES.

1. By whose authority was the Constitution established?

2. What six distinct purposes are declared in the "enacting clause" with which it opens?

3. What imperfect union had already existed? 298, 299.

4. How long had the United States existed as a nation when the Constitution was adopted?

Article I.

5. To whom is the law-making power entrusted ? Section 1.

6. Of what two bodies does Congress consist?

7. By whom and how often is a Representative chosen? Section 2.

8. Of what age and nationality must he be? Section 2, Clause 2.

9. Can an inhabitant of Maine be elected to represent a district in Nevada?

10. What was the least number of persons that were entitled to a Representative when the Constitution was adopted ? Section 2, Clause 3.

11. What number constitutes a Congressional District now? Aus. 130,533.

12. What is the whole number of United States Senators? Section 3.

13. How long does a Senator serve ?

14. What are his qualifications as to age and citizenship? Section 3, Clause 3.

15. Who presides in the Senate? Section 3, Clause 4.

16. In what case does the Vice-president vote?

17. How would his place in the Senate be filled in case of his death, absence, or promotion to the Presidency ? Section 3, Clause 5.

18. How many Vice-presidents have succeeded to the highest office?

19. What judicial powers are vested in the Senate? Section 3, Clause 6.

20. What punishment can be inflicted in eases of impeachment? Section 3, Clause 7.

21. How often, and on what day, docs Congress assemble? Section 4,

Clause 2.

22. Who decides upon the qualifications of members? Section 5, Clause 1.

23. What are the privileges of members of Congress? Section 6, Clause 1.

24. Can they hold any office under the Government? Section 6, Clause 2.

25. What house originates bills for raising the public revenues? Section 7, Clause 1.

26. What part has the President in making laws? Section 7, Clause 2

27. In what two cases can a law become effective without the President's signature? Section 7, Clause 2.

28. Recite the powers and duties of Congress as enumerated in the eighteen clauses of Section 8.

29. In what eases only can a writ of habeas corpus be refused to an arrested person? Section 9, Clause 2.

30. What is a writ of habeas corpus See Andrews's "Manual of the Constitution," pages 146, 147.

31. Can a law authorize the punishment of an offense that was committed before the law was made? Section 9, Clause 3.

32. Can Congress favor one state more than another in imposing taxes and duties? Section 9. Clause 5.

33. Can a citizen of the United States accept gifts, offices, or titles from a foreign government? Section 9, Clause 7.

34. What restrictions are laid on the actions of the several States? Section 10.

Article II.

35. What is required of a candidate for the Presidency as to age, citizenship, and residence? Section 1, Clause 5.

36. What powers are exercised by the President alone? Section 2, Clauses 1 and 3.

37. What, in concurrence with the Senate? Section 2, Clause 2.

38. What additional duties are demanded of him? Section 3.

39. How and for what reasons can a President be removed? Section 4.

Article III.

40. How long do Judges of the Supreme Court hold their office? Section 1.

41. What cases are judged by the Supreme Court? Section 2.

42. What is the difference between original and appellate jurisdiction? See Andrews's "Manual of the Constitution," page 206.

43. In what court must a robber of the mails be tried?

44. What is meant by "trial by jury"? Section 2, Clause 3. Andrews's "Manual of the Constitution," page 213.

45. What constitutes treason against the United States? Section 3, Clause 1.

46. Can the children of a traitor be made to suffer in person or property for their father's crime? Section 3, Clause 2.

Article IV.

47. What duties do the several states owe to each other? Sections 1 and 2.

48. By what authority and under what conditions can new states be admitted? Section 3.

49. What claim can any state make on the General Government? Section 4.

Article V.

50. How can amendments be made in the Constitution?

Article VI.

51. What constitutes the supreme law of the land ? Section 2.

Amendments.

52. What was the general purpose of the ten Amendments proposed by the first Congress and accepted by the states? Articles I-X.

53. Can any one be legally[7] called in question for religious belief or practice in the United States? Article I.

54. What are the rights of the accused under Articles V to VIII.

55. How was the mode of electing executive officers settled in 1803 and 1804? Article XII.

56. Under what description were slaves alluded to in the original Constitution? Article I, Section 2, Clause 3; and Section 9, Clause 1.

57. What was the Thirteenth Amendment, ratified in December, 1865?

58. How are "citizens" defined in the Fourteenth Amendment? Section 1.

59. How is the number of Representatives made dependent on the free exercise of the right to vote? XIV, Section 2.

60. What class of persons were excluded from civil office by Amendment XIV, Section 3.

www.ingramcontent.com/pod-product-compliance
Lightning Source LLC
Chambersburg PA
CBHW071910110426
R18126600001B/R181266PG42743CBX00016B/13